Visible Learning Guide to Student Achievement

Visible Learning Guide to Student Achievement critically examines the major influences shaping student achievement today. A revision of the *International Guide to Student Achievement*, this updated edition provides readers with a more accessible compendium of research summaries – with a particular focus on the school sector. As educators throughout the world seek to enhance learning, the information contained in this book provides practitioners and policymakers with relevant material and research-based instructional strategies that can be readily applied in classrooms and schools to maximize achievement.

Rich in information and empirically supported research, it contains seven sections, each of which begins with an insightful synthesis of major findings and relevant updates from the literature since the publication of the first *Guide*. These are followed by key entries, all of which have been recently revised by the authors to reflect research developments. The sections conclude with user-friendly tables that succinctly identify the main influences on achievement and practical implications for educators.

Written by world-renowned bestselling authors John Hattie and Eric M. Anderman, this book is an indispensable reference for any teacher, school leader and parent wanting to maximize learning in our schools.

John Hattie is Laureate Professor at the Melbourne Graduate School of Education at the University of Melbourne. He is the author of *Visible Learning*, *Visible Learning for Teachers*, *Visible Learning and the Science of How We Learn*, *Visible Learning into Action*, *10 Mindframes for Visible Learning*, *Visible Learning Feedback* and *Visible Learning Insights* and co-editor of the *International Guide to Student Achievement*.

Eric M. Anderman is Professor of Educational Psychology in the Department of Educational Studies at The Ohio State University. He is a recipient of the Richard E. Snow Early Career Achievement Award from the American Psychological Association (APA), and he served as President of Division 15 of APA in 2008. He is a fellow of both APA and the American Educational Research Association. In addition to authoring and editing several books, he serves on the editorial boards of several major journals. He currently is the editor of the *Theory into Practice* journal.

Visible Learning Guide to Student Achievement

Schools Edition

Edited by John Hattie and
Eric M. Anderman

LONDON AND NEW YORK

First published 2020
by Routledge
2 Park Square, Milton Park, Abingdon, Oxon OX14 4RN

and by Routledge
52 Vanderbilt Avenue, New York, NY 10017

Routledge is an imprint of the Taylor & Francis Group, an informa business

© 2020 selection and editorial matter, John Hattie and Eric M. Anderman; individual chapters, the contributors

The right of John Hattie and Eric M. Anderman to be identified as the authors of the editorial material, and of the authors for their individual chapters, has been asserted in accordance with sections 77 and 78 of the Copyright, Designs and Patents Act 1988.

All rights reserved. No part of this book may be reprinted or reproduced or utilised in any form or by any electronic, mechanical, or other means, now known or hereafter invented, including photocopying and recording, or in any information storage or retrieval system, without permission in writing from the publishers.

Trademark notice: Product or corporate names may be trademarks or registered trademarks, and are used only for identification and explanation without intent to infringe.

British Library Cataloguing-in-Publication Data
A catalogue record for this book is available from the British Library

Library of Congress Cataloging-in-Publication Data
Names: Hattie, John, editor. | Anderman, Eric M.
Title: Visible learning guide to student achievement / [edited by] John Hattie and Eric M. Anderman.
Other titles: International guide to student achievement.
Description: Schools Edition. | Abingdon, Oxon ; New York, NY : Routledge, 2020. | Revised edition of: International guide to student achievement. | Includes bibliographical references and index.
Identifiers: LCCN 2019023362 (print) | LCCN 2019023363 (ebook) | ISBN 9780815367239 (hardback) | ISBN 9780815367246 (paperback) | ISBN 9781351257848 (ebook)
Subjects: LCSH: Academic achievement—Cross-cultural studies.
Classification: LCC LB1062.6 .I72 2020 (print) | LCC LB1062.6 (ebook) | DDC 370.152—dc23
LC record available at https://lccn.loc.gov/2019023362
LC ebook record available at https://lccn.loc.gov/2019023363

ISBN: 978-0-8153-6723-9 (hbk)
ISBN: 978-0-8153-6724-6 (pbk)
ISBN: 978-1-351-25784-8 (ebk)

Typeset in Bembo and Helvetica Neue
by Apex CoVantage, LLC

Printed and bound in Great Britain by
TJ International Ltd, Padstow, Cornwall

Contents

List of contributors   *viii*

1 Understanding achievement   1

2 Influences from the student   6

    2.1 Gender influences   12
        Judith Gill
    2.2 Learning difficulties in school   20
        R. Allan Allday and Mitchell L. Yell
    2.3 Indigenous and other minoritized students   26
        Russell Bishop
    2.4 Personality influences – the Big Five and achievement   33
        Meera Komarraju
    2.5 Motivation   40
        Dale H. Schunk and Carol A. Mullen
    Summary table: influences from the student   44

3 Influences from the home   51

    3.1 Home environment   55
        Burkhard Gniewosz and Jacquelynne S. Eccles
    3.2 Socioeconomic status and student achievement   61
        Erin Bumgarner and Jeanne Brooks-Gunn
    3.3 Parent involvement in learning   66
        Wendy S. Grolnick, Rachel E. Lerner, Jacquelyn N. Raftery-Helmer, and
        Elizabeth S. Allen
    Summary table: influences from the home   72

4	Influences from the school		75
	4.1	Ability grouping *Ed Baines*	79
	4.2	Class size *John Hattie*	86
	4.3	Financing schools *Eric A. Hanushek*	92
	4.4	Influences of school layout and design on student achievement *C. Kenneth Tanner and Sheila J. Bosch*	98
	4.5	Middle school transitions *Eric M. Anderman and Marissa S. Green*	104
	Summary table: influences from the school		110

5	Influences from teachers and classrooms		114
	5.1	Homework and academic achievement *Jianzhong Xu*	121
	5.2	The role of formative assessment in student achievement *Jerome V. D'Agostino, Emily M. Rodgers, and Aryn C. Karpinski*	126
	5.3	Collaboration in the classroom *Noreen M. Webb*	132
	5.4	Pedagogical content knowledge *Julie Gess-Newsome*	139
	5.5	Emotion and achievement in the classroom *Thomas Goetz and Nathan C. Hall*	145
	5.6	Teacher-student relationships *Heather A. Davis and Christopher T. Dague*	153
	5.7	Classroom management and student achievement *H. Jerome Freiberg*	160
	5.8	Academic motivation and achievement in classrooms *Lynley H. Anderman and Robin Sayers*	166
	5.9	Nontraditional teacher preparation *Belinda G. Gimbert and Ryan Kapa*	173
	Summary table: influences from teachers and classrooms		181

6	Influences from the curriculum		189
	6.1	Successful mathematics achievement is attainable *Patti Brosnan, Aaron Schmidlin, and Melva R. Grant*	195
	6.2	Bilingual education programs and student achievement *Jill Fitzgerald and Jackie Eunjung Relyea*	203
	6.3	Language teaching curricula *Eli Hinkel*	210

	6.4	Response to intervention and multitiered systems of supports	216
		Paul J. Riccomini and Gregory W. Smith	
	6.5	Writing instruction	222
		Mark Torrance and Raquel Fidalgo	
	6.6	Role of discussion in reading comprehension	231
		Ian A. G. Wilkinson and Kathryn Nelson	
	6.7	Achievement in adolescent health education	238
		Megan Sanders, Rashea Hamilton, and Eric M. Anderman	
		Summary table: influences from the curriculum	243
7	Influences from teaching strategies	247
	7.1	Metacognitive strategies	253
		Linda Baker	
	7.2	The role of questions in academic achievement	259
		Scotty D. Craig	
	7.3	Teacher immediacy	264
		Ann Bainbridge Frymier	
	7.4	Problem-based learning	270
		David Gijbels, Piet Van den Bossche, and Sofie Loyens	
	7.5	Direct instruction	277
		Gregory Arief D. Liem and Andrew J. Martin	
	7.6	Goal orientation	285
		Andrew J. Martin	
	7.7	Multimedia learning	291
		Richard E. Mayer	
	7.8	Reciprocal teaching	297
		Annemarie Sullivan Palincsar	
	7.9	Technology-supported learning and academic achievement	303
		Peter Reimann and Anindito Aditomo	
	7.10	Study skills	310
		Dale H. Schunk and Carol A. Mullen	
	7.11	Problem solving	315
		R. Taconis	
		Summary table: influences from teaching strategies	320

Index 325

Contributors

Anindito Aditomo
University of Surabaya

R. Allan Allday
University of Kentucky

Elizabeth S. Allen
Cornell Weill Medicine

Eric M. Anderman
The Ohio State University

Lynley H. Anderman
The Ohio State University

Ed Baines
UCL Institute of Education

Linda Baker
University of Maryland, Baltimore County

Russell Bishop
University of Waikato

Sheila J. Bosch
The University of Florida

Jeanne Brooks-Gunn
Columbia University

Patti Brosnan
The Ohio State University

Erin Bumgarner
Abt Associates

Scotty D. Craig
Arizona State University

Jerome V. D'Agostino
The Ohio State University

Christopher T. Dague
The Citadel

Heather A. Davis
Montessori Institute of San Diego

Jacquelynne S. Eccles
University of California, Irvine

Raquel Fidalgo
University of León, Spain

Jill Fitzgerald
The University of North Carolina at Chapel Hill

H. Jerome Freiberg
University of Houston

Ann Bainbridge Frymier
Miami University

Julie Gess-Newsome
Oregon State University-Cascades

David Gijbels
University of Antwerp

Judith Gill
University of South Australia

Belinda G. Gimbert
The Ohio State University

Burkhard Gniewosz
University of Salzburg

Thomas Goetz
University of Konstanz and Thurgau University of Teacher Education

Melva R. Grant
Old Dominion University

Marissa S. Green
The Ohio State University

Wendy S. Grolnick
Clark University

Contributors

Nathan C. Hall
McGill University

Rashea Hamilton
Washington Student Achievement Council

Eric A. Hanushek
Stanford University

John Hattie
University of Melbourne

Eli Hinkel
Seattle Pacific University

Ryan Kapa
The Ohio State University

Aryn C. Karpinski
Kent State University

Meera Komarraju
Southern Illinois University

Rachel E. Lerner
Clark University

Gregory Arief D. Liem
National Institute of Education, Nanyang Technological University

Sofie Loyens
Erasmus University, Rotterdam, and University College Roosevelt, Middelburg and Erasmus University Rotterdam

Andrew J. Martin
University of New South Wales, Australia

Richard E. Mayer
University of California, Santa Barbara

Carol A. Mullen
Virginia Tech

Kathryn Nelson
The Ohio State University

Annemarie Sullivan Palincsar
University of Michigan

Jacquelyn N. Raftery-Helmer
Worcester State University

Peter Reimann
University of Sydney

Jackie Eunjung Relyea
North Carolina State University

Paul J. Riccomini
Pennsylvania State University

Emily M. Rodgers
The Ohio State University

Megan Sanders
Colorado School of Mines

Robin Sayers
The Ohio State University

Aaron Schmidlin
The Ohio State University

Dale H. Schunk
The University of North Carolina at Greensboro

Gregory W. Smith
University of Southern Mississippi

R. Taconis
Eindhoven School of Education

C. Kenneth Tanner
The University of Georgia

Mark Torrance
Nottingham Trent University

Piet Van den Bossche
University of Antwerp and Maastricht University

Noreen M. Webb
University of California, Los Angeles

Ian A. G. Wilkinson
The University of Auckland

Jianzhong Xu
Mississippi State University

Mitchell L. Yell
University of South Carolina

CHAPTER 1

Understanding achievement

The first edition of the *International Guide to Student Achievement* was designed as a comprehensive resource examining and summarizing influences on student achievement. In that book, we asked an international array of scholars to discuss the major research-based correlates of achievement. The primary aim of this revised edition (*Visible Learning Guide to Student Achievement*) is to provide educators with a more user-friendly compendium of research summarizing these major influences – and with a particular focus on the school sector. As educators throughout the world seek to improve student learning outcomes and thus to enhance achievement, the information presented in this book provides practitioners and policy makers with up-to-date research on academic achievement, along with relevant research-based instructional strategies.

The original *Guide* contained nine distinct sections. In that first edition, each section contained a series of short chapters focusing on a larger thematic topic. For example, one section ("Influences from the Teacher") contained 18 brief entries, each written by experts, regarding the various ways in which teachers influence student achievement. Each entry had a similar organizational structure, including (a) an introduction, (b) a brief summary of research evidence, (c) recommendations, and (d) conclusions.

Although the previous edition was rich in information, it did not include summary information for each section that provided educators and policy makers with a brief synthesis of major research findings in each area. In this updated edition, each section begins with a brief summary of the major influences on achievement associated with that particular section. This is followed by a few of the key entries from the original *Guide*, all of which have been recently updated by the authors to reflect recent research developments. Each chapter then concludes with a user-friendly "summary table" that synopsizes the key research-based influences on achievement from that chapter. Both the summaries provided at the start of each chapter and the summary tables provided at the end of each chapter succinctly identify the major influences on achievement, as well as practical implications for educators. All of the summary information reflects both the entries from the original *Guide* and research findings from the updated entries.

What is achievement?

In this section, we briefly (re)introduce the elusive concept of "achievement," in order to provide a framework for the book. **Academic achievement** is a universally valued educational outcome. Valuing of high achievement is engrained in the fabric of many societies. Parents want their children to achieve at high levels, administrators want their schools to be high performing, regional school leaders (e.g., superintendents) want their regions' aggregated achievement to be strong, and even politicians want local and national data to be indicative of high achievement. Indeed, throughout much of the world, children learn from an early age that high achievement is necessary in order to succeed both professionally and financially.

It is impossible to avoid the constant messaging that emphasizes the value of achievement in society. For example, the valuing of achievement is accentuated through highly publicized results of large-scale internationally comparative studies (e.g., the Programme for International Assessment [PISA] and the Trends in International Mathematics Science study [TIMMS]), which regularly report that students in some countries achieve at higher levels than others. Achievement scores are also used as a tool to measure the effectiveness of schools or of specific teachers (with these scores being reported widely and publicly). There are even reminders about the importance of achievement in seemingly unrelated aspects of daily life; for example, it is not uncommon for real estate agents to emphasize that a home that is for sale is in a high-achieving neighborhood and thus has more financial value (Seo & Simons, 2009).

Defining achievement

Whereas achievement is highly coveted, there is no universal agreement on what truly constitutes "achievement." Achievement can be defined in many ways. In the first edition of this book, Guskey (2013) wrote an introductory chapter that provided a framework for understanding this broad construct. Guskey defined achievement, in its simplest terms, as "the accomplishment of something" (p. 3). Guskey noted that in education, achievement is closely tied to learning goals; these could be a student's personal learning goals, curricular goals or teacher's instructional goals, as well as a host of other types of goals.

Guskey identified several significant points that should be considered in discussions of student achievement. Those include the following:

- Learning goals (and achievement outcomes that are tied to those goals) can be classified across three dimensions: *cognitive goals*, *affective goals*, and *psychomotor*

goals. Thus, assessments of achievement can focus on cognitive, affect, or psychomotor outcomes (or any combination of those outcomes).
- There are many conceptualizations of cognitive, affective, and psychomotor achievement outcomes. For example, there are many types of achievement outcomes that can be assessed in the cognitive domain (e.g., memorization of facts, ability to solve problems, etc.), the affective domain (e.g., engagement, socioemotional outcomes), and the psychomotor domain (e.g., running speed, performing a specific gymnastics routine).
- School curricula often emphasize cognitive achievement outcomes; nevertheless, achievement in the affective and psychomotor domains, while often not assessed regularly, represent achievement outcomes that should not be ignored. In recent years, educators have begun to recognize the importance of affective outcomes in particular (e.g., Collaborative for Academic, Social, and Emotional Learning, 2019; Frey, Fisher, & Smith, 2019).
- Although achievement can be thought of as a summative construct that encompasses multiple content areas, achievement is usually examined within specific content areas (e.g., mathematics, reading, chemistry, etc.). Moreover, there is some variation in content areas that are taught and assessed across countries.
- Achievement can be conceptualized both in terms of *attainment* of knowledge or skills (i.e., what a student has learned at a particular point in time) or *improvement* in knowledge or skills (i.e., changes in academic performance over time). Both attainment and improvement are valued outcomes, but they represent different types of achievement and need to be assessed differently.
- Measures of achievement are not all created equal; some measures more accurately assess achievement than do others. Thus, the reliability and validity of measures of achievement should be considered in the reporting of achievement outcomes.
- Measures of achievement are designed for many purposes. For example, measures of achievement can be used to assess:
  - Learning upon completion of a specific unit of instruction
  - Learning within a specific course
  - Readiness for postsecondary education
  - Eligibility for instructional support services

It is essential that the purpose for which an achievement measure was designed is aligned with the ways that achievement outcomes derived from those measures are being reported and used.

What variables are associated with achievement?

This book is about correlates of and influences on achievement. Some of the most commonly considered correlates of achievement include demographic variables (e.g., socioeconomic status, age, or gender), noncognitive variables (e.g., motivation and engagement), school-related variables (e.g., school size, school grade configurations, etc.), and instructional practices (e.g., grouping practices, technology usage, etc.) (Hattie & Anderman, 2013; Hattie, 2009). But in addition to the more typically discussed correlates, achievement also is related to an enormously wide range of other variables (some of which may seem quite odd!). Indeed, a careful examination of the research literature indicates that scholars also have examined the relations of achievement to variables as diverse as body-mass index (which is weakly and negatively related to achievement) (He, Chen, Fan, Cai, & Huang, 2019), homelessness (which is, for the most part, related to lower achievement) (Manfra, 2018), and dietary intake (which is related to achievement through a variety of mechanisms) (Burrows, Goldman, Pursey, & Lim, 2017), among others.

The remaining chapters in this book include discussions of correlates of achievement within specific categories. We have tried to provide information about the correlates of achievement that are most often discussed in the literature and valued by practitioners. The original *Guide* contained nine distinct sections; in this updated version, the former "sections" have been repurposed into shorter chapters. The chapters specifically examine the following influences on achievement:

- Influences from the student
- Influences from the home
- Influences from the school
- Influences from teachers and classrooms
- Influences from the curriculum
- Influences from teaching strategies

In the original *Guide*, we included separate sections examining influences from teachers and classrooms; in this new version, those have been combined into one comprehensive chapter. The original *Guide* also contained two sections that are not included in this updated book. Those included an initial section that contained six entries examining multiple perspectives on understanding the broad concept of achievement and a final section that examined achievement from an international perspective, wherein there were distinct entries examining achievement across a variety of nations (e.g., Russia, Finland, Ghana, and South Korea).

Summary

We believe that this new edition will serve as a practical and useful guide. School personnel throughout the world constantly work toward enhancing students' academic achievement. We hope that the information contained in this book, which is all rooted in science, can help educators, administrators, and policy makers in their daily work. Numerous interventions, innovations, and novel instructional practices are introduced daily in schools throughout the world; it is our hope that this book can assist educators in critically examining their daily practices and the implementation of new strategies in light of research on correlates of academic achievement.

References

Burrows, T., Goldman, S., Pursey, K., & Lim, R. (2017). Is there an association between dietary intake and academic achievement: A systematic review. *Journal of Human Nutrition and Dietetics*, *30*(2), 117–140. https://doi.org/10.1111/jhn.12407

Collaborative for Academic, Social, and Emotional Learning (CASEL). (2019). *What is SEL?* Retrieved from https://casel.org/what-is-sel/

Frey, N., Fisher, D., & Smith, D. (2019). *All learning is social and emotional*. Alexandria, VA: ASCD.

Guskey, T. R. (2013). Defining student achievement. In J. Hattie & E. M. Anderman (Eds.), *International guide to student achievement* (pp. 3–6). New York, NY: Routledge/Taylor & Francis Group.

Hattie, J. (2009). *Visible learning: A synthesis of over 800 meta-analyses relating to achievement*. New York, NY: Routledge.

Hattie, J., & Anderman, E. M. (2013). *International guide to student achievement*. New York, NY: Routledge.

He, J., Chen, X., Fan, X., Cai, Z., & Huang, F. (2019). Is there a relationship between body mass index and academic achievement? A meta-analysis. *Public Health (Elsevier)*, *167*, 111–124. https://doi.org/10.1016/j.puhe.2018.11.002

Manfra, L. (2018). Impact of homelessness on school readiness skills and early academic achievement: A systematic review of the literature. *Early Childhood Education Journal*. https://doi.org/10.1007/s10643-018-0918-6

Seo, Y., & Simons, R. A. (2009). The effect of school quality on residential sales price. *Journal of Real Estate Research*, *31*(3), 307–327.

CHAPTER 2

Influences from the student

The entries in this chapter focus on influences from the student. By "influences from the student," we are referring to four distinct types of influences on achievement. First, sometimes academic achievement differs based on student demographic differences. For example, there often is much rhetoric in the media about gender differences in achievement or the effects of socioeconomic status on achievement; variables such as gender and socioeconomic status vary by student and interact with the larger social contexts in which students reside to exert their influences on achievement. In this chapter, our contributing authors present evidence to help separate fact from fiction with regard to these descriptive variables.

Academic achievement is also related to students' attitudes and dispositions (i.e., students' feelings, perceptions, and psychological characteristics), as well as to cognitive variables (e.g., students' current levels of cognitive development). These variables also vary greatly among students; thus within any given classroom anywhere in the world, there is likely to be variability in students' motivation, engagement, attitudes toward school, level of cognitive development, etc. Some of the entries in this chapter examine variables that are malleable (e.g., attitudes, motivation, and engagement), whereas other chapters focus on more enduring variables (e.g., personality traits). The chapters on cognitive variables focus in particular on the relations of developmental aspects of cognition to achievement.

Finally, there are many social (i.e., contextual) variables that affect individual students' academic achievement. Whereas a cohort of students may be situated within the same social context (e.g., 30 students may all be learning in the same classroom, with the same teacher, at the same time), each student experiences that classroom uniquely; thus, social variables influence achievement depending largely on how individual students perceive and interpret these social variables. Some examples include peer relationships, preschool learning environments, and students' social goals.

The entries that appeared in the previous edition are listed below. (Entries with an asterisk have been updated for this edition.)

Entry to School
Collette Tayler

Piagetian Approaches
Philip Adey and Michael Shayer

Entry to Tertiary Education
Emer Smyth

Physical Activity
Janet Clinton

Gender Influences★
Judith Gill

Engagement and Opportunity to Learn
Phillip L. Ackerman

Behavioral Engagement in Learning
Jennifer Fredricks

Goal Setting and Academic Achievement
Dominique Morisano and Edwin A. Locke

Self-Reported Grades and GPA
Marcus Credé and Nathan R. Kuncel

Conceptual Change
Stella Vosniadou and Panagiotis Tsoumakis

Social Motivation and Academic Motivation
Tim Urdan

Attitudes and Dispositions
Robert D. Renaud

Personality Influences★
Meera Komarraju

Academic Self-Concept
Herbert W. Marsh and Marjorie Seaton

Self-Efficacy
> *Mimi Bong*

Motivation★
> *Dale H. Schunk and Carol A. Mullen*

Friendship in School
> *Annemaree Carroll, Stephen Houghton, and Sasha Lynn*

Indigenous and Other Minoritized Students★
> *Russell Bishop*

Low Academic Success
> *David A. Bergin*

Learning Difficulties in School★
> *R. Allan Allday and Mitchell L. Yell*

We briefly describe some of the major student influences on achievement below; these are summarized in the summary table at the end of the chapter.

Demographic differences

Educators, policy makers, and researchers often focus on the relations of individual differences to achievement. Many of these discussions focus on the relations of demographic characteristics of students (e.g., gender and ethnicity) to achievement. Whereas some patterns do emerge, they generally are small when they do. For example, while there is a fairly widespread assumption that males achieve at higher levels in math than do females and that females achieve at higher levels in language arts than do males, evidence for such differences is extremely limited. When gender differences do emerge, they are more pronounced among students from disadvantaged backgrounds. In addition, males are more likely to be diagnosed with attention deficit hyperactivity disorder (which can impact achievement), and females tend to receive higher teacher-assigned grades than do males (Gill, this volume; Voyer & Voyer, 2014).

The relations of ethnicity to achievement are also often discussed and debated. In general, research suggests that ethnic differences in academic achievement are small to nonexistent (Bishop, this volume). In discussions of the relations between ethnicity and achievement, it often is more useful to examine variation within specific ethnic groups, rather than comparing one group to another on measures of achievement (Davis-Kean & Jager, 2014). Research does suggest that achievement varies *within* ethnic groups, with higher achievement being associated in particular with (a) students learning from teachers who value the unique experiences that students bring into the classroom and (b) having a positive racial/ethnic identity (Bishop, this volume; Miller-Cotto & Byrnes, 2016).

Attitudes and dispositions

Students' attitudes toward learning, as well as more enduring personality characteristics, also are related to academic achievement. Fortunately, many of students' attitudes and beliefs are malleable. This means that teachers and parents can positively influence attitudes and beliefs, particularly when those beliefs hinder achievement.

Many of the entries in the original *Guide* focused on student motivation. Motivation is a broad term that encompasses a variety of mental processes that facilitate the attainment of one's goals (Schunk & Mullen, this volume). Whereas, historically, motivation was viewed as being caused by personality traits and the desire to satisfy basic human needs, motivation researchers now generally view student motivation as having both cognitive and social components (Weiner, 1990). Thus, students' motivation in academic settings is influenced both by what students think (i.e., the cognitive components) and a variety of social influences (e.g., peers, instructional practices, etc.).

The goals that students pursue represent an important component of academic motivation. Research clearly indicates that the goals that students have affect their achievement; these include both goals that students set for themselves and goals that are imposed on students by their teachers, their parents, and their peers (e.g., Rawsthorne & Elliot, 1999; Schunk, 1985). One aspect of motivation that is related strongly to goals is self-efficacy; self-efficacy refers to the belief that one can successfully engage with and complete a specific task (e.g., solve an algebra problem) (Bandura, 2013). Self-efficacy is enhanced when students set short-term, slightly challenging goals and achieve success at reaching those goals (Schunk, 1984). Other motivation variables that vary across students and that are related to achievement include students' attributions (i.e., the reasons to which students attribute academic successes and failures), intrinsic and extrinsic motivation (i.e., motivation to engage with a task because it is enjoyable [intrinsic] or in order to receive a reward or avoid a punishment [extrinsic]), values (i.e., students' beliefs about the importance, usefulness, and likability of a task), and goal orientations (i.e., the reasons why students engage with a task). (For reviews, see Anderman & Anderman, 2014 or Anderman & Wolters, 2006.)

All these motivation variables shape students' perceptions of their own abilities (i.e., their *academic self-concepts*). Academic self-concept can represent both a general perception of one's ability (i.e., a student may see him- or herself as being "smart" or being "dumb"), as well as domain-specific academic self-concepts (i.e., a student may see him- or herself as being "smart" at math but "dumb" at language arts) (Marsh & Seaton, 2013). The relation between academic self-concept and achievement is reciprocal: if a student has a high academic self-concept in a particular domain (e.g., in the study of biology), that positive self-concept will positively affect achievement; in turn, the high achievement that the student earns in biology further feeds into the student's self-concept of ability.

Academic engagement is related to motivation, albeit somewhat differently. Students who are academically engaged are actively involved in their academic learning (Lei, Cui, & Zhou, 2018). There are three types of engagement: cognitive engagement (e.g., using effective self-regulatory strategies while participating in a classroom activity), behavioral engagement (e.g., behaving appropriately and exerting effort during a classroom activity), and emotional engagement (e.g., expressing joy while participating in a classroom activity) (Fredricks, 2013; Fredricks, Blumenfeld, & Paris, 2004). Students who are highly engaged in their studies achieve at higher levels than those who are less engaged (Ackerman, 2013).

Cognitive

In any discussion of the relations of cognitive variables to achievement, it is essential to recognize the powerful positive relationship between a student's prior achievement and subsequent achievement (Richardson, Abraham, & Bond, 2012). Nevertheless, there often is substantial variability in cognitive abilities among students, and some of this variability is attributable to development. From a developmental perspective, Piaget's classic conceptualization of four stages of cognitive development helps us frame these individual differences. The four stages proposed by Piaget (i.e., sensorimotor, preoperational, concrete operations, and formal operations) are not rigidly aligned with specific chronological ages; rather, researchers and educators have consistently and vehemently argued that movement into a higher stage is gradual and occurs differently for different children (Adey & Shayer, 2013). Thus, two children who share a birth date may be at very different places in terms of their cognitive development; this is not to suggest that the child who appears to be more advanced cognitively is "smarter" than the other child; rather, they are just experiencing cognitive development at different rates.

Another cognitive variable that has been examined by educators in recent years is conceptual change. Conceptual change occurs when current knowledge structures (i.e., long-held beliefs) change in order to facilitate the learning of new information that conflicts with one's prior knowledge. Although conceptual change is often discussed in the domain of science, conceptual change can occur in all academic domains (Vosniadou & Mason, 2012) and is influenced by cognitive, motivational, and affective variables (Sinatra, Kienhues, & Hofer, 2014). Certain instructional methods (e.g., teaching with analogies or asking students to make predictions) can facilitate conceptual change and, ultimately, greater achievement (Vosniadou & Tsoumakis, 2013).

Social

The chapter also contains several entries that focus on relationships of student-level variables to achievement from a social perspective. Whereas the word "social" implies interactions involving more than one person (i.e., beyond individual differences), students experience the social milieu of schools in different ways. Whereas students are always in social settings while they are at school, their perceptions, experiences, and interpretations of the events that occur in their schools vary, thus leading to differential effects on achievement. Moreover, social or "contextual" variation both within and across classrooms also affects achievement differentially across individual students.

Students' friendships emerge as a particularly salient and obvious influence on achievement. Friendships affect achievement in numerous ways, and friendships have differential effects on achievement as children move from the early school years into secondary school settings (Carroll, Houghton, & Lynn, 2013). In general, research indicates that both working with friends on schoolwork and having friendships are positively related to achievement (Wentzel, Jablansky, & Scalise, 2018). Moreover, students' friendships also influence their educational goals (Urdan, 2013); thus, a student who maintains friendships with peers who value school is likely to also value school and thus set achievement-oriented goals.

The larger social contexts of schools and classrooms also affect achievement. For example, achievement is affected by the ability of one's student peers within a school; specifically, individual students who attend schools along with many high-ability peers may have lower academic self-concepts, which may in turn affect achievement (the "Big-Fish-Little-Pond-Effect") (Becker & Neumann, 2018; Marsh & Seaton, 2013). In addition, the training of teachers who work in a given school also can have differential effects on achievement; for example, young children whose teachers have received substantial training in child development tend to experience achievement benefits (Tayler, 2013).

2.1

Gender influences

Judith Gill

Introduction

Few topics have generated such vigorous and ongoing debates in recent decades as have those concerning the relationship between gender and achievement. In the 1970s, when the talk was about sex differences in learning outcomes, it seemed that many educationists were inclined to believe the nostrums of early psychology, wherein young people were understood to have innate and inevitable differences in their capacity to learn that were reliably demonstrable in learning outcomes. This thinking was about to undergo rapid and fundamental change with the move from thinking of "sex" as fixed and innate to "gender," which was seen as produced by the learner's social context in conjunction with his or her innate potentials. By 2011, the term "sex" had virtually disappeared from the public lexicon and been replaced by "gender" on forms for individual inscription and social reporting and accounting. This change in terminology followed from research results demonstrating that the old truths were no longer universally applicable in terms of male and female differences in learning outcomes, along with science's incapacity to account for the differences that were seen to occur. The following text will offer a broad overview of what we now know about gender and achievement and what we still do not know.

Research evidence

In the mid-1970s, the first major review was conducted into sex differences in thinking. Based on hundreds of preceding American studies on the topic, Maccoby and Jacklin (1974) produced their analysis of the combined results and concluded that there were very few reliable and consistent differences in mental functioning between boys and girls: so few, in fact, that they advised great caution in restating them for fear of perpetuating some of the myths. The researchers insisted that there was far greater variation within either population of girls or boys than between them. The one item they cautiously identified concerns the superior performance of boys from age ten in mental spatial rotation – a feature often associated with superior mathematical performance in males, although its explanatory capacity is much more limited. Subsequently, a prominent British researcher published his review of the British studies of sex differences in cognition and came to the same conclusion (Fairweather, 1976). In this case, he added that the differences were least likely to appear the younger the population tested, giving support to the idea that what were still called sex differences in thinking were socially produced rather than innately given. Despite the clarity of these findings, the high repute of the researchers, and the fact that the finding of no or very little difference continues to be demonstrated (Halpern & Mamay, 2000; Hyde & Linn, 2006), these results did not indicate the end of the story.

The decades following the 1970s produced many examples of research investigating gender differences in schooling outcomes in terms of the subjects girls and boys chose to study, the scores they obtained, their proceeding to tertiary education, and their capacity to engage in the highest levels of intellectual life. Initially, this research typically showed girls trailing boys in a range of performance measures, most notably grades in math and science. Additionally, it was noticed that the gender gaps in student achievement were seen to increase with age, suggesting that schooling processes may work to increase these gender differences rather than reduce them. This perception led to many studies of classroom treatments in the attempt to identify ways in which teaching practice might be implicated in the construction of gender difference (Gill, 1992; Sadker & Sadker, 1994).

During the 1980s and 1990s, there was much activity inspired by feminist efforts to address gender inequity in girls' schooling. Classroom research was dedicated to monitoring the inclusion of girls and their interests, teaching materials were scrutinized to avoid featuring males at the expense of females across the broad spectrum of adult roles, and girls were targeted and encouraged to enroll in nontraditional subject areas, especially math and science. In many respects the movement to improve girls' educational outcomes was successful: girls now are seen to get higher grades than boys, and more of them complete school. Girls are enrolling in math and science in significant numbers in high school, albeit not quite as commonly as are boys, and many progress to university and choose courses not open to women of previous generations.

While the success story holds true for many middle-class girls, if less so for girls from disadvantaged backgrounds, by the mid-1990s the situation for boys had become a cause for widespread concern. Boys began to emerge as significantly less successful than girls in terms of learning outcomes. Researchers write of a "small but pervasive tendency for females to score better on standardized tests and to achieve more post school qualifications" (Gibb, Fergusson, & Horwood, 2008, p. 63). Increasing numbers of research papers appeared, addressing what became known as the "crisis" in boys' education. Studies showed boys as more likely than girls to get referrals for behavioral issues, to present with reading problems, to be identified with ADHD, and to drop out of school before completion. For example, US statistics for the 2003–2004 school year show that 26% of female students became school dropouts, compared to 34% of male students. Reports of male underachievement have come from across the developed world (Thiessen & Nickerson, 1999; Tinklin, Croxford, Ducklin, & Frame, 2001; Weaver-Hightower, 2003; Younger & Warrington, 2005). Tallies of high school graduations show girls as the more successful group: more of them go on to university and more of them gain undergraduate degrees – albeit in the fields of education and health, which are not renowned for providing access to the status and power of some other professions. By 2009, for the first time in the United States, more women than men graduated with master's degrees. By this time the focus in investigations of gender equity in education had turned to the situation of boys. As New Zealand researchers Gibb et al. concluded, "The trend of male underachievement has been evident for at least the last decade" (Gibb et al., 2008, p. 63). Male underachievement is particularly prevalent among boys from disadvantaged backgrounds whose situation is made more evident with the demise of ready employment in unskilled trades and manufacturing. However, it is also the case that middle-class boys continue in the main to do well in school. However, the media hype around the "boys' crisis" was constructed around a gender wars scenario as though all girls were doing well and all boys were not. Of course, the situation is much more complex (Gill & Starr, 2001; for a fuller discussion, see Gill, Esson, & Yuen, 2016).

While girls appear as more reliable in terms of passing grades than their male peers, one area still stands out in the research and popular understanding of gender differences in enrollment and achievement: namely science, engineering, technology, and mathematics (STEM). Numerous studies have attempted to demonstrate and explain gender differences in achievement in these areas and have led to a mixed bag of conclusions. For example, it has been alleged that girls' lower achievements in these areas are largely due to their choosing against these courses in high school and, consequently, having less experience with numerical and scientific ways of thinking. This situation leads to the question of whether the girls would do better if they were not able to choose courses of study. However when senior school results for these subjects are compared, a higher proportion of girls is frequently found among the high performers, which is explained in terms of the more selective group of girls who form the minority enrollment in these areas. On the other hand, studies continue to show that, among the very high performers as evidenced by competitions such as the Mathematics Olympiad and industry-led, country-specific prizes, boys are consistently more likely than girls to be among the winners (Ellison & Swanson, 2009).

One interesting outcome of the Programme for International Student Assessment (PISA) analyses is that the variation in student performance within the participating European countries is many times larger than the variation between countries. However, differences in test items and survey methodologies make generalizations extremely difficult, with at least one study showing that the gender difference in reading is a product of the test items rather than the individual responses (Lafontaine & Monseur, 2009). Moreover, PISA results suggest that the most consistent and visible gender difference relates to girls' advantage in reading, a gender gap that emerges early and is maintained with age, such that by age 15, there were "significant differences in favor of females reported for virtually all European countries" (Eurydice, 2010, p. 34). There is some indication in this work that the recorded differences result from different patterns of school attendance, with boys tending to start school later and being more likely to be required to repeat a year, thus testing that records achievement against age should also account for difference in schooling patterns and treatments.

In mathematics, the gender differences were less pronounced and less stable than those for reading. A 1995 survey showed that gender difference in mathematics in the fourth year of schooling was small or nonexistent. A similar "no difference" outcome was found at year eight. It was not until the final year of secondary school that the males emerged with significantly higher mathematical achievement in all countries except Hungary (Eurydice, 2010, p. 35). Other, comparable tests found similarly inconsistent results, with gender gaps visible only intermittently across age and culture.

A more promising line of research has been carried out by Hyde and colleagues, who argue that there is a much more consistent and demonstrable similarity between males and females in mathematics and science capabilities than there is a difference (Hyde & Linn, 2006). Based on a meta-analysis of gender differences in mathematics across a sample of 100 studies testing more than three million students, Hyde's team was able to show the traditional gap in favor of males had disappeared, an outcome that had been predicted by neuroscientist researchers for some time (Rogers, 2001). This latter case repeats a theme from analyses of the gender and achievement research: that is, the differences that used to be understood as a result of the genetic makeup of males and females have, in reality, been produced by their different treatment within the social context. Hyde notes that the lack of gender difference in math achievement does not explain the ongoing gender disparity in STEM enrollments, which continue to favor males. Recent research suggests that such differences in enrollment patterns may be a product of culturally laden gender-appropriate perceptions in concert with different levels of self-confidence and individual capacity.

Psychological research has revealed consistent male/female differences in the capacity to hold to an image of a successful self. For example, Renold and Allan, in an English study, describe a bright girl who "deprecated her achievements whenever she was praised and systematically denied her flair for academic work" (Renold & Allan, 2007, 463). These writers describe the girls as struggling with the "precarious balance" between achieving academically and acceptable femininity. In a Canadian study, Pomerantz and Raby (2011, p. 555) write of bright girls holding "academic achievements close to their chest as a secret to be guarded" in a paper identifying the complexity of girls' engagements with narratives of academic success. In their analysis of the range of contradictory discourses around girls' performance of academic identities, the need to mask ability for fear of contaminating the idealized construction of acceptable femininity is a familiar theme. The widely reported analysis of gender equality in the OECD studies of student achievement levels suggested that highly able girls "choke" on the pressure they experience from friends, family, and themselves, a situation which renders them unable to perform at their best.

> Given girls' keen desire to succeed in school and to please others, their fear of negative evaluations, and their lower self confidence in mathematics and science, it is hardly surprising high-achieving girls choke under often self-imposed pressure.
>
> (OECD, 2015)

This report seems to blame the girls for being girls – wanting to "please others" and having "lower self confidence" and putting pressure on themselves. In the final analysis, the report presents the girls as underachieving: an outcome that is "hardly surprising" – indeed almost expected. The girls' shortcomings have been identified as their own fault! Not surprisingly, then, the conclusion is somewhat ambivalent:

> [G]ender disparities in performance do not stem from innate differences in aptitude, but rather from students' attitudes towards learning and their behaviour in school, from how they choose to spend their leisure time, and from the confidence they have – or do not have – in their own abilities as students.
>
> (OECD, 2015, p. 3)

Despite the increasing recognition of girls as top students, the idea that their success comes at a price is a reiterated theme in educational research. Questions about female academic success continue to be raised, as seen in the OECD report mentioned earlier and in studies of the difficulties of successful women in male-dominated professions, which identify outcomes that suggest the ongoing complex negotiations required for girls and women achievers (Mills, Franzway, Gill, & Sharp, 2014).

Having rejected the explanation of gender differences in educational outcomes as being due to lack of intellectual capacity, the challenge for research is to explain the persistent gender differences that continue to occur. One explanation for this phenomenon is that the girls are responding (both consciously and subconsciously) to contextual cues that continually reinforce the idea of male superiority and leadership as gender-based entitlements and that this image becomes grounded in the habitus of girls and women. Hence, in striving for an acceptable form of femininity, girls avoid positioning themselves as success stories, especially in terms of public roles when they could be seen as in competition with men. While this syndrome of female underestimation of ability and hiding success compared with male overestimation of ability and lauding their success was initially demonstrated in the 1970s, research continues to reveal the same feature in studies of professional women right up to the present time (Sandberg, 2013; Heilman & Okimoto, 2007). As summarized by Sheryl Sandberg in her bestselling book about women and leadership:

> I believe this bias [against women's success] is at the very core of why women are held back. It is also at the very core of why women hold themselves back. For men, professional success comes with positive reinforcement every step of the way. For women, even when they're recognized for their achievements, they're often regarded unfavorably.
>
> (Sandberg, 2013, p. 40)

Given that this syndrome – of males being celebrated for success and females being downgraded – appears as early as elementary school, the challenge is surely for teachers to create an environment in which success is recognized and celebrated without the gender-related overtones.

Researchers have called for greater gender sensitivity in teachers, along with programs in teacher education that alert potential teachers to the ways in which they may operate to reinforce traditional limitations – or to help students overcome them. The ideal educational experience is that all students understand themselves as "can-do" learners as the optimum preparation for becoming fully participative and engaged citizens.

Summary and recommendations

Much has been learned in recent years from the research on gender and achievement. We now know that the traditional generalizations have little basis in hard evidence and that boys and girls are much more likely to have similar abilities than to be divided in terms of capacity. If we must talk of gender differences in educational outcomes – and we take seriously the warnings of researchers about not wishing to further the difference case! – we should say only that girls as a group emerge as the more reliable scholars in terms of passing grades, whereas there are some indications that boys are more spread across the scale, with some found among the very high achievers as well as others at the lowest underachieving end. By and large, however, the evidence that there is a far greater area of similarity than of difference between girls and boys in terms of learning capacities appears most compelling.

The implications for teaching that follow are that teachers should encourage the young people in their charge to explore and learn unhampered by outdated gender roles. The research shows that gender differences are more often developed in terms of the learner's social context than as a result of innate propensities. The challenge for teachers is to develop all students in ways that maximize potential. This is surely best done by using teaching methods and materials that include men and women as equal active participants in the world beyond school.

References

Ellison, G., & Swanson, A. (2009). The gender gap in secondary school mathematics at high achievement levels. *Journal of Economic Perspectives, 24*(2), 109–128.

Eurydice. (2010). *Gender differences in educational outcomes: European commission*. Retrieved from http://eacea.ec.europa.eu/education/eurydice/documents/thematic_reports/120EN.pdf

Fairweather, H. (1976). Sex differences in cognition. *Cognition, 4*(3), 231–280.

Gibb, S. J., Fergusson, D., & Horwood, L. J. (2008). Gender differences in educational achievement to age 25. *Australian Journal of Education, 52*(1), 63–78.

Gill, J. (1992). *Differences in the making: The construction of gender in Australian schooling* (Unpublished doctoral dissertation), Adelaide University, Australia.

Gill, J., Esson, K., & Yuen, R. (2016). *A girl's education? Schooling and the formation of gender, identities and future visions*. London: Palgrave Macmillan.

Gill, J., & Starr, K. (2001). Sauce for the goose? Deconstructing the boys-in-education push. *Discourse: Studies in the Cultural Politics of Education, 23*(3), 323–334.

Halpern, D. F., & Mamay, M. L. (2000). The smarter sex: A critical review of sex differences in intelligence. *Educational Psychology Review, 12*(2), 229–246. Retrieved from https://springerlink3.metapress.com/ behavioral-science/

Heilman, M. E., & Okimoto, T. G. (2007). Why are women penalized for success at male tasks? The implied communality deficit. *Journal of Applied Psychology, 92*(1), 81–92.

Hyde, J. S., & Linn, M. (2006, October 27). Gender similarities in mathematics and science. *Science, 314*, 599–600.

Lafontaine, D., & Monseur, C. (2009). Gender gap in comparative studies of reading comprehension: To what extent do the test characteristics make a difference? *European Educational Research Journal, 8*(1), 69–79.

Maccoby, E., & Jacklin, C. N. (1974). *The psychology of sex differences*. Stanford, CA: Stanford University Press.

Mills, J., Franzway, S., Gill, J., & Sharp, R. (2014). *Challenging knowledge, sex and power: Gender, work and engineering*. New York, NY: Routledge.

OECD (Organization for Economic Cooperation and Development). (2015). *The ABC of gender equality in education*. Paris: OECD Publishing.

Pomerantz, S., & Raby, R. (2011). Oh she's so smart: Girls' complex engagement with post / feminist narratives of academic success. *Gender and Education, 23*(5) 549–564.

Renold, E., & Allan, A. (2007). Bright and beautiful: High achieving girls, ambivalent femininities and the feminization of success in the primary school. *Discourse: Studies in the Cultural Politics of Education, 27*(4), 457–473.

Rogers, L. (2001). *Sexing the brain*. New York, NY: Columbia University Press.

Sadker, M., & Sadker, D. (1994). *Failing at fairness: How our schools cheat girls*. New York, NY: Simon & Schuster.

Sandberg, S. (2013). *Lean in: Women work and the will to lead*. Sydney: Random House.

Thiessen, V., & Nickerson, C. (1999). *Canadian gender trends in education and work*. Ottawa, Canada: Human Resources Development.

Tinklin, T., Croxford, L., Ducklin, A., & Frame, B. (2001). *Gender and pupil performance in Scotland's schools*. Edinburgh, Scotland: Edinburgh University Press.

Weaver-Hightower, M. (2003). The "boy turn" in research on gender and education. *Review of Educational Research, 73*(4), 471–498.

Younger, M., & Warrington, M. (2005). *Raising boys' achievement*. London: Department for Education and Skills.

2.2
Learning difficulties in school

R. Allan Allday and Mitchell L. Yell

Introduction

Learning difficulties present a myriad of academic and behavioral challenges to schools and teachers due to their effect on achievement. Numerous factors are associated with learning difficulties; however, these factors typically funnel into similar outcomes that are often linked to low academic achievement and poor social functioning. Identifying factors that lead to learning difficulties requires pinpointing the primary sources of influence within schools.

Three distinct groups (i.e., students, teachers, and schools) contain specific factors and characteristics that impact school achievement. For example, student factors, such as presence of a disability, socioeconomic status, or family involvement, can affect achievement. Teachers who lack training in effective practices for struggling learners and effective classroom and behavior-management strategies can magnify learning difficulties. Finally, school factors can affect student achievement through the established school-wide climate and expectations. Each of these groups (i.e., student, teacher, and school) influences achievement, and they are interconnected; therefore, focusing on these three groups can help identify effective practices that can increase the success of students with learning difficulties.

Research evidence

Defining school achievement is necessary before addressing how student, teacher, and school factors can impact academic and behavioral success. It also requires consideration of a school's role in a student's life: that is, schools function as mediators to prepare students for successful competitive employment and a socially well-adjusted adult life. In order to prepare students to achieve these outcomes, schools must focus on the attainment of the academic and behavioral skills necessary for productive and socially engaged adults. For the purpose of this discussion, achievement is defined as success within the school environment in the areas of academic functioning (e.g., reaching skill mastery, performing at or above expected levels) and behavioral functioning (e.g., exhibiting appropriate social skills, engaging in school-appropriate behavior).

Student factors

There are a number of causal mechanisms that affect students prior to entering primary school. The presence of a disability, whether physical, intellectual, or behavioral, can impact school success (Lane, Carter, Pierson, & Glaeser, 2006). Other mechanisms, such as family structures and neighborhoods (Herberle, Thomas, Wagmiller, Briggs-Gowan, & Carter, 2014; White & Renk, 2012) affect student outcomes. Considering these mechanisms, it is clear that individual students enter primary school with different skills and experiences that will impact academic successes as well as social productivity (e.g., social skills, behavioral regulation).

Academic and behavioral challenges often occur simultaneously within the student and impact school success (Algozzine, Wang, & Violette, 2011). Academic challenges among students with learning difficulties can be exacerbated through their behavior. Students with learning difficulties may engage in inappropriate behavior to escape academic tasks (Burke, Hagan-Burke, & Sugai, 2003). In contrast, students with learning difficulties may experience negative peer interactions (Baumeister, Storch, & Geffken, 2008) and withdraw from academic engagement to avoid peer interaction. Student responses to academic tasks and social situations within the school directly impact achievement and social successes.

Schools and teachers can only plan for student characteristics, but are limited in what they can control outside of school functions. For example, schools cannot control the presence of a disability, familial structures, or neighborhoods; however, schools can control experiences within the school building. Providing students with effective teachers and a school environment that supports learning is vital to negate the effects of student characteristics. The following sections relate to how teacher and school characteristics can improve academic achievement and limit learning difficulties.

Teacher characteristics

Teachers are the most important mediators of knowledge within schools. They must understand how to initiate learning so that the full spectrum of students can be successful. As inclusion of students with academic and behavioral difficulties increases in the general education classroom (i.e., mainstreaming), teachers must be effective in providing instruction to students with a wide spectrum of skills. Instructional practices and classroom/behavior management strategies are two primary factors that can hinder a teacher's ability to address learning difficulties effectively.

Instructional practices often affect student behavior. Scott, Hirn, and Alter (2014) reported results of over 1,000 observations showing that student engagement increased and disruptive behavior decreased as teachers were providing instruction. This suggests that teachers who are actively instructing their students will increase student learning behaviors (i.e., engagement). Teachers who are well trained to instruct students with learning difficulties understand that effective instructional practices can be successful with *any* student. Unfortunately, some teachers are ill prepared to instruct students who learn at slower paces or require additional academic or behavioral supports (Allday, Neilsen-Gatti, & Hudson, 2013). Therefore, un- or underprepared teachers may avoid students with learning difficulties for lack of understanding of how to remedy the challenges. For example, students who struggle with new concepts tend to slow the pace of instruction. This slowing of instruction can cause the struggling learner to be overlooked or unintentionally ignored by teachers. It helps in maintaining lesson pacing to overlook low-performing students; however, it does not address those students' learning difficulties.

A solid foundation in classroom and behavior management is a second factor that can limit teacher effectiveness in improving achievement. Teachers who do not have good management skills are more likely to remove students from the classroom. The likelihood of a student gaining academic skills decreases when that student is removed from the learning environment. Teachers with a strong foundational understanding of management principles know that students who struggle academically may be more apt to exhibit problem behaviors in order to escape task demands. Utilizing group contingencies can assist teachers in combating problem behaviors (Maggin, Pustejovsky, & Johnson, 2017). Another challenge for teachers with poor management skills is stopping instruction to address problem behavior. The more frequently a teacher stops the lesson, the less content that can be covered during instruction. Proximity control and effective questioning are two strategies effective classroom managers can use to continue lessons while addressing problem behavior.

Moving forward in reducing or eliminating learning difficulties, teachers must better prepare to teach students who have academic and behavioral challenges. Specifically, teachers must embrace teaching methods known to be effective (e.g., direct instruction) and be more hesitant to use unproven methods. Often, teachers can use simple techniques such as guided notes or increased opportunities to respond to assist students with learning difficulties. For example, Konrad, Joseph, and Eveleigh (2009) conducted a meta-analysis supporting the use of guided notes in improving academic achievement of students with learning difficulties. MacSuga-Gage and Simonsen (2015) found in their systematic review of literature that teacher-directed opportunities to respond improved both academic and behavioral outcomes. Utilizing research-validated methods increases the possibility of maximum content coverage and overcoming academic deficits.

Teachers must learn strategies to reduce challenging behavior while promoting socially appropriate alternative behaviors. As with academics, teachers can use simple management strategies (e.g., proximity control, effective questioning) to address student behavior. When teachers employ proven methods to increase positive behaviors, they should see an increase in academic achievement.

School characteristics

Effective schools provide environments that encourage academic growth and reinforce socially appropriate behaviors. Effective schools meet student needs through hard work and staff perseverance and overcome many factors that potentially impede school effectiveness. For instance, learning can be affected by issues posed by low socioeconomic status in a school, as well as urban or rural challenges. Schools, however, can focus on factors in which they have more control, such as developing a learning climate and collaborative teamwork that builds upon student success.

Historically, schools have taken a punitive approach to managing behavior that disrupts the learning environment. Although this approach is effective with many students, it is less effective in reducing problem behaviors of students with chronic behavior problems. Often, students with consistent problem behaviors receive progressively more intense levels of punishment (e.g., from office referrals to suspensions to expulsions). Students who receive suspensions and expulsions are disadvantaged in academic achievement because of removal from the learning environment. For schools to address the learning difficulties of students with challenging behaviors, it is necessary to address student engagement in the learning environment.

A second school-wide factor that can affect achievement is an atmosphere of collaborative teamwork with the school. Schools that fail to create effective communication between administration and staff limit their effectiveness. Students with learning difficulties may exhibit different behaviors with different teachers. When teachers fail to communicate effective strategies for particular students, they may decrease the likelihood of student success in all classes. An additional challenge in communication among school staff is the sharing of academic and behavioral data. If teachers view data as "my data" versus "our data," then they may be less likely to work collaboratively in analyzing the data and developing interventions.

Addressing learning difficulties at a school-wide level requires individual schools and districts to be prepared to address their students' various academic and behavioral issues. School-wide positive behavior supports and interventions (PBIS) have proven to be a successful method of addressing some of these issues (Horner & Sugai, 2015). PBIS has been an endeavor aimed at creating a welcoming learning environment that promotes socially appropriate behavior. Within the system of PBIS, there are several effective practices that can help schools better meet the needs of students with learning difficulties. Specifically, school staff must collaboratively define common objectives, develop teaching methods for expectations, follow through with set procedures, and evaluate program effectiveness (Sugai & Horner, 2002). Freeman et al. (2015) examined the effects of PBIS from 883 high schools. The authors noted that, among the school data examined, office discipline referrals (ODRs) decreased and attendance increased when PBIS was implemented with fidelity. These two findings support the reduction of learning difficulties through increased access to instruction. This approach (i.e., PBIS) addresses student and teacher behavior through encouraging positive behavior and requires that schools train their teachers in effective practices.

Summary and recommendations

Identifying factors that support and maintain learning difficulties in school is a challenge that researchers, educators, and school administrators must continue to resolve. These factors can be numerous and complex but present themselves in various forms of academic and behavior problems. It is unknown if academic or behavior problems arise first; therefore, teachers and schools should work to *teach* academic skills and to *teach* behavior skills (Algozzine et al., 2011). Two goals can be reached through teaching academic and behavior skills. First, learning difficulties in schools can be reduced when students are presented with effective instruction. Second, academic achievement can be increased when schools and teachers reinforce positive student behaviors.

References

Algozzine, B., Wang, C., & Violette, A. S. (2011). Reexamining the relationship between academic achievement and social behavior. *Journal of Positive Behavior Interventions, 13*, 3–16.

Allday, R. A., Neilsen-Gatti, S., & Hudson, T. M. (2013). Preparation for inclusion in teacher education pre-service curricula. *Teacher Education and Special Education, 36*, 298–311.

Baumeister, A. L., Storch, E. A., & Geffken, G. R. (2008). Peer victimization in children with learning disabilities. *Child and Adolescent Social Work Journal, 25*, 11–23.

Burke, M. D., Hagan-Burke, S., & Sugai, G. (2003). The efficacy of function-based interventions for students with learning disabilities who exhibit escape-maintained problem behaviors: Preliminary results from a single-case experiment. *Learning Disabilities Quarterly, 26*, 15–25.

Freeman, J., Simonsen, B., McCoach, D. B., Sugai, G., Lombardi, A., & Horner, R. (2015). Relationship between school-wide positive behavior interventions and supports and academic, attendance, and behavioral outcomes in high schools. *Journal of Positive Behavior Interventions, 18*, 41–51.

Herberle, A. E., Thomas, Y. M., Wagmiller, R. L., Briggs-Gowan, M. J., & Carter, A. S. (2014). The impact of neighborhood, family, and individual risk factors on toddler's disruptive behavior. *Child Development, 85*, 2046–2061.

Horner, R. H., & Sugai, G. (2015). School-wide PBIS: An example of applied behavior analysis implemented at a scale of social importance. *Behavior Analysis in Practice, 8*, 80–85.

Konrad, M., Joseph, L. M., & Eveleigh, E. (2009). A meta-analytic review of guided notes. *Education and Treatment of Children, 32*, 421–444.

Lane, K., Carter, E., Pierson, M., & Glaeser, B. (2006). Academic, social, and behavioral characteristics of high school students with emotional disturbances or learning disabilities. *Journal of Emotional and Behavioral Disorders, 14*, 108–117.

MacSuga-Gage, A. S., & Simonsen, B. (2015). Examining the effects of teacher-directed opportunities to respond on student outcomes: A systematic review of the literature. *Education & Treatment of Children, 38*, 211–240.

Maggin, D. M., Pustejovsky, J. E., & Johnson, A. H. (2017). A meta-analysis of school-based group contingency interventions for students with challenging behavior: An update. *Remedial and Special Education, 38*, 353–370.

Scott, T. M., Hirn, R. G., & Alter, P. J. (2014). Teacher instruction as a predictor for student engagement and disruptive behaviors. *Preventing School Failure, 58*, 193–200.

Sugai, G., & Horner, R. (2002). The evolution of discipline practices: School-wide positive behavior supports. *Child and Family Behavior Therapy, 24*, 23–50.

White, R., & Renk, K. (2012). Externalizing behavior problems during adolescence: An ecological perspective. *Journal of Child and Family Studies, 21*, 158–171.

2.3 Indigenous and other minoritized students

Russell Bishop

Introduction

A seemingly intractable problem that besets modern education in the Western world is how to raise the achievement levels of indigenous and other minoritized students so that the educational disparities that afflict these students can be addressed. The term *minoritized* refers to a people who have been ascribed the characteristics of a minority (Shields, Bishop, & Mazawi, 2005). To be minoritized, one does not need to be in the numerical minority but only to be treated as if one's position and perspective are of less worth, to be silenced or marginalized. Hence, for example, in schools on the Navajo reservation with over 95% of the population being Navajo or in Bedouin schools, we find characteristics of the students similar to those we may find among Māori in mainstream schools in which they are actually in the numerical minority. Also included in this category are the increasing number of migrants into European countries, populations of color or poverty, and those whose abilities and sexual persuasions do not belong to the perceived mainstream.

There are numerous explanations for why indigenous and other minoritized groups from around the world continue to suffer from the immediate and long-term effects of educational disparities on employment, social well-being, and health. These theories include deficit notions about the paucity of literature in the children's homes, the lack of positive educational experiences and expertise among their families, the lack of motivation among particular groups of students, the negative impacts of peer cultures, the impact of the generally low socioeconomic status of the families, the impact of child poverty and abuse, the lack of positive role models (including those of successful members of indigenous and other minoritized groups in schools), and the neocolonial nature of the school system. It is a feature of most of these theories that they focus either on the problems that the child and their families present to the school or that the school presents to the families. Less common are explanations that focus on what actually happens between the participants in education: that is, the relationships that exist within the school's classrooms and between the school and the families within the wider society or the impact of the power imbalances that exist in the wider society that are reflected and reproduced within the nation's classrooms.

Research evidence

Fundamental to this analysis of explanatory theories about the phenomena of low achievement among indigenous and other minoritized students is the understanding that when teaching occurs, progress is decided upon and practices are modified as "a direct reflection of the beliefs and assumptions the teacher holds about the learner" (Bruner, 1996, p. 47). This means that "our interactions with others are deeply affected by our everyday intuitive theorizing about how other minds work" (Bruner, 1996, p. 45). To Foucault (1972), such theorizing is seen in the images that teachers create in their minds when explaining their experiences of interacting with indigenous and other minoritized students. These images are expressed in the metaphors they use that are part of the language or the discourses around education that have already existed for considerable periods of time and that struggle against each other for explanatory power. It is through these metaphors that teachers subsequently organize classroom relationships and activities. Hence, discourses have a powerful influence on how teachers and those with whom they interact understand or ascribe meaning to particular experiences and what eventually happens in practice. In short, particular discourses will provide teachers with a complex network of explanatory images and metaphors, which are then manifest in their positioning, which then will determine, in large part, how they think and act in relation to indigenous and other minoritized students.

The impact of teachers' discursive positioning on indigenous and other minoritized student achievement is seen when it is understood that some discourses hold solutions to problems that affect these students while others do not. For example, if the discourse that the teacher is drawing from explains indigenous and other minoritized students' achievement problems in their classroom as being due to inherent or culturally based deficiencies of the children or of their parents and families (Valencia, 2012; Vass, 2012), then the relationships and interactions that teachers develop with these children will be negative, and they will engage students in low-quality pedagogic content and skill programs such as remedial activities or resort to traditional transmission strategies. In addition, and perhaps not surprisingly, indigenous and other minoritized students will react to this experience negatively, with consequent negative implications for their attendance (they will often vote with their feet), engagement and motivation for learning (they will be met with behavior modification programs and assertive discipline), and achievement (which remains lower than that children of the majority cultural groups in the classroom, and in many cases in the world, the gaps continue to widen).[1] Conversely, if the discourse offers positive explanations and solutions, then teachers will more likely be able to act in an agentic manner, seeing themselves as being able to develop quality caring and learning pedagogic relationships with indigenous and other minoritized students. When such contexts for learning are developed, as evidenced in the Te Kotahitanga project (Bishop, Berryman, Powell, & Teddy, 2007; Bishop, Berryman, Tiakiwai, & Richardson, 2003; Bishop, 2011; Bishop, Ladwig, & Berryman, 2014; Ministry of Education, 2015), which focuses on improving the achievement of indigenous Māori students in mainstream public secondary schools in New Zealand, Māori students respond positively with measurable increases in engagement, attendance, retention, motivation (Bishop, Berryman, Powell et al., 2007; Meyer et al., 2010), and achievement (Bishop, Berryman, Wearmouth, Peter, & Clapham, 2011; Meyer et al., 2010; Sleeter, 2011). Further studies support this conclusion (Castagno & Brayboy, 2008). The first example considered the determinants of student leadership in schools, thereby determining the keys to improving student achievement (Dempster, 2011). The argument is that "it is the immediacy of the sense of connection and belonging they experience with their teachers and their peers that governs the sense of identification students have with their schools. Only then is engagement in all aspects of learning, curricular and cocurricular, enhanced, and once this occurs, the desire to take on leadership responsibilities in matters of school citizenship is elevated" (p. 97). Dempster continues by suggesting that

> how well children and young people are treated by their families, teachers and peers is a fundamental influence on how well they become connected to their schools. Furthermore, there is support for the proposition that experience of reasonable empowerment and a climate of participatory social engagement (both factors influencing leadership), are known to develop in students the very social, emotional and cognitive attributes that facilitate improvements in academic achievement.
>
> (p. 97)

The second example is a meta-analysis by Cornelius-White (2007) based on 119 studies with 1,450 effects, which was based on 355,325 students, 14,851 teachers, and 2,439 schools. In this analysis, there was a correlation of 0.34 ($d = 0.72$) across all person-centered teacher variables and all student outcomes (achievement and attitudes). Hattie (2009) uses these results to argue that in classrooms "with person-centered teachers, there are more engagements, more respect of self and others, there are fewer resistant behaviors, there is greater non-directivity (student initiative and student-regulated activities), and there are higher student achievement outcomes" (p. 119).

The third example is our own research into means of changing teacher theorizing and practice in ways that will bring about improvements in the schooling experiences and achievement of Māori students in mainstream public schools. In 2001, we began the research for Te Kotahitanga by talking with groups of Māori students in years 9 and 10, together with members of these students' families, school principals, and teachers, about their collective schooling experiences. From these interviews, a series of narratives of experience were developed (Bishop & Berryman, 2006). In contrast to the majority of their teachers, who tended to dwell upon the problems that the children's deficiencies caused them, the children clearly identified that the main influence on their educational achievement was the quality of the in-class relationships and interactions they had with their teachers. They also explained how teachers could create a context for learning in which Māori students' educational achievement could improve by teachers changing the ways they related to and interacted with Māori students in their classrooms. It was clear from their experiences that if Māori students were to achieve at higher levels and educational disparities were to be reduced, then teachers must relate to and interact with these students in a different manner from the most commonly occurring approaches.

From these interviews, we developed an Effective Teaching Profile (ETP) (Bishop, Berryman, Tiakiwai et al., 2003) that formed the basis of the Te Kotahitanga professional development innovation, which is now running in 49 secondary schools in New Zealand. In these schools, the most effective implementers of the ETP are those who see Māori student schooling experiences improve dramatically and achievement rise to the highest levels in norm-referenced standardized tests.

Fundamental to the ETP are teachers' understandings of the need to explicitly reject deficit theorizing as a means of explaining Māori students' educational achievement levels and their taking an agentic position in their theorizing about their practice. In order for teachers to attain these understandings, they need to be provided with learning opportunities for critically evaluating where they discursively position themselves when constructing their own images, principles, and practices in relation to Māori and other minoritized students in their classrooms. They also need an opportunity to consider the implications of their discursive positioning on their own agency and for Māori students' learning. Practitioners need to be able to express their professional commitment and responsibility to bringing about change in indigenous and other minoritized students' educational achievement by accepting professional responsibility for the learning of all their students, not just those who they can relate to readily. These central understandings are then manifested in these teachers' classrooms when effective teachers demonstrate on a daily basis that they care for the students as culturally located individuals; they have high expectations for students' learning; they are able to manage their classrooms and curriculum so as to promote learning; they are able to engage in a range of discursive learning interactions with students or facilitate students to engage with others in these ways; they know a range of strategies that can facilitate learning interactions; they collaboratively promote, monitor, and reflect upon student's learning outcomes so as to modify their instructional practices in ways that will lead to improvements in Māori student achievement; and they share this knowledge with the students (Bishop, 2011).

Summary and recommendations

Positive classroom relationships and interactions are built upon positive, nondeficit, agentic thinking by teachers about students and their families. Agentic thinking views the students as having many experiences that are relevant and fundamental to classroom interactions. This agentic thinking by teachers means they see themselves as being able to solve problems that come their way and as having recourse to skills and knowledge that can help all their students, and they believe that all of their students can achieve, no matter what. Agentic thinking is fundamental to the creation of learning contexts in classrooms where young Māori people are able to be themselves as Māori, to bring who they are into the classroom, where Māori students' humor is acceptable, where students can care for and learn with each other, where being different is acceptable, and where the power of Māori students' own self-determination is fundamental to classroom relations and interactions. Indeed, the interdependence of self-determining participants in the classroom creates vibrant learning contexts, which in turn are characterized by the growth and development of quality learning relations and interactions, increased student attendance, and engagement and achievement both in school and on nationally based measures.

Fundamental to these classrooms is teachers' discursive (re)positioning, which is a necessary but often overlooked condition for educational reform; the sufficient conditions are the skills and experience teachers need to develop effective caring and learning relationships. In this way, theorizing from within a relational discourse addresses the limitations of the culturalist position that promotes quality teaching but gives limited consideration to the impact of power differentials within the classroom, school, and society such as those that manifest themselves in teachers drawing upon deficit discourses to explain their use of ineffective pedagogies. It also is preferable to the structuralist position that promotes a redistribution of resources and wealth in society yet gives only limited consideration to the agency of teachers and school leaders and policy makers at all levels of education, allowing them to abrogate their responsibilities. While both of these considerations are necessary, what is missing from much current debate about the influences on (indigenous and other minoritized) students' achievement is a model that promotes effective and sustainable educational reform drawn from a relational discourse.

Note

1. It is interesting that when challenged over their "closing the gaps" policy in the early 1990s, the then–New Zealand government chose to abandon the policy and instead focus on "realising Māori student potential." However, there are a number of problems with this new focus. First, it is a much more elusive target and is extremely difficult to define and, in fact, is left undefined, in government policy documents (Ministry of Education, 2008), other than statements about Māori students having unlimited potential and abilities.

Second, most teachers that we interviewed during our research used deficit terms when they spoke of Māori students (Bishop et al., 2003). This means that the power of defining what constitutes Māori potential is, in practice, left to a group of people who think Māori potential is limited, not unlimited. In policy terms, to leave the determination of Māori potential in the hands of what is essentially a non-Māori teaching force, most of whom see Māori potential as being limited, can only be described as careless. Rather, it is essential to have an outcome measure that is not open to sabotage by deficit thinking, which does not go away just because antideficit thinking is suggested in a policy document.

References

Bishop, R. (2011). *Freeing ourselves: An indigenous response to neo- Colonial dominance in research, classrooms, schools and education systems.* Rotterdam: Sense Publications

Bishop, R., & Berryman, M. (2006). *Culture speaks: Cultural relationships and classroom learning.* Wellington, NZ: Huia.

Bishop, R., Berryman, M., Powell, A., & Teddy, L. (2007). *Te Kotahitanga: Improving the educational achievement of Māori students in mainstream education Phase 2: Towards a whole school approach.* Report to the Ministry of Education. Wellington, NZ: Ministry of Education.

Bishop, R., Berryman, M., Tiakiwai, S., & Richardson, C. (2003). *Te Kotahitanga: The experiences of year 9 and 10 Māori students in mainstream classrooms.* Final report to Ministry of Education. Wellington, NZ: Ministry of Education.

Bishop, R., Berryman, M., Wearmouth, J., Peter, M., & Clapham, S. (2011). *Te Kotahitanga: Improving the educational achievement of Māori students in English-medium schools: Report for Phase 3 and Phase 4: 2008–2010* (pp. 1–228). Report to the Ministry of Education. Wellington, NZ: Ministry of Education. Retrieved from www.educationcounts.govt.nz/publications/maori/english-medium-education/9977

Bishop, R., Ladwig, J., & Berryman, M. (2014, February). The centrality of relationships for pedagogy: The *Whanaungatanga* Thesis. *American Educational Research Journal, 51*(1), 184–214.

Bruner, J. (1996). *The culture of education.* Cambridge, MA: Harvard University Press.

Castagno, A., & Brayboy, B. (2008). Culturally responsive schooling for indigenous youth: A review of the literature. *Review of Educational Research, 78*(4), 941–993.

Cornelius-White, J. (2007). Learner-centered teacher-student relationships are effective: A meta-analysis. *Review of Educational Research, 77*(1), 113–143.

Dempster, N. (2011). Leadership and learning: Making connections down under. In T. Townsend & J. MacBeath (Eds.), *International handbook: Leadership for learning* (pp. 89–102). Dordrecht, The Netherlands: Springer.

Foucault, M. (1972). *The archaeology of knowledge.* New York, NY: Pantheon.

Hattie, J. (2009). *Visible learning: A synthesis of over 800 meta-analyses relating to achievement.* New York, NY: Routledge.

Meyer, L., Penetito, W., Hynds, A., Savage, C., Hindle, R., & Sleeter, C. (2010). *Evaluation of Te Kotahitanga: 2004–2008.* Wellington, NZ: Jessie Hetherington Centre for Educational Research, Victoria University. Retrieved from www.educationcounts.govt.nz/publications/maori_educa-tion/78910

Ministry of Education. (2008). *Ka Hikitia – Managing for success: The Māori education strategy 2008–2012.* Wellington, NZ: Ministry of Education.

Ministry of Education. (2015). *Ka Hikitea, A Demonstration Report: Effectiveness of Te Kotahitanga, Phase 5, 2010–2012*. Wellington, NZ: Ministry of Education.

Shields, C. M., Bishop, R., & Mazawi, A. E. (2005). *Pathologizing practices: The impact of deficit thinking on education*. New York, NY: Peter Lang Publishing Inc.

Sleeter, C. (Ed.). (2011). *Professional development for culturally responsive and relationship-based pedagogy* (pp. 163–177). New York: Peter Lang Publishing Inc.

Valencia, R. (2012). *The evolution of deficit thinking: Educational thought and practice*. London: RoutledgeFalmer.

Vass, G. (2012). So, what is wrong with indigenous education? Perspective, position and power beyond a deficit discourse. *The Australian Journal of Indigenous Education, 41*(2), pp. 85–89.

2.4

Personality influences – the Big Five and achievement

Meera Komarraju

Introduction

Student success is a central goal of educational organizations worldwide. In achieving this objective, educators are encouraged to look beyond cognitive ability and investigate psychosocial factors that influence academic achievement. A spotlight on nonintellectual factors is needed, particularly at the college level, where students' ability within a cohort is restricted by admission criteria (Furnham, Monsen, & Ahmetoglu, 2009). In highly selective programs that enroll students who are more homogeneous in intellectual ability, differences in student achievement at the time of graduation are explained by noncognitive factors. For instance, two students entering a college or university may have similar standardized test scores and high school grade-point averages (GPA) yet the degree of success they achieve in college is influenced by noncognitive variables such as personality, motivation, self-efficacy, information processing style, intellectual engagement, and effort regulation. This chapter focuses mainly on untangling the relationship between the Big Five personality traits and academic achievement.

Research evidence

Over the past three decades, the Big Five theory of personality has emerged as a robust and parsimonious conceptual framework of personality. Empirical evidence establishes it as an important predictor of academic achievement assessed as course grades, overall exam scores, or college GPA (O'Connor & Paunonen, 2007). Of the Big Five personality traits, conscientiousness is the single most consistent and strongest significant predictor of academic performance beyond cognitive ability (Conrad, 2006; Furnham & Chamorro-Premuzic, 2004; Higgins, Peterson, Pihl, & Lee, 2007; Noftle & Robins, 2007). Regarding the relationship between the four other Big Five traits (openness, agreeableness, extraversion, and neuroticism) and academic achievement, research findings are inconsistent or nonexistent (Chamorro-Premuzic & Furnham, 2003). For instance, in a meta-analysis that included about 25 studies, O'Connor and Paunonen (2007) report a mean correlation of .24 between conscientiousness and academic performance and mixed results for openness and extraversion. A more recent meta-analysis of 20 studies also found conscientiousness to be the strongest predictor of GPA, followed by openness and agreeableness (Vedel, 2014). Likewise, another meta-analysis of primary education revealed that conscientiousness and openness in children, as rated by adults, significantly predicted academic performance (Poropat, 2014). A longitudinal study of Swedish children in upper secondary education showed, that after controlling for intelligence, conscientiousness and neuroticism were positively associated with academic performance (Rosander & Backstrom, 2014). Similarly, high conscientiousness, high openness, and low extraversion predicted academic achievement in Russian and Slovenian children (Zupančič, Kavčič, Slobodskaya, & Akhmetova, 2016). This body of research suggests that, although cognitive ability scores inform us about what students can do, their personalities unveil what they are likely to do. For example, students who score high on conscientiousness are more likely to be hardworking, thorough, disciplined, and achievement oriented, and those who score high on neuroticism are more likely to be anxious, worried, and inclined to give up or avoid coming to class if they think they are not doing well (Chamorro-Premuzic & Furnham, 2003). In attempting to unravel the relationship between personality traits and achievement, researchers have focused on several intermediate or causal mechanisms, including achievement motivation, perfectionism striving, self-regulation, deep processing of information, regular class attendance, and coping strategies.

A comprehensive meta-analysis of 65 studies by Judge and Ilies (2002) revealed that the link between personality and motivation is complex. They found consistent associations between three types of performance motivation (goal setting, expectancy, and self-efficacy) and two personality traits, conscientiousness (in a positive direction) and neuroticism (in a negative direction). On further scrutiny, Chamorro-Premuzic and Furnham (2003) state that, although some of the broad personality traits (conscientiousness positively, and extraversion and neuroticism negatively) explain 15% of the variance in exam grades, the narrower facets (achievement striving, self-discipline, and activity) have a stronger relationship and explain much more (about 30%) variance in exam scores. Since conscientiousness and achievement motivation (the capacity to persist in the face of difficulties, obstacles, or failures) are both significant predictors of GPA, even after controlling for standardized entrance exam test scores (Richardson & Abraham, 2009), some researchers have examined their interrelationship more closely. Conscientiousness seems to include a component of achievement motivation as highly conscientious students seem to be motivated to succeed (Higgins et al., 2007). This is supported by Noftle and Robins's (2007) finding that the relationship between conscientiousness and GPA is mediated by students' self-reports of how much effort they put into their studying and their perceptions of their overall academic ability as well as verbal ability. There is also support for the notion that students who are driven to accomplish are more likely to obtain higher GPAs if they are also more conscientiousness; they need to be disciplined and organized, follow through, and remain persistent despite facing difficulties (Komarraju, Karau, & Schmeck, 2009). As conscientiousness is associated with both intrinsic and extrinsic motivation, highly conscientious students might remain internally motivated despite fluctuations in environmental rewards (Hart, Stasson, & Mahoney, 2007). Highly conscientious students are also likely to be orderly, strive for perfectionism, and aspire to high standards (Kim, Chen, MacCann, Karlov, & Kleitman, 2015). They tend to do well academically as they strive for perfection, avoid procrastination, and cautiously review details to reduce errors (Boysan & Kiral, 2017; Rikoon et al., 2016). This empirical evidence draws attention to the achievement motivation component of personality traits (particularly conscientiousness) in explaining academic achievement.

Besides achievement motivation, self-regulation has emerged as a causal mechanism that influences student performance and achievement. Almost two decades ago, Pintrich (2000) highlighted the importance of self-regulation and then Bidjerano and Dai (2007) noted that effort regulation fully mediated the individual relationships between GPA and the personality traits of conscientiousness and agreeableness. Pintrich (2000) found that highly conscientious individuals tend to be better self-managers and are able to regulate themselves more effectively. Conscientious students also display greater metacognition (Kelly & Donaldson, 2016) as well as proactive and initiating behavior as they plan, monitor, gather feedback, and reflect on whether or not their learning strategies are working (Bidjerano & Dai, 2007). They are responsible, disciplined, achievement oriented, organized, and proactive as they are driven to achieve their goals (Higgins et al., 2007). Conscientious students who display autonomous motivation and seek to make independent choices are more likely to be motivated to pursue high academic performance (Zhou, 2015). Likewise, conscientious West Point military cadets tend to do well academically as they exert self-control and manage their interpersonal behavior more intentionally (Mayer & Skimmyhorn, 2017). Conscientious students also tend to be efficient when multitasking and use step-by-step processing (Stock & Beste, 2015) and are able to manage and control their emotions, making them more likely to achieve higher GPAs (Ivcevic & Brackett, 2014). In a cross-national sample (the US and South Korea), conscientiousness and emotional stability predicted self-efficacy as well as performance (Stajkovic, Bandura, Locke, Lee, & Sergent, 2018). The qualities of being organized, efficient, self-disciplined, and self-directed are crucial in college because, unlike in high school, parents and teachers no longer offer constant reminders or monitoring, and students have to self-regulate and manage themselves.

The extent to which students process information deeply and meaningfully appears to be an important determinant of achievement. Highly conscientious students appear to use deep and strategic learning strategies that help them achieve higher academic performance (Duff, Boyle, Dunleavy, & Ferguson, 2004). In addition, Chamorro-Premuzic and Furnham (2008) note that 40% of the variance in academic performance measured through end-of-year comprehensive essay exams was explained incrementally by ability, two personality traits (conscientiousness and openness), and learning strategies. What is particularly noteworthy is the finding that individuals with high ability performed well because they were more open (displayed intellectual curiosity), and those who were more open performed well because they processed information more deeply. Other researchers also support the importance of elaborative and meaningful processing of information for academic performance. To illustrate, students scoring high on the Big Five personality trait of openness also reported using critical analysis and deep processing, leading to greater comprehension, and this was associated with academic achievement even after controlling for ability and attendance or effort (Farsides & Woodfield, 2003). Similarly, in a study predicting national secondary school exam performance for 212 secondary school students, Furnham et al. (2009) found that, although intelligence tests predicted a majority of the variance in the academic performance test, a deep processing and achieving learning approach was a significant predictor of exam scores. Thus, empirical evidence certainly highlights the importance of a deep and thoughtful approach to learning as a link between personality traits and academic achievement.

Classroom behaviors that are associated with personality traits, such as attending classes, conforming to task directions, and participating in group discussions, appear to have important roles in achieving academic success. For example, class absences incrementally predict final course grades beyond intelligence and the Big Five traits; conscientious and agreeable students are more likely to attend class seminars, and those attending regularly achieve better performance (Farsides & Woodfield, 2003; Conrad, 2006). Dollinger, Matyja, and Huber (2008) offer similar empirical support through their findings that the variance in exam scores is predicted not only by factors that are not under the control of students such as verbal ability, personality traits, and past performance, but also by controllable factors such as attendance and hours spent working or studying. In taking a closer look at the facets of the Big Five, McCann, Duckworth, and Roberts (2009) found that industriousness was a stronger predictor of absenteeism, compared to the broad conscientiousness factor, and perfectionism was a stronger predictor of cognitive test scores and attaining high academic honors, compared to the broad conscientiousness factor. These results are supported by Kappe and van der Flier (2010), who found that conscientiousness was positively associated with attending lectures, acquiring skills, working on group projects, obtaining on-the-job training, and completing a thesis. They also found that extraversion was positively associated with performance on tasks involving interacting with others and expressing or articulating ideas, neuroticism was negatively associated with performance under time pressure or being observed, and openness was negatively associated with conforming to group project deadlines. Thus, these results suggest that the Big Five personality traits influence preferred ways of behaving that influence task accomplishment and academic achievement.

As students interact with their academic careers, they often face unexpected situations and obstacles. How well they cope with adversity appears to be related to the personality traits of conscientiousness and neuroticism. For instance, Perera, McIlveen, and Oliver (2015) found that first-year Australian college students who were more conscientious displayed higher levels of attentional control, narrowed their focus to avoid distraction, and continued planning and persisting in the face of obstacles. In contrast, students reporting higher levels of neuroticism were more likely to experience higher levels of affective-physiological stimulation in stressful situations and became inhibited and disengaged academically, rather than actively managing the stressors. Similarly, Chinese undergraduate business majors with a proactive personality were more likely to seek opportunities and perform well academically in the face of challenging and stressful situations (Zhu, Wei, & Wang, 2017).

Summary and recommendations

This review establishes that personality traits have a distal influence on academic achievement through mechanisms such as motivation, self-regulation, deep processing, attendance behavior, encouraging perfection striving, reducing procrastination, and enhancing coping strategies that are more proximal to achievement. Schools and teachers could utilize this information to construct syllabi, curriculum, classroom interventions, and learning environments that foster and reward achievement motivation, self-regulatory efforts, deep processing, and conscientious behavior (particularly industriousness). In particular, educators could implement interventions that help students who might be experiencing stressful or adjustment issues by developing effective coping strategies that enhance academic engagement. Future researchers could further our understanding of the link between the Big Five personality traits (specifically, facets of conscientiousness and neuroticism) and academic achievement by exploring other causal mechanisms.

References

Bidjerano, T., & Dai, D. Y. (2007). The relationship between the big-five model of personality and self-regulated learning strategies. *Learning and Individual Differences, 17,* 69–81.

Boysan, M., & Kiral, E. (2017). Associations between procrastination, personality, perfectionism, self-esteem and locus of control. *British Journal of Guidance and Counselling, 45,* 284–296.

Chamorro-Premuzic, T., & Furnham, A. (2003). Personality traits and academic examination performance. *European Journal of Personality, 17,* 237–250.

Chamorro-Premuzic, T., & Furnham, A. (2008). Personality, intelligence and approaches to learning as predictors of academic performance. *Personality and Individual Differences, 44,* 1596–1603.

Conrad, M. A. (2006). Aptitude is not enough: How personality and behavior predict academic performance. *Journal of Research in Personality, 40,* 339–346.

Dollinger, S. J., Matyja, A. M., & Huber, J. L. (2008). Which factors best account for academic success: Those which college students can control or those they cannot? *Journal of Research in Personality, 42*, 872–885.

Duff, A., Boyle, E., Dunleavy, K., & Ferguson, J. (2004). The relationship between personality, approach to learning and academic performance. *Personality and Individual Differences, 36*, 1907–1920.

Farsides, T., & Woodfield, R. (2003). Individual differences and undergraduate academic success: The roles of personality, intelligence, and application. *Personality and Individual Differences, 34*, 1225–1243.

Furnham, A., & Chamorro-Premuzic (2004). Personality and intelligence as predictors of statistics examination grades. *Personality and Individual Differences, 37*, 943–955.

Furnham, A., Monsen, J., & Ahmetoglu, G. (2009). Typical intellectual engagement, big five personality traits, approaches to learning and cognitive ability predictors of academic performance. *British Journal of Educational Psychology, 79*, 769–782.

Hart, J. W., Stasson, M. F., & Mahoney, J. M. (2007). The big five and achievement motivation: Exploring the relationship between personality and a two-factor model of motivation. *Individual Differences Research, 5*, 267–274.

Higgins, D. M., Peterson, J. B., Pihl, R. O., & Lee, A. G. M. (2007). Prefrontal cognitive ability, intelligence, big five personality, and the prediction of advanced academic and workplace performance. *Journal of Personality and Social Psychology, 93*, 298–319.

Ivcevic, Z., & Brackett, M. (2014). Predicting school success: Comparing conscientiousness, grit, and emotion regulation ability. *Journal of Research in Personality, 52*, 29–36.

Judge, T. A., & Ilies, R. (2002). Relationship of personality to performance motivation: A meta-analytic review. *Journal of Applied Psychology, 87*, 797–807.

Kappe, R., & van der Flier, H. (2010). Using multiple and specific criteria to assess the predictive validity of the big five personality factors on academic performance. *Journal of Research in Personality, 44*, 142–145.

Kelly, D., & Donaldson, D. I. (2016). Investigating the complexities of academic success: Personality constrains the effects of metacognition. *The Psychology of Education Review, 40*, 17–23.

Kim, L. E., Chen, L., MacCann, C., Karlov, L., & Kleitman, S. (2015). Evidence for three factors of perfectionism: Perfectionistic strivings, order, and perfectionistic concerns. *Personality and Individual Differences, 84*, 16–22.

Komarraju, M., Karau, S. J., & Schmeck, R. R. (2009). Role of the big five personality traits in predicting college students' academic motivation and achievement. *Learning and Individual Differences, 19*, 47–52.

Mayer, J. D., & Skimmyhorn, W. (2017). Personality attributes that predict cadet performance at West Point. *Journal of Research in Personality, 66*, 14–26.

McCann, C., Duckworth, A. L., & Roberts, R. D. (2009). Empirical identification of the major facets of conscientiousness. *Learning and Individual Differences, 19*, 451–458.

Noftle, E. E., & Robins, R. W. (2007). Personality predictors of academic outcomes: Big five correlates of GPA and SAT Scores. *Journal of Personality and Social Psychology, 93*, 116–130.

O'Connor, M. C., & Paunonen, S. V. (2007). Big five personality predictors of post-secondary academic performance. *Personality and Individual Differences, 43*, 971–990.

Perera, H. N., McIlveen, P., & Oliver, M. E. (2015). The mediating roles of coping and adjustment in the relationship between personality and academic achievement. *British Journal of Educational Psychology, 85*, 440–457.

Pintrich, P. R. (2000). The role of goal orientation in self-regulated learning. In M. Boekaerts, P. R. Pintrich, & M. Zeidner (Eds.), *Handbook of self-regulation* (pp. 451–501). San Diego, CA: Academic Press.

Poropat, A. E. (2014). A meta-analysis of adult-rated child personality and academic performance in primary education. *British Journal of Educational Psychology*, *84*, 239–252.

Richardson, M., & Abraham, C. (2009). Conscientiousness and achievement motivation predict performance. *European Journal of Personality*, *23*, 589–605.

Rikoon, S. H., Brenneman, M., Kim, L. E., Khorramdel, K., MacCann, C., Burrus, J., & Roberts, R. D. (2016). Facets of conscientiousness and their differential relationships with cognitive ability factors. *Journal of Research in Personality*, *61*, 22–34.

Rosander, P., & Backstrom, M. (2014). Personality traits measured at baseline can predict academic performance in upper secondary school three years late. *Scandinavian Journal of Psychology*, *55*, 611–618.

Stajkovic, A. D., Bandura, A., Locke, E. A., Lee, D., & Sergent, K. (2018). Test of three conceptual models of influence of the big five personality traits and self-efficacy on academic performance: A meta-analytic path-analysis. *Personality and Individual Differences*, *120*, 238–245.

Stock, A., & Beste, C. (2015). Conscientiousness increases efficiency of multicomponent behavior. *Scientific Reports, 5–15713*, 1–7.

Vedel, A. (2014). The Big Five and tertiary academic performance: A systematic review and meta-analysis. *Personality & Individual Differences*, *71*, 66–76.

Zhou, M. (2015). Moderating effect of self-determination in the relationship between Big Five personality and academic performance. *Personality & Individual Differences*, *86*, 385–389.

Zhu, Y., Wei, H., & Wang, Y. (2017). Challenge-hindrance stress and academic achievement: Proactive personality as moderator. *Social Behavior and Personality*, *45*(3), 441–452.

Zupančič, M., Kavčič, T., Slobodskaya, H. R., & Akhmetova, O. A. (2016). Broad and narrow personality traits predicting academic achievement over compulsory schooling: A cross-sectional study in two countries. *Journal of Early Adolescence*, *36*, 783–806.

2.5 Motivation

Dale H. Schunk and Carol A. Mullen

Introduction

Motivation is the process whereby goal-directed activities are instigated and sustained (Schunk, Meece, & Pintrich, 2014). We do not directly observe motivation but rather its outcomes: selection of activities, effort, persistence, and achievement. Because motivation always involves goals, it is necessary to characterize one's level of motivation relative to those goals. To illustrate, imagine that high school students Kevin and Alex have a test tomorrow. Kevin's goal is to make a good grade, so he studies for four hours. In contrast, Alex's goal is to pass the test, so he studies for 30 minutes, spending the bulk of his evening social networking with friends. While both students are motivated, Kevin has higher academic motivation in contrast with Alex, whose social motivation is higher.

Research evidence

There are various theories of motivation (Schunk et al., 2014). Historically, theorists viewed motivation as reflecting such processes as instincts, needs, and drives. Humanistic psychologists, Abraham Maslow and Carl Rogers among them, emphasized the need for personal growth, achieving wholeness, and self-actualization. Conversely, behavioral psychologists contended that motivation was superfluous because reinforcement strengthened behavior, and punishment weakened it. Motivation reflected the rate and duration of behavior. These historical views construed motivation as something that affected the performance of previously learned behaviors more than new learning.

As cognitive theories of learning gained ascendance in the 1960s, researchers began investigating cognitive and affective variables that can influence learning and performance (Shuell, 1986). One can have a goal to learn a skill (learning goal) or to demonstrate a learned skill (performance goal). Researchers currently explore the conditions, variables, and attitudes that affect motivated learning.

Motivation can influence what, when, and how people learn (Schunk et al., 2014). Students approach learning tasks with different goals, self-efficacy (perceived capabilities) for learning, values (perceived importance of learning), and affects (e.g., excitement, fear). They decide how they will work on the task (i.e., their learning strategy). While engaged in learning, learners are influenced by instructional (e.g., materials, feedback) and contextual variables (e.g., peers, environmental conditions). They monitor their understanding and gauge their learning progress. Perceptions of progress build self-efficacy and sustain motivation. When difficulties arise, they may seek help or alter their strategy. Following task engagement, they may reflect and make attributions (perceived causes) for their outcomes (e.g., success due to hard work). Students who believe they are progressing toward valued goals are apt to sustain their motivation, self-efficacy, and positive affect. In mentoring relationships, students (i.e., protégés) benefit the most when they and their mentors share the desire to attain success and, thus, hold high achievement motivation. As achievement motivation increases, protégés may be more motivated to learn from their relationships and mentors, and to engage in mentoring as well (Schunk & Mullen, 2013).

Reviews of motivational research support the influence of these processes on learning and achievement. Goal properties have motivational effects (Locke & Latham, 2002). Goals that incorporate specific standards of performance can be attained relatively quickly; in contrast, goals that are moderately difficult are more likely to sustain motivation and lead to better performance than are goals that are general (e.g., "Do your best"), long-term, and overly easy or challenging. Self-evaluations of goal progress build self-efficacy and motivation (Schunk et al., 2014).

Self-efficacy influences learning and achievement through effort and persistence (Schunk & DiBenedetto, 2016). Multon, Brown, and Lent (1991) found that self-efficacy related positively to academic outcomes and accounted for 14% of their variance. Effects were stronger for older (high school, college) students and when self-efficacy and performance measures reflected specific rather than general tasks (e.g., standardized tests).

Values have been shown to relate positively to achievement-related choices, including course enrollments, occupational choices, college majors, and sports participation (Wigfield, Tonks, & Klauda, 2016). Pekrun (2016) reported that positive affective states influence motivation and learning through their effects on cognitive engagement and use of strategies.

Attribution research shows that successes ascribed to internal and stable causes, such as ability (e.g., "I'm good at this"), result in higher expectancies for future successes than attributions to external and unstable causes, such as luck (e.g., "I made lucky guesses") (Graham & Taylor, 2016). For difficulties, more adaptive attributions are those to unstable and controllable causes, such as low effort (e.g., "I didn't study enough") and poor strategy (e.g., "I used the wrong method").

Studies on the effects of interventions designed to promote motivation have shown that motivation and achievement are enhanced by the following: having learners pursue proximal and specific goals; teaching them to set their own goals;

having students observe peer models who learn by expending effort and persisting; showing students video recordings of their own performances demonstrating learning; rewarding students for their performance improvements; stressing the value of learning to students, and providing them with feedback linking their improved performances to increased effort (Schunk et al., 2014).

Certain variables can moderate the influence of motivation on learning and achievement. Children's cognitive capacity limits their abilities to represent distant goals in thought, segment long-term goals into short-term goals, and evaluate their progress (Schunk et al., 2014). They also may overestimate what they can do. They are motivated by goals that can be attained quickly and by immediate consequences of actions. With cognitive development, children's capabilities for goal setting and self-evaluation improve.

Cultural factors also affect motivation. Researchers have found that self-efficacy often is lower among non-Western (e.g., Asian) students than for students from Western Europe, Canada, and the United States (Klassen, 2004); however, the former students' self-efficacy aligns more closely with their actual performances, whereas the Western students overestimate what they can do. How students interpret perceived causes may vary due to culture. In some cultures, ability may be thought of as uncontrollable (similar to intelligence), whereas individuals in other cultures may interpret it more akin to specific skills that can be learned. Academic motivation may suffer when the practices of schools and students' cultures conflict (e.g., individual versus group learning) (Kumar & Maehr, 2010).

Student differences in mind-sets and interests can affect motivation. Persons with *fixed* mind-sets assume that capabilities are set and that one cannot change much, whereas those holding *growth* mind-sets equate ability with learning (Dweck, 2006). Students with growth mind-sets may be more motivated to set learning goals and evaluate their progress, believing they can improve their skills.

Students also vary in their interests. Some may be *intrinsically* motivated to engage in activities for their own sake, whereas others may be *extrinsically* motivated as means toward ends (e.g., praise, rewards). Whether offering students rewards decreases their intrinsic motivation is a source of debate (Cameron & Pierce, 2002). Research shows that rewards given commensurate with performance improvements convey that students are becoming more capable and can foster motivation and self-efficacy (Schunk et al., 2014).

Motivation is a complex topic, and questions continue. One is whether motivation – which presumably operates before, during, and after task engagement – is distinct from *volition* or the processes that protect concentration and effort from distractions while a student is working on a task or activity (Schunk et al., 2014). Whether motivation and volition are separate or overlap, it is useful to think of motivation at different phases of task engagement. Thus, choice of activities is a motivational outcome but often is not relevant because students may not be able to decide whether to engage in particular learning.

A second question is how motivation fits with cognitive accounts of learning. Motivational processes have cognitive referents (e.g., self-efficacy beliefs), which presumably are stored along with other cognitive information. Early cognitive learning theorists were not settled on this score, but recent cognitive theories address motivation (Winne & Hadwin, 2008).

Summary and recommendations

Research on academic motivation has implications for educational practice. Motivation is improved when students set goals and evaluate their progress. If rewards are used, they should be given contingent on students' improving their capabilities. It is also helpful to show students how learning will help them perform better. Learners can be taught to attribute learning difficulties to causes they can control, such as low effort or poor use of strategies. Lastly, linking learning to students' interests can improve motivation. For example, teachers' creative use of technology should appeal to today's students, thereby increasing their motivation to learn.

References

Cameron, J., & Pierce, W. D. (2002). *Rewards and intrinsic motivation: Resolving the controversy*. Westport, CT: Bergin & Garvey.

Dweck, C. S. (2006). *Mindset: The new psychology of success*. New York, NY: Random House.

Graham, S., & Taylor, A. Z. (2016). Attribution theory and motivation in school. In K. R. Wentzel & D. B. Miele (Eds.), *Handbook of motivation at school* (2nd ed., pp. 11–33). New York, NY: Routledge.

Klassen, R. M. (2004). Optimism and realism: A review of self-efficacy from a cross-cultural/perspective. *International Journal of Psychology, 39*, 205–230.

Kumar, R., & Maehr, M. L. (2010). Schooling, cultural diversity, and student motivation. In J. L. Meece & J. S. Eccles (Eds.), *Handbook of research on schools, schooling, and human development* (pp. 308–324). New York, NY: Routledge.

Lei, H., Cui, Y., & Zhou, W. (2018). Relationships between student engagement and academic achievement: A meta-analysis. *Social Behavior and Personality: An International Journal, 46*(3), 517–528. https://doi-org.proxy.lib.ohio-state.edu/10.2224/sbp.7054

Locke, E. A., & Latham, G. P. (2002). Building a practically useful theory of goal setting and task motivation: A 35-year odyssey. *American Psychologist, 57*, 705–717.

Multon, K. D., Brown, S. D., & Lent, R. W. (1991). Relation of self-efficacy beliefs to academic outcomes: A meta-analytic investigation. *Journal of Counseling Psychology, 38*, 30–38.

Pekrun, R. (2016). Academic emotions. In K. R. Wentzel & D. B. Miele (Eds.), *Handbook of motivation at school* (2nd ed., pp. 120–144). New York, NY: Routledge.

Schunk, D. H., & DiBenedetto, M. K. (2016). Self-efficacy theory in education. In K. R. Wentzel & D. B. Miele (Eds.), *Handbook of motivation at school* (2nd ed., pp. 34–54). New York, NY: Routledge.

Schunk, D. H., Meece, J. L., & Pintrich, P. R. (2014). *Motivation in education: Theory, research, and applications* (4th ed.). Boston, MA: Pearson Education.

Schunk, D. H., & Mullen, C. A. (2013). Toward a conceptual model of mentoring research: Integration with self-regulated learning. *Educational Psychology Review, 25*(3), 361–389.

Shuell, T. J. (1986). Cognitive conceptions of learning. *Review of Educational Research, 56*, 411–436.

Wigfield, A., Tonks, S. M., & Klauda, S. L. (2016). Expectancy-value theory. In K. R. Wentzel & D. B. Miele (Eds.), *Handbook of motivation at school* (2nd ed., pp. 55–74). New York, NY: Routledge.

Winne, P. H., & Hadwin, A. F. (2008). The weave of motivation and self-regulated learning. In D. H. Schunk & B. J. Zimmerman (Eds.), *Motivation and self-regulated learning: Theory, research, and applications* (pp. 297–314). New York, NY: Taylor & Francis.

Summary table: influences from the student

Category	Variable	Considerations
Demographics	**Gender differences** in achievement are minimal; when they do occur, they are generally more pronounced among students from disadvantaged backgrounds. An exception is that males are more likely to be diagnosed with ADHD and to drop out of school than are females.	*Students may believe that girls and boys have different abilities, even though in reality differences are minimal.*
	There is some evidence of lower achievement for children who were born **preterm** and were **underweight** at the time of birth, particularly through middle childhood.	*These students may need additional academic support.*
	Indigenous and minoritized students sometimes do not experience the same academic successes that their majority peers experience.	*Indigenous and minoritized students are more likely to achieve at high levels when teachers value the experiences that these students bring to the classroom and acknowledge power differentials and the ways that classroom discourse affects power structures in the classroom.*
Attitudes and Dispositions	**Personality** is not strongly related to academic achievement. The one exception is that high levels of the personality trait of conscientiousness are related positively to achievement.	*Conscientiousness seems to be related to a greater likelihood of students engaging in specific behaviors and using strategies (e.g., avoiding procrastination) that facilitate academic achievement. An awareness of these relationships can guide educators in providing supports to students so that they learn, practice, and use effective strategies.*

(Continued)

Category	Variable	Considerations
	Student **engagement** is related positively to academic achievement; however, high-ability students may still achieve at high levels, even when their engagement is less than optimal.	*Programs to address low student engagement need to focus in particular on enhancing engagement in lower-achieving students.*
	Behavioral engagement is a broad construct; in general, behavioral engagement is characterized by positive conduct (e.g., following classroom rules), involvement in learning (e.g., paying attention), and involvement in school activities. Behavioral engagement is related to academic achievement and to retention in school.	*Teachers can promote behavioral engagement by creating a caring social environment in the classroom, establishing clear rules and expectations, and infusing the curriculum with meaningful activities.*
	When students set specific and somewhat challenging academic **goals**, they achieve at higher levels.	*Students often need to be instructed in how to set appropriate goals. Students will persist with academic goals if they feel confident that they are making progress toward the goal; thus, teachers should provide students with feedback on progress toward goal attainment.*
	Motivation refers to the processes that facilitate the attainment of one's goals. Motivation is a very broad term that encompasses many processes and that vary across students, across tasks, and over time. Examples of these processes include students' self-efficacy beliefs, attributional beliefs, and their beliefs about the value of a task.	*Educators can promote motivation (and, ultimately, higher achievement) by helping students (a) set specific, reachable goals and (b) evaluate their progress toward achieving those goals. Motivation also can be promoted by providing exposure to examples of peers who can successfully engage in and succeed at specific tasks, rewarding students for improvement, and fostering the development of positive value beliefs toward a particular task or subject area.*
	Students' **attitudes** toward academics are related to achievement but not very strongly. The relationship appears to be strongest among upper elementary students.	*Although the relation is not strong, teachers should still do all that they can to support the development of positive attitudes toward specific academic subject domains. Creating positive experiences in classrooms can simultaneously affect both attitudes and student motivation to achieve.*

(Continued)

Category	Variable	Considerations
	Academic self-concept refers to a student's perception of his or her ability. Academic self-concept within a particular domain (e.g., math) is most strongly related to achievement in that domain.	*The relation between academic self-concept and achievement is reciprocal: having a high self-concept of ability in a particular domain (e.g., math) leads to higher achievement in that domain and that high achievement, in turn, can further enhance one's academic self-concept. Thus teachers should focus both on improving students' academic self-concepts, and improving their achievement (e.g., by giving them useful feedback and helping them make appropriate attributions).*
	Academic **self-efficacy** refers to the belief that one can successfully engage with and complete a particular academic task. A student who feels highly efficacious toward a particular academic task (e.g., solving algebra problems) is likely to experience success with that task.	*Self-efficacy beliefs are more strongly related to achievement when the beliefs are specific to the task at hand, as opposed to general beliefs about one's overall ability. Teachers can help students become efficacious at tasks by (a) setting moderately challenging short-term goals, (b) helping students to develop skills by creating experiences in which students can master tasks, (c) observing models that can successfully engage with the task, (d) providing feedback that fosters the development of adaptive attributions, and (e) helping students to become confident as they are presented with increasingly complex versions of the task.*
Cognitive	When new information that is presented in class conflicts with a student's prior knowledge and beliefs, effective learning of the new information often requires **conceptual change**.	*It is possible to facilitate conceptual change through classroom instruction; however, conceptual change does not occur quickly. In order to teach for conceptual change, educators must acknowledge that it takes time to change long-held beliefs and incomplete or inaccurate prior knowledge. There are a variety of evidence-based strategies that can be used; some examples include teaching with analogies, introducing alternative explanations with refutational texts, and asking students to make predictions, which are followed by evidence that conflicts with the predictions.*

(Continued)

Category	Variable	Considerations
	When students experience **learning difficulties**, these difficulties may be attributable to a wide range of causes. Such difficulties may be attributable to student characteristics (e.g., a disability), teacher characteristics (e.g., instructional practices), or school characteristics (e.g., school-wide approaches to discipline for bad behavior). Learning difficulties often occur as a result of more than one of these factors.	*It is often difficult to discover the root causes of students' learning difficulties. Educators should not conclude that the problem lies solely within the student. Sometimes achievement is hindered due to teacher behaviors or school policies. Moreover, learning difficulties may arise as a result of multiple causes simultaneously (e.g., both a characteristic of the student and the use of an ineffective instructional practice).*
	Piaget's four stages of cognitive development are still useful tools in the planning of instruction. The four stages represent broad ranges of cognitive development, and appropriate instruction at each stage facilitates student learning.	*Educators should not think of Piaget's stages as rigid categorizations; educators must realize that children and adolescents of the same chronological age may be at different stages of cognitive development. Thus, two children who are each ten years old may differ in their readiness to learn from an identical curriculum.*
	Prior achievement (including self-reported grades) is a very strong predictor of future achievement.	*Students who have achieved highly in the past are likely to continue to achieve at high levels in the future; nevertheless, if some students have not done well in school in the past, they still have the potential to learn at high levels, but they may need extra instruction and support.*
Social Influences	Early and effective **preschool experiences** are very important predictors of subsequent academic achievement. Students who experience **low academic success** during the early grades often continue to experience these difficulties during the later grades.	*Exposure to effective early childhood educational programs can greatly benefit students in both the short and the long-term. Given that children vary in their exposure to effective programs, teachers must acknowledge that students do not come to school equally prepared.*
	Children experience academic benefits when teachers of young children (e.g., kindergarten teachers) have received appropriate **training in child development**.	*School administrators should provide professional development for teachers of young children so that educators are prepared for the unique needs of young learners.*

(Continued)

Category	Variable	Considerations
	The secondary school that a student attends impacts the likelihood of **enrolling in post-secondary education**.	*In some secondary schools, there is a strong emphasis on college preparation; in such schools, most (if not all) students are expected to attend college. This is often tied to socioeconomic status (i.e., these schools often enroll students from affluent neighborhoods).*
	Students' **social goals** are related to academic motivation and, in turn, to achievement. Social goals can both facilitate and hinder achievement, depending on the types of social goals that the student pursues and the academic behaviors of the students' peer group.	*Teachers can better help students achieve if they are attuned to both students' goals and the social dynamics of students in their classrooms. If a student's peers value education and doing well in school, then the student is likely to also value education and doing well; however, if peers devalue education, that can undermine a student's academic achievement.*
	Friendships affect achievement, although these effects vary with age. Young children develop friendships through playing with others. During middle childhood, higher achievement is generally associated with greater peer acceptance. The effects of friendships on achievement grow stronger during adolescence as students tend to be friendly with peers who have similar interests and similar attitudes toward school.	*Teachers should be aware that friendships affect achievement, although the effects of friendships on achievement change as children grow older. Adolescents who affiliate with peers who do not value academics may benefit from opportunities to engage in school-based activities that are well supervised and that provide opportunities for those adolescents to develop relationships with new peer groups that value education.*
	Greater **physical activity** is related to higher achievement.	*Provide opportunities for students to be physically active during the school day; such activity may enhance both academic achievement and emotional well-being.*
	The Big-Fish-Little-Pond Effect refers to situations in which students who learn in schools or classrooms populated by high-ability students have lower academic self-concepts than students who learn among average- or lower-ability students. This can affect achievement, in that students may not work to their potential in environments that undermine their ability beliefs.	*Teachers and administrators need to carefully consider the many effects of grouping students by ability. Whereas it is often easier for teachers to instruct classrooms comprised of students of similar abilities, not all students benefit equally from such environments.*

Note: This table summarizes information presented by authors who contributed chapters to section 2 of the first edition of The International Guide to Student Achievement, as well as to revised chapters included in the present chapter.

Additional references

Ackerman, P. L. (2013). Engagement and opportunity to learn. In J. Hattie & E. M. Anderman (Eds.), *International guide to student achievement* (pp. 39–41). New York, NY: Routledge/Taylor & Francis Group.

Adey, P., & Shayer, M. (2013). Piagetian approaches. In J. Hattie & E. M. Anderman (Eds.), *International guide to student achievement* (pp. 28–30). New York, NY: Routledge/Taylor & Francis Group.

Anderman, E. M., & Anderman, L. H. (2014). *Classroom motivation*. Boston, MA: Pearson.

Anderman, E. M., & Wolters, C. A. (2006). Goals, values, and affect: Influences on student motivation. In P. A. Alexander & P. H. Winne (Eds.), *Handbook of educational psychology* (pp. 369–389). Mahwah, NJ: Lawrence Erlbaum Associates Publishers.

Bandura, A. (2013). The role of self-efficacy in goal-based motivation. In E. A. Locke & G. P. Latham (Eds.), *New developments in goal setting and task performance* (pp. 147–157). New York, NY: Routledge/Taylor & Francis Group. Retrieved from http://proxy.lib.ohio-state.edu/login?url=http://search.ebscohost.com/login.aspx?direct=true&db=psyh&AN=2013-00428-010&site=ehost-live

Becker, M., & Neumann, M. (2018). Longitudinal big-fish-little-pond effects on academic self-concept development during the transition from elementary to secondary schooling. *Journal of Educational Psychology, 110*(6), 882–897. Retrieved from http://proxy.lib.ohio-state.edu/login?url=http://search.ebscohost.com/login.aspx?direct=true&db=eric&AN=EJ1187706&site=ehost-live

Carroll, A., Houghton, S., & Lynn, S. (2013). Friendship in school. In J. Hattie & E. M. Anderman (Eds.), *International guide to student achievement* (pp. 70–73). New York, NY: Routledge/Taylor & Francis Group.

Davis-Kean, P. E., & Jager, J. (2014). Trajectories of achievement within race/ethnicity: "Catching Up" in achievement across time. *Journal of Educational Research, 107*(3), 197–208. https://doi-org.proxy.lib.ohio-state.edu/10.1080/00220671.2013.807493

Fredricks, J. (2013). Behavioral engagement in learning. In J. Hattie & E. M. Anderman (Eds.), *International guide to student achievement* (pp. 42–44). New York, NY: Routledge/Taylor & Francis Group.

Fredricks, J. A., Blumenfeld, P. C., & Paris, A. H. (2004). School Engagement: Potential of the Concept, State of the Evidence. *Review of Educational Research, 74*(1), 59–109.

Marsh, H. W., & Seaton, M. (2013). Academic self-concept. In J. Hattie & E. M. Anderman (Eds.), *International guide to student achievement* (pp. 62–63). New York, NY: Routledge/Taylor & Francis Group.

Miller-Cotto, D., & Byrnes, J. P. (2016). Ethnic/racial identity and academic achievement: A meta-analytic review. *Developmental Review, 41*, 51–70.

Rawsthorne, L. J., & Elliot, A. J. (1999). Achievement goals and intrinsic motivation: A meta-analytic review. *Personality & Social Psychology Review (Lawrence Erlbaum Associates), 3*(4), 326. https://doi.org/10.1207/s15327957pspr0304pass:_3

Richardson, M., Abraham, C., & Bond, R. (2012). Psychological correlates of university students' academic performance: A systematic review and meta-analysis. *Psychological Bulletin, 138*(2), 253–387. https://doi-org.proxy.lib.ohio-state.edu/10.1037/a0026838

Schunk, D. H. (1984). Enhancing self-efficacy and achievement through rewards and goals: Motivational and informational effects. *Journal of Educational Research, 78*(1), 29–34.

Retrieved from http://proxy.lib.ohio state.edu/login?url=http://search.ebscohost.com/login.aspx?direct=true&db=eric&AN=EJ307667&site=ehost-live

Schunk, D. H. (1985). Participation in goal setting: Effects on self-efficacy and skills of learning-disabled children. *The Journal of Special Education*, *19*(3), 307–317. https://doi.org/10.1177/002246698501900307

Sinatra, G. M., Kienhues, D., & Hofer, B. K. (2014). Addressing challenges to public understanding of science: Epistemic cognition, motivated reasoning, and conceptual change. *Educational Psychologist*, *49*(2), 123–138.

Tayler, C. (2013). Entry to school. In J. Hattie & E. M. Anderman (Eds.), *International guide to student achievement* (pp. 25–27). New York, NY: Routledge/Taylor & Francis Group.

Urdan, T. (2013). Social motivation and academic motivation. In J. Hattie & E. M. Anderman (Eds.), *International guide to student achievement* (pp. 54–56). New York, NY: Routledge/Taylor & Francis Group.

Vosniadou, S., & Mason, L. (2012). Conceptual change induced by instruction: A complex interplay of multiple factors. In K. R. Harris, S. Graham, T. Urdan, S. Graham, J. M. Royer, & M. Zeidner (Eds.), *APA educational psychology handbook, Vol 2: Individual differences and cultural and contextual factors* (pp. 221–246). Washington, DC: American Psychological Association. https://doi-org.proxy.lib.ohio-state.edu/10.1037/13274-009

Vosniadou, S., & Tsoumakis, P. (2013). Conceptual change. In J. Hattie & E. M. Anderman (Eds.), *International guide to student achievement* (pp. 51–53). New York, NY: Routledge/Taylor & Francis Group.

Voyer, D., & Voyer, S. D. (2014). Gender differences in scholastic achievement: A meta-analysis. *Psychological Bulletin*, *140*(4), 1174–1204. https://doi-org.proxy.lib.ohio-state.edu/10.1037/a0036620

Weiner, B. (1990). History of motivational research in education. *Journal of Educational Psychology*, *82*(4), 616–622. Retrieved from http://proxy.lib.ohio-state.edu/login?url=http://search.ebscohost.com/login.aspx?direct=true&db=eric&AN=EJ440457&site=ehost-live

Wentzel, K. R., Jablansky, S., & Scalise, N. R. (2018). Do friendships afford academic benefits? A meta-analytic study. *Educational Psychology Review*, *30*(4), 1241–1267. https://doi.org/10.1007/s10648-018-9447-5

CHAPTER 3

Influences from the home

Whereas the amount of time that children and adolescents spend at school varies, youth throughout the world spend much of the remainder of their nonschool time at home. As we review in this chapter, research clearly indicates that numerous aspects of the home environment affect learning and achievement, throughout childhood and adolescence. For example, during early childhood, research indicates that home influences are two to three times stronger than are the influences of childcare (U.S. Department of Health and Human Services, 2006).

The effects of home environments are particularly salient early in life, because they are predictive of many aspects of school readiness. Children who start formal schooling with lower levels of preparation on average do not achieve as well over time. In particular, experiences with literacy and numeracy are predictive of subsequent academic achievement. Recent data from the *Longitudinal Study of Australian Children* indicates that four aspects of home environments have particularly strong effects on the development of reading and math skills in children: activities (e.g., playing games at home), reading with adults, the number of books in the home, and out-of-home activities (e.g., going to the library) (Australian Institute of Family Studies, 2018). Children often acquire reading and math skills that lead to later academic success through participation in high-quality preschool programs. However, participation in such programs is highly dependent on home influences (e.g., income, neighborhood where the family resides, etc.). (e.g., Burger, 2010).

Even during adolescence, when youth are seeking greater independence from adults, aspects of the home environment still can have dramatic effects on adolescent adjustment and learning (Sacks, Moore, Shaw, & Cooper, 2014). In particular, having positive relationships (i.e., supportive relationships built on trust and communication) with parents is predictive of academic success (Steinberg, 2014). Moreover, parental involvement with adolescents' academic learning is positively related to achievement (Pomerantz, Kim, & Cheung, 2011).

The chapters included in the original *Guide* focused on a number of key aspects of the home environment that affect academic achievement. These included socioeconomic status, parental involvement in learning (including family-school partnerships), family status (e.g., resident versus nonresident fathers, maternal working status), and television viewing. Some of these factors are malleable (e.g., television viewing), whereas others are more systemic in nature (e.g., socioeconomic status). These chapters also indicate that both the beliefs and the behaviors of parents and caregivers affect academic achievement. That section, which was edited by Andrew Martin (University of Sydney), included the entries and authors listed below (entries marked with an asterisk have been updated for this edition):

Resident and Nonresident Fathers
William Jeynes

Home Environment★
Burkhard Gniewosz and Jacquelynne S. Eccles

Socioeconomic Status and Student Achievement★
Erin Bamgarner and Jeanne Brooks-Gunn

Welfare Policies
Lisa A. Gennetian and Pamela A. Morris

Family-School Partnerships and Academic Achievement
Andrew J. Martin

Parent Involvement in Learning★
Wendy S. Grolnick, Jacquelyn N. Raftery-Helmer, and Elizabeth S. Flamm

Maternal Employment and Achievement
Rachel G. Lucas-Thompson and Wendy A. Goldberg

Television and Academic Achievement
Andrew J. Martin

Next, we summarize some of the most important findings regarding the effects of home environments on achievement. These findings fit into three broad categories: (a) beliefs, (b) behaviors, and (c) structural influences.

Beliefs

Parents and guardians hold beliefs about various aspects of education (as do all of us!). These include beliefs about their children's abilities as well as more general beliefs about the value of education. Both parents' general beliefs about education and specific beliefs about a child's ability are related to students' academic achievement. These beliefs exert their influences on achievement primarily because parents' beliefs affect their behaviors, and those behaviors, in turn, influence academic achievement (Elliott & Bachman, 2018; Simpkins, Fredricks, & Eccles, 2015). Thus, for example, a parent who believes that education is valuable may spend more time engaging in activities with young children (e.g., reading together), and those activities (e.g., reading together) build literacy skills that better prepare those children for academic success.

Researchers have examined parents' beliefs about children's abilities. A consistent finding that emerges from this literature is that when parents believe that a child is capable of learning in a particular academic domain (e.g., mathematics), achievement in that domain is higher for those students (Gniewosz & Eccles, this volume). Specifically, when parents have high-competence beliefs for a child (i.e., the parents believe that the child can successfully learn mathematics), the child is likely to also hold high-competence beliefs (i.e., the child is likely to believe that she or he will be able to learn math); the child's positive beliefs about his or her abilities then lead to greater achievement.

In addition, parents' more generalized beliefs about education also impact achievement. When parents hold high expectations for achievement, students tend to achieve at higher levels. Moreover, parents' beliefs about the overall importance of education also are predictive of student achievement. When parents value education, they are more likely to engage in practices that are conducive to achievement (e.g., assuring that students spend sufficient time each evening working on schoolwork).

Behaviors

In addition to parents' and guardians' beliefs, the actual behaviors of caregivers also affect achievement. There is a large body of literature that demonstrates that parenting styles affect numerous outcomes. These "styles" refer to the ways that parents interact with children and adolescents across a variety of life domains. Research consistently indicates that an authoritative parenting style (characterized by warm relationships, allowing youth to experience autonomy, and having a clear set of reasonable rules) is most consistently related to academic achievement (e.g., Masud, Thurasamy, & Ahmad, 2015; Pinquart, 2016).

Researchers also have examined many aspects of parental involvement with academics. Results of numerous studies indicate that greater parental involvement is related to higher achievement (e.g., Grolnick, Lerner, Raftery-Helmer, & Allen, this volume; Wilder, 2014). Parents can be involved in children's academic lives in a number of ways, and several aspects of parent involvement seem to be particularly important in terms of achievement. In particular, when parents provide opportunities outside school that support children's cognitive development (e.g., having books in the home, spending time reading together), achievement is enhanced. Achievement is also related positively to parental involvement and participation in school-related activities. Parental involvement also occurs through simple daily interactions; for example, when parents ensure that their children have both allocated time and support to complete their homework, achievement is enhanced (e.g., Gonida & Cortina, 2014). School personnel can work toward developing partnerships with parents and guardians; such partnerships can enhance student achievement, particularly when the partnerships specifically focus on students' learning and behavior, as well as on enhancing parental expectations for student success (Martin, 2013).

In addition, parents can influence the amount of time that children spend watching television or using social media. Effects of television viewing on achievement are complex, but research overall indicates that high-quality educational programs can enhance children's academic preparedness for school; however, when children watch too much television, it may affect the amount of time that they can spend playing (Kostyrka-Allchrome, Cooper, & Simpson, 2017; Martin, 2013).

Structural influences

Although parents' beliefs and behaviors affect achievement, we must recognize that some of these beliefs and behaviors are intertwined with structural variables that may be out of the parents' control. For example, one of the most robust findings is the positive relation between socioeconomic status (SES) and academic achievement (Bamgarner & Brooks-Gunn, this volume). Children and adolescents who have more resources available to them tend to achieve at higher levels in school. Nevertheless, the relations between SES and achievement are complex. When fewer resources are available to families, there are several ramifications. For example, parents may need to spend more time at work (and thus can spend less time becoming involved in their children's academic pursuits); the quality of affordable health care may be low (thus potentially making children more vulnerable to illness, which could affect school attendance and learning); and the quality and availability of food may be limited (thus affecting nutrition). Although low SES is related to lower achievement, this research does not indicate that students with fewer resources are universally destined to achieve at lower levels.

Some of the chapters in the *Guide* also report on research showing that the presence of parents in the home is also related to achievement. On average, the presence of fathers in the home is related to greater achievement (Jeynes, 2015). Moreover, the positive effects of parental involvement in education on achievement are equally strong for fathers and mothers (Kim & Hill, 2015). In addition, whereas there is often a belief that maternal employment is detrimental to achievement, this is not necessarily the case; maternal employment can be related to positive outcomes for youth, particularly in families that will truly benefit from that income (Lucas-Thompson & Goldberg, 2013).

We next present updated versions of several of the chapters that appeared in the original *Guide*. The chapter then concludes with a table that summarizes the main takeaway points.

3.1 Home environment

Burkhard Gniewosz and Jacquelynne S. Eccles

Introduction

Theoretical and empirical approaches to the investigation of learning processes and educational achievement have been profoundly enriched by adding an ecological perspective, which examines the multiple effects and interrelatedness of social elements in an environment. Learning and its outcomes do not occur in a vacuum. Processes leading to positive or negative academic outcomes are embedded in multiple contexts. The school is one (admittedly very important) context among others, such as the peer group or the home environment. Educators probably have experienced the difficulties emerging in the family or peer context that can often hamper their influences on learners. It is important to understand the complex interactions working within and between the contexts to provide an optimal learning environment. In this entry, the focus is on the home environment as being an important context for students' academic achievement (see also Eccles, 2007; Gniewosz & Walper, 2017; Wigfield et al., 2015).

Research evidence

Who the parents/caregivers are

When we look at the parental background characteristics that affect children's academic achievement, the socioeconomic background is of tremendous importance. A meta-analysis based on the review of 74 samples (>100,000 students) by Sirin (2005) provided strong evidence for the link between (a) parental income, education, and occupation and (b) various academic achievement outcomes (domain-specific grades, GPA, general and domain-specific achievement). The aim was to explain achievement differences between students by the parental social background. About 9% of these differences were due to differences in the social status of the parents. This result still shows in recent meta-analyses, such as the visible learning study by Hattie (2015). One interpretation of this association is that the financial and social background of a family determine the opportunity structure through which parents can positively affect their children's academic development. Many of the ways in which parents might benefit their children are a lot easier to provide if the parents have financial and social resources. Moreover, if the parents have to work two jobs to support their family, the stress level can be increased, and the time available to support the children becomes limited. Both stressors are linked to a less-supportive home environment.

The parents' socioeconomic background is linked to educational transitions, such as the change from elementary to secondary school, as well. In ability-tracked systems, such as the German school system, these transitions serve as selective filters for college-bound or vocational educational tracks. There is evidence that parental socioeconomic status is related to the probability of being admitted to the college-bound school track, even if achievement, migration status, and other student characteristics are the same (Dumont, Maaz, Neumann, & Becker, 2014). The likelihood of attending the college-bound track is higher for students from better-off families, independent of their grades and achievements.

Although this is largely ignored by educators, parents affect their children through genetic transmission as well. Academic success is, to a considerable extent, explained by interindividual differences in cognitive competences and personality characteristics – all of them highly heritable (Petrill & Wilkerson, 2000). Recent research showed that up to 9% of the variance in academic achievement can be explained by a genome-wide polygenic score that aggregates a wide range of genetic variations (Selzam et al., 2016). Johnson, McGue, and Iacono (2007) also showed strong genetic influences on achievement development through adolescence. However, this genetic predisposition interacts with the environment. There is no deterministic relationship of genetic predisposition and academic success. Students' academic outcomes can be promoted, regardless of genetics. Nonetheless, the initial differences between students can be explained, in part, by within-family genetic transmission.

What parents believe

Parents' general attitudes, beliefs, and values play a very important role as effects on students' academic development within the home environment. If parents think that education is important, fun, or useful, their offspring are more likely to also value schooling (e.g., Gniewosz & Noack, 2012; Simpkins et al., 2012). Social learning processes are assumed to lead to this intergenerational transmission of values. Parents can communicate their beliefs in several ways. They can directly communicate the importance of doing homework and learning. Furthermore, if parents behave in ways consistent with their values, they communicate by being role models, and social learning processes can result in the intergenerational transmission of academic values. Subsequently, if students value education highly, they will engage more in learning activities, and thus, achievement can be improved.

Parents' child-specific beliefs and expectations can also affect students' academic development through their impact on their children's developing self-perceptions. Students at the same achievement level whose parents hold positive competence perceptions about their children will have more favorable competence beliefs themselves than students with less confident parents. In turn, these competence beliefs are strongly linked to subsequent academic engagement and achievement (Gniewosz, Eccles, & Noack, 2015; Pesu, Viljaranta, & Aunola, 2016; Wigfield et al., 2015).

The beliefs held by the parents are affected by their gender-related domain-specific stereotypes. Oftentimes, parents expect higher performances in the mathematical domain for their sons while they consider daughters as more competent in the verbal domain, independent of the children's actual performances (e.g., Tiedemann, 2000). Considering the aforementioned impact of the parental child-specific beliefs on the students' self-perceptions, parents' stereotypes influence the students' academic development. The same processes are likely to be associated with other socially defined group memberships.

What parents do

Parents' values and beliefs are strongly linked to the extent to which parents get involved in their children's' school matters. If parents value academics highly, they will spend more time with their children in academic activities (Gniewosz & Noack, 2012). In addition to these indirect effects, parental behaviors directly affect students' motivation and subsequent achievement through the provision of important resources. One example is that parents provide learning materials or private tutoring if needed. Here, the parental financial background becomes an obvious factor in a child's academic success. It is much easier for better-off families to pay for these materials or the tutoring. In this case, the question "what parents do" becomes the question "what parents can afford to do."

Not all the resources that are provided by parents are tangible. The way parents interact with their children can be understood as a resource, as well. An authoritative parenting style, characterized by warmth, support for the child's autonomy, and clear rules, enhances students' motivation and strategy use in learning activities (e.g., Aunola, Viljaranta, Lehtinen, & Nurmi, 2013). Providing students with a supportive home environment in a general sense satisfies the students' need for autonomy. This basic need is of tremendous importance for the students' motivation to learn, especially during adolescence. If the general parenting style supports the students' needs, then the students will be more academically engaged, which will result in better achievement in terms of grades or test results.

Moreover, the direct involvement of parents in their children's schooling and learning is important for their academic outcomes (Castro et al., 2015). Parents differ in the nature of their involvement. This involvement of parents can be categorized into personal, cognitive, and behavioral (Grolnick & Slowiaczek, 1994). *Personal involvement* means that the parents can elicit the affective experience in their children that their parents care about education and school matters. The children of personally involved parents enjoy parent-child interactions around school, leading to a positive feeling toward school. Parents who show a high *cognitive involvement* expose their children to intellectually stimulating activities, such as book reading, museum trips, or solving sudoku puzzles. This can convey the intrinsically rewarding qualities of education-related activities. Moreover, students can have mastery experiences in these stimulating activities, improving their ability and value beliefs within an out-of-school setting. These decontextualized educational experiences are important for the development of students' valuing of intellectual academic activities and thus subsequently affect achievement. Parents who are *behaviorally involved* participate in parent-teacher interactions, join the PTA, take part in school activities, and so on. Thus, parental involvement in school matters conveys a notion about parents' valuing of education. High parental involvement indicates that the parents value school, which can be linked to the students valuing school through intergenerational value transmission. In terms of social learning, parental academic involvement can serve as a positive role model and thus reinforce the students' academic involvement, which, in turn, affects academic engagement and performance.

Summary and recommendations

A meta-analysis by Jeynes (2007) combined the results of 52 studies (in sum, >300,000 students) on home-environment predictors of students' academic achievement (operationalized as grades and test scores in secondary school). Several dimensions were compared regarding their association with academic achievement outcomes. Unfortunately, this study did not distinguish between longitudinal and cross-sectional studies. Therefore, it is not possible to determine if home-environment variables affect achievement or vice versa. However, comparing the effect sizes allows for a differential evaluation of the strength of the association. Parental educational expectations turned out to be the best predictor of academic achievement. If the student's parents maintained high expectations of the student's ability to achieve at high levels, the student performed better. The second strongest source of influence was parenting style (see earlier) followed by homework support (an indicator of *personal involvement*). The communication between parents and students about school activities predicted the achievement as well. Furthermore, whether and how frequently parents attended and participated in school functions and activities was associated with higher achievement levels of the students as well (indicators of *behavioral involvement*). The associations of the home-environment characteristics and the achievement outcomes were by and large the same for European American and minority students.

As outlined previously, there are several ways for the home environment to affect students' academic development. The described routes of influence are not independent of each other or independent of influences from other contexts. For example, if schools do not provide opportunities for parents to participate in school activities or teacher-parent interaction, then there will be little chance to influence the students' academic development positively through behavioral involvement. On a macro level, there are societal factors that determine the ways parents can be part of students' education. Societies differ in their social norms about the extent that parents should participate in their children's education. Thus, values that are shared within a society affect the parents' values, which in turn predict their individual involvement. Finally, as noted at the start of this entry, if parents have few economic resources and their lives are stressed due to other factors linked to their health, their socioeconomic or historical constraints, or characteristics of their children or other family-related constraints, then their ability to provide opportunities for their children is likely to be constrained as well.

References

Aunola, K., Viljaranta, J., Lehtinen, E., & Nurmi, J-E. (2013). The role of maternal support of competence, autonomy and relatedness in children's interests and mastery orientation. *Learning and Individual Differences, 25*, 171–177. doi:10.1016/j.lindif.2013.02.002

Castro, M., Expósito-Casas, E., López-Martín, E., Lizasoain, L., Navarro-Asencio, E., & Gaviria, J. L. (2015). Parental involvement on student academic achievement: A meta-analysis. *Educational Research Review, 14*(0), 33–46. doi:http://dx.doi.org/10.1016/j.edurev.2015.01.002

Dumont, H., Maaz, K., Neumann, M., & Becker, M. (2014). Soziale Ungleichheiten beim Übergang von der Grundschule in die Sekundarstufe I: Theorie, Forschungsstand, Interventions- und Fördermöglichkeiten [Social disparities at the transition into secondary school: Theoretical conceptions and empirical evidence]. *Zeitschrift für Erziehungswissenschaft, 17*(2), 141–165. doi:10.1007/s11618-013-0466-1

Eccles, J. S. (2007). Families, schools, and developing achievement-related motivations and engagement. In J. E. Grusec & P. D. Hastings (Eds.), *Handbook of socialization* (pp. 665–691). New York, NY: The Guilford Press.

Gniewosz, B., Eccles, J. S., & Noack, P. (2015). Early adolescents' development of academic self-concept and intrinsic task value: The role of contextual feedback. *Journal of Research on Adolescence, 25*(3), 459–473. doi:10.1111/jora.12140

Gniewosz, B., & Noack, P. (2012). What you see is what you get: The role of early adolescents' perceptions in the intergenerational transmission of academic values. *Contemporary Educational Psychology, 37*(1), 70–79. doi:10.1016/j.cedpsych.2011.10.002

Gniewosz, B., & Walper, S. (2017). Bildungsungleichheit – Alles eine Frage der Familie?! [Social disparities in education – All a question of the family ?!]. In T. Eckert & B. Gniewosz (Eds.), *Bildungsgerechtigkeit* (pp. 187–200). Wiesbaden: Springer Fachmedien.

Grolnick, W., & Slowiaczek, M. L. (1994). Parents' involvement in children's schooling: A multidimensional conceptualization and motivational model. *Child Development, 65*(1), 237–252.

Hattie, J. (2015). The applicability of visible learning to higher education. *Scholarship of Teaching and Learning in Psychology, 1*(1), 79–91. doi:10.1037/stl0000021

Jeynes, W. H. (2007). The relationship between parental involvement and urban secondary school student academic achievement – A meta-analysis. *Urban Education, 42*(1), 82–110. doi:10.1177/0042085906293818

Johnson, W., McGue, M., & Iacono, W. G. (2007). How parents influence school grades: Hints from a sample of adoptive and biological families. *Learning and Individual Differences, 17*(3), 201–219. doi:10.1016/j.lindif.2007.04.004

Pesu, L., Viljaranta, J., & Aunola, K. (2016). The role of parents' and teachers' beliefs in children's self-concept development. *Journal of Applied Developmental Psychology, 44*, 63–71. doi:http://dx.doi.org/10.1016/j.appdev.2016.03.001

Petrill, S. A., & Wilkerson, B. (2000). Intelligence and achievement: A behavioral genetic perspective. *Educational Psychology Review, 12*(2), 185–199.

Selzam, S., Krapohl, E., von Stumm, S., O'Reilly, P. F., Rimfeld, K., Kovas, Y., . . . Plomin, R. (2016). Predicting educational achievement from DNA. *Molecular Psychiatry, 22*, 267. doi:10.1038/mp.2016.107

Simpkins, S. D., Fredricks, J. A., & Eccles, J. S. (2012). Charting the Eccles' expectancy-value model from mothers' beliefs in childhood to youths' activities in adolescence. *Developmental Psychology, 48*(4), 1019–1032. doi:10.1037/a0027468

Sirin, S. R. (2005). Socioeconomic status and academic achievement: A meta-analytic review of research. *Review of Educational Research, 75*(3), 417–453. doi:10.3102/00346543075003417 75

Tiedemann, J. (2000). Parents' gender stereotypes and teachers' beliefs as predictors of children's concept of their mathematical ability in elementary school. *Journal of Educational Psychology, 92*(1), 144–151. doi:10.1037/0022–0663.92.1.144

Wigfield, A., Eccles, J. S., Fredricks, J. A., Simpkins, S., Roeser, R. W., & Schiefele, U. (2015). Development of achievement motivation and engagement. In *Handbook of child psychology and developmental science* (pp. 657–700). Hoboken, NJ: John Wiley & Sons, Inc.

3.2

Socioeconomic status and student achievement

Erin Bumgarner and Jeanne Brooks-Gunn

Introduction

Decades of research have confirmed that socioeconomic status (SES) plays a significant role in children's academic achievement (Bradley & Corwyn, 2002; Duncan & Brooks-Gunn, 1997; Duncan, Ziol-Guest, & Kalil, 2010; Sirin, 2005; Smith, Brooks-Gunn, & Klebanov, 1997). Cognitive differences between children from high- and low-SES families have been documented by kindergarten entry (Duncan, Brooks-Gunn, & Klebanov, 1994; Larson, Russ, Nelson, Olson, & Halfon, 2015) and even in infancy (Clearfield & Niman, 2012; Klebanov, Brooks-Gunn, McCarton, & McCormick, 1998). These differences persist into school years and even adulthood (Duncan, Kalil, & Ziol-Guest, 2017). Recent longitudinal evidence shows that these trends have worsened in recent decades; as income disparities have grown, so have the achievement gaps between the highest- and lowest-income children (Reardon, 2011). This research shows that the high- versus low-achievement gaps are now twice the size of the black-white achievement gap – a pattern that has reversed over the past 50 years. SES is a comprehensive, multifaceted construct, which extends beyond poverty status alone to describe social stratification within a given society (Mueller & Parcel, 1981). Therefore, the most sophisticated measures of SES often combine aspects of income, education, and occupation (Duncan & Magnuson, 2003).

Research evidence

A majority of research examining the pathways between SES and children's achievement scores has drawn on two models. First, the parental investment model (Becker & Tomes, 1986) posits that economic hardship prevents parents from purchasing materials, experiences, and resources for their children because they must invest more in immediate, basic needs (Mayer, 1997). As a consequence, children of these parents are less likely to have access to resources that foster positive development, such as child care, cognitively stimulating activities in the home, and medical insurance (Yeung, Linver, & Brooks-Gunn, 2002). A second model, the family stress model (Conger & Elder, 1994), proposes that economic hardship causes significant strain on parents' emotional well-being and increases marital conflict. As a result, parents are less likely to provide warm, responsive, and consistent parenting (Smith & Brooks-Gunn, 1997). This is problematic because these parenting skills have significant positive implications for a child's cognitive, language, and social development (Collins, Maccoby, Steinberg, Hetherington, & Bornstein, 2000).

While these two models focus exclusively on family processes as the direct pathway, more current literature has begun exploring how other contexts serve as pathways. For example, the literature suggests that neighborhoods also serve as pathways between SES and achievement (Kohen, Brooks-Gunn, Leventhal, & Hertzman, 2002; Leventhal & Brooks-Gunn, 2000, 2004). This literature finds poor parents are restricted in their choice of neighborhoods and are therefore more likely to live in areas characterized by social disorganization and limited resources for child development. Other pathways include physical health, sleep quality, teacher and caregiver quality, school environment, and type of early care arrangement (Bassok, Finch, Lee, Reardon, & Waldfogel, 2016; Hoyniak, Bates, Staples, Rudasill, Molfese, & Molfese, 2018; Sirin, 2005).

Beyond the pathways that connect SES to achievement, research has explored how various mechanisms determine the strength of this association. Using income as a proxy for SES, research has found achievement scores and cognitive outcomes to be particularly sensitive to poverty during the first few years of life (Clearfield & Niman, 2012; Smith et al., 1997). This can be explained by the cumulative nature of skill development, such that a solid foundation of skills makes subsequent learning easier and more efficient (Heckman, 2006). In addition to timing, both the length and depth of poverty influence how severely SES impacts achievement outcomes (Duncan, Yeung, Brooks-Gunn, & Smith, 1998).

As we move forward in our understanding of the relation between SES and achievement, it is important to keep in mind several critiques and recommendations that have been made thus far. First, the majority of research on SES has focused on the economic aspects of SES. Several studies have begun looking at the unique contribution of parental education and occupation as predictors of children's academic achievement (Brooks-Gunn, Han, & Waldfogel, 2010; Magnuson, 2007; Reardon, 2011). Nevertheless, future research will need to explore how parental education, occupation, and income work in isolation and in various configurations to predict children's academic achievement (Conger, Conger, & Martin, 2010).

Second, the majority of literature looking at the relation between SES and academic achievement has been based on cross-sectional analyses of large datasets. The most convincing studies, however, are longitudinal, use fixed-effects models, and include a rich array of controls. Randomized trials are always preferable; however, as of yet, there are only a few that have explored this line of research (Costello, Compton, Keeler, & Angold, 2003). Despite this limitation, however, the effect sizes in many studies are modest and consistent, thus confirming that SES has important implications for children's academic achievement (Bassok et al., 2016; Dearing, McCartney, & Taylor, 2001; Reardon, 2011; Sirin, 2005).

Third, caution should be used when generalizing results because the relative impact of pathways between SES and academic outcomes may vary depending on the context and culture. For example, in the United States, research has indicated that two of the most significant mediating pathways are the cognitive stimulation provided within the home and parenting style (Guo & Harris, 2000). In other countries, however, particularly the poorest, SES may have the most impact on academic outcomes via pathways such as nutrition and access to health care (Grantham-McGregor et al., 2007).

Finally, despite the need for more research, researchers, policy makers, and schools must continue developing more effective policies and interventions. Without them, the impact of SES on academic achievement is often sustained into adulthood (Duncan et al., 2017; Schweinhart et al., 2005). In the presence of limited resources, the decision regarding which type of intervention to implement is critical. There is no single intervention or policy that can inoculate against the negative effects of SES on children (Brooks-Gunn, 2003). Nevertheless, current research suggests that early high-quality investments in young children's experiences can be a cost effective method for protecting against long-term negative consequences of poverty on academic outcomes later in life (Bassok et al., 2016; Heckman, 2006).

Summary and recommendations

In sum, the literature has found that SES has important implications for children's academic achievement that develop early and can persist for a lifetime (Bradley & Corwyn, 2002; Clearfield & Niman, 2012; Duncan et al., 2010; Duncan et al., 2017; Reardon, 2011; Smith et al., 1997). There are multiple causal pathways through which SES exerts its influence on academic achievement, including the home learning environment, parenting styles, child care arrangements, health, teaching methods, and neighborhood conditions (Bassok et al., 2016; Hoyniak et al., 2018; Sirin, 2005). The depth, duration, and timing of poverty are determinants of how severely SES impacts children's academic performance (Smith et al., 1997). In the face of limited resources, it is critical that all parties come together to develop more effective policies that are cost effective, of high quality, and able to provide an equal playing field for young children (Bassok & Latham, 2017; Currie, 1997; Heckman, 2006).

References

Bassok, D., Finch, J. E., Lee, R., Reardon, S. F., & Waldfogel, J. (2016). Socioeconomic gaps in early childhood experiences: 1998 to 2010. *AERA Open, 2*(3), 2332858416653924.

Bassok, D., & Latham, S. (2017). Kids today: The rise in children's academic skills at kindergarten entry. *Educational Researcher, 46*(1), 7–20.

Becker, G. S., & Tomes, N. (1986). Human capital and the rise and fall of families. *Journal of Labor Economics, 4*, S1–S139.

Bradley, R., & Corwyn, R. (2002). Socioeconomic status and child development. *Annual Review of Psychology, 53*, 371–399.

Brooks-Gunn, J. (2003). Do you believe in magic? What we can expect from early childhood intervention programs. *Social Policy Report, Society for Research in Child Development, 17*, 3–13.

Brooks-Gunn, J., Han, W-J., & Waldfogel, J. (2010). First-year maternal employment and child development in the first seven years. *Monographs of the Society for Research in Child Development, 75*(2), 1–19.

Clearfield, M. W., & Niman, L. C. (2012). SES affects infant cognitive flexibility. *Infant Behavior and Development, 35*(1), 29–35.

Collins, W., Maccoby, E., Steinberg, L., Hetherington, E., & Bornstein, M. (2000). Contemporary research on parenting: The case of nature and nurture. *American Psychologist, 55*, 215–232.

Conger, R. D., Conger, K. J., & Martin, M. J. (2010). Socioeconomic status, family processes, and individual development. *Journal of Marriage and Family, 72*, 685–704.

Conger, R. D., & Elder, G. H. (1994). *Families in troubled times: Adapting to change in rural America.* Hawthorne, NY: Aldine de Gruyter.

Costello, J., Compton, S., Keeler, G., & Angold, A. (2003). Relationships between poverty and psychopathology: A natural experiment. *Journal of the American Medical Association, 290*, 2023–2029.

Currie, J. (1997). Choosing among alternative programs for poor children. *Children and Poverty, 7*(2), 113–131.

Dearing, E., McCartney, K., & Taylor, B. (2001). Change in family income-to-needs matters more for children with less. *Child Development, 72*, 1779–1793.

Duncan, G. J., & Brooks-Gunn, J. (Eds.). (1997). *Consequences of growing up poor.* New York, NY: Russell Sage.

Duncan, G. J., Brooks-Gunn, J., & Klebanov, P. K. (1994). Economic deprivation and early-childhood development. *Child Development, 65*, 296–318.

Duncan, G. J., Kalil, A., & Ziol-Guest, K. M. (2017). Increasing inequality in parent incomes and children's schooling. *Demography, 54*(5), 1603–1626.

Duncan, G. J., & Magnuson, K. A. (2003). Off with Hollingshead: Socioeconomic resources, parenting and child development. In M. H. Bornstein & R. H. Bradley (Eds.), *Socioeconomic status, parenting and child development* (pp. 83–106). Mahwah, NJ: Erlbaum.

Duncan, G. J., Yeung, W. J., Brooks-Gunn, J., & Smith, J. R. (1998). How much does childhood poverty affect the life chances of children? *American Sociological Review, 63*(3), 406.

Duncan, G. J., Ziol-Guest, K., & Kalil, A. (2010). Early-childhood poverty and adult attainment, behavior, and health. *Child Development, 81*, 306–325.

Grantham-McGregor, S., Cheung, Y., Cueto, S., Glewwe, P., Richter, L., Strupp, B., & The International Child Development Steering Group. (2007). Developmental potential in the first 5 years for children in developing countries. *The Lancet, 369*, 60–70.

Guo, G., & Harris, K. M. (2000). The mechanisms mediating the effects of poverty on children's intellectual development. *Demography, 37*, 431–447.

Heckman, J. (2006). Skill formation and the economics of investing in disadvantaged children. *Science, 312*, 1900–1902.

Hoyniak, C. P., Bates, J. E., Staples, A. D., Rudasill, K. M., Molfese, D. L., & Molfese, V. J. (2018). Child sleep and socioeconomic context in the development of cognitive abilities in early childhood. *Child Development*. Advance online publication. doi:10.1111/cdev.13042

Klebanov, P. K., Brooks-Gunn, J., McCarton, C., & McCormick, M. C. (1998). The contribution of neighborhood and family income to developmental test scores over the first three years of life. *Child Development, 69*, 1420–1436.

Kohen, D. E., Brooks-Gunn, J., Leventhal, T., & Hertzman, C. (2002). Neighborhood income and physical and social disorder in Canada: Associations with young children's competencies. *Child Development, 73*, 1845–1860.

Larson, K., Russ, S. A., Nelson, B. B., Olson, L. M., & Halfon, N. (2015). Cognitive ability at kindergarten entry and socioeconomic status. *Pediatrics, 135*(2), e440–e448.

Leventhal, T., & Brooks-Gunn, J. (2000). The neighborhoods they live in: The effects of neighborhood residence upon child and adolescent outcomes. *Psychological Bulletin, 126*, 309–337.

Leventhal, T., & Brooks-Gunn, J. (2004). A randomized study of neighborhood effects on low-income children's educational outcomes. *Developmental Psychology, 40*, 488–507.

Magnuson, K. (2007). Maternal education and children's academic achievement during middle childhood. *Developmental Psychology, 43*, 1497–1512.

Mayer, S. (1997). *What money can't buy: Family income and children's life chances*. Cambridge, MA: Harvard University Press.

Mueller, C. W., & Parcel, T. L. (1981). Measures of socioeconomic status: Alternatives and recommendations. *Child Development, 52*, 13–30.

Reardon, S. (2011). The widening academic achievement gap between the rich and the poor: New evidence and possible explanations. In R. Murnane & G. Duncan (Eds), *Whither opportunity? Rising inequality and the uncertain life chances of low-income children* (pp. 91–116). New York, NY: Sage Found.

Schweinhart, L., Montie, J., Xiang, Z., Barnett, W., Belfield, C., & Nores, M. (2005). *Lifetime effects: The high/scope Perry preschool study through age 40*. Ypsilanti, MI: High/Scope Press.

Sirin, S. (2005). Socioeconomic status and academic achievement: A meta-analytic review of research. *Review of Educational Research, 75*(3), 417–453.

Smith, J. R., & Brooks-Gunn, J. (1997). Correlates and consequences of harsh discipline for young children. *Archives of Pediatric and Adolescent Medicine, 151*, 777–786.

Smith, J. R., Brooks-Gunn, J., & Klebanov, P. K. (1997). The consequences of living in poverty for young children's cognitive and verbal ability and early school achievement. In G. J. Duncan & J. Brooks-Gunn (Eds.), *Consequences of growing up poor* (pp. 132–189). New York, NY: Russell Sage.

Yeung, J., Linver, M., & Brooks-Gunn, J. (2002). How money matters for young children's development: Parental investment and family processes. *Child Development, 73*(6), 1861–1879.

3.3 Parent involvement in learning

Wendy S. Grolnick, Rachel E. Lerner, Jacquelyn N. Raftery-Helmer, and Elizabeth S. Allen

Introduction

There is great interest among educators, psychologists, and policy makers in enhancing parent involvement in children's learning. Research identifies parent involvement as a key mechanism for closing achievement gaps between more and less advantaged and majority and minority youth (Dearing, Kreider, Simpkins, & Weiss, 2006; Hara, 1998; Hayes, 2012). Further, facilitating parent involvement was included as a major goal of the reauthorized Elementary and Secondary Education Act (Every Student Succeeds Act of 2015, 2015–2016). This action reflects the understanding that parent involvement is a significant factor in students' achievement and school adjustment.

Parent involvement in children's learning is typically defined broadly. For example, Grolnick and Slowiaczek (1994) defined parent involvement as parents' dedication of tangible and intangible resources to children in a given domain. Gonzalez-DeHass, Willems, and Holbein (2005) defined parent involvement in children's schooling as "parenting behaviors directed toward children's education" (p. 101). Hill and Taylor (2004) defined school involvement as "parents' interaction with schools and with their children to promote academic success" (p. 1491). These definitions are purposefully broad to include the many ways that parents can be involved in their children's educations.

Research evidence

A burgeoning literature supports the importance of parent involvement in children's learning for children's achievement across a range of ages and populations. In particular, Jeynes's (2005) meta-analysis of 41 studies, which included over 20,000 elementary-age students, addressed the relations between parent involvement and academic achievement and showed large effects of parent involvement on both children's grades and standardized test scores. These results held when controlling for socioeconomic status, race, and other demographic factors. In a second meta-analysis of 52 studies of secondary school children (Jeynes, 2007), there were also positive effects of parent involvement on both grades and standardized test scores. Though the effects were somewhat smaller for the older students than those for the elementary students, they were still appreciable. In a meta-analysis of 50 studies of middle school students, Hill and Tyson (2009) found a highly significant effect of parent involvement on children's achievement. Finally, Ma, Shen, Krenn, Hu, and Yuan's (2016) meta-analysis of 46 studies focusing on the period of early childhood and elementary education found a significant effect of parental involvement on children's learning outcomes, including students' achievement in language, math, and science. Thus, across all age groups and in a variety of populations, there appears to be a robust connection between parent involvement and children's achievement.

While research clearly demonstrates overall relations between parent involvement and children's achievement, it is crucial to understand what parents are doing that effectively supports children's achievement. Thus, researchers have divided parent involvement into different types. Notably, Epstein's (1986) home-school partnership model identified six types of involvement: (a) basic responsibilities of families to provide a supportive environment for children's adequate health, safety, and well-being; (b) school-home communication, such as through conferences, notes, and report cards; (c) involvement at school, including volunteering and attending school events; (d) involvement in learning activities at home, including helping with homework; (e) involvement in advocacy, governance, or decision-making, such as in school councils or PTOs; and (f) family collaboration with other stakeholders, such as businesses or agencies in the community that can facilitate children's learning.

Several studies have examined the efficacy of some of these different types of involvement. Jeynes (2005, 2007) divided the studies in his meta-analyses into communication, homework, parental expectations, reading, attendance, and participation at school. He found the strongest effects for parental expectations. In their study of low-income ethnic minority children, McWayne, Hampton, Fantuzzo, Cohen, and Sekino (2004) divided parent involvement into a supportive home learning environment that included behaviors such as talking about school and structuring the home environment to support learning; direct involvement, including involvement in school activities and direct communication between families and school; and inhibited involvement, including time and language constraints and competing responsibilities that interfere with involvement. They found the strongest effects for the supportive environment type of involvement, particularly for kindergarten children. Using a longitudinal design, Sy, Gottfried, and Gottfried (2013) divided parent involvement into academic instruction, which included parent assistance in the development of children's academic skills through educational activities, and academic socialization, which included parental communication of academic expectations, values, and beliefs. Although parent academic instruction in early childhood had strong effects on early reading achievement, parent academic socialization had strong effects on reading achievement throughout childhood and adolescence. In their meta-analysis of studies of middle school children, Hill and Tyson (2009) examined school-based involvement, home-based strategies, and academic socialization such as communicating expectations for the value of education. There were no significant effects of home-based involvement, significant effects for school-based involvement, and the strongest effects for academic socialization on children's achievement (class grades, test scores, track placement, and other measures of achievement). Overall, research suggests that the strongest parent involvement findings are for the attitudes, expectations, and values parents convey to their children, especially their older children.

While research has considered the level and type of parent involvement, it is crucial to also consider *how* parents are involved in their children's academics (Pomerantz, Moorman, & Litwack, 2007). Parents can be involved in an autonomy-supportive way, by taking their children's perspectives and providing them choices, or in a controlling way, by pressuring them and solving problems for them. A few studies have focused on the degree to which parents are autonomy supportive versus controlling in their involvement and children's achievement. For instance, Steinberg, Lamborn, Dornbusch, and Darling (1992) found that parents' involvement in their children's schooling was more associated with children's academic achievement when it was implemented in an authoritative (i.e., including autonomy support) manner rather than an authoritarian (i.e., including parental control) manner. Similarly, when completing a homework-like task with their children in the laboratory, parents who displayed a more controlling style had children who were less successful on similar tasks later when performing on their own (Grolnick, Gurland, DeCourcey, & Jacob, 2002).

Another question that researchers have asked is how, or through what processes, parent involvement might affect children. Grolnick and Slowiaczek (1994) differentiated between two models for such effects. The direct effects model suggests that parent involvement affects children's achievement by helping them attain the academic skills they need to succeed: for example, math and reading skills. A second model suggests that parent involvement affects children's achievement by facilitating children's motivation (i.e., their confidence in their abilities, their sense that they can control their own successes and failures in school, and their engagement in school for more autonomous versus controlled reasons). In a study of 203 middle school students, these authors tested this model by examining relations between three types of parent involvement: behavior at school, cognitive/intellectual activities with their children, and personal involvement, which was asking about and keeping up on children's school activities and progress and children's motivation and school performance. For both mothers and fathers, the results supported the motivational model, indicating that involvement at school and in cognitive/intellectual activities facilitated students' perceived competence and perceived control over academic successes and failures, which were then associated with children's school performance.

Other studies demonstrating the link between parent involvement and children's motivation further support the motivation model. For example, Sanders (1998) found positive relations between parent encouragement of academic endeavors and achievement and children's positive academic self-concept, school behavior, and perception of the importance of achievement for future success. Fan and Williams (2010) showed that parents' educational aspirations for their children as well as their school-based involvement were positively associated with children's academic self-efficacy, school engagement, and intrinsic motivation. A review of multiple studies by Gonzalez-DeHass et al. (2005) concluded that there is ample support that parent involvement facilitates children's perceived competence, perceived control, and value for the educational endeavor.

Hoglund, Jones, Brown, and Aber (2015) explored three models that considered the relation between parent involvement and children's achievement. The parent socialization model suggests that parent involvement promotes children's adjustment. The child adjustment model suggests that children's adjustment contributes to parents' involvement. Finally, the transactional model argues that there are bidirectional relations between parent involvement and children's adjustment. These models were tested with a sample of 941 low-income, racially diverse third- and fourth-graders in a study that included three types of parent involvement: homework assistance, home-school conferencing, and school-based support. Results supported the child adjustment model, such that when children were struggling in school, their parents showed higher levels of homework assistance and home-school conferencing. While the results of this study may be specific to the types of involvement examined, they illustrate the importance of considering that parents may influence and also respond to children's behavior through their involvement.

Summary and recommendations

Given evidence of the strength and breadth of effects of parent involvement, it is not surprising that boosting parent involvement is a key goal for educational policy and school reform. While research has clearly shown that characteristics of parents such as education and income predict involvement, with, for example, levels of involvement being higher for more educated and higher-income families (e.g., Bhargava & Witherspoon, 2015; Grolnick, Benjet, Kurowski, & Apostoleris, 1997; Horvat, Weininger, & Lareau, 2003; Wang & Sheikh-Khalil, 2014), there is also evidence that teachers and schools can make a difference in parents' levels of involvement. For example, Epstein (1986) showed that when teachers believed strongly in parent involvement, parents reported that they received the most ideas for home learning activities from the teacher and felt they had an increased understanding of what their child was learning in school. Beyond what teachers can do, there are many school-wide efforts that are successfully enhancing parent involvement. For example, schools that are members of the National Network of Partnership Schools (NNPS; Sanders & Epstein, 2000) set goals for implementing family-school partnerships and monitoring progress toward these goals. Schools with these partnership programs have more parent involvement both at home and at school than non-partnership schools (Sheldon & Van Voorhis, 2004). Future school efforts should consider why parents are involved in their children's schooling in order to further increase parent involvement. A recent study found that mothers who are involved because they believe the activities are important or fun have higher levels of involvement and display a more positive affect when involved than mothers who are involved to avoid external consequences or feelings of guilt (Grolnick, 2015). Similarly, Jungert et al. (2015) found that when parents invest in their parenting role because it is meaningful or important to them, they display a more autonomy-supportive parenting style. Thus, to promote parent involvement, school initiatives should not use coercive, punitive, or guilt-evoking methods but should focus on helping parents see the value of their involvement for their children.

In sum, parents' involvement in children's learning is a major resource for children's academic achievement. Facilitating this crucial resource will require the active efforts of all stakeholders who have children's success and well-being as their goal.

References

Bhargava, S., & Witherspoon, D. P. (2015). Parental involvement across middle and high school: Exploring contributions of individual and neighborhood characteristics. *Journal of Youth and Adolescence*, *44*(9), 1702–1719.

Burger, K. (2010). How does early childhood care and education affect cognitive development? An international review of the effects of early interventions for children from different social backgrounds. *Early Childhood Research Quarterly*, *25*(2), 140–165.

Dearing, E., Kreider, H., Simpkins, S., & Weiss, H. B. (2006). Family involvement in school and low-income children's literacy: Longitudinal association between and within families. *Journal of Educational Psychology*, *98*, 653–664.

Epstein, J. L. (1986). Parents' reactions to teacher practices of parent involvement. *The Elementary School Journal*, *86*, 277–294.

Every Student Succeeds Act of 2015, Pub. L. No. 114–95 § 114 Stat. 1177 (2015–2016).

Fan, W., & Williams, C. M. (2010). The effects of parental involvement on students' academic self-efficacy, engagement and intrinsic motivation. *Educational Psychology*, *30*, 53–74.

Gonida, E. N., & Cortina, K. S. (2014). Parental involvement in homework: Relations with parent and student achievement-related motivational beliefs and achievement. *British Journal of Educational Psychology*, *84*(3), 376–396. https://doi-org.proxy.lib.ohio-state.edu/10.1111/bjep.12039

Gonzalez-DeHass, A., Willems, P., & Holbein, M. (2005). Examining the relationship between parental involvement and student motivation. *Educational Psychology Review*, *17*(2), 99–123.

Grolnick, W. S. (2015). Mothers' motivation for involvement in their children's schooling: Mechanisms and outcomes. *Motivation and Emotion*, *39*(1), 63–73.

Grolnick, W. S., Benjet, C., Kurowski, C. O., & Apostoleris, N. (1997). Predictors of parent involvement in children's schooling. *Journal of Educational Psychology*, *89*, 538–548.

Grolnick, W. S., Gurland, S. T., DeCourcey, W., & Jacob, K. (2002). Antecedents and consequences of mothers' autonomy support: An experimental investigation. *Developmental Psychology, 38*(1), 143–155.

Grolnick, W. S., & Slowiaczek, M. L. (1994). Parents' involvement in children's schooling: A multidimensional conceptualization and motivational model. *Child Development, 65*, 237–252.

Hara, S. R. (1998). Parent involvement: The key to improved student achievement. *School Community Journal, 8*(2), 9–19.

Hayes, D. (2012). Parental involvement and achievement outcomes in African American adolescents. *Journal of Comparative Family Studies, 43*, 567–582.

Hill, N. E., & Taylor, L. C. (2004). Parental school involvement and children's academic achievement: Pragmatics and issues. *Current Directions in Psychological Science, 13*, 161–164.

Hill, N. E., & Tyson, D. F. (2009). Parental involvement in middle school: A meta-analytic assessment of the strategies that promote achievement. *Developmental Psychology, 45*(3), 740–763.

Hoglund, W. L., Jones, S. M., Brown, J. L., & Aber, J. L. (2015). The evocative influence of child academic and social-emotional adjustment on parent involvement in inner-city schools. *Journal of Educational Psychology, 107*(2), 517–532.

Horvat, E. M., Weininger, E. B., & Lareau, A. (2003). From social ties to social capital: Class differences in the relations between schools and parent networks. *American Educational Research Journal, 40*, 319–351.

Jeynes, W. H. (2005). A meta-analysis of the relation of parental involvement to urban elementary school student academic achievement. *Urban Education, 40*, 237–269.

Jeynes, W. H. (2007). The relationship between parental involvement and urban secondary school student academic achievement: A meta-analysis. *Urban Education, 42*, 82–110.

Jungert, T., Landry, R., Joussemet, M., Mageau, G., Gingras, I., & Koestner, R. (2015). Autonomous and controlled motivation for parenting: Associations with parent and child outcomes. *Journal of Child and Family Studies, 24*(7), 1932–1942.

Kim, S. won, & Hill, N. E. (2015). Including Fathers in the Picture: A Meta-Analysis of Parental Involvement and Students' Academic Achievement. *Journal of Educational Psychology, 107*(4), 919–934.

Ma, X., Shen, J., Krenn, H. Y., Hu, S., & Yuan, J. (2016). A meta-analysis of the relationship between learning outcomes and parental involvement during early childhood education and early elementary education. *Educational Psychology Review, 28*(4), 771–801.

McWayne, C., Hampton, V., Fantuzzo, J., Cohen, H. L., & Sekino, Y. (2004). A multivariate examination of parent involvement and the social and academic competencies of urban kindergarten children. *Psychology in the Schools, 41*, 363–377.

Pomerantz, E. M., Moorman, E. A., & Litwack, S. D. (2007). The how, whom, and why of parents' involvement in children's academic lives: More is not always better. *Review of Educational Research, 77*(3), 373–410.

Sanders, M. G. (1998). The effects of school, family, and community support on the academic achievement of African American adolescents. *Urban Education, 33*, 385–409.

Sanders, M. G., & Epstein, J. L. (2000). The National Network of Partnership Schools: How research influences educational practice. *Journal of Education for Students Placed at Risk, 5*, 61–76.

Sheldon, S. B., & Van Voorhis, F. L. (2004). Partnership programs in U. S. schools: Their development and relationship to family involvement outcomes. *School Effectiveness and School Improvement, 15*, 125–148.

Steinberg, L., Lamborn, S. D., Dornbusch, S. M., & Darling, N. (1992). Impact of parenting practices on adolescent achievement: Authoritative parenting, school involvement, and encouragement to succeed. *Child Development, 63*(5), 1266–1281.

Sy, S. R., Gottfried, A. W., & Gottfried, A. E. (2013). A transactional model of parental involvement and children's achievement from early childhood through adolescence. *Parenting, 13*(2), 133–152.

Wang, M. T., & Sheikh-Khalil, S. (2014). Does parental involvement matter for student achievement and mental health in high school? *Child Development, 85*(2), 610–625.

Summary table: influences from the home

Category	Variable	Considerations
Beliefs	Parents' **beliefs about the importance of education** affect achievement.	*Achievement is higher when (a) parents believe in the value of education, and (b) parents support and encourage behaviors that are consistent with these beliefs (e.g., encouraging students to study and to do homework).*
	Parents' **competence beliefs** about their children refer to parents' beliefs about how well a child is able to learn.	*Positive parental competence beliefs are related to greater achievement in students.*
	Parental educational expectations refer to parents' expectancies about the quality and amount of education that their children will attain.	*When parents hold high expectations for academic achievement, students achieve at higher levels.*
Behaviors	An **authoritative parenting style** is a style in which parents express support and warmth and allow for the child to have some autonomy but also have and consistently enforce rules.	*Authoritative parenting is related to greater academic achievement.*
	Parental involvement with academics includes (a) consistently demonstrating that the parents care about education, (b) providing opportunities for cognitive growth (e.g., reading books together), and (c) participating in school-related activities (e.g., participating in school activities).	*Parental involvement yields positive influences on achievement because it leads to more positive feelings about school and learning, it sends the message to students that learning can be "fun" (i.e., it facilitates the development of positive motivational beliefs), and it can facilitate the development of effective study and learning strategies. Not all parents are able to attend school events, but, nevertheless, parents can be involved through supports provided at home.*

(Continued)

Category	Variable	Considerations
	Maternal employment refers to families in which the mother is employed.	*There are no direct negative effects of maternal employment on achievement. However, other variables that are related to maternal employment (e.g., SES, family structure) may affect achievement.*
	Parents should expect that homework gets completed and should **provide appropriate time and support to encourage homework completion**.	*When parents support students' efforts to complete homework, students achieve at higher levels.*
	Family-school partnerships occur when school personnel work cooperatively with parents to support student success.	*These partnerships are effective when they focus on (a) students' learning and behavior and (b) improving parents' expectations for student success. Partnerships should allow for equal input from parents and schools.*
Structural Influences	**Socioeconomic status (SES)** is measured in numerous ways but generally is comprised of parental education, parental income, and status of parental occupations.	*Higher SES is related to greater academic achievement. SES exerts its influence in many ways. For example, SES is related to the resources available in the home, children's health, neighborhood environments, child care, and numerous other variables that affect achievement. Nevertheless, welfare programs aimed at low-income households are not related to achievement gains.*
	Genetic influences refer to characteristics of children that have been biologically transmitted to them. Genetics do contribute to personality and some cognitive competencies.	*Genetics are related to academic achievement, but genetic influences interact with environmental factors in influencing achievement.*
	Family structure refers to the individuals who reside in the same household as a student.	*Students achieve at higher levels when there are two parents in the household; research indicates that the absence of the father is related to lower achievement.*
	Television viewing refers to the amount and quality of programming viewed by children outside school.	*There are small negative effects of viewing television on achievement. However, these effects are complex and also depend on age, quality of programming, whether watching television affects sleep, etc.*

Note: This table summarizes information presented by authors who contributed chapters to section 3 of the first edition of The International Guide to Student Achievement, as well as to revised chapters included in the present chapter.

Additional references

Australian Institute of Family Studies. (2018). *Growing up in Australia: The longitudinal study of Australian children: Annual statistical report 2017*. Department of Social Services and Australian Institute of Family Studies, Commonwealth of Australia.

Elliott, L., & Bachman, H. J. (2018). Parents' educational beliefs and children's early academics: Examining the role of SES. *Children & Youth Services Review, 91*, 11–21. https://doi-org.proxy.lib.ohio-state.edu/10.1016/j.childyouth.2018.05.022

Jeynes, W. H. (2015). A meta-analysis: The relationship between father involvement and student academic achievement. *Urban Education, 50*(4), 387–423.

Kostyrka-Allchorne, K., Cooper, N. R., & Simpson, A. (2017). The relationship between television exposure and children's cognition and behaviour: A systematic review. *Developmental Review, 44*, 19–58. https://doi-org.proxy.lib.ohio-state.edu/10.1016/j.dr.2016.12.002

Lucas-Thompson, R. G., & Goldberg, W. A. (2013). Maternal employment and achievement. In J. Hattie & E. M. Anderman (Eds.), *International guide to student achievement* (pp. 104–106). New York, NY: Routledge/Taylor & Francis Group.

Martin, A. J. (2013). Television and academic achievement. In J. Hattie & E. M. Anderman (Eds.), *International guide to student achievement* (pp. 107–109). New York, NY: Routledge/Taylor & Francis Group.

Masud, H., Thurasamy, R., & Ahmad, M. S. (2015). Parenting styles and academic achievement of young adolescents: A systematic literature review. *Quality & Quantity: International Journal of Methodology, 49*(6), 2411–2433. https://doi-org.proxy.lib.ohio-state.edu/10.1007/s11135-014-0120-x

Pinquart, M. (2016). Associations of parenting styles and dimensions with academic achievement in children and adolescents: A meta-analysis. *Educational Psychology Review, 28*(3), 475–493. Retrieved from http://proxy.lib.ohio-state.edu/login?url=http://search.ebscohost.com/login.aspx?direct=true&db=eric&AN=EJ1110201&site=ehost-live

Pomerantz, E. M., Kim, E. M., & Cheung, C. S. (2011). Parents' involvement in children's learning. In K. Harris, S. Graham, & T. Urdan (Eds.), *Educational psychology handbook* (pp. 417–440). Washington, DC: American Psychological Association.

Sacks, V., Moore, K. A., Shaw, A., & Cooper, P. M. (2014). *The family environment and adolescent well-being*. Bethesda, MD: Child Trends. Retrieved from www.childtrends.org/wp-content/uploads/2015/08/2014-52FamilyEnvironmentRB.pdf

Simpkins, S. D., Fredricks, J. A., & Eccles, J. S. (2015). The role of parents in the ontogeny of achievement-related motivation and behavioral choices: V Parent belief and behavior models. *Monographs of the Society for Research in Child Development, 80*(2), 85–97. https://doi-org.proxy.lib.ohio-state.edu/10.1111/mono.12161

Steinberg, L. (2014). *Age of opportunity: Lessons from the new science of adolescence*. New York, NY: Houghton Mifflin.

U.S. Department of Health and Human Services. (2006). *The NICHD study of early child care and youth development*. Washington, DC: U.S. Department of Health and Human Services/NIH. Retrieved from www.nichd.nih.gov/sites/default/files/publications/pubs/documents/seccyd_06.pdf

Wilder, S. (2014). Effects of parental involvement on academic achievement: A meta-synthesis. *Educational Review, 66*(3), 377–397. https://doi-org.proxy.lib.ohio-state.edu/10.1080/00131911.2013.780009

CHAPTER 4

Influences from the school

Academic achievement is affected at multiple organizational levels. Whereas some effects occur at the classroom level, students are always nested within larger school structures. Thus, the policies and practices implemented at the school level often affect the types of instructional practices that are implemented in individual classrooms. Moreover, when effective policies are implemented consistently across classrooms and grade levels, they can have strong cumulative effects on achievement.

In the original *Guide*, we invited authors to comment on a variety of influences from the school. That section, which was edited by Catherine Bradshaw (University of Virginia), included the entries and authors listed below.

Charter Schools and Academic Achievement
Ann Allen

Ability Grouping★
Ed Baines

Evaluating and Improving Student-Teacher Interactions
Anne H. Cash and Bridget K. Hamre

Mixed-Grade Elementary School Classes and Student Achievement
Linley Cornish

School-Based Mental Health
Erin Dowdy, Matthew P. Quirk, and Jenna K. Chin

Achievement in Faith-Based Schools
L. Mickey Fenzel

Class Size★
John Hattie

Financing Schools★
  Eric A. Hanushek

Influences of School Layout and Design on Student Achievement★
  C. Kenneth Tanner

Grade Retention
  Shane R. Jimerson and Jacqueline A. Brown

Inclusive Education
  Geoff Lindsay

School-Wide Positive Behavior Interventions and Supports and Academic Achievement
  Kent McIntosh, Sophie V. Ty, Robert H. Horner, and George Sugai

School Connectedness
  Clea McNeely

Teacher Mentoring, Coaching, and Consultation
  Elise T. Pas and Daniel S. Newman

The Link between Student Mobility and Academics
  Bess Rose and Catherine P. Bradshaw

Service-Learning
  Shelley H. Billig

Single-Sex Schools and Academic Achievement
  Shirley L. Yu and Isabel Rodriguez-Hejazi

Summer School and Student Achievement in the United States
  Jordan D. Matsudaira

Within Class Grouping: Arguments, Practices, and Research Evidence
  Yiping Lou

Special Education and Academic Achievement
  Benjamin Zablotsky and Michael S. Rosenberg

Social and Emotional Learning and Academic Achievement
  Jessika Zmuda and Catherine P. Bradshaw

Middle School Transitions★
  Eric M. Anderman

Four of the chapters (noted with an *) have been updated for the new edition and are presented later in the chapter.

Next we present a brief overview of some of the major school-level influences on achievement. We have organized this into discussions of (a) the organizational features of schools, (b) services provided by schools, and (c) instructional practices that are implemented throughout schools.

Organizational features of the school

"Organization" is a broad term that refers to numerous aspects of schooling. Organizational features are largely determined by school administrators, and many are dependent on funding. Moreover, some of these structures are easily malleable, whereas others are extremely difficult if not impossible to change.

One of the most salient organizational features of the school is the grade configuration. Whereas there are numerous determinants of these configurations, most schools utilize fairly standard configurations, with elementary or primary schools serving young children, middle schools serving early adolescents, and high schools serving older adolescents. There are few effects of these configurations, although when instruction is not developmentally appropriate, students can experience declines in achievement as they transition into the higher grades (e.g., from elementary school into middle school). Moreover, although most schools separate students into distinct grade levels, some schools are organized with mixed-grade classrooms (i.e., students from different grade levels are placed in the same classroom). Such arrangements are not deleterious to achievement, but benefits seem to only accrue when schools organize these classrooms into truly nongraded classrooms (i.e., classrooms where work is individually tailored to student needs, regardless of the students' grade levels).

Another organizational feature of schools is class size. Although many argue that smaller class sizes lead to higher achievement, research suggests that class size is not strongly related to achievement. Rather, the types of instructional practices used by teachers are what really make a difference in terms of achievement. Thus, a student who is enrolled in a small class (e.g., one with 8 students) but who receives poor instruction will probably not achieve as well as a student who is enrolled in a larger class (e.g., one with 25 students) but who receives evidence-based instruction and academic support.

Finally, some schools are affiliated with specific faiths or organizations. Students who attend faith-based schools (e.g., Catholic schools) often achieve at higher levels than students who attend non-faith-based schools. These effects are quite likely attributable to the faith-based schools having fewer behavioral infractions and a positive, supportive school climate. Moreover, charter schools also continue to grow in number. Attending a charter school (i.e., a school that receives public funds but is independently operated) generally does not yield sizeable achievement benefits, despite much public rhetoric.

Services provided by the school

Schools also are characterized by the types of services that are available to students and families. The provision of services is tied to school budgets, which are affected by local and national economic conditions. When available, these services can address a variety of needs, including academic and wellness/mental health needs.

Schools can provide a wide range of mental-health services. Student mental health can be addressed via the provision of services from school counselors, school psychologists, school social workers, and other mental-health professionals. Although the quality and duration of services varies, research generally suggests that when students are experiencing social or emotional stressors, the provision of mental-health support is related to increased academic achievement for those students.

Services designed to support academic success also at times are implemented at the school level. For example, some schools adopt school-wide programs that focus on students' socioemotional learning (SEL). Whereas there are many extant SEL programs, research suggests that when schools implement SEL programs that are evidence-based and when those programs are implemented with fidelity, students' achievement is enhanced.

Instructional practices

Whereas instructional practices are often determined by classroom teachers, there are many instructional practices that are implemented (or mandated) at the school level. In order to be effective, these practices must be implemented appropriately and consistently. Moreover, the practices need to be tailored to the developmental readiness of the students. Thus a practice that is effective with a fifth-grade student may not be effective for a first-grade student.

Grouping practices also are often mandated by school policy. This includes both between-class grouping (e.g., grouping students into "advanced" or "regular" algebra) and within-class grouping (i.e., arranging students into small learning groups within a classroom). Despite popular beliefs, there is little research indicating that the use of between-class ability grouping is related to academic achievement. Within-class grouping can be homogeneous (i.e., students are organized into groups of peers with similar abilities) or heterogeneous (i.e., students are organized into groups of peers with varying abilities). Whereas all students experience some achievement benefits from working in small groups, lower-ability students benefit more from working in heterogenous groups, whereas average-ability students benefit more from participation in homogeneous groups.

We next present updated versions of four of the chapters that appeared in the original *Guide*. The chapter then concludes with a table that summarizes the main takeaway points.

4.1 Ability grouping

Ed Baines

Introduction

Grouping students on the basis of some estimate or judgment of their academic ability is a widely used approach in many countries to the organization of pupils for instructional purposes, though its exact nature varies between and within countries. This review examines the nature and rationale for the use of ability grouping; it also summarizes findings relating to academic achievement and explanatory processes.

Organizing pupils in groups on the basis of ability provokes strong debates among educators, politicians, and parents. Its use is based on a belief that all students' attainment can be increased if instruction, learning support, the curriculum, resources, teacher expertise, and so on are targeted at students according to similar ability level. However, many concerns are expressed about the potentially negative effects of ability grouping, particularly in relation to equality of opportunity and access to curriculum, resources, and instructional expertise. Homogenous ability grouping also tends to organize students by socioeconomic background (SEB) and across racial lines (Oakes, 2005). Consequently, many argue that it exacerbates and sustains existing societal divisions (Archer et al., 2018).

It is important to acknowledge that the notion of "ability" as something that can be measured with reliability is questionable (Ireson & Hallam, 2001), and we know that schools rarely base decisions about ability grouping placement solely on measures of aptitude or attainment but also on other factors relating to the students concerned. The term "ability grouping" is thus something of a misnomer, and many researchers prefer alternatives such as "attainment grouping" or a specific term for the particular nature of the grouping (e.g., "streaming").

Homogenous ability grouping can take different forms and be present at different organizational levels within the school system. Students may be grouped by ability *within* classrooms (within-class ability grouping) and may receive differentiated instruction. *Tracking* or *streaming* refers to the allocation of students to different classes on the basis of similar ability levels for all academic subjects. The curriculum offered may differ between tracks/streams to match the perceived student level. Another form of ability grouping, known as *setting* or *regrouping*, is similar to tracking but is particular to the curriculum area studied and therefore allows students to be in different ability group levels for different academic subjects. In these circumstances, the same curriculum is usually accessed by all students. The opposite of ability grouping is *heterogeneous-ability grouping*, sometimes known as *mixed-ability grouping*, in which group composition reflects the school intake (although even here there are complexities as schools can also be selective). This review will only consider literature relating to ability grouping within schools and classes. Readers interested in other forms of ability grouping should refer elsewhere (e.g., Chmielewski, 2014; Schoffield, 2010).

Research evidence

There is a long history of research on ability grouping, including several meta-analyses and literature reviews. Findings from recent international studies, particularly the ongoing triennial PISA research, indicate consistent effects of ability grouping in relation to performance in reading, mathematics, and science assessments. The PISA studies involved data collections from 15-year-old students and their schools across up to 65 countries. This research compared the academic performance of students who had experienced homogenous ability grouping for all curricula with those that experienced some ability grouping or none at all and found that the more schools grouped by ability the lower the overall performance. Findings also indicate that the earlier that differentiation starts, the greater the gap in achievement becomes by SEB, without any improvement in achievement overall. After controlling for student and school SEB, recent PISA studies found no independent relation between the grouping of students by ability and performance in reading or in mathematics. The PISA research concludes that "school systems that seek to cater to different students' needs through a high level of differentiation in the institutions, grade levels and classes have not succeeded in producing superior overall results, and in some respects they have lower-than-average and more socially unequal performance" (Organisation for Economic Co-operation and Development [OECD], 2010, p. 13; see also OECD, 2012).

Another international study of students (aged nine to ten years) in 40 countries utilized data from the 2006 Progress in International Reading Literacy Study (PIRLS) to examine the effects of ability grouping on reading achievement (Chiu, Chow, & Joh, 2017). This research utilized parental ratings of past literacy skills as well as measures of SEB, classmates' family characteristics, and school and teacher characteristics. Tracking was associated with lower reading achievement, whereas mixing within classes was connected to higher reading achievement. In particular, higher reading achievement was apparent when a student's classmates were reported (by parents) to have had stronger literacy skills in the past or very weak skills, had a higher SEB or where there was more diversity in SEB and when classmates had higher reading attitudes or when there was diversity in reading attitudes. The authors explain that the mixing of students in classes enables sharing of attitudes to reading leading to positive consequences and enables positive help giving and seeking opportunities where both more able and less able students benefit.

However, international comparison studies are often limited by their cross-sectional and correlational nature and are unable to offer causal explanations. Analyses are constrained to making crude comparisons of types/levels of ability grouping and are unable to determine the effects of more flexible or informal systems as used in many schools or of uncontrolled variables (e.g. curriculum coverage, student composition, teacher expertise/experience, and so on).

Meta-analyses of experimental and correlational studies examining the effect of homogenous ability grouping on achievement also show little overall benefit for the achievement of all students, and where trends are reported, effect sizes are small (Kulik & Kulik, 1982; Slavin, 1987, 1990). Studies of tracked systems and comparisons of the achievement performance of high-, middle-, and low-ability students show inconsistencies in reported effect sizes, though most are generally small (Hattie, 2002). A recent second-order meta-analysis reviewed 13 previous meta-analyses involving 172 unique primary studies (Steenbergen-Hu, Makel, & Olszewski-Kubilius, 2016) and found no evidence of a significant effect of between-class ability grouping on academic performance, either overall or in relation to prior attainment level. However, the majority of studies on ability grouping tend to involve the different groups undertaking broadly the same curriculum yet part of the purpose of ability grouping is to enable differentiation. Research that focuses on the co-occurrence of tracking and a differentiated curriculum shows more marked effects, which suggests that gifted and high-attaining students tend to perform better in homogeneous ability classes, whereas those in the low-ability range tend to fare worse in ability groups than in heterogeneous classes (Hallinan & Kubitschek, 1999; Schoffield, 2010).

Few studies have focused on the practice of "setting" in schools yet there are advantages to this approach over tracking, most notably a greater flexibility in reassignment and potentially a closer match between instruction and individuals' level of ability. Slavin's (1987) meta-analysis included seven studies comparing setting and heterogeneous grouping at the elementary school level in terms of performance in reading or mathematics. Results were inconclusive. More recently a naturalistic longitudinal study of the impact of setting on 6,000 secondary school students from 45 UK comprehensive schools found that the strength of setting experiences within a curriculum (from entirely mixed ability to rigorous setting experiences across the three years examined) showed no effect on student's performance in national English, mathematics, and science assessments at 13 to 14 years and in a follow-up at 15 to 16 years (Ireson & Hallam, 2001; Ireson, Hallam, & Hurley, 2005). Similarly there was little evidence of an increased achievement gap. However, at 13 to 14 years, low-ability students in mathematics made slightly more progress in response to mixed-ability grouping, and high-ability students benefited from a more rigorous setting. Analyses were controlled for SEB, previous attainment, and other background variables.

Studies of the effects of within-class ability grouping on achievement are rare. The advantage of within-class grouping over between-class grouping is its closer relationship with learning and teaching purposes, greater flexibility in reassignment, and greater opportunity for sustained interaction with teachers and peers. Meta-analyses indicate that within-class ability grouping may have modest to marked effects on student achievement in comparison to nongrouping or heterogeneous grouping (Lou et al., 1996), and a secondary meta-analysis of five meta-analyses reports significant small positive effects of within-class grouping on academic attainment with students at all levels benefiting (Steenbergen-Hu et al., 2016). Consistent with other findings on ability grouping, a number of studies suggest that low-attaining students appear to benefit most from mixed-ability grouping. With average effect sizes varying markedly between studies and within meta-analyses, the effects of within-class ability grouping are unclear. This may be due to variations in task, instruction, and interaction type and the group sizes that students within these groups experience (Baines, Blatchford, & Kutnick, 2003). As within-class ability grouping can be utilized for a range of pedagogic purposes (e.g., group instruction, peer-interactive learning) and may be embedded within a lesson involving other pedagogic practices, it is difficult to identify effects on performance beyond small-scale experimental designs (Blatchford, Kutnick, Baines, & Galton, 2003). Studies of within-class grouping with an enriched or accelerated curriculum (e.g., for use with "talented" students) suggest more substantial effect sizes than heterogeneous grouping (Lou et al., 1996), though this may be due to the different curricula undertaken.

Potential causal mechanisms

Although there is some disagreement in quantitative analyses about the impact of ability grouping between classrooms on academic achievement, effect sizes seem uniformly small to absent, suggesting that there is little to be explained (Hattie, 2002, 2009). Interestingly, though, qualitative studies have illustrated how student experiences vary between low-, middle-, high-, and heterogeneous-ability groups, thus providing insights into explanatory processes.

Qualitative studies suggest that teachers have higher expectations of students in higher-ability groups and lower expectations of students in lower-ability groups (Boaler, Wiliam, & Brown, 2000). These expectations are reflected in curriculum and examination demands and through teacher-pupil interaction. Expectations may have marked effects on student motivation with some students benefiting from the pressure of high expectations while others are turned off learning by low expectations. Interestingly, studies have found that when students are located in ability groups above their achievement level, they tend to make better progress than students of equivalent ability in groups that are at approximately the right level (Ireson et al., 2005). Placement in a lower group depresses students' academic progress regardless of attainment level.

Studies also indicate that teachers alter their pedagogic approach according to their expectations about the ability range of the classes they teach (Boaler et al., 2000). This, of course, is part of the point of homogeneous-ability grouping, but when accompanied by low expectations, it may function to lower the challenging and motivating nature of teaching and learning. Research conveys a depressing picture of the low level and fragmented nature of teaching and learning in low-ability groups. By contrast higher-ability classes experience more interactive, challenging, sustained, and responsive teaching. They may also have more highly experienced/qualified teachers (Oakes, 2005). Studies suggest that, where setting is accompanied by didactic instruction, there is a wider disparity in academic performance across sets than when within-class groups and individualized instruction are used alongside setting (e.g. Wiliam & Bartholomew, 2004). Varying pedagogic approaches may go some way to explaining the variable effects associated with ability grouping.

Summary and recommendations

Although there are seemingly obvious advantages to homogenous ability grouping, the evidence is less convincing. Some studies report marked variability between schools, thus explaining inconsistent findings. Either way, research suggests that it is not the activity of between-class ability grouping per se that leads to the observed small effects on achievement but rather its interaction with curriculum, classroom, and student social and demographic characteristics.

A key attraction to the use of between-class ability grouping is that it enables instruction at a single level and direct instruction. However, ability groups are never completely homogenous, and treating them as such can be problematic. A one-size-fits-all approach to instruction will tend to meet the needs of some students in the class while either constraining the learning of others or making them struggle to keep up. Without efficient and flexible structures to allow students to change groups, students may become disenchanted with learning. Research suggests that more could be done to make strategic and flexible use of within-class grouping practices for learning purposes. This may mean sometimes strategically mixing abilities for particular activities (e.g., peer-interactive learning) and at other times sustaining a more homogenous ability range to enable differentiation and support for students of all ability levels (e.g., through small-group instruction). When enmeshed with other pedagogic practices, such an approach may provide motivating, challenging, and mutually reinforcing instructional contexts that enhance student learning while engaging constructively with student diversity.

References

Archer, L., Francis, B., Miller, S., Taylor, B., Tereshchenko, A., Mazenod, A. . . . Travers, M-C. (2018). The symbolic violence of setting: A Bourdieusian analysis of mixed methods data on secondary students' views about setting. *British Educational Research Journal, 44*(1), 119–140.

Baines, E., Blatchford, P., & Kutnick, P. (2003). Grouping practices in classrooms: Changing patterns over primary and secondary schooling. *International Journal of Educational Research, 39*(1), 9–34.

Blatchford, P., Kutnick, P., Baines, E., & Galton, M. (2003). Toward a social pedagogy of classroom group work. *International Journal of Educational Research, 39*(1), 153–172.

Boaler, J., Wiliam, D., & Brown, M. (2000). Students' experiences of ability grouping: Disaffection, polarisation and the construction of failure. *British Educational Research Journal, 26*, 631–648.

Chiu, M. M., Chow, B. W-Y., & Joh, S. W. (2017). Streaming, tracking and reading achievement: A multilevel analysis of students in 40 countries. *Journal of Educational Psychology, 109*(7), 915–934. http://dx.doi.org/10.1037/edu0000188

Chmielewski, A. K. (2014). An international comparison of achievement inequality in within- and between-school tracking systems. *American Journal of Education, 120*(3), 293–324.

Hallinan, M. T., & Kubitschek, W. N. (1999). Curriculum differentiation and high school achievement. *Social Psychology of Education, 2*, 1–22.

Hattie, J. A. C. (2002). Classroom composition and peer effects. *International Journal of Educational Research, 37*, 449–481.

Hattie, J. A. C. (2009). *Visible learning: A synthesis of over 800 meta-analyses relating to achievement*. London: Routledge.

Ireson, J., & Hallam, S. (2001). *Ability grouping in education*. London: Chapman.

Ireson, J., Hallam, S., & Hurley, C. (2005). What are the effects of ability grouping on GCSE attainment? *British Educational Research Journal, 31*, 443–458.

Kulik, C-L., & Kulik, J. (1982). Effects of ability grouping on secondary school students: A meta-analysis of evaluation findings. *American Educational Research Journal, 19*, 415–428.

Lou, Y., Abrami, P., Spence, J., Chambers, B., Poulsen, C., & d'Apollonia, S. (1996). Within-class grouping: A meta-analysis. *Review of Educational Research, 66*, 423–458.

Oakes, J. (2005). *Keeping track: How schools structure inequality*. New Haven, CT: Yale University Press.

OECD (Organisation for Economic Co-operation and Development). (2010). *PISA 2009 results: What makes a school successful? Resources, policies and practices* (Vol. 4). Paris: OECD Publishing. http://dx.doi.org/10.1787/9789264091559-en

OECD. (2012). *Equity and quality in education: Supporting disadvantaged students and schools*. OECD Publishing. http://dx.doi.org/10.1787/9789264130852-en

Schoffield, J. W. (2010). International evidence on ability grouping with curriculum differentiation and the achievement gap in secondary schools. *Teachers College Record, 112*, 1492–1528.

Slavin, R. (1987). Ability grouping and student achievement in the elementary schools: A best-evidence synthesis. *Review of Educational Research, 57*, 293–336.

Slavin, R. (1990). Ability grouping in secondary schools: A best-evidence synthesis. *Review of Educational Research, 60*, 471–499.

Steenbergen-Hu, S., Makel, M. C., & Olszewski-Kubilius, P. (2016). What one hundred years of research says about the effects of ability grouping and acceleration on K-12 students' academic achievement: Findings of two second-order meta-analyses. *Review of Educational Research, 86*(4), 849–899.

Wiliam, D., & Bartholomew, H. (2004). It's not which school but which set you're in that matters: The influence of ability grouping practices on student progress in mathematics. *British Educational Research Journal, 30*, 279–295.

4.2 Class size

John Hattie

Introduction

It is not difficult to find claims for both sides of the argument about whether or not reducing class sizes leads to enhancements in learning outcomes. One side argues that reducing class size leads to more individualized instruction, higher-quality instruction, greater scope for innovation and student-centered teaching, increased teacher morale, fewer disruptions, less student misbehavior, and greater ease in engaging students in academic activities. On the other side, there is a voluminous literature that does not support the claim that learning outcomes are markedly enhanced when class sizes are reduced. It is possible to locate eight meta-analyses (based on 176 studies of over half a million students), and the overall average effects were positive but very small ($d = .15$). Further, there are so many major reviews representing a variety of designs including meta-analysis, longitudinal studies, and cross-cohort studies; they are from several countries (the United States, the United Kingdom, Israel, Bolivia) and from across all grades and use some of the most sophisticated statistical methods available. There is remarkable consistency across the effect sizes from these many diverse studies that the effects are positive but small.

Research evidence

Glass and Smith (1978) completed the first meta-analysis on this topic, synthesizing 77 studies, and found that, when classes were reduced from 25 to 15, the effects were, on average, very small (.09). They also synthesized 59 studies covering 371 effects relating to class size and non-achievement-based outcomes such as self-concept, interpersonal regard, engagement, quality of instruction, teacher attitude, and school climate (Smith & Glass, 1980) – and the effects were similarly "negligible."

The best-known study is the Tennessee Student-Teacher Achievement Ratios study (STAR), which involved a random assignment of about 6,500 students in 329 classrooms in 79 schools entering kindergarten. Teachers and students were assigned for three years to a regular class (22–26 students) or a small class (13–17 students) (Achilles & Finn, 2000). The overall effects (.15 to .27) increased as students spent additional years in a small class (about .12 for each year) and were double for minority students, but there were no effects for motivation and self-concept. In follow-up studies of these students, there remained small effects favoring those from smaller classes in achievement, engagement in learning, and higher graduation rates with fewer dropouts (Finn, Gerber, & Boyd-Zaharias, 2005).

Other large-scale studies have found similar low effects – the Wisconsin study (Molnar et al., 1999), Connecticut (Hoxby, 2000), and California (Jepsen & Rivkin, 2002) – as have various econometric studies (Argaw & Puhani, 2017; Hanushek, Rivkin, & Taylor, 1996; Krueger, 1999) and value-added studies (Ludwig & Bossi, 1999). Akerhielm (1995) used the National Education Longitudinal Study (NELS), based on a US nationally representative sample of over 24,000 eighth-graders. She found an overall effect size of .18 for science and .13 for history and concluded that "the incremental benefits may not surpass the incremental costs of decreasing class size" (p. 239). Gilraine, Macartney, and McMillan (2018) used a sophisticated differencing approach and found an effect of 0.11 in mathematics scores. Shen and Konstantopoulos (2017) investigated class-size reduction impacts on reading achievement in eight European countries: Bulgaria, Germany, Hungary, Italy, Lithuania, Romania, Slovakia, and Slovenia. There were no significant class-size effects on reading achievement across all but Romania (which were still very small but positive) and across all years (see also Gary-Bobo & Mahjoub, 2013; Konstantopoulos & Traynor, 2014; Pong & Pallas, 2001; Wößmann, 2005).

Similar findings have been reported in non-Western countries. Fuller (1987) reviewed nine studies in developing countries (Botswana, Thailand, India, Chile, Iran, Egypt, Kenya, Malaysia, Puerto Rico, Tanzania, Bolivia, and Argentina) and found no difference in learning outcomes relating to class size. Wößmann and West (2002) investigated the effect of class size on student achievement across many countries using the Third International Mathematics and Science Study (TIMSS) data. They were unable to detect a statistically significant effect of class size on student achievement for most school systems. Indeed, many of the countries where class sizes were greatest were among the highest performers across the comparable countries (including most Western countries – see Blatchford, Chan, Galton, Lai, & Lee, 2016).

Across all these studies, there is a high degree of overlap in the effects between larger and smaller classes. Some teachers are more effective than others almost irrespective of class size. Analyses of interactions across differing class sizes has shown few differences in the percent of student-initiated questions, the percent of student-initiated comments, the percent of students off task, student engagement, or time waiting for help. There are slight increases in on-task behavior and in social interaction but more direct-teacher and whole-group instruction in smaller classes. The typical arguments supporting smaller classes is that they increase on-task behavior and allow greater amounts of individual attention; less whole-class teaching; more prosocial interactions, peer interactions, and student-initiated questions; and greater curricula coverage – although there is more evidence not supporting these claims than supporting them (Evertson & Folger, 1989). Finn, Gerber, Achilles, and Boyd-Zaharias (2001), for example, found that teachers in STAR smaller classes spent increased time in direct instruction, although less time on managerial organizational tasks. Bourke (1986) found no relationship between class size and student engagement, more whole-class teaching and no more individualization in smaller classes, as well as fewer teacher-student interactions and fewer student questions.

Finn et al. (2001) undertook the most comprehensive review of potential reasons to account for the small overall effect size when reducing class sizes. Their claim was that the major effects of smaller class sizes related to the "visibility of the individual" – in smaller classes, there is increased pressure to participate: "students in a small class can't easily avoid being noticed and the teacher cannot readily ignore any pupil(s) even if s/he would like to" (p. 10). As a consequence, students are more likely to take responsibility for their learning, be less involved in social loafing, and have a greater sense of belonging and higher levels of group cohesiveness. Thus, if any effects accrue from smaller classes, the reasons relate to what students rather than teachers do in smaller versus larger classes (see also Blatchford, 2011).

The cost of class size reduction is high (teacher salaries, buildings) and ongoing and, compared with many other innovations, prohibitive. Brewer, Krop, Gill, and Reichardt (1999) estimated the costs of reducing class sizes to 18 students in years one to three in the United States would require hiring an additional 100,000 teachers, at a cost of $US 5 to 6 billion per year, and adding 55% more classrooms. To reduce again from 18 to 15 students would cost a further $US 5 to 6 billion per year. Instead, they estimate that this investment could be used to raise teachers' salaries by $20,000 per year, although the most effective investments are probably in teacher expertise, which makes much larger enhancements to student learning (see also Blatchford, Goldstein, Martin, & Browne, 2002).

Summary and recommendations

The conclusion is that it may be more effective to ask, "Why, given the seemingly obvious advantages for reducing class size, has it *not* led to the expected substantial positive impacts on student achievement?" The major reason seems to be that teachers of smaller classes seem to adopt the same teaching methods they were using in larger classes and thus not optimizing the opportunities presented by having fewer students. Glass, Cahen, Smith, and Filby (1982) reported that the nature of the instruction rarely changed when classes were reduced from 40 to 20 students. A poor/good teacher with 30 students may remain a poor/good teacher even with only 20 students. Even in smaller classes, teachers continue to teach as if there were 30 students in front of them. In a sense, why shouldn't they? What has worked for them (successfully, at least in their eyes) in one context is surely adaptable to many other situations (Hattie, 2007, 2018). There is little change in instructional practices in smaller classes – in the structure of lessons, teaching practices, opportunities, or content coverage. Perhaps retraining would change this (but see Stasz & Stecher, 2000).

The effects of reducing class size are small, which should not be surprising when teachers don't appear to change their teaching behaviors even when provided with opportunities in smaller classes to teach in different ways. The major issue is less whether class size makes a difference (as it appears not) but whether there are teaching strategies that optimize student learning in smaller classes. The slight increase, for example, for the junior classes may be that teachers of these classes are more likely to adopt the teaching principles and behaviors that optimize small-group learning. Given the enormous costs and the high levels of advocacy by teachers and parents for lower class size, it is necessary to rephrase the key question from "Does class size reduction positively influence student achievement?" to "How can we optimize teaching in small classes?" There is much merit in following through on Blatchford's (2011) recommendation to move from what he termed first- to third-generation research on class size. He posited at least three generations of research on class size. The first generation of research was directed at effects of class size on academic outcomes, the second generation was related to understanding the classroom processes that might be involved in moving to smaller classes, and the third generation addresses the most effective pedagogies in classes of different sizes.

References

Achilles, C. M., & Finn, J. D. (2000). Should class size be a cornerstone for educational policy? In M. C. Wang & J. D. Finn (Eds.), *How small classes help teachers do their best* (pp. 299–324). Philadelphia, PA: Temple University Center for Research in Human Development in Education.

Akerhielm, K. (1995). Does class size matter? *Economics of Education Review, 14*(3), 229–241.

Argaw, B., & Puhani, P. A. (2017). Does class size matter for school tracing outcomes after elementary school? Quasi-experimental evidence using administrative panel data from Germany. *GLO Discussion Paper, No. 155*. Global Labor Organization (GLO), Maastricht.

Blatchford, P. (2011). Three generations of research on class-size effects. In K. R. Harris, S. Graham, & T. Urdan (Eds.), *APA educational psychology handbook: Vol. 2. Individual differences and cultural and contextual factors* (pp 529–554). Washington, DC: American Psychological Association.

Blatchford, P., Chan, K. W., Galton, M., Lai, K. C., & Lee, J. C. K. (Eds.). (2016). *Class size: Eastern and Western perspectives*. New York: Routledge.

Blatchford, P., Goldstein, H., Martin, C., & Browne, W. (2002). A study of class size effects in English school reception year classes. *British Educational Research Journal, 28*(2), 169–185.

Bourke, S. (1986). How smaller is better: Some relationships between class size, teaching practices, and student achievement. *American Educational Research Journal, 23*(4), 558–571.

Brewer, D. J., Krop, C., Gill, B. P., & Reichardt, R. (1999). Estimating the cost of national class size reductions under different policy alternatives. *Educational Evaluation and Policy Analysis*, *21*(2), 179–192.

Evertson, C. M., & Folger, J. K. (1989, March). *Small class, large class: What do teachers do differently?* Paper presented at American Educational Research Association, San Francisco, CA.

Finn, J. D., Gerber, S. B., Achilles, C. M., & Boyd-Zaharias, J. (2001). The enduring effects of small classes. *Teachers College Record*, *103*(2), 145–183.

Finn, J. D., Gerber, S. B., & Boyd-Zaharias, J. (2005). Small classes in the early grades, academic achievement, and graduating from high school. *Journal of Educational Psychology*, *94*, 214–223.

Fuller, B. (1987). What school factors raise achievement in the third world? *Review of Educational Research*, *57*(3), 255–292.

Gary-Bobo, R. J., & Mahjoub, M. B. (2013). Estimation of class-size effects, using "Maimonides' Rule" and other instruments: The case of French junior high schools. *Annals of Economics and Statistics (ANNALES D'ÉCONOMIE ET DE STATISTIQUE)*, 193–225.

Gilraine, M., Macartney, H., & McMillan, R. (2018). *Education reform in general equilibrium: Evidence from California's class size reduction* (No. w24191). Cambridge, MA: National Bureau of Economic Research.

Glass, G. V., Cahen, L. S., Smith, M. K., & Filby, N. N. (1982). *School class size: Research and policy*. Beverly Hills, CA: Sage.

Glass, G. V., & Smith, M. L. (1978). *Meta-analysis of research on the relationship of class size and achievement*. San Francisco, CA: Far West Laboratory for Educational Research & Development.

Hanushek, E. A., Rivkin, S. G., & Taylor, L. L. (1996). Aggregation and the estimated effects of school resources. *Review of Economics and Statistics*, *78*, 611–627.

Hattie, J. A. (2018). The right question in the debates about class size: Why is the (positive) effect so small? In M. Gilraine, H. Macartney, & R. McMillan (Eds.), *Education reform in general equilibrium: Evidence from California's class size reduction* (pp. 105–119) (No. w24191). Cambridge, MA: National Bureau of Economic Research.

Hattie, J. A. C. (2007). The paradox of reducing class size and improved learning outcomes. *International Journal of Education*, *42*, 387–425.

Hoxby, C. M. (2000). The effects of class size on student achievement: New evidence from population variation. *Quarterly Journal of Economics*, *115*(4), 1239–1285.

Jepsen, C., & Rivkin, S. (2002). What is the trade-off between smaller classes and teacher quality? *NBER Working Paper Series 9205*. Retrieved from www.nber.org/papers/w9205

Konstantopoulos, S., & Traynor, A. (2014). Class size effects on reading achievement using PIRLS data: Evidence from Greece. *Teachers College Record*, *116*(2), n2.

Krueger, A. B. (1999). Experimental estimates of education production functions. *Quarterly Journal of Economics*, *114*(2), 497–532.

Ludwig, J., & Bossi, L. J. (1999). The puzzling case of school resources and student achievement. *Educational Evaluation and Policy Analysis*, *21*(4), 385–403.

Molnar, A., Smith, P., Zahorik, J., Palmer, A., Halbach, A., & Ehrle, K. (1999). Evaluating the SAGE program: A pilot program in targeted pupil-teacher reduction in Wisconsin. *Educational Evaluation and Policy Analysis*, *21*(2), 165–177.

Pong, S. L., & Pallas, A. (2001). Class size and eighth-grade math achievement in the United States and abroad. *Educational Evaluation and Policy Analysis, 23*(3), 251–273.

Shen, T., & Konstantopoulos, S. (2017). Class size effects on reading achievement in Europe: Evidence from PIRLS. *Studies in Educational Evaluation, 53*, 98–114.

Smith, M. L., & Glass, G. V. (1980). Meta-analysis of research on class size and its relationship to attitudes and instruction. *American Educational Research Journal, 17*(4), 419–433.

Stasz, C., & Stecher, B. M. (2000). Teaching mathematics and language arts in reduced size and non-reduced size classrooms. *Educational Evaluation and Policy Analysis, 22*(4), 313–329.

Wößmann, L. (2005). Educational production in Europe. *Economic Policy, 43*, 445–493.

Wößmann, L., & West, M. R. (2002). *Class-size effects in school systems around the world: Evidence from between-grade variation in TIMSS*. Retrieved from ftp://repec.iza.org/RePEc/Discussionpaper/dp485.pdftie)

4.3 Financing schools

Eric A. Hanushek

Introduction

Around the world, schools are overwhelmingly controlled and operated by governments, and governmental policies directly affect much of what goes on in schools. The financing of schools has traditionally been addressed from two different perspectives. For the longest period, the central issues have revolved around how money for schools is raised and how it is distributed to local schools. These issues fit naturally into the policy debates around where a society's resources should be invested, along with the related question of how much is spent on schools. Over the past half century, however, a second perspective has entered into the debates: namely, how student performance relates to the financing of schools. This latter perspective has dramatically shifted the policy discussions about school finance. It has also made it clear that finance discussions cannot be separated from broader educational policy discussions because it is important to integrate finance incentives with other policies designed to improve achievement.

Research evidence

The new finance focus comes from investigations of the impact of finance on student outcomes. Hundreds of estimates using accepted statistical approaches provide a clear picture of the relationship between resources and achievement. Although they do not always agree, the majority of the studies have found that differences in either the absolute spending level or spending increases bear little or no consistent relationship to student achievement (e.g., Hanushek, 2003, 2006). Perhaps the best-known study on this issue was one of the first, *Equality of Educational Opportunity* (Coleman et al., 1966), the "Coleman Report." This report was one of the first attempts to apply statistical analyses to student achievement in what is now commonly referred to as "educational production functions." In 1964, the US Congress funded this massive study to assess the reasons for the continued failure to close the black-white achievement gap. The report suggested that variation in school resources had little or nothing to do with differences in student achievement and that almost all the test score gap was attributable to the widely varying social and economic conditions of black and white citizens.

The findings of the Coleman Report were extremely controversial, but, since its publication in 1966, a vast literature has confirmed many of the original conclusions. Studies have examined spending and related resources, such as class size, teacher experience, teacher education, teacher credentials, and other possible school inputs – all without finding a consistent or systematic influence on student achievement. For example, with regard to pupil-teacher ratios, almost three-quarters of all studies report no significant relationship with achievement. The studies that do indicate a statistically significant relationship are evenly divided between those showing the expected negative impact of a higher pupil-teacher ratio and those showing a positive impact on achievement (Hanushek, 2003, 2006). Even though the now-famous STAR study from Tennessee found positive impacts in a random-assignment experimental study during the 1980s (Word et al., 1990), the Tennessee STAR study is balanced not only by hundreds of other studies reaching the opposite conclusion, but also by the disappointing results of California and many other US states that have introduced programs for reducing class sizes in grades K–3 and other grades (see the research in Ehrenberg, Brewer, Gamoran, & Willms, 2001). Similarly, there is no support for any consistent relationship between the level of a teacher's education and student achievement (Hanushek & Rivkin, 2006). Fewer than 10% of the studies on this topic find a statistically significant positive impact of additional teacher education on student achievement. Teacher experience has historically shown a stronger relationship with performance, but recent studies have consistently found that the impact of experience is concentrated in the first year or two of teaching with little or no positive impact resulting from additional experience.

It is important to highlight these issues in the discussion of finances because class size reductions and increases in teacher salaries have been very important over the past century in the tremendous increases in real expenditure per pupil in schools (Hanushek & Rivkin, 1997). Class-size reduction programs have been very popular even though they are perhaps the most expensive of all school reform programs and even though research suggests that they are unlikely to be generally associated with improved student achievement. Because the primary determinants of teacher pay – experience and education level – do not have a consistent link with achievement, what teachers are paid also shows little consistent relationship with achievement. A teacher who has been successful in improving her students' achievement is as likely to have a low salary as a high salary (Hanushek & Rivkin, 2004). Further, since salaries make up the largest component of school district expenditures, variations in instructional expenditures also have little consistent relationship with achievement.

Some studies have found statistically significant positive effects of school spending, and people who wish to advocate for more spending tend to cite just these. Nonetheless, particularly with the spending studies, the relatively few studies finding a positive relationship with achievement tend to be the lowest-quality studies. These studies disproportionately rely on aggregate state evidence, where omission of any measures of state policy differences is likely to introduce bias in the estimated effects of spending differences (Hanushek, 2003). Further, these results are not simply a peculiarity of the United States. The same results are found across countries, as reviewed by Woessmann (2007a). Quite consistently, the analysis of performance on international achievement tests suggests that things other than resources are most important for student outcomes (Hanushek & Woessmann, 2011).

Another line of research has examined teacher quality measured on an outcome basis as a potentially important influence on student achievement. As opposed to assessing quality on the basis of measured teacher characteristics such as teacher education or experience, this work has concentrated on whether some teachers consistently produce more gains in student achievement than others. Working with extensive longitudinal data on individual students from different US states, these studies have confirmed large differences among teachers in terms of outcomes in the classroom (see Hanushek, 1971; Hanushek & Rivkin, 2010). This research, which also finds that differences in teacher effectiveness are not closely related to commonly observed characteristics of teachers, leads to a different conclusion than the Coleman Report. Teachers and schools differ dramatically, but, as found in the Coleman Report, it is not the simple measured characteristics that are important.

The inability to identify specific teacher qualities makes it difficult to regulate having high-quality teachers in classrooms. It also contributes to a conclusion that changes in the institutional structure and incentives of schools are fundamental to improving school outcomes. The simplest statement is *If one is concerned about student performance, one should gear policy to student performance*. Perhaps the largest problem with the current organization of most schools in most countries is that nobody's job or career is closely related to student performance. Relatedly, popular input policies, such as lowering class size, do nothing to change the structure of incentives.

One potential alternative is to alter the structure of school finance to include performance incentives for teachers and other school personnel. Existing international evidence suggests some clear general policies related to the institutional structure of schools that are important, and these have direct ramifications for the structure of school finance (Hanushek & Woessmann, 2011). Foremost among these, the performance of a system is affected by the incentives that actors face. That is, if the actors in the education process are rewarded (extrinsically or intrinsically) for producing better student achievement, and if they are penalized for not producing high achievement, then achievement is likely to improve. The incentives to produce high-quality education, in turn, are created by the institutions of the education system – the rules and regulations that explicitly or implicitly set rewards and penalties for the people involved in the education process.

From existing work, three interrelated institutional policies come to the forefront: promoting more competition, so that parental demand will create strong incentives to individual schools; autonomy in local decision-making, so that individual schools and their leaders will take actions to promote student achievement; and an accountability system that identifies good school performance and leads to rewards based on this. The evidence is summarized in Woessmann (2007b). It is also a central part of considerations of why some nations have done better in terms of international test scores (Mourshed, Chijioke, & Barber, 2010). One of the key channels by which these institutions affect performance is clearly through ensuring a strong teacher force in the schools. Each of the institutions provides incentives to improve on student outcomes, and the most direct way to do this comes through improving the effectiveness of teachers.

The exact form of such incentives will vary across different countries. For example, the United States relies considerably on individual states to organize and finance the schools. Historically, the states have differed considerably, but none of them has relied very much on incentives for performance. It is easy, however, to establish a school finance system that emphasizes performance incentives (Hanushek & Lindseth (2009).

One of the big issues in doing this is thinking about performance incentives for teachers, even though these have not proved popular in many places where they are discussed. One reason for the general resistance by teachers to incentive systems like performance pay is a concern about what will be rewarded. Research shows, for example, that families make a huge difference in the education of students. An implication of this is that the finance system should not reward or punish teachers for the portion of education they are not responsible for. If some students come to school better prepared than others, their teachers should not receive extra rewards. Similarly, if students come from disadvantaged backgrounds that leave them less well prepared for schools, we should not punish their teachers.

Pursuing this approach requires an aggressive system of performance measurement. It is necessary to track the progress of individual students and to relate this progress to the teachers who are responsible for it. This does not necessarily mean a system of individual rewards as opposed to group rewards for teachers in a school, but it does mean accurately measuring the performance of schools. Nor does it mean that test-based measures should be exclusively used. This area – designing accountability systems – is an obvious area for governmental leadership (although not necessarily ignoring local preferences and capacity).

The international evidence again suggests that countries that rely more on performance rewards for teachers show higher achievement, other things being equal (Woessmann, 2011). Whereas the evaluations of specific forms of performance pay are just now beginning to be developed (Podgursky & Springer, 2007; Dee & Wyckoff, 2015), there are signs that schools are generally moving toward experimenting with such ideas.

Summary and recommendations

The main message of current research is thus that school finance questions must be put into a larger context. Recent international research shows that higher achievement has very strong impacts on the economic well-being both of individuals (Hanushek, Schwerdt, Wiederhold, & Woessmann, 2015) and of nations (Hanushek & Woessmann, 2015a, 2015b). It is not possible, however, to expect higher achievement of students from simply providing extra resources to schools. Some specific thought must be given to how any resources affect the incentives of people in the schools. One cannot expect to improve student achievement and outcomes simply by putting more resources into the existing schools. Thus, the traditional focus of school finance policy on the flows of resources is misguided because it conflicts with an outcome basis for decision-making. While there is some uncertainty about the specific details of programs, the most promising school finance policies and institutions are the ones that promote higher achievement (instead of simply providing more resources to schools). The modern way to view school finance is how the support of schools relates to incentives.

References

Coleman, J. S., Campbell, E. Q., Hobson, C. J., McPartland, J., Mood, A. M., Weinfeld, F. D., & York, R. J. (1966). *Equality of educational opportunity*. Washington, DC: U.S. Government Printing Office.

Dee, T. S., & Wyckoff, J. (2015). Incentives, selection, and teacher performance: Evidence from IMPACT. *Journal of Policy Analysis and Management, 34*(2), 267–297.

Ehrenberg, R. G., Brewer, D. J., Gamoran, A., & Willms, J. D. (2001). Class size and student achievement. *Psychological Science in the Public Interest, 2*(1), 1–30.

Hanushek, E. A. (1971). Teacher characteristics and gains in student achievement: Estimation using micro data. *American Economic Review, 60*(2), 280–288.

Hanushek, E. A. (2003). The failure of input-based schooling policies. *Economic Journal, 113*(485), F64–F98.

Hanushek, E. A. (2006). School resources. In E. A. Hanushek & F. Welch (Eds.), *Handbook of the economics of education* (pp. 865–908). Amsterdam, Netherlands: North Holland.

Hanushek, E. A., & Lindseth, A. A. (2009). *Schoolhouses, courthouses, and statehouses: Solving the funding-achievement puzzle in America's public schools*. Princeton, NJ: Princeton University Press.

Hanushek, E. A., & Rivkin, S. G. (1997). Understanding the twentieth-century growth in U.S. school spending. *Journal of Human Resources, 32*(1), 35–68.

Hanushek, E. A., & Rivkin, S. G. (2004). How to improve the supply of high quality teachers. In D. Ravitch (Ed.), *Brookings papers on education policy 2004* (pp. 7–25). Washington, DC: Brookings Institution Press.

Hanushek, E. A., & Rivkin, S. G. (2006). Teacher quality. In E. A. Hanushek & F. Welch (Eds.), *Handbook of the economics of education* (pp. 1051–1078). Amsterdam, Netherlands: North Holland.

Hanushek, E. A., & Rivkin, S. G. (2010). Generalizations about using value-added measures of teacher quality. *American Economic Review, 100*(2), 267–271.

Hanushek, E. A., Schwerdt, G., Wiederhold, S., & Woessmann, L. (2015). Returns to skills around the world: Evidence from PIAAC. *European Economic Review, 73*, 103–130.

Hanushek, E, A., & Woessmann, L. (2011). The economics of international differences in educational achievement. In E. A. Hanushek, S. Machin, & L. Woessmann (Eds.), *Handbook of the economics of education* (Vol. 3, pp. 89–200). Amsterdam, Netherlands: North Holland.

Hanushek, E. A., & Woessmann, L. (2015a). *The knowledge capital of nations: Education and the economics of growth*. Cambridge, MA: MIT Press.

Hanushek, E. A., & Woessmann, L. (2015b). *Universal basic skills: What countries stand to gain*. Paris: Organisation for Economic Co-operation and Development.

Mourshed, M., Chijioke, C., & Barber, M. (2010). *How the world's most improved school systems keep getting better*. New York, NY: McKinsey.

Podgursky, M. J., & Springer, M. G. (2007). Teacher performance pay: A review. *Journal of Policy Analysis and Management, 26*(4), 909–949.

Woessmann, L. (2007a). International evidence on expenditure and class size: A review. In *Brookings papers on education policy 2006/2007* (pp. 245–272). Washington, DC: Brookings.

Woessmann, L. (2007b). International evidence on school competition, autonomy and accountability: A review. *Peabody Journal of Education, 82*(2–3), 473–497.

Woessmann, L. (2011). Cross-country evidence on teacher performance pay. *Economics of Education Review, 30*(3), 404–418.

Word, E., Johnston, J., Bain, H. P., DeWayne Fulton, B., Zaharies, J. B., Lintz, M. N., … Breda, C. (1990). *Student/teacher achievement ratio (STAR), Tennessee's K-3 class size study: Final summary report, 1985–1990*. Nashville, TN: Tennessee State Department of Education.

4.4 Influences of school layout and design on student achievement

C. Kenneth Tanner and Sheila J. Bosch

Introduction

Recently, the intricate activity of relating an official learning environment, such as school building layout, to students' learning and behavior is receiving increased emphasis in research and formal writing. This is in contrast to the traditional "nuts and bolts" commentary on facilities of bygone years. A significant question is "How do we capture consistency of measurement of school design and then relate it to a student's acquisition of knowledge?" We recommend that measurement should, as Flygt suggests, include objective-subjective assessments representative of both the functional/technical and the ethical/aesthetical dimensions of a facility (Flygt, 2009).

Based on previous research, we propose that aspects of the interplay of knowledge, beliefs, behaviors, and experience in reference to a place (the school's physical environment) are tied to cognition or acquisition of knowledge (Figure 4.1). Knowledge acquisition may be measured rather reliably by standardized test scores. Other researchers have also linked these two areas simultaneously. For example, Rollero and De Piccoli (2010) maintain that affective and cognitive dimensions, defined as place attachment and identification, characterize the relationship between people and places. They demonstrated that the affective and the cognitive dimensions (a) are directly predicted by different demographical and psychosocial variables and (b) are strictly associated with the perception of the place and its inhabitants. Furthermore, they contend that cognitive and affective dimensions are two distinct but correlated components.

Beginning in 1997, researchers at the School Design and Planning Laboratory, formerly at the University of Georgia and under the direction of Dr. C. Kenneth Tanner, discovered that no valid and reliable measurements existed that would indicate if or how much the school's physical environment contributes to or influences students' cognitive learning. Hence, the researchers began to explore a way to link place and cognitive learning. Up until then, the literature showed that school environments were usually built on whims, standardized codes, and unsupported "best practices" or hearsay evidence among educational planners and decision makers.

Influences from the school

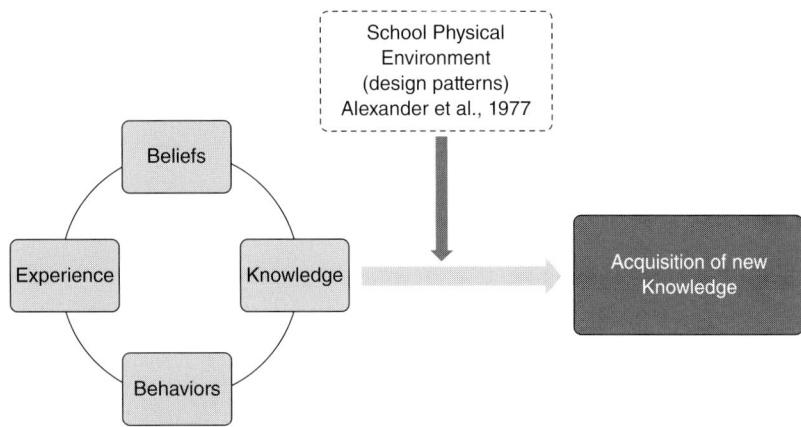

Figure 4.1 Conceptual framework suggesting that the physical environment moderates the effects that knowledge, beliefs, behaviors and experience have on the acquisition of new knowledge within a school setting.

To strengthen the argument, the University of Georgia researchers encouraged educators to examine the issue of "best practices in building schools," which often go unchallenged regarding whose best practices and what, when, where, and how they might influence various educational and cultural settings (Tanner & Lackney, 2006, pp. 263–322). Overall, the University of Georgia researchers avoided using best practices as a basis for planning and designing schools.

Instead, we (Dr. Tanner led the researchers) began identifying aspects of places where students learn; these are called "design patterns," adapted from the work of Alexander, Ishikawa, and Silverstein (1977). Our primary assumption was that design patterns in the school's physical environment influence student achievement; therefore, "Each pattern describes a problem which occurs over and over again in our environment, and then describes the core of the solution to that problem, in such a way that you can use this solution a million times over, without ever doing it the same way twice" (Alexander et al. 1977, p. x). That is, we assumed that place and cognitive dimensions were related in various ways. Readers interested in more detail on the physical environment as we have defined it may refer to additional works such as Sommer (1969), Tanner and Lackney (2006, pp. 263–322) and Tanner (2009).

More recently, Tanner (2015) completed a meta-analysis of the work he directed at the University of Georgia. This comprehensive work demonstrated that 12 out of 15 families of design patterns were associated with statistically significant differences in student test scores. These include movement and circulation; natural light – daylighting and views; safety and security; display spaces and places for student artifacts and mini-museums; storage places for personal artifacts; quiet places and spaces; green spaces; outdoor rooms – any safe place that is not indoors; instructional neighborhoods with more open plans, flex zones, quiet zones, and teaching-planning areas; technology for teaching and learning; color configurations with appropriate variation and contrast; and overall impression. Each family of design patterns investigated represents best practices that are usually associated with students' affective, behavioral, and cognitive responses to school design. Research-informed design propositions and recommendations are provided as well. What follows is a small subset of research evidence related to school design and student achievement.

Designing schools – research evidence

There is ample evidence that a school's physical environment affects student achievement. In a study of 153 classrooms in 27 primary schools (n = 3,766 students), Barrett and colleagues (Barrett, Davies, Zhang, & Barrett, 2015) found that 16% of the variation in student progress could be explained by seven design elements, including light, temperature, air quality, ownership, flexibility, complexity, and color. Fiske (1995) indicated that the organization of space has a profound effect on learning and that students feel better connected to a building that anticipates their needs and respects them as individuals. When children attend a school designed with their needs in mind, they notice it and demonstrate a more natural disposition toward respectful behavior and a willingness to contribute to the classroom community (Herbert, 1998). Maxwell (2016) demonstrated that associations between school building condition and student achievement are mediated by student perceptions of social climate and attendance. In other words, students in schools with better physical environments tend to have higher perceptions of the schools' social climate, better attendance, and thereby higher academic achievement.

The process used in planning greatly influences school design. Collaboration among stakeholders in planning and designing a school is a significant step in achieving the right design solutions. Both the planner and the stakeholders (including parents, students, principals, and teachers) learn from each other. Participation can lead to the ultimate agreement about what the future should look like and includes awareness and perception. Awareness involves persuading participants to speak the same language; perception takes awareness forward to the next milestone because it facilitates an understanding of the physical, social, cultural, and economic ramifications for the project outcomes (Sanoff, 1994). Without such participation, stakeholders often have limited awareness of and perceptions about school design. For example, Schabmann and colleagues (Schabmann et al., 2016) surveyed 1,164 school principals in Austria and found that, although principals understand the important role of school architecture in education, they feel ill-informed about innovative design solutions that promote learning.

The need exists for the development of spaces that engage, challenge, and arouse a student's imagination. Taylor and Vlastos (1975) suggested that educational architecture is a "three-dimensional textbook." This means that the learning environment is a functional art form, a place of beauty, and a motivational center for learning. School buildings are visual objects, and, as such, they can be stimulating in terms of both their intrinsic design and their use.

Architectural design should include a friendly entrance that is age appropriate and highly visible. Huge, overpowering entrances are intimidating to young children, for example. The entrance should evoke a welcoming feeling, not instill fear (Alexander et al., 1977). To stakeholders, the school administrative offices should be centralized for convenience and connection. Main buildings have an obvious reference point, a feature that heightens the sense of community. Variation of ceiling heights and intimacy gradients help blend public and private places in schools and give the effect of drawing people into an area. The issue of scale must also be emphasized in planning the school layout. Meek (1995) contributed to the issue of scale when she wrote about Crow Island School: "Then you are at the front door, and what you notice is that the door handle is too low. Too low for you, just right for children" (p. 53).

Movement and circulation

For many years, researchers in the field of environmental psychology have been interested in research on movement classifications, described as links to main entrances, pathways with goals, circulation patterns, density or freedom of movement, personal space, and social distance. At the University of Georgia, we always asked questions about too much or too little space and then referred to issues of social and personal distance to develop a stem for a measurement scale to be used in assessing existing places and spaces for learning.

Regarding personal and social distance, Wohlwill and Van Vliet (1985) summarized the effects of high student density as a hindrance to movement. "It appears as though the consequences of high-density conditions that involve either too many children or too little space are: excess levels of stimulation; stress and arousal; a drain on resources available; considerable interference; reductions in desired privacy levels; and loss of control" (pp. 108–109). Works such as this have led to the assertion that a high-density school has a negative influence on achievement (Weinstein & David, 1987). Our decision about freedom of movement has been consistent: an overcrowded school is not conducive to teaching and learning. It is not the size of the school that plays the positive or negative role in student achievement so much as it is the density – number of students per square and cubic unit of measurement.

Some other major conclusions from research at the University of Georgia are summarized as follows (Tanner, 2015): The issue of density may be viewed through psychological implications implied in "territoriality of place." Since the school is a social system within the cultural environment, social distance as it relates to crowding and density is a function of school design. This line of reasoning should be made for school size and the size of classrooms. Special attention should be given to circulation classifications that permit student traffic to flow quickly from one part of the building to another. Movement within the school should be a conscious and perceptible environmental exchange, and complex structures that cause crowding should be avoided. School design should include pathways both inside and outside of the building. Pathways may link structures together and lead into the natural environment.

Daylight and views

The presence of natural light in classrooms improves student learning. An extensive research effort, including a controlled study of over 21,000 students in California, Washington, and Colorado, found that students with the most "day lighting" in their classrooms progressed 20% faster on mathematics and 26% faster on reading tests over a period of one year than students having less daylight in their classrooms (Heschong Mahone Group, 1999). "We also identified another window-related effect, in that students in classrooms where windows could be opened were found to progress 7–8% faster than those with fixed windows. This occurred regardless of whether the classroom also had air conditioning" (p. 62). Rather than being a distraction that disrupts the learning process, an argument often used from the "conventional wisdom" side, windows provide a necessary relief for students (Kuller & Lindsten, 1992).

Exposing children to harmful forms of lighting in poorly designed schools is reason enough for us to seriously consider Alexander's et al. (1977) notion of optimizing daylight. Windows (views) overlooking life are another positive aspect of design amenable to translation from the theories of "pattern language" to the school environment. In a randomized controlled experiment, Li and Sullivan (2016) demonstrated that students with window views of green spaces performed better on tests measuring attention and showed higher levels of stress recovery than students with views of built environments and those with no windows. Other researchers found schools having more trees, on average, had higher reading and mathematics standardized test scores when school size, student-teacher ratio and free lunch participation were controlled (Kweon, Ellis, Lee, & Jacobs, 2017)

Light is the most important environmental input, after food and water, in controlling bodily functions (Wurtman, 1975). Lights of different colors affect blood pressure, pulse, respiration rates, brain activity, and biorhythms. Full-spectrum light, required to influence the pineal gland's synthesis of melatonin, which in turn helps determine the body's output of the neurotransmitter serotonin, is critical to a child's health and development (Ott, 1973). To help reduce the imbalances caused by inadequate exposure to the near ultraviolet and infrared ends of the spectrum, full-spectrum bulbs that approximate the wavelengths provided by sunshine should replace standard bulbs. There is ample evidence that people need daylight to regulate circadian rhythms (Alexander et al., 1977, p. 527). Poorly lit and windowless classrooms can cause students to experience a daily form of jet lag while forms of florescent lighting may affect some students and teachers by causing mild seizures.

Summary and recommendations

There is a growing body of literature supporting the important role the physical school environment plays in student achievement. Research suggests that the following selected physical characteristics of learning environments will improve student performance: allow ample space for learning to avoid overcrowding, design for abundant circulation patterns, maintain scale as a guide, require plenty of natural light in the classroom, and demand extensive stakeholder participation in planning and designing a school.

References

Alexander, C., Ishikawa, S., & Silverstein, M. (1977). *A pattern language.* New York, NY: Oxford University Press.

Barrett, P., Davies, F., Zhang, Y., & Barrett, L. (2015). The impact of classroom design on pupils' learning: Final results of a holistic, multi-level analysis. *Building and Environment*, *89*, 118–133. https://doi.org/10.1016/j.buildenv.2015.02.013

Fiske, E. B. (1995). Systematic school reform: Implications for architecture. In A. Meek (Ed.), *Designing places for learning* (pp. 1–10). Alexandria, VA: ASCD.

Flygt, E. (2009). Investigating architectural quality theories for school evaluation: A critical review of evaluation instruments in Sweden. *Educational Management, Administration & Leadership*, *37*(5), 645–666.

Herbert, E. A. (1998). Design matters: How school environment affects children. *Educational Leadership*, *56*, 69–70.

Heschong Mahone Group. (1999). *Daylighting in schools*. Fair Oaks, CA: Author. (11626 Fair Oaks Blvd. #302, Fair Oaks, CA 95628)

Kuller, R., & Lindsten, C. (1992). Health and behavior of children in classrooms with and without windows. *Journal of Environmental Psychology*, *12*, 305–317.

Kweon, B-S., Ellis, C. D., Lee, J., & Jacobs, K. (2017). The link between school environments and student academic performance. *Urban Forestry & Urban Greening*, *23*, 35–43. https://doi.org/10.1016/j.ufug.2017.02.002

Li, D., & Sullivan, W. C. (2016). Impact of views to school landscapes on recovery from stress and mental fatigue. *Landscape and Urban Planning*, *148*, 149–158. https://doi.org/10.1016/j.landurbplan.2015.12.015

Maxwell, L. E. (2016). School building condition, social climate, student attendance and academic achievement: A mediation model. *Journal of Environmental Psychology*, *46*, 206–216. https://doi.org/10.1016/j.jenvp.2016.04.009

Meek, A. (Ed.). (1995). *Designing places for learning*. Alexandria, VA: ASCD.

Ott, J. (1973). *Health and light*. New York, NY: Simon & Schuster.

Rollero, C., & De Piccoli, N. (2010). Place attachment, identification and environment perception: An empirical study. *Journal of Environmental Psychology*, *30*(2), 198–205.

Sanoff, H. (1994). *School design*. New York, NY: Van Nostrand Reinhold.

Schabmann, A., Popper, V., Schmidt, B. M., Kühn, C., Pitro, U., & Spiel, C. (2016). The relevance of innovative school architecture for school principals. *School Leadership & Management*, *36*(2), 184–203. https://doi.org/10.1080/13632434.2016.1196175

Sommer, R. (1969). *Personal space*. Englewood Cliffs, NJ: Prentice-Hall.

Tanner, C. K. (2009). Effects of school design on student outcomes. *Journal of Educational Administration*, *47*(3), 376–394.

Tanner, C. K. (2015, August 13). *Effects of school architectural designs on students' accomplishments: A meta-analysis*. Retrieved from https://efc.gwu.edu/2015/08/13/effects-of-school-architectural-designs-on-students-accomplishments-a-meta-analysis/

Tanner, C. K., & Lackney, J. A. (2006). *Educational facilities planning: Leadership, architecture, and management*. Boston, MA: Allyn & Bacon.

Taylor, A. P., & Vlastos, G. (1975). *School zone: Learning environments for children*. New York, NY: Van Nostrand Reinhold.

Weinstein, C. S., & David, T. G. (Eds.). (1987). *Spaces for children: The built environment and child development*. New York, NY: Plenum Press.

Wohlwill, J. F., & van Vliet, W. (1985). *Habitats for children: The impacts of density*. Hillsdale, NJ: Erlbaum.

Wurtman, R. J. (1975). The effects of light on the human body. *Scientific American*, *233*, 68–77.

4.5

Middle school transitions

Eric M. Anderman and Marissa S. Green

Introduction

Education researchers and policy makers have sought to better understand the transition of students from schools that serve children into schools that serve early adolescents for many years. This is an important area of research because transitions between schools during the early adolescent years often occur at the onset of puberty. Thus, these transitions occur while students, parents, and teachers are simultaneously dealing with the academic, social, and motivational issues that occur during the adolescent years. It is important for educators, policy makers, researchers, and parents to understand this transitional period so that effective learning environments can be provided for early adolescents. For many students, the transition represents a time when motivation and achievement change noticeably, often in a negative direction.

Research evidence

Results of most studies of academic achievement at the transition indicate that in general, achievement declines for most students as they move into new school settings during early adolescence. In particular, when students attend schools that primarily serve early adolescents (e.g., schools with grade configurations of sixth through eighth grade or seventh through ninth grade in many countries), their academic achievement is often lower than it was when they attended a school that primarily served younger children. Most studies indicate that both standardized test scores and teacher-assigned grades are lower for students who transition to a new school during early adolescence than for those students who remain at the same school through mid-adolescence (e.g., students who attend schools that serve both children and early adolescents together, such as schools with kindergarten through eighth-grade configurations) (Akos, Rose, & Orthner, 2015; Gutman,

Peck, Malanchuk, Sameroff, & Eccles, 2017; Ryan, Shim, & Makara, 2013; Simmons & Blyth, 1987; Warburton, Jenkins, & Coxhead, 1983). Although many of the studies of achievement across the transition have been conducted in the United States, studies conducted in Australia and England have yielded similar findings (e.g., Hopwood, Hay, & Dyment, 2017; Warburton et al., 1983).

Many studies of school transitions have also examined students' motivation toward academic achievement. Several researchers have found that students' attitudes toward achievement become particularly negative after the transition (e.g., Eccles, Midgley, & Adler, 1984; Oie & Fujii, 2017). Specifically, students report that they perceive school to be less interesting, useful, and important than they did when they were in elementary school. These shifting attitudes toward school are related to the changes in achievement that occur for many students.

The transition from elementary school into middle school coincides with the onset of adolescent physical, cognitive, and psychological development (Patrick & Drake, 2009). Students and their social worlds are changing rapidly, and these changes are related to academic achievement in important ways. Physically, adolescents are going through puberty; their bodies are growing and changing rapidly. They are growing taller, weighing more than they did in the past, and developing adult sexual characteristics. Cognitively, adolescents are developing the ability to think about more complex topics; they are now able to entertain abstract possibilities and engage in more cognitively complex academic work at school. Socially, adolescents are becoming more involved with their peers, more self-conscious, and more interested in dating and sexuality. Although in the past, many researchers attributed the declines in achievement and motivation specifically to the physiological changes associated with puberty, research conducted in recent years has demonstrated that these negative shifts in academic behaviors are not attributable to pubertal development (Anderman, 2012, for a review). Rather, these shifts often are attributable to the types of academic environments and instructional practices of middle schools (Ryan et al., 2013).

In general, although adolescents are going through many major changes during the same period when they transition from elementary schools into middle-grade schools, the new school environments often do not meet these students' needs. When adolescents' developmental needs are not met, motivation and achievement suffer. Researchers have argued and demonstrated that this is a problem of "stage-environment fit": adolescents are at a stage of development where they would benefit from specific types of educational environments that many middle-grade schools do not provide (Booth & Gerard, 2014; Eccles & Midgley, 1989; Symonds & Hargreaves, 2016).

More specifically, researchers have argued that early adolescents are best served by school environments that provide (a) warm, caring relationships with teachers; (b) cognitively challenging academic work; (c) the opportunity to express autonomy and make choices during the school day; and (d) a sense of belonging in the school community (Buehler, Fletcher, Johnston, & Weymouth, 2015; Wang & Eccles, 2013). However, research indicates that many (although certainly not all) middle-grade schools are characterized by environments in which teachers and students have poor, confrontational relationships; in which students often are asked to complete many worksheets and given undemanding, repetitive assignments; in which students do not get the opportunity to make choices about how they spend their time or about the academic tasks with which they engage; and in which students often do not feel like they "belong" (Anderman, 2012; Givens Rolland, 2012; Wang & Eccles, 2012). This mismatch between what adolescents need from a developmental perspective and what they are provided within schools, causes many of them to become disengaged with school; this disengagement adversely affects their motivation and ultimately their achievement (Wang & Eccles, 2012). Although schools have changed somewhat in response to research on this topic, there is still room for improvement (Dickinson, 2013; Rose, 2015).

One of the other reasons often cited for declines in achievement across this transition is the increasing focus on grades, competition, and relative ability that is prominent in schools serving early adolescents. As students enter middle schools, grading practices become more focused on ability and less on effort than they were during elementary school (Anderman & Maehr, 1994; Givens Rolland, 2012). Studies indicate that during elementary school, students often report that the purpose of schooling is to truly learn and master academic material; however, after the transition, students perceive that the mastery of academic content is less important than during elementary school; rather, obtaining high grades and demonstrating one's academic ability rise in importance after the transition (Anderman & Midgley, 1997; Mensah, 2015). Thus performance on "tests" becomes much more important to students, teachers, and parents after the transition. Increased focus on grades and ability during adolescence is an international phenomenon, as suggested by studies conducted in the United States, as well as in South Korea (Bong, 2009), China (Liu, 2003), and Japan (Oie & Fujii, 2017). Many students become less engaged with school after the transition because for many, learning is simply no longer an enjoyable enterprise; whereas learning was "fun" during elementary school, it often becomes competitive and provokes anxiety after the transition.

One of the reasons why grades and ability differences become particularly salient after the transition is the increased emergence of between-class ability grouping. During the elementary grades, students generally spend most of the day in the same classroom, with the same students and teacher. Although sometimes elementary educators engage in teaming practices wherein different teachers will instruct the students in different subjects (e.g., reading, social studies), most grouping of students occurs within the classroom. However, the entry into middle schools often marks the beginning of between-class ability grouping; students often are separated into remedial, basic, or advanced tracks. Research indicates that such practices may be detrimental to the achievement-related attitudes of students, particularly those who are in the lower-ability tracks (Oakes & Lipton, 1990). The achievement of lower-ability students in particular may be adversely affected after the transition due to their restricted access to more advanced academic content that could improve their learning and achievement (e.g., Giersch, 2016; Umansky,

2016). Research also indicates that there often is an inequitable balance of student ethnicity and socioeconomic status in classes that are grouped by ability (e.g., Stark, 2014; Thijs & Verkuyten, 2014; Umansky, 2016).

Students' ability beliefs and achievement values also change across the transition. Research indicates that, after the transition, students are likely to report that they are less confident in their abilities and have less value for a variety of subjects than they did before the transition (Oie & Fujii, 2017; Ryan et al., 2013; Wigfield, Eccles, Mac Iver, Reuman, & Midgley, 1991). In particular, students often report losing confidence in their abilities in mathematics after they move into the middle grades. Recent research has also demonstrated that this decrease in students' valuing of mathematics is particularly pronounced for students who struggle with behavioral difficulties (Metsäpelto et al., 2017). Students' intrinsic motivation to learn (i.e., learning for the sake of learning) also decreases as students move from elementary schools into middle schools (Harter, Whitesell, & Kowalski, 1992).

These decrements in ability beliefs, achievement values, and intrinsic motivation are important because they affect future achievement for adolescents. Students' beliefs about their abilities in specific subject areas are predictive of their subsequent achievement in those areas: for example, a student who believes that she is an outstanding science student is likely to continue to get high science grades in the future, whereas a student who does not believe that she has the ability to learn science well will quite likely not obtain good science grades in the future. In addition, students' valuing of academic subjects during early adolescence is predictive of subsequent involvement with those subjects: for example, students who value mathematics are more likely to choose to enroll in elective math courses later in adolescence and are even more likely to choose a math-intensive major upon entering college (Musu-Gillette, Wigfield, Harring, & Eccles, 2015; Wigfield & Eccles, 1992).

Summary and recommendations

In summary, research indicates that, in general, academic achievement declines across school transitions that occur during early adolescence. Although most research has been conducted in the United States, studies that have been conducted in other countries generally also indicate that students become more focused on grades and extrinsic outcomes after the transition. Many students become less interested in their academic subjects after the transition, and this lack of interest can affect their achievement. Moreover, many students' beliefs about their abilities decline after the transition. Many of these unfortunate changes in motivation, ability beliefs, and achievement are attributed to the fact that the environments provided by many middle level schools do not meet the developmental needs of early adolescents. Nevertheless, decrements in achievement and motivation are not inevitable; when schools utilize instructional practices that are developmentally appropriate, achievement and motivation do not necessarily need to decline (Anderman,

Maehr, & Midgley, 1999; Buehler et al., 2015; Wang & Eccles, 2013; Simmons & Blyth, 1987). In sum, early adolescents are likely to flourish academically after a school transition when school personnel are committed to (a) promoting positive teacher-student relationships, (b) providing students with academic work that is both challenging and developmentally appropriate, (c) providing students with the opportunity to express autonomy, and (d) ensuring that all students feel that they belong in their school, these schools are at an advantage to help lessen the impact of this difficult school transition on their students.

References

Akos, P., Rose, R. A., & Orthner, D. (2015). Sociodemographic moderators of middle school transition effects on academic achievement. *Journal of Early Adolescence*, *35*(2), 170–198.

Anderman, E. M. (2012). Adolescence. In K. Harris & T. Urdan (Eds.), *APA handbook educational psychology Vol. 3: Applications to learning and teaching* (pp. 43–61). Washington, DC: American Psychological Association.

Anderman, E. M., & Maehr, M. L. (1994). Motivation and schooling in the middle grades. *Review of Educational Research*, *64*(2), 287–309.

Anderman, E. M., Maehr, M. L., & Midgley, C. (1999). Declining motivation after the transition to middle school: Schools can make a difference. *Journal of Research and Development in Education*, *32*, 131–147.

Anderman, E. M., & Midgley, C. (1997). Changes in achievement goal orientations, perceived academic competence, and grades across the transition to middle-level schools. *Contemporary Educational Psychology*, *22*(3), 269–298.

Bong, M. (2009). Age-related differences in achievement goal differentiation. *Journal of Educational Psychology*, *101*(4), 879–896.

Booth, M. Z., & Gerard, J. M. (2014). Adolescents' stage-environment fit in middle and high school: The relationship between students' perceptions of their schools and themselves. *Youth & Society*, *46*(6), 735–755.

Buehler, C., Fletcher, A. C., Johnston, C., & Weymouth, B. B. (2015). Perceptions of school experiences during the first semester of middle school. *School Community Journal*, *25*(2), 55–83.

Dickinson, T. S. (2013). *Reinventing the middle school*. New York: Routledge.

Eccles, J. S., & Midgley, C. (1989). Stage-environment fit: Developmentally appropriate classrooms for young adolescents. In C. Ames & R. Ames (Eds.), *Research on motivation in education: Goals and cognitions* (Vol. 3, pp. 139–186). New York, NY: Academic Press.

Eccles, J. S., Midgley, C., & Adler, T. F. (1984). Grade-related changes in the school environment: Effects on achievement motivation. In J. G. Nicholls & M. L. Maehr (Eds.), *Advances in motivation and achievement: The development of achievement motivation* (pp. 283–331). Greenwich, CT: JAI.

Giersch, J. (2016). Academic tracking, high-stakes tests, and preparing students for college: How inequality persists within schools. *Educational Policy*, 1–29.

Givens Rolland, R. (2012). Synthesizing the evidence on classroom goal structures in middle and secondary schools: A meta-analysis and narrative review. *Review of Educational Research*, *82*(4), 396–435.

Gutman, L. M., Peck, S. C., Malanchuk, O., Sameroff, A. J., & Eccles, J. S. (2017). VI: Academic functioning. *Monographs of the Society for Research in Child Development*, *82*(4), 95–105.

Harter, S., Whitesell, N. R., & Kowalski, P. S. (1992). Individual differences in the effects of educational transitions on young adolescents' perceptions of competence and motivational orientation. *American Educational Research Journal*, *29*(4), 777–807.

Hopwood, B., Hay, I., & Dyment, J. (2017). Students' reading achievement during the transition from primary to secondary school. *The Australian Journal of Language and Literacy*, *40*(1), 46–58.

Liu, P. (2003). Transition from elementary to middle school and change in motivation: An examination of Chinese students. *Journal of Research in Childhood Education*, *18*(1), 71–83.

Mensah, E. (2015). Middle level students' goal orientations and motivation. *Journal of Education and Training Studies*, *3*(2), 20–33.

Metsäpelto, R. L., Taskinen, P., Kracke, B., Silinskas, G., Lerkkanen, M. K., Poikkeus, A. M., & Nurmi, J. E. (2017). Changes in achievement values from primary to lower secondary school among students with and without externalizing problems. *Learning and Individual Differences*, *58*, 75–82.

Musu-Gillette, L. E., Wigfield, A., Harring, J. R., & Eccles, J. S. (2015). Trajectories of change in students' self-concepts of ability and values in math and college major choice. *Educational Research and Evaluation*, *21*(4), 343–370.

Oakes, J., & Lipton, M. (1990). Tracking and ability grouping: A structural barrier to access and achievement. In J. I. Goodlad & P. Keating (Eds.), *Access to knowledge: An agenda for our nation's schools* (pp. 187–204). New York, NY: College Entrance Examination Board.

Oie, M., & Fujii, T. (2017). Development of mathematics motivation across the transition from elementary to junior high school in Japan. *Psychology*, *8*(2), 287–301.

Patrick, H., & Drake, B. M. (2009). Middle school. In E. M. Anderman & L. H. Anderman (Eds.), *Psychology of classroom learning* (Vol. 2, pp. 775–778). Detroit, MI: Gale/Cengage.

Rose, M. (2015). School reform fails the test. *The American Scholar*, 18–30.

Ryan, A. M., Shim, S. S., & Makara, K. A. (2013). Changes in academic adjustment and relational self-worth across the transition to middle school. *Journal of Youth and Adolescence*, *42*(9), 1372–1384.

Simmons, R. G., & Blyth, D. A. (1987). *Moving into adolescence: The impact of pubertal change and school context*. New York, NY: Aldine de Gruyter.

Stark, L. (2014). Naming giftedness: Whiteness and ability discourse in US schools. *International Studies in Sociology of Education*, *24*(4), 394–414.

Symonds, J., & Hargreaves, L. (2016). Emotional and motivational engagement at school transition: A qualitative stage-environment fit study. *The Journal of Early Adolescence*, *36*(1), 54–85.

Thijs, J., & Verkuyten, M. (2014). School ethnic diversity and students' interethnic relations. *British Journal of Educational Psychology*, *84*(1), 1–21.

Umansky, I. M. (2016). Leveled and exclusionary tracking: English learners' access to academic content in middle school. *American Educational Research Journal*, *53*(6), 1792–1833.

Wang, M. T., & Eccles, J. S. (2012). Adolescent behavioral, emotional, and cognitive engagement trajectories in school and their differential relations to educational success. *Journal of Research on Adolescence*, *22*(1), 31–39.

Wang, M. T., & Eccles, J. S. (2013). School context, achievement motivation, and academic engagement: A longitudinal study of school engagement using a multidimensional perspective. *Learning and Instruction*, *28*, 12–23.

Warburton, S., Jenkins, W. L., & Coxhead, P. (1983). Science achievement and attitudes and the age of transfer to secondary school. *Educational Research, 25*, 177–183.

Wigfield, A., & Eccles, J. S. (1992). The development of achievement task values: A theoretical analysis. *Developmental Review, 12*(3), 265–310.

Wigfield, A., Eccles, J. S., Mac Iver, D., Reuman, D. A., & Midgley, C. (1991). Transitions during early adolescence: Changes in children's domain-specific self-perceptions and general self-esteem across the transition to junior high school. *Developmental Psychology, 27*(4), 552–565.

Summary table: influences from the school

Category	Definition of Influence	Achievement Effects and Considerations
Organizational Features of the School	**Charter Schools** are public schools that operate independently. Charter schools have their own governing boards.	*Although charter schools are popular, particularly among parents, it has been difficult to document strong effects on achievement, particularly due to student mobility and varying school resources.*
	Single-sex schools are schools that enroll either males or females, but not both.	*Research indicates that, overall, attending a single-sex school has positive effects on achievement. Research to date has not clearly identified the mechanisms within single-sex schools that yield these effects.*
	Faith-based schools are schools that are affiliated with a religion or a set of religious beliefs.	*Students enrolled in faith-based schools on average achieve at higher levels than students who attend non-faith-based schools. This is likely related to an emphasis on academics, strong monitoring of student behavior, a positive school climate, and greater racial accord.*
	Mixed-grade classrooms at the elementary school level are characterized by classrooms that enroll students from multiple grade levels (e.g., a class containing third, fourth, and fifth graders).	*Whereas there are no negative effects on achievement for mixed-grade classrooms, the only type of mixed-grade classroom that has been found to benefit student achievement is the use of non-graded classes (i.e., classes in which students are not identified by their age or grade level). These positive effects probably are a result of the use of individualized and developmentally appropriate curricula.*

(Continued)

Category	Definition of Influence	Achievement Effects and Considerations
	The **middle school transition** occurs when students move from elementary grade schools (e.g., grades K–5 or K–6) into middle-grade schools (e.g., grades 6–8 or 7–9).	*Achievement often declines as students make this transition. However, when educators use developmentally appropriate instructional practices in middle schools, achievement is unlikely to decline.*
	Class size refers to the number of students who are placed in a particular classroom.	*Class size is only related in limited ways to achievement; the types of instructional strategies that teachers use are a much more important determinant than the size of the class. Reducing class sizes without the use of evidence-based instructional practices is unlikely to yield significant achievement gains.*
	School finance refers to how all aspects of the organization of a school are funded.	*Research suggests that simply providing more resources (i.e., additional funding) to schools is not related directly to greater achievement. When financial resources serve as incentives to school personnel to utilize instructional strategies that promote learning, then achievement may increase.*
	School layout refers to all aspects of the physical design of schools.	*Physical characteristics of schools that are related to student achievement include providing sufficient space to avoid overcrowding; layouts that allow for efficient movement between classrooms and that prevent crowding; and the availability of sufficient natural light.*
Services Provided by the School	**School-based mental health** refers to the provision of mental-health services for students within the school building.	*The provision of mental-health support in schools is related to higher achievement, particularly for students who are experiencing socioemotional distress.*
	Inclusive education or **mainstreaming** is a practice wherein students who have been identified as being eligible for special education services spend as much time as possible in traditional classrooms and are not isolated from their non–special education peers.	*Research suggests that there are achievement benefits for students with mild/moderate learning difficulties. Although there are social benefits to inclusive education, the actual type of instruction and support that is provided is much more important (in terms of achievement) than the physical placement of the students within the school.*

(Continued)

Category	Definition of Influence	Achievement Effects and Considerations
	School-wide Positive Behavior Interventions and Supports (SWPBIS) is a school-wide approach to improving student outcomes by focusing on the prevention of behavioral problems, primarily through instruction in social competencies.	*The use of SWPBIS is related to increased student achievement, when students also receive evidence-based, high-quality instruction. Many schools are now implementing **Multitiered Systems of Support (MTSS)**, which represent systemic efforts to train teachers to effectively address both student learning and student behavior.*
	Mentoring, **coaching**, and **consulting** are services provided to support teachers; these services are provided by individuals who work with teachers on a variety of strategies so that the teachers can more effectively influence student achievement.	*These support services for teachers can lead to positive effects on student achievement when they are based on solid empirical research and when they can be implemented with sufficient time (both on a daily basis and across several academic years).*
	Summer school programs provide students with opportunities for academic remediation (and, occasionally, for academic enrichment) during the summer months.	*Participation in summer school programs has a small positive effect on academic achievement.*
	Special education is a process for providing appropriate instruction for students with documented disabilities.	*Special education is extremely broad in scope; thus it is difficult to assess overall effects of special education (for all disabilities) on achievement. Research does indicate that an approach referred to as **Response to intervention (RTI)** can have positive effects on reading and math achievement in students who are at risk for academic difficulties, or who have been designated as eligible for special education services. RTI is a multitiered approach, in which the academic progress of all students is monitored; when students are performing poorly, they receive tiered interventions, increasing in intensity and duration as needed.*
Instructional Practices	**Service learning** is an instructional strategy wherein a class assignment or project is aligned with a needs of the community; the project is generally carried out within the community setting.	*Whereas service learning can improve students' academic engagement, civic engagement, and socioemotional well-being, research to date has not documented major positive effects on achievement outcomes.*

(Continued)

Category	Definition of Influence	Achievement Effects and Considerations
	Between-class ability grouping occurs when students are organized into classes based on their academic abilities in a particular subject domain.	*There are few significant achievement advantages for students who are grouped by ability for instruction.*
	Within-class grouping is a practice in which students are organized into small learning groups within a classroom.	*There are two types of grouping.* **Heterogeneous** *grouping occurs when groups consist of students of mixed academic ability;* **homogeneous** *grouping occurs when students are grouped together with other students of similar academic ability. Learning in small groups is related to higher achievement for all students. Lower-ability students benefit more from participation in heterogeneous groups; average-ability students benefit more from participation in homogeneous groups; high-ability students' achievement is not jeopardized when they are in heterogenous groups.*
	Grade retention occurs when students are required to repeat a grade in school.	*Research indicates that there are no benefits to achievement associated with grade retention, compared to promotion of a student into the subsequent grade in school.*
	There are many instruments and strategies available for **evaluating and improving student-teacher interactions**.	*The use of validated, standardized instruments and protocols for evaluating such interactions can indirectly lead to improved student achievement, since administrators are better able to assess how learning is occurring throughout a school and to provide supports and professional development for teachers who are using strategies that do not support student learning.*
	Social and emotional learning programs (SEL) that are implemented at the school level are systematic, research-based programs that foster the development of positive relationships and regulation of emotions among students.	*The utilization of school-wide SEL programs is related to increased academic achievement, provided that (a) research-based programs with strong empirical support are used, and (b) the programs are implemented by school personnel with fidelity.*

Note: This table summarizes information presented by authors who contributed chapters to section 4 of the first edition of The International Guide to Student Achievement, as well as to revised chapters included in the present chapter.

CHAPTER 5

Influences from teachers and classrooms

Overview

The entries in this chapter summarize research on the effects of teachers and classrooms on students' academic achievement. Some of the entries focus specifically on attributes of the teacher, whereas others focus more broadly on instructional practices that are implemented within classrooms (and presumably *by teachers*). These distinctions are sometimes obvious and sometimes abstract.

It is difficult if not impossible at times to separate the effects of classrooms from the effects of teachers on achievement (e.g., Meyer, 2013). In the previous edition of this book, we invited authors to contribute separate chapters focusing on either teachers or classrooms. The section on classrooms was edited by Julianne Turner, and the section on teachers was edited by Anita Woolfolk Hoy. For this updated edition, we have synthesized the research on teachers and classrooms into a single, more readily usable chapter. The entries that appeared in the previous edition are listed below (entries with an asterisk have been updated for this edition):

Classroom Instructional Contexts
Debra K. Meyer

Academic Motivation and Achievement in Classrooms★
Lynley H. Anderman

Elementary Classroom Management
Inge R. Poole and Carolyn M. Evertson

Emotion and Achievement in the Classroom★
Thomas Goetz and Nathan C. Hall

Secondary Classroom Management
  Anne Gregory and Jennifer R. Jones
Homework and Academic Achievement★
  Jianzhong Xu
The Role of Formative Assessment in Student Achievement★
  Aryn C. Karpinski and Jerome V. D'Agostino
Peer Influences in Elementary School
  Gary W. Ladd
Acceleration for All
  Henry M. Levin and Pilar Soler
Ability Grouping
  Janet Ward Schofield
Collaboration in the Classroom★
  Noreen M. Webb
Teacher-Student Relationships★
  Heather A. Davis
National Board for Professional Teaching Standards
  Mary E. Dilworth
Classroom Management and Student Achievement★
  H. Jerome Freiberg
Fostering Student Creativity in the Era of High-Stakes Testing
  Bree Frick
Nontraditional Teacher Preparation★
  Belinda G. Gimbert
Quality of Teaching
  Laura Goe
Methods for Studying Teacher and Teaching Effectiveness
  Alexander Gröschner, Tina Seidel, and Richard J. Shavelson
Teachers' Expectations
  Lee Jussim

Teacher Enthusiasm and Student Learning
> *Melanie Keller, Knut Neumann, and Hans E. Fischer*

Teachers' Cultural and Professional Identities and Student Outcomes
> *Revathy Kumar and Linda Alvarado*

Teacher Intelligence: What Is It and Why Do We Care?
> *Andrew J. McEachin and Dominic J. Brewer*

Pedagogical Content Knowledge*
> *Julie Gess-Newsome*

Teacher Beliefs about Teaching and Learning: The Role of Idea-Oriented Pedagogy
> *Richard Prawat*

School Reform
> *Linda Valli and Carla Finkelstein*

Teacher Efficacy
> *John A. Ross*

Teachers' Epistemological Beliefs and Achievement
> *Gregory Schraw, Joanne Brownlee, and Lori Olafson*

Teacher Motivation and Student Achievement Outcomes
> *H. M. G. Watt and P. W. Richardson*

The Relation of Teacher Characteristics to Student Achievement
> *Xin Ma*

We have organized our discussion of this topic into three categories: (a) teachers' attitudes and beliefs, (b) classroom contexts, and (c) teachers' preparation and professional development growth. We briefly summarize some of the major findings related to achievement within each of these dimensions next.

Teachers' attitudes and beliefs

Teachers develop a wide array of beliefs and attitudes throughout their careers. Some of these beliefs emerge early, when teachers first enter the classroom, whereas others develop over time. These beliefs are extremely important, because teachers' beliefs influence their behaviors and interactions with students in the classroom (Buehl & Beck, 2015). When teachers are aware of their personal attitudes and beliefs about how students learn, they may be more likely to consider changing their practices (Levin, 2015).

Teachers' *efficacy beliefs* are among the most studied teacher beliefs. High teacher efficacy is characterized by the belief that a teacher has the competence and knowledge base to be able to positively affect students' learning. Research clearly and consistently indicates that teacher efficacy is positively associated with student achievement (e.g., Klassen & Tze, 2014; Ross, 2013); when teachers believe that they can be effective teachers, they are more likely to utilize instructional strategies that lead to achievement gains.

A number of other teacher beliefs also are related to student achievement. Just as students need to be sufficiently motivated to engage with their academic work, teachers also need to be motivated to engage with their professional work. Teachers are more effective at their jobs when they work in environments that support their motivation. Teachers' motivation is enhanced when teachers are able to set reasonable goals at work and are provided with supports to help them achieve those goals. Teacher motivation also is enhanced when administrators allow teachers to have some autonomy (i.e., to be able to make decisions about instructional practices) (Watt & Richardson, 2013). When teachers are motivated at work, they are likely to express greater enthusiasm during their interactions with students, and students achieve at higher levels when they perceive their teachers as being enthusiastic (Keller, Neumann, & Fischer, 2013).

More general teacher beliefs also affect student learning. Teachers' *epistemological beliefs* have been identified as being particularly important. Epistemological beliefs refer to teachers' general beliefs about the nature of knowledge and the acquisition of knowledge (Schraw & Olafson, 2002). Epistemological beliefs are predictive of the types of instructional practices that teachers use (e.g., Roth & Weinstock, 2013). Specifically, when teachers believe that learning takes time and that all students can learn (if provided with the appropriate supports), their students are more likely to achieve at higher levels (Schraw, Brownlee, & Olafson, 2013).

Classroom context

Anyone who has walked into a classroom understands that a classroom has a "feel" to it; in lay terms, this is what we mean by the *classroom context*. The context of a classroom is attributable to many factors, and the context may be perceived in different ways by different students. The classroom context is affected by many variables – the layout of the room, the teacher's personality, the topic being taught, the types of assignments that are given, the relationships between peers and with the teacher, behavior management, and a host of other variables (Meyer, 2013).

The policies and practices of the classroom teacher (as well as the policies that are implemented at the school or district level) contribute to the contexts of classrooms. When these policies and practices are malleable and can be readily changed or adapted, classroom contexts can change dramatically; however, when these practices are set in stone and rarely if ever change, then classroom contexts remain quite stable. The types of policies and practices that teachers use in their classrooms are influenced by their own beliefs, by school policies, and by their *pedagogical content knowledge* (i.e., their knowledge of their subject area, of effective instructional practices, and of the unique social contexts of their schools and students) (Gess-Newsome, this volume).

Classroom contexts are important for both young children and adolescents. For example, research indicates that executive functioning in young children is enhanced when teachers create classroom contexts that are perceived as being structured, emotionally supportive, and cognitively stimulating (Vandenbroucke, Spilt, Verschueren, Piccinin, & Baeyens, 2018). Among adolescents, classroom contexts that are responsive to adolescents' developmental needs promote learning and motivation (e.g., Anderman & Mueller, 2010); such classroom contexts are characterized by warm teacher-student relationships, opportunities for students to experience autonomy, and assessment policies that foster mastery of content (as opposed to high-stakes assessment) (e.g., Eccles et al., 1993; Eccles & Roeser, 2009).

Social relationships and the classroom context. The social relationships among teachers and students are major determinants of classroom contexts. A classroom that is characterized by positive, supportive relationships creates an entirely different atmosphere from a classroom that is characterized by discordant, hostile relationships. Whereas having "warm fuzzy" relationships between teachers and students is desirable, perhaps even more important is a relationship in which the student perceives that the teacher truly cares about each student's individual learning (Davis & Dague, this volume). For example, if a student is struggling with a particular unit in an algebra course, a classroom context in which the teacher notices that the student is struggling and offers appropriate instructional support will have a greater positive effect on that student's achievement than will merely having a "warm fuzzy" relationship with that student.

Peer interactions vary across classrooms. In some classrooms, peers regularly work together and interact around academic content; in other classrooms, students may work independently and remain in the same seats most of the time. Research suggests that when teachers support positive peer interactions in the classroom and manage student behavior effectively, achievement is enhanced (e.g., Gregory & Jones, 2013). Nevertheless, teachers need to be particularly cognizant of students who are rejected, victimized, or bullied by their peers; such interactions create an aversive classroom context that can hinder achievement (Ladd, 2013; Wentzel, 2017).

Academic tasks and the classroom context. The types of academic tasks that teachers use in their classrooms on a daily basis also contribute to the classroom context. Think about your own experiences in classrooms; you probably recall some classes in which there were many structured assignments, others where perhaps there were just a few high-stakes end-of-semester exams, and still others where you perhaps received regular feedback on your classwork and your progress. The choices that teachers make about the kinds of academic tasks that they will use with their students and the kind of feedback that they will provide shape the perceived contexts of classrooms and thus influence student achievement (Anderman & Anderman, 2014).

The assessment of student learning can be accomplished via the use of a wide range of academic tasks. Achievement can be assessed in many ways (e.g., via tests, quizzes, presentations, projects, essays, etc.). Regardless of the type of assessment that is used, achievement is enhanced when assessments are formative in nature. *Formative assessments* generally are informal, frequent assessments of students' performance on academic tasks; they are particularly effective because students receive regular feedback about their progress (D'Agostino, Rodgers, & Karpinski, this volume). In contrast, although *high-stakes assessments* are often emphasized and even required, research indicates that these types of assessments are not strongly related to improved student achievement (Valli & Finkelstein, 2013).

The frequency and quality of *homework* assignments also contribute to classroom context and to student achievement. Although teachers often assign homework in order to reinforce what was learned during class, homework only seems to positively affect achievement when the assignments are of high quality and when students have sufficient preparation to complete the assignment; if students do not have the necessary resources or know the appropriate cognitive strategies that they will need to complete the assignment, then the homework may not enhance their learning. Moreover, although homework is an academic task that tends to be given to youth of all ages, research suggests that homework is more strongly related to achievement for adolescents compared to younger children (Cooper, Robinson, & Patall, 2006; Xu, this volume).

Motivation and classroom context. Many educators believe that academic motivation solely resides within the student; students either come to class "motivated" or "not motivated" to learn. In addition, student motivation does affect classroom context – a classroom filled with 25 excited students engaged in interesting group projects creates a very different context than a classroom filled with 25 students seated at their desks and yawning. Despite the common belief that motivation resides solely within the student, research clearly indicates that the instructional practices used by teachers on a daily basis have powerful influences on student motivation. Ultimately, the quality of student motivation, in turn, affects students' academic achievement (Anderman & Gray, 2017; Anderman & Sayers, this volume; Cerasoli, Nicklin, & Ford, 2014).

Motivation and achievement are optimized when students feel *efficacious* (i.e., they believe that they can be successful in their studies), when they experience *autonomy* (i.e., they are able to make some decisions and to have some choices), and when they *value* academic content (i.e., they believe that what they are learning in class is useful, important, and interesting) (Anderman & Sayers, this volume; Jussim, 2013; Wigfield, Rosenzweig, & Eccles, 2017). Moreover, achievement is enhanced when students hold a *growth mind-set* (i.e., when students believe that their intelligence is malleable and that they can learn just about anything if they exert appropriate effort and have appropriate supports) (Dweck, 2016).

In any discussion of motivation and classroom context, the ways that students are grouped for instruction are particularly relevant. For example, whereas the use of *ability grouping* (i.e., tracking) is quite typical in many classrooms, research suggests that grouping students by ability generally benefits high-achieving students but has limited positive effects for most other students (Schofield, 2013). Whereas it may seem wise to put all the lowest achieving students together into the same classroom, this practice can have detrimental effects on motivation and achievement (the students in that classroom may see themselves as "the dumb kids"). In addition, whereas there is a widely held belief that arranging students into collaborative groups (i.e., collaborative learning) leads to higher achievement, beneficial effects only emerge when students understand how to work effectively in a group and when the collaborative groups are carefully organized and monitored by classroom teachers (Webb, this volume).

Teachers' preparation and professional development

Teachers generally need to obtain certification and/or a license in order to be employed as a professional educator. Many prospective educators participate in traditional teacher training programs, generally administered through colleges and universities. Nevertheless, in recent years, there has been a growth in *alternative licensure* programs. These programs provide alternative routes for prospective teachers to become licensed. Although these different pathways to certification are available, research suggests that, overall, student achievement is not related to the type of certification (alternative or traditional) that a teacher has (Gimbert & Kapa, this volume). Although alternative licensure programs may provide a viable and sometimes practical route to grow the teacher workforce (particularly in shortage areas), the quality of the instructional strategies that teachers use in the classroom matters much more than their path to licensure.

Once teachers are in the workforce, there are many opportunities for professional development and continuing education. Professional development opportunities vary dramatically in terms of content, quality, and duration. Research indicates that professional development opportunities for teachers can lead to student achievement growth, although gains in student achievement generally only occur when the professional development opportunities are of sufficient duration, are aligned with the local context of the school, are supported by school administrators, and are likely to challenge prevailing beliefs and misconceptions that teachers hold about instruction and learning (Goe, 2013; Yoon, Duncan, Lee, Scarloss, & Shapley, 2007).

5.1 Homework and academic achievement

Jianzhong Xu

Introduction

Typically defined as "tasks assigned to students by schoolteachers that are meant to be carried out during nonschool hours" (Cooper, 1989, p. 7), homework is a "complicated thing" (Corno, 1996), influenced by more factors than any other instructional activities (Cooper, 2007). It is a widespread educational activity extending across cultures, ages, and ability levels (Chen & Stevenson, 1989; Fan, Xu, Cai, He, & Fan, 2017; Warton, 2001). Indeed, for most school-age children, homework is an important part of their daily routine (Cooper et al., 2006; Fan et al., 2017). It is also an issue of tremendous everyday importance for parents and teachers alike (Trautwein, 2007). Not surprisingly, homework has been a perennial topic of public interest and an active area of investigation among educational researchers (Cooper et al., 2006).

Research evidence

Reviews of homework research (e.g., Cooper, 1989; Cooper et al., 2006; Fan et al., 2017; Keith, 1986; Walberg, 1991) provide generally consistent evidence for a positive influence of homework on academic achievement. In their synthesis of 69 studies conducted in the United States from 1987 to 2003, Cooper et al. (2006) found, with rare exceptions, that homework had a positive effect on academic achievement. They categorized the 69 studies into three basic design types. The first type included six studies that used experimental designs to compare homework and no-homework conditions. The six studies all revealed a positive effect of homework on unit tests, with effect sizes varying between $d = .39$ and $d = .97$.

The second type used data from 31 cross-sectional studies, most using multiple regression analyses or structural equation modeling. The large majority of these studies revealed positive and generally significant relationships between the amount of homework and achievement when various potentially confounding variables were controlled.

The third type involved the calculation of a simple bivariate correlation between the time the student spent on homework and the measure of achievement. These 32 studies included 69 separate correlations based on 35 separate samples of students. Of the 69 correlations, 50 were in a positive direction and 19 in a negative direction, with a weighted average correlation of $r = .24$ (which can be converted to d = .49).

Recently, Fan et al. (2017) systematically investigated prior research on the homework-achievement relationship in mathematics/science, based on 28 studies conducted from 1986 to 2015. These 28 studies included 61 effect sizes from 41 independent samples. The overall relationship between homework and mathematics/science achievement was $r = 0.22$ ($d = .45$) for the effect-size based meta-analysis (i.e., k = 61). Mathematics and science domains revealed a relatively small difference ($r = 0.21$ vs. $r = 0.23$). Taken together, these findings suggest that homework had a positive effect on mathematics/science achievement.

Whereas its overall findings were largely in line with the prior findings on the homework-achievement relationship (Cooper, 1989; Cooper et al., 2006), Fan et al.'s meta-analysis (2017) provides new insights by examining several moderators of the homework-mathematics/science achievement, including grade level, geographical region, and homework indicator.

Fan et al. (2017) found that the homework-achievement relationship in mathematics/science was stronger for elementary school students ($r = .36$) and high school students ($r = .30$) than for middle school students ($r = .15$). These findings are not in line with previous findings, in which Cooper et al. (2006) found a stronger correlation at the secondary school level ($r = .25$) than at the elementary school level ($r = -.04$). One plausible explanation is that Fan et al.'s study (2017) focused on the homework-achievement relationship in mathematics/science. For younger children, more frequent and short homework assignments may be more effective than fewer yet long assignments (Cooper, 1989, 2007); mathematics assignments in particular tend to be short and more frequent in elementary grades. In addition, whereas the transition to middle school is difficult for many students (Gutman & Midgley, 2000), developmental declines are particularly evident in mathematics/science (e.g., competence beliefs and intrinsic motivation) (Gottfried, Marcoulides, Gottfried, & Oliver, 2009), which may reduce the amount of gain that middle school students could anticipate from doing mathematics/science homework.

Whereas the studies in Cooper et al.'s study (2006) were all conducted in the United States, the studies in Fan et al. (2017) included studies conducted in other countries, thereby providing new perspective concerning geographical region association. Results revealed that the studies with US samples had the largest effect size ($r = .28$), the studies with Asian samples had the smallest effect size ($r = .08$), and the studies with European samples had an effect size between the previous two samples ($r = .12$). One likely explanation is that, compared with US students, Asian students spend substantially more time on after-school private tutoring (Chen &

Chang, 2015; Lee, 2007). This emphasis on private tutoring may water down the role of formal education in Asian countries. Thus, the homework-achievement relationship may be less apparent for Asian students, especially as private tutoring tends to extend to weekends and holidays (Fan et al., 2017).

Fan et al. (2017) further categorized the studies into several groups, based on how homework was operationalized in these studies. Results revealed that the effect sizes from the studies based on "homework effort" and "homework completion" were larger ($r = .31$ and $r = .59$) than those in the studies based on "homework frequency" and "time spent on homework" ($r = .12$ and $r = .15$). Although these findings are largely consistent with other homework studies (e.g., Cooper, Lindsay, Nye, & Greathouse, 1998; Trautwein, 2007), previous homework meta-analyses have not examined these homework indicators as a moderator in the relationship between homework and academic achievement.

Summary and recommendations

Many previous studies have examined the relationship between homework and achievement. Although moderated by grade level, geographical region, homework indicator, and achievement domain, results from these studies generally support the notion that the relationship between homework and academic achievement is a positive one for students across countries. Recently, a number of studies indicate that other factors (i.e., in addition to homework effort and homework completion) may play a more important role in academic achievement than homework time, including homework quality (e.g., Dettmers, Trautwein, Lüdtke, Kunter, & Baumert, 2010) and self-efficacy (e.g., Zimmerman & Kitsantas, 2005).

Consequently, instead of focusing on the quantity of homework, there is a critical need for teachers to improve the effectiveness of their instruction by designing more interesting, well-selected, and adequately difficult and challenging homework assignments (Dettmers et al., 2010; Epstein & Van Voorhis, 2001). This is particularly important, as engaging and interesting homework assignments can boost students' self-efficacy and responsibility for learning (Ramdass & Zimmerman, 2011) and as homework quality is positively related to students' homework effort (Dettmers et al., 2010).

Also, it would be important to pay more direct attention to the effort students put into homework, as various homework distractions (e.g., TV viewing and text messaging) may interfere with their attempt to follow through on their homework assignments (Xu, 2015) and as spending a lot of time on homework may signify a rather inefficient, unmotivated homework style (Trautwein, 2007). In addition, it would be important for teachers to model and provide students with explicit instructions on how better to manage their homework, including organizing the workspace, setting priorities, managing time, monitoring motivation, and coping with negative emotions (Xu, 2013). Finally, it would be important to listen to students' perspectives about what teachers can do to help them better manage homework, which would enable educators to provide more appropriate support in their effort at homework management (e.g., by making homework more interesting and by providing individualized homework feedback). This, in turn, will further promote students' self-efficacy, self-regulatory skills, and responsibility for managing their own homework.

References

Chen, C., & Stevenson, H. W. (1989). Homework: A cross-cultural examination. *Child Development, 60*, 551–561.

Chen, S. Y., & Chang, H. Y. (2015). Out-of-school time-use portfolios and Taiwanese children's reading achievement. *US-China Education Review, 5*, 336–348.

Cooper, H. (1989). *Homework.* White Plains, NY: Longman.

Cooper, H. (2007). *The battle over homework: Common ground for administrators, teachers, and parents* (3rd ed.). Thousand Oaks, CA: Corwin.

Cooper, H., Lindsay, J. J., Nye, B., & Greathouse, S. (1998). Relationships among attitudes about homework, amount of homework assigned and completed, and student achievement. *Journal of Educational Psychology, 90*, 70–83.

Cooper, H., Robinson, J. C., & Patall, E. A. (2006). Does homework improve academic achievement? A synthesis of research, 1987–2003. *Review of Educational Research, 76*, 1–62.

Corno, L. (1996). Homework is a complicated thing. *Educational Researcher, 25*(8), 27–30.

Dettmers, S., Trautwein, U., Lüdtke, O., Kunter, M., & Baumert, H. (2010). Homework works if homework quality is high: Using multilevel modeling to predict the development of achievement in mathematics. *Journal of Educational Psychology, 102*, 467–482.

Epstein, J. L., & Van Voorhis, F. L. (2001). More than minutes: Teachers' roles in designing homework. *Educational Psychologist, 36*, 181–193.

Fan, H., Xu, J., Cai, Z., He, J., & Fan, X. (2017). Homework and students' achievement in math and science: A 30-year meta-analysis, 1986–2015. *Educational Research Review, 20*, 35–54.

Gottfried, A. E., Marcoulides, G. A., Gottfried, A. W., & Oliver, P. H. (2009). A latent curve model of parental motivational practices and developmental decline in math and science academic intrinsic motivation. *Journal of Educational Psychology, 101*, 729–739.

Gutman, L. M., & Midgley, C. (2000). The role of protective factors in supporting the academic achievement of poor African American students during the middle school transition. *Journal of Youth and Adolescence, 29*, 223–248.

Keith, T. Z. (1986). *Homework.* West Lafayette, IN: Kappa Delta Pi.

Lee, J. (2007). Two worlds of private tutoring: The prevalence and causes of after-school mathematics tutoring in Korea and the United States. *Teachers College Record, 109*, 1207–1234.

Ramdass, D., & Zimmerman, B. J. (2011). Developing self-regulation skills: The important role of homework. *Journal of Advanced Academics, 22*, 194–218.

Trautwein, U. (2007). The homework-achievement relation reconsidered: Differentiating homework time, homework frequency, and homework effort. *Learning and Instruction, 17*, 372–388.

Walberg, H. J. (1991). Does homework help? *School Community Journal, 1*(1), 13–15.

Warton, P. M. (2001). The forgotten voices in homework: Views of students. *Educational Psychologist, 36*, 155–165.

Xu, J. (2015). Investigating factors that influence conventional distraction and tech-related distraction in math homework. *Computers & Education, 81*, 304–314.

Xu, J., & Wu, H. (2013). Self-regulation of homework behavior: Homework management at the secondary school level. *Journal of Educational Research, 106*, 1–13.

Zimmerman, B. J., & Kitsantas, A. (2005). Homework practices and academic achievement: The mediating role of self-efficacy and perceived responsibility beliefs. *Contemporary Educational Psychology, 30*, 397–417.

5.2 The role of formative assessment in student achievement

Jerome V. D'Agostino, Emily M. Rodgers, and Aryn C. Karpinski

Introduction

Formative assessment (FA) is a process of collecting information on student progress during instruction and using that information to guide subsequent teaching to maximize the likelihood that students will attain the planned objectives. FA commonly is misconstrued as a type of test, which has led to improper FA implementation. Sometimes tests labeled as "FA" are administered in school settings with little or no interim evaluation of learning and/or instructional revision, which is a practice that is not FA. Nonetheless, there are certain test properties that enhance the effectiveness of the FA process. Further, the parameters that define FA and that distinguish it from other concepts have not been clearly articulated. It has been argued that FA and scaffolding essentially are the same instructional strategies (Shepard, 2005) and that FA is simply summative assessment (SA) with the addition of student feedback (Taras, 2005).

Though FA, scaffolding, feedback, and SA are related and share certain properties, the terms are not completely overlapping. FA is distinguished from summative assessment (SA) in that the purpose of SA is to determine the degree to which the student attained the learning outcomes at the end of an instructional period without the assumption that subsequent instruction will occur to address any detected shortcomings in the student's knowledge or skill set. Though feedback often is provided to students during the FA process and feedback and FA commonly are linked together, FA does not require that a teacher provide a student direct feedback, but instead, the feedback resulting from FA could remain with the teacher for instructional modification and evaluation purposes. Scaffolding, on the other hand, centers on the amount and kind of help that a teacher provides during instruction and encompasses other strategies, such as delaying a response to allow the student time to process this situation, which is not a defining feature of FA.

It is difficult to pinpoint exactly the person or persons who first proposed FA. Scriven (1967) was the first to suggest the term's formative and summative evaluation to distinguish between the different evaluative purposes, but the concept of FA was first formulated much earlier. The importance of FA is rooted in reconceptualizations of curriculum by individuals such as Charters (1923), who construed curriculum as sequential tasks that a learner needs to develop to reach learning objectives. Early developments in mastery learning coincided with the creation of tests designed specifically to track student progress (Washburne, 1922). Tyler (1949) built upon Charter's earlier work to offer a more dynamic model of curriculum and instruction development that included a major emphasis on assessing the degree to which students had attained specified learning objectives and to rely on the test results to refine future instruction. Developments in criterion-referenced testing in the early 1960s (Glaser, 1963) helped forge test properties that are more amenable for FA.

Key elements

As stated, it is not the test but the process that defines FA, yet there are certain test properties that a measure used for FA purposes should possess. First and foremost, an effective FA test typically aligns with the learning objectives the instruction is designed to address. The test items should map on well to the objectives and measure them in a valid manner. Thus, items designed to measure each objective should properly reflect the content and expected cognitive demand level of the objective. Second, the test should yield criterion-referenced scores on an array of key outcomes that define the domain to be tested. Tests that produce a single overall score or only norm-referenced interpretations are not very informative if the goal is to understand a student's strengths and areas in need of improvement.

A good FA measure also should contain items that are instructionally sensitive. Once the student has partially or fully obtained the objective, items that measure the objective should become more attainable to the student if those items properly reflect the objective. Because FA is founded on the assumption of student learning, or change, the measure should yield scores that capture various levels of achievement. The range of growth that can be adequately measured by the test should be congruent with the overall intent of instruction. Lastly, the scores produced by the test should be in a form that is meaningful for the teacher and student, and thus, the scores can be used to communicate student progress and guide instructional decisions.

Research evidence

Educators do not require empirical evidence to know that FA is a critical component of effective instruction. Ongoing assessment to track student progress and address any necessary instructional needs obviously contribute to a constructive learning situation. Empirical research would be needed, however, to better understand how to structure FA so that it is integrated into instruction and to design useful FA tests. To date, however, such research is in short supply. Numerous research studies have been conducted on topics related to FA, such as providing student feedback, but few studies have focused directly on the impact of FA on student achievement and other outcomes. Two reasons for the relative lack of direct FA research are (1) researchers have not been clear about what does and does not constitute FA in practice, and (2) FA often correlates with other attributes of effective teaching and, thus, is hard to isolate.

Researchers and others often cite a research review by Black and Wiliam (1998) to make claims about the effectiveness of FA. Black and Wiliam concluded that FA has a rather large impact on student learning, with effect sizes between .4 and .7 (see also Wiliam, Lee, Harrison, & Black, 2004). More recently, critics of the methodology employed by Black and Wiliam have raised serious doubts about the validity of their findings (see Bennett, 2011; Dunn & Mulvenon, 2009). Black and Wiliam relied heavily on other meta-analyses, only some of which directly addressed the impact of FA, and the ones that did study FA directly focused on certain subpopulations.

Black and Wiliam (1998) drew on a meta-analysis conducted by Fuchs and Fuchs (1986), which examined the effects of FA but with an emphasis on special education students. Combining 21 studies, they computed a weighted effect size of .70, with 83% of the students in the studies representing special education categories. The meta-analysis also focused on FA practices that were integrated into interventions designed for special populations (e.g., behavior modification).

Another meta-analysis Black and Wiliam utilized examined the effects of one component of FA – feedback (Kluger & DeNisi, 1996). They reviewed several thousand manuscripts on teacher feedback and found an average effect of .4. The effects varied considerably, however, and a number of them were negative. In attempting to account for variations in effect sizes, Kluger and DeNisi identified certain features of feedback that either promoted or detracted from effectiveness in terms of increased student achievement. Feedback interventions that only directed students' attention back to themselves through praise or other affective cues typically yielded negative effects. Efforts to focus students' attention toward the task, including emphasis on what students did correctly and where they needed improvement, tended to produce positive effects on learning. Thus, praise alone without substantive feedback was deleterious.

Besides prior research syntheses, Black and Wiliam (1998) cited primary studies, but taken together, those studies addressed various facets either related to or comprising FA but not FA directly. Fontana and Fernandes (1994) examined 25 math teachers who were trained in self-evaluation methods. Frequent self-evaluation as part of the classroom assessment process has been theorized to be a key factor in enhancing student performance. After training the students, ages 8 to 14, in self-evaluation, the mean gain in math achievement for the younger students was about twice that of the control group.

Similar findings in another study also demonstrated the value of self-evaluation in motivation and achievement. Schunk (1996) found that students who used frequent self-evaluation and focused on *how* to solve problems had raised achievement outcomes compared to students who merely solved for the correct answer. With regards to self-evaluation as part of FA, it has been found that teaching students to self-assess increases understanding and the quality of work. Additionally, engaging students' prior knowledge to support new learning (i.e., knowledge transfer and generalization) allows for a direct impact of FA on achievement. This transfer is supported when a variety of activities are used in assessing and instructing students. Additionally, studies have demonstrated that students who understand the learning goals and criteria for evaluation and have opportunities to reflect on their work show greater progress than those who do not (Fontana & Fernandes, 1994).

Given the lack of details that Black and Wiliam (1998) followed in their analysis, it is not clear if an actual meta-analysis was conducted or if they simply reported a range of average effects from prior meta-analyses on related topics (Bennett, 2011). Furthermore, because they included studies or reviews on a very heterogeneous array of topics, it remains questionable if FA has an impact on student outcomes in the .4 to .7 range. Wiliam and Leahy (2007) point out, nonetheless, a more recent review (Nyquist, 2003) found similar results, albeit in higher education with a focus on feedback. Issues with the Black and Wiliam study do not cast doubt on the conclusion that FA has a positive impact on student achievement, mainly because most of the included studies pertained to topics within the broad domain of FA. In a more recent meta-analysis, Lee, Chung, Abedi, and Rashedi (2018) reported an effect size of .28 for FA based on 32 randomized controlled trials or quasi-experiments, which is outside the Black and Wiliam .4 to .7 range yet, given the more select inclusion criteria employed by Lee et al., may be a more accurate estimate of the FA effect.

There have been several studies conducted since the Black and Wiliam (1998) review that provide some understanding of the importance of FA. Ruiz-Primo and Furtak (2007) examined informal FA practices, which are FA practices that can take place during any teacher-student interaction and are not always planned. The results illustrated that using informal strategies (e.g., informal conversations between teachers and students focusing on the teachers' occurrences of eliciting, recognizing, and using information from their students) led to improved student performance compared to teachers that did not implement such strategies. In addition, Fox-Turnbull (2006) investigated the relation between "teacher knowledge of FA feedback" (i.e., teachers asking students higher-level or open-ended questions to extend their thinking) and student achievement. It was found that teacher knowledge had an impact on the use and quality of FA feedback, which had a positive influence on students' achievement.

Summary and recommendations

FA is the process of appraising student attributes during an instructional period to monitor learning and to design subsequent instruction to provide the student an opportunity to reach desirable learning outcomes. FA is not a type of test, but there are certain key properties of measures that are more conducive for FA effectiveness. Prior research on FA is scattered and ill-defined, mainly because the critical features of FA have not been clearly articulated, and it is difficult to disentangle the effects of FA from other instructional strategies. Instead of determining the overall impact of FA, more useful research could contribute to a better understanding of how to best arrange FA in specific instructional situations and settings. The effect of FA may indeed be very contextual, and therefore, there may not be one effective fixed effect.

Based on her review of the research on topics related to FA, Brookhart (2007) made the following recommendations to maximize the effect of FA on student achievement: (a) provide meaningful assessment activities linked to key objectives; (b) have a method of detecting strengths, weaknesses, and present performance levels; (c) have a clear understanding of the reference levels for students to attain; (d) measure the gap between the present and reference levels; (e) communicate the gap effectively to students; and (f) provide students follow-up activities to continually monitor progress toward closing the gap. Each of these recommendations takes proper training and skill to implement correctly. The foundation of those skills should be a cornerstone of teacher education programs and professional development opportunities.

References

Bennett, R. E. (2011). Formative assessment: A critical review. *Assessment in Education: Principles, Policy, and Practice, 18*, 5–25.

Black, P., & Wiliam, D. (1998). Assessment and classroom learning. *Assessment in Education: Principles, Policy, and Practice, 5*(1), 7–74.

Brookhart, S. M. (2007). Expanding views about formative classroom assessment: A review of the literature. In J. H. McMillan (Ed.), *Formative classroom assessment: Theory into practice* (pp. 43–62). New York, NY: Teachers College Press.

Charters, W. W. (1923). *Curriculum construction.* New York, NY: Palgrave Macmillan.

Dunn, K. E., & Mulvenon, S. W. (2009). A critical review of research on formative assessment: The limited scientific evidence of the impact of formative assessment in education. *Practical Assessment, Research, & Evaluation, 14*(7), 1–11. Retrieved from http://pareonline.net/getvn.asp?v=14&n=7

Fontana, D., & Fernandes, M. (1994). Improvements in mathematics performance as a consequence of self-assessment in Portuguese primary school pupils. *British Journal of Educational Psychology, 64*, 407–417.

Fox-Turnbull, W. (2006). The influences of teacher knowledge and authentic formative assessment on student learning in technology education. *International Journal of Technology & Design Education, 16*(1), 53–77.

Fuchs, L. S., & Fuchs, D. (1986). Effects of systematic formative evaluation: A meta-analysis. *Exceptional Children, 53*, 199–208.

Glaser, R. (1963). Instructional technology and the measurement of learning outcomes. *American Psychologist, 18*, 519–521.

Kluger, A. N., & DeNisi, A. (1996). The effects of feedback interventions on performance: A historical review, a meta-analysis, and a preliminary feedback intervention theory. *Psychological Bulletin, 119*, 254–284.

Lee, H., Chung, H. Q., Abedi, J, & Rashedi, R. (2018, April). *A systemic review of formative assessment: Efficacy and characteristics*. Paper presented at the Annual Meeting of the American Educational Research Association, New York, NY.

Nyquist, J. B. (2003). *The benefits of reconstruing feedback as a larger system of formative assessment: A meta-analysis* (Unpublished Master's thesis), Vanderbilt University.

Ruiz-Primo, M. A., & Furtak, E. M. (2007). Exploring teachers' informal formative assessment practices and students' understanding in the context of scientific inquiry. *Journal of Research in Science Teaching, 44*(1), 57–84.

Schunk, D. H. (1996). Goal and self-evaluative influences during children's cognitive skill learning. *American Educational Research Journal, 33*, 359–382.

Scriven, M. (1967). The methodology of evaluation. In R. W. Tyler, R. M. Gagne, & M. Scriven (Eds.), *Perspectives of curriculum evaluation* (pp. 39–83). Chicago, IL: Rand McNally.

Shepard, L. A. (2005). Linking formative assessment to scaffolding. *Educational Leadership, 63*(3), 66–70.

Taras, M. (2005). Assessment – Summative and formative – Some theoretical reflections. *British Journal of Educational Studies, 53*, 466–478.

Tyler, R. W. (1949). *Basic principles of curriculum and instruction*. Chicago, IL: The University of Chicago Press.

Washburne, C. W. (1922). Educational measurement as a key to individual instruction and promotion. *Journal of Educational Research, 5*(3), 195–206.

Wiliam, D., & Leahy, S. (2007). A theoretical foundation for formative assessment. In J. H. McMillan (Ed.), *Formative classroom assessment: Theory into practice* (pp. 29–42). New York, NY: Teachers College Press.

Wiliam, D., Lee, C., Harrison, C., & Black, P. (2004). Teachers developing assessment for learning: Impact on student achievement. *Assessment in Education, 11*(1), 49–65.

5.3 Collaboration in the classroom

Noreen M. Webb

Introduction

Recognizing that students can learn by working with and helping each other, school districts, state departments of education, national research organizations, and curriculum specialists have long recommended the use of collaborative group work in classrooms. Research reviews and meta-analyses showing positive effects of group collaboration on student achievement compared with other forms of instruction that involve little interaction between students (e.g., teacher-led whole-class instruction, individual work) date back several decades (Slavin, 1983). Even positive reviews, however, acknowledge that placing students in collaborative groups does not guarantee that learning will take place. Consequently, much research has explored the mechanisms by which working with other students benefits or hinders student learning and the many ways in which collaborative work might be orchestrated for maximum benefit (Esmonde, 2009; O'Donnell, 2006; Webb & Palincsar, 1996).

Research evidence

Perspectives on the benefits of peer interaction

According to social-behavioral perspectives (Slavin, 1983), working with other students will lead to increased effort, greater learning, and more liking of the task and other students than instructional settings without such opportunities for peer engagement. When students work toward a common goal, especially a group or cooperative goal that group members can attain only if the group is successful, they will feel individually accountable and personally responsible for what happens in the group and, consequently, will work hard and encourage others to do the same. Socially cohesive groups motivate students to help each other because they care about the group and its members. To promote a sense of group identification and concern for others, some cooperative learning methods use team building and development of social skills (e.g., active listening, stating ideas freely, taking turns, making decisions democratically) to help group members trust and support each other, communicate accurately and effectively, and resolve conflicts constructively.

Cognitive/developmental perspectives on learning from peers focus on the cognitive processes occurring during group collaboration. In the Piagetian perspective (Piaget, 1932), cognitive conflict arises when learners perceive a contradiction between their existing understanding and what they hear or see in the course of interacting with others. To resolve the conflict, learners reexamine and question their own ideas and beliefs, seek additional information, and try out new ideas, which leads to higher levels of reasoning and learning. In the Vygotskian perspective, learning can occur when a more expert person helps a less expert person (Vygotsky, 1978). Through a process sometimes called scaffolding or guided participation, the more skilled person enables the less competent person to carry out a task or solve a problem that the latter student could not perform without assistance. The less proficient student can internalize skills and knowledge that he or she has practiced and developed so that they become part of the individual's repertoire.

From a cognitive elaboration perspective (O'Donnell, 2006), giving and receiving explanations may lead students to restructure their own knowledge and understanding. Explaining material to others may promote learning by encouraging explainers to rehearse information, reorganize and clarify material in their own minds, recognize misconceptions and gaps in understanding, strengthen connections between new information and previously learned information, internalize and acquire new strategies and knowledge, and develop new perspectives and understanding (Chi, 2000). When they receive explanations, students can compare their own knowledge with what is being presented, correct misconceptions, and recognize and fill in gaps in their own knowledge. Maximum benefits will accrue when learners apply the explanations received to try to solve the problem or carry out the task themselves.

Through co-construction of knowledge (Barron, 2000), students can collaboratively build knowledge and problem-solving strategies that no group member has at the start by acknowledging, clarifying, correcting, building upon, and connecting each other's ideas and suggestions. Co-construction may require highly coordinated interaction among group members, characterized by students paying close attention to and acknowledging, repeating, and elaborating on each other's ideas.

Debilitating interpersonal processes

Groups may not function in ways that are optimal for learning (Webb & Palincsar, 1996): students can be left out of group collaboration; extroverted students may dominate group work at the expense of introverted students; and high-status students tend to be more active, assertive, talkative, and influential than low-status individuals. Other students may choose not to participate. They may engage in social loafing or diffusion of responsibility, which arises when one or more group members sit back and let others do the work. This free-rider effect may turn into a sucker effect when the group members who are working discover that they have been taken for a free ride and start to contribute less in order to avoid being suckers (Salomon & Globerson, 1989). To combat tendencies toward such unbalanced participation, cooperative learning methods often assign group members responsibilities for specific aspects of a group project or require group members to learn and teach different portions of the material to each other.

Students may fail to seek help when they need it or fail to obtain effective help when they seek it (Nelson-Le Gall, 1992). Students may not be able to monitor their own comprehension well enough to realize they need help. Or they may decide not to seek help for fear of being judged academically or socially incompetent, to conform to perceived classroom norms to work independently, because they believe themselves unable to benefit from help, or because they believe others do not have the competence or knowledge to provide help. Students who do seek help may select potential helpers who are nice or kind or who have high status, rather than those who have task-relevant skills. Or students may have ineffective help-seeking strategies, such as asking vague, indirect, confusing, or unfocused questions, rather than questions that are explicit, precise, direct, and targeted to a specific aspect of the problem or task (the latter being easier for groups to answer).

Too little or too much conflict may be detrimental

Infrequent conflict may reflect suppression of disagreements, either from the domination of one group member over the others or from social pressures not to challenge others. Too much conflict may prevent group members from moving forward, especially if they engage in an adversarial or conflictual style of argumentation instead of a co-constructive style in which they work together to critique suggestions and create new solutions.

Group functioning may also suffer from uncoordinated communication (Barron, 2000), marked by low levels of attention to, and uptake of, members' suggestions (even correct ones) and by students advocating and repeating their own positions and ideas, and ignoring or rejecting others' suggestions. Lack of coordination and joint attention may undermine many of the processes by which individuals can gain by collaborating with others, such as resolving conflicts and co-constructing knowledge, as well as reduce group cohesion and students' motivation to work together.

Other negative socioemotional processes, such as rudeness, hostility, and unresponsiveness, may also impede group members' participation and learning. Rudely disagreeing with others and ignoring their suggestions may prevent groups from solving problems correctly. Aggressiveness, hostility, and insulting behavior may lead to unconstructive and bitter arguments and may cause students to withhold knowledge and ideas from the group or to decide not to seek help.

Empirical evidence links these processes to learning outcomes. For example, explanation (Howe et al., 2007) and engagement with others' ideas (Webb et al., 2014) are positively related to learning outcomes, whereas rudeness and disagreement are negatively related (Chiu & Khoo, 2003). Learning measures in these studies typically consist of individually administered achievement tests, although the quality of the collaborative group's problem or task solution sometimes serves as the outcome measure.

Summary and recommendations

Preparing students for collaboration. To promote beneficial peer interaction and inhibit detrimental group dynamics, teachers can carry out activities prior to collaboration, such as building students' communication skills. Students can receive instruction in taking turns speaking, engaging in active listening, asking clear and precise questions, making and asking for suggestions and explanations, expressing and requesting ideas and opinions, using persuasive talk, summarizing conversations, checking others' answers, and monitoring others' understanding and the progress of the group (Veenman, Denessen, van den Akker, & van der Rijt, 2005). Some programs focus on skills specifically related to explaining and high-level reasoning, including providing reasons to justify assertions, opinions, and suggestions; giving explanations rather than answers; anticipating objections; and challenging others with counterarguments (Mercer, Dawes, Wegerif, & Sams, 2004). To prevent low-status students from being marginalized in group interaction, teachers can alter high-status students' expectations about low-status students' competence. Methods include providing low-status students with academic and nonacademic skills that they then teach to high-status students and having teachers point out the multiple abilities that are needed for task completion and highlighting special abilities that low-status students bring to the task (Cohen, 1994).

Structuring collaborative work. Some peer-learning approaches assign students roles to play or require students to carry out specific activities while collaborating, such as learning leader (or recaller) and active listener, in which the recaller summarizes material and the listener is responsible for detecting errors, identifying omissions, and seeking clarification, and tutor, who gives explanations, corrections, and feedback to the tutee (Fuchs et al., 1997).

Specific activities to carry out during collaborative work may include asking each other high-level questions, jointly answering questions to help groups reflect on problems and strategies before solving them (King, 1997), and responding to written prompts to give elaborated explanations justifying answers and beliefs (Mevarech & Kramarski, 2003). Sometimes the teacher takes a leadership role to model strategies (e.g., generating questions about the text they have read, summarizing the text, and generating predictions) before gradually helping students learn to carry them out in their groups. Collaborative work may also be structured as debates, in which groups are subdivided into teams who master material on different sides of an issue, debate the issue with the other team, and then work as a group to synthesize the two positions (Johnson & Johnson, 1994).

Teachers' instructional practices

Teachers can monitor group collaboration and intervene when groups exhibit communication problems, such as some students dominating the interaction and preventing useful dialogue or failing to justify their opinions and ideas. To improve communication, teachers can remind students about their obligations (e.g., share their thinking and solution methods with others, challenge each other's solutions) and make specific communication suggestions (e.g., stop another student and ask for help). Teachers can also increase the incidence of explaining in collaborative groups by asking students probing and clarifying questions, identifying discrepancies in students' work, and offering indirect hints about directions to take (Gillies, 2004), prompting for reasons and evidence, and modeling the articulation of clear arguments and counterarguments (Chinn, Anderson, & Waggoner, 2001) and by refraining from providing direct supervision (Galton & Williamson, 1992).

The nature of teacher discourse with students during whole-class instruction and the norms teachers negotiate with the class about expected interpersonal exchanges may also influence group collaboration. Pressing students to explain and justify their problem-solving strategies and generalizations and elaborate on their ideas and opinions can increase the incidence of student explanations during group work as well as during classroom discussion (Kazemi & Stipek, 2001). Teachers can negotiate norms for active student participation by discussing students' responsibilities to explain, defend, evaluate, and challenge their own and others' thinking when interacting with others and discussing examples of genuine dialogue between students (Yackel, Cobb, & Wood, 1991).

Teachers can also encourage active participation of students through the use of complex tasks or open-ended problems without clear-cut answers or procedures that require the combined expertise of everyone in the group. Such tasks encourage groups to recognize and value the different contributions that students can make, whereas narrowly defined tasks or problems, especially those that can be completed by one student with the requisite skills, may limit the participation of some students (Cohen, 1994).

References

Barron, B. (2000). Achieving coordination in collaborative problem-solving groups. *Journal of the Learning Sciences, 9*, 403–436.

Chi, M. T. H. (2000). Self-explaining expository texts: The dual processes of generating inferences and repairing mental models. In R. Glaser (Ed.), *Advances in instructional psychology: Educational design and cognitive science* (pp. 161–238). Hillsdale, NJ: Erlbaum.

Chinn, C. A., Anderson, R. C., & Waggoner, M. A. (2001). Patterns of discourse in two kinds of literature discussion. *Reading Research Quarterly, 36*(4), 378–411.

Chiu, M. M., & Khoo, L. (2003). Rudeness and status effects during group problem solving: Do they bias evaluations and reduce the likelihood of correct solutions? *Journal of Educational Psychology, 95*, 506–523.

Cohen, E. G. (1994). Restructuring the classroom: Conditions for productive small groups. *Review of Educational Research, 64*, 1–35.

Esmonde, I. (2009). Ideas and identities: Supporting equity in cooperative mathematics learning. *Review of Educational Research, 79*, 1008–1043.

Fuchs, L. S., Fuchs, D., Hamlett, C. L., Phillips, N. B., Karns, K., & Dutka, S. (1997). Enhancing students' helping behavior during peer-mediated instruction with conceptual mathematical explanations. *Elementary School Journal, 97*, 223–249.

Galton, M., & Williamson, J. (1992). *Group work in the primary classroom*. London: Routledge.

Gillies, R. M. (2004). The effects of communication training on teachers' and students' verbal behaviours during cooperative learning. *International Journal of Educational Research, 41*, 257–279.

Howe, C., Tolmie, A., Thurston, A., Topping, K., Christie, D., Livingston, K., . . . Donaldson, C. (2007). Group work in elementary science: Towards organisational principles for supporting pupil learning. *Learning and Instruction, 17*, 549–563.

Johnson, D. W., & Johnson, R. T. (1994). *Learning together and alone: Cooperative, competitive, and individualistic learning* (4th ed.). Boston, MA: Allyn & Bacon.

Kazemi, E., & Stipek, D. (2001). Promoting conceptual thinking in four upper-elementary mathematics classrooms. *Elementary School Journal, 102*(1), 59–80.

King, A. (1997). ASK to Think-Tel why: A model of transactive peer tutoring for scaffolding higher level complex learning. *Educational Psychologist, 32*, 221–235.

Mercer, N., Dawes, L., Wegerif, R., & Sams, C. (2004). Reasoning as a scientist: Ways of helping children to use language to learn science. *British Educational Research Journal, 30*, 359–377.

Mevarech, A. R., & Kramarski, B. (2003). The effects of metacognitive training versus worked-out examples on students' mathematical reasoning. *British Journal of Educational Psychology, 73*, 449–471.

Nelson-Le Gall, S. (1992). Children's instrumental help-seeking: Its role in the social acquisition and construction of knowledge. In R. Hertz-Lazarowitz & N. Miller (Eds.), *Interaction in cooperative groups: The theoretical anatomy of group learning* (pp. 49–68). New York, NY: Cambridge University Press.

O'Donnell, A. M. (2006). The role of peers and group learning. In P. A. Alexander & P. H. Winne (Eds.), *Handbook of educational psychology* (pp. 781–802). Mahwah, NJ: Erlbaum.

Piaget, J. (1932). *The language and thought of the child* (2nd ed.). London: Routledge and Kegan Paul.

Salomon, G., & Globerson, T. (1989). When teams do not function the way they ought to. *International Journal of Educational Research, 13*, 89–99.

Slavin, R. (1983). *Cooperative learning*. New York, NY: Longman.

Veenman, S., Denessen, E., van den Akker, A., & van der Rijt, J. (2005). Effects of a cooperative learning program on the elaborations of students during help seeking and help giving. *American Educational Research Journal, 42*(1), 115–151.

Vygotsky, L. S. (1978). *Mind in society: The development of higher psychological processes* (M. Cole, V. John-Steiner, S. Scribner, & E. Souberman, Eds. & Trans.). Cambridge, MA: Harvard University Press.

Webb, N. M., Franke, M. L., Ing, M., Wong, J., Hernandez, C. H., Shin, N., & Turrou, A. C. (2014). Engaging with others' mathematical ideas: Interrelationships among student participation, teachers' instructional practices and learning. *International Journal of Educational Research, 63*(1), 79–93.

Webb, N. M., & Palincsar, A. S. (1996). Group processes in the classroom. In D. Berliner & R. Calfee (Eds.), *Handbook of educational psychology* (pp. 841–873). New York, NY: Palgrave Macmillan.

Yackel, E., Cobb, P., & Wood, T. (1991). Small-group interactions as a source of learning opportunities in second-grade mathematics. *Journal for Research in Mathematics Education, 22*, 390–408.

5.4

Pedagogical content knowledge

Julie Gess-Newsome

Introduction

What teachers know should affect classroom practice and thus student learning. Research linking teachers' characteristics to student achievement, however, has not supported this assumption. Teacher content knowledge as traditionally measured by standardized tests, courses taken, and grade-point average, has only weak positive relationships to student achievement (Ferguson & Womack, 1993). See Gröschner, Seidel, and Shavelson (2013) for more complete discussions of teacher characteristics and content knowledge.

Such findings have puzzled researchers for nearly 40 years. In considering the dilemma, Shulman (1986) proposed a "missing paradigm" in educational research. The construct, pedagogical content knowledge, challenged past practices of examining knowledge of subject matter and pedagogy separately. Instead, pedagogical content knowledge (PCK), recognizes the melding of subject-matter expertise with pedagogical strategies and knowledge of the learner to produce high-quality classroom practice. For Shulman and the researchers who followed, PCK is a unique knowledge base held by teachers that allows them to consider the structure and importance of an instructional topic, recognize the features that will make it more or less accessible to students, and justify the selection of teaching practices based on learning needs. With PCK, neither content knowledge nor generic teaching skills alone are sufficient to be an effective teacher.

Research evidence

Nature of PCK

Since 1986, research concerning PCK focused on defining its nature and constituent parts. Shulman (1987) defined PCK as one of seven professional knowledge bases needed for teaching. Other knowledge bases included subject-matter knowledge, pedagogical knowledge, curricular knowledge, knowledge of students, knowledge of context, and knowledge of educational goals. Building from earlier work (Grossman, 1990; Wilson, Shulman, & Rickert, 1988) and applied to the field of science, Magnusson, Krajcik, and Borko (1999) defined PCK as the transformation of subject-matter knowledge and beliefs, pedagogical knowledge and beliefs, and knowledge and beliefs about context into a distinct knowledge base for teaching. In their model, PCK included orientations to teaching (such as inquiry, didactic, and conceptual change) that shaped and were shaped by knowledge of science curricula, knowledge of students' understanding of science, knowledge of instructional strategies, and knowledge of assessment of scientific literacy.

Although variations exist, most definitions of PCK include the following components:

- *Content knowledge*, including depth, breadth, and accuracy of content knowledge; connections within and between topics and the nature of the discipline; and fluency with multiple modes of representation or examples of a topic;
- *Pedagogical knowledge*, including a rationale linking teaching strategies to learning, strategies for eliciting student prior understandings, and strategies to promote student examination of their own thinking;
- *Contextual knowledge*, including understanding how student variations, such as student prior conceptions, impact instructional decisions (Gess-Newsome, Taylor, Carlson, Gardner, Wilson, & Stuhlsatz, 2017).

There is mounting evidence that PCK exists on a continuum, both across and within teachers, and influences teaching. Working from the assumption that depth of content knowledge is a precursor to PCK, early studies examined the differences between teachers. Some examined teaching practice resulting from varying teacher preparation programs (Grossman, 1990). Others compared teaching practices in self-described high- and low- knowledge areas or examined teacher planning for content topics within and outside their area of specialization (Hashweh, 1987) or across experience levels (Borko & Livingston, 1989). These studies demonstrated that depth of content knowledge resulted in differing teaching practices, providing initial support for the PCK construct. When teaching high-knowledge areas, teachers were more likely to present new information, ask high-level questions, review student work, encourage open-ended and student-initiated activities, recognize student misconceptions, and vary from or augment curricular materials. In low-knowledge areas, classroom practices were more teacher- and curriculum-centered with fewer opportunities for student-directed instruction. Student questioning in low-knowledge areas was infrequent and student misconceptions ignored or reinforced (Gess-Newsome, 1999).

When examining the development of PCK over time, the results are mixed. Hashweh (1987) compared how biology and physics teachers went about planning a topic in their content area and one outside their area. Teachers had a richer, more integrated knowledge base for the topics that they taught, indicating that PCK develops with the experience of teaching a topic multiple times. Such findings reinforce those of other studies that examine the impact of professional development on PCK (Barnett & Hodson, 2001; van Driel, Verloop, & deVos, 1998). Many of these studies note that examining student work or misconceptions is a particularly effective means of increasing teachers' careful consideration of content and pedagogical knowledge on classroom practice. In contrast, studies in Germany (Baumert et al., 2010; Krauss, Baumert, & Blum, 2008) found limited growth in PCK and CK across a mathematics teacher's career. Through looking at natural variation in teacher preparation programs in Germany, the most rigorous programs that included mathematics preparation similar to a master's degree produced teachers with CK (multitopic mathematical content knowledge) and PCK scores that exceeded those of teachers who received less rigorous content preparation. Interestingly, CK and PCK scores did not change with years of teaching experience following graduation. An analysis across preservice teachers within a preparation program showed that two-thirds of the growth occurred during formal university coursework, with the last third occurring during the final 18-month apprentice teaching. The authors suggest that such perplexing results point to the idea of deliberate practice theory (Ericsson, Krampe, & Tesch-Römer, 1993). This theory proposes that change does not come with simple repetition of a task but from thoughtful reflection, motivation to grow, and guidance through expert feedback. While the authors note that such professional development does not commonly exist in Germany, preservice preparation programs often include such characteristics, as do some of the professional development opportunities reported in other studies.

PCK and student achievement

Two large studies in mathematics are among the few to provide initial evidence that teachers with strong PCK are more likely to increase student achievement. In a study of how the mathematical knowledge needed for teaching impacts student achievement, Hill, Rowan, and Ball (2005) examined US elementary mathematics teachers' knowledge in the first and third grades. Key to this study was a multiple-choice test that assessed teacher mathematical knowledge of commonly taught topics: number concepts, operations, patterns, functions, and algebra. The test focused specifically on the knowledge that teachers use in the classroom rather than general mathematical knowledge and included tasks that involved mathematical explanations, alternative representations of mathematical ideas, and unusual solution methods. For example, one task asked teachers to examine and assess three different approaches to a multidigit multiplication problem, 35×25. The goal of the task was to capture both common mathematical knowledge and knowledge specialized for teaching. Teachers' content knowledge for teaching mathematics (CKT-M) significantly and positively predicted student achievement at both grade levels. CKT-M was the strongest teacher-level predictor of academic achievement exceeding teacher background characteristics such as number of mathematics and methods courses, certification, and years of teaching experience. The only variable that approached CKT-M in explaining student achievement was student socio-economic status (SES). Teachers in the lowest 20 to 30% of CKT-M scores had significantly lower student achievement gains, though further increases in teacher knowledge did not additionally influence student gains. Such findings suggest that there is a minimum threshold of CK needed to improve student achievement but diminishing returns beyond that point.

In the Baumert et al. (2010) study described previously, 13 open-ended content items on various mathematics topics assessed profound mathematical content knowledge taught in school and measured secondary mathematics teacher content knowledge. The test represented a content knowledge level that fell between that of a good secondary student and the knowledge taught at the university. Three knowledge dimensions defined PCK of mathematics: mathematical tasks, student thinking, and multiple representations. PCK scores predicted a higher quality of instruction, defined by student thinking (called cognitive activation), lesson correspondence to the grade-appropriate curriculum, individual student learning support, and classroom management, which in turn predicted student achievement. In fact, PCK scores explained 39% of student achievement variance. The importance of PCK for student achievement was more important in low-SES students than for high-SES students.

The Baumert et al. study (2010) further examined the interaction of the various categories of knowledge related to PCK. Content knowledge was not a predictor of high-quality instruction, supporting the hypothesis that PCK and CK are theoretically and empirically distinct. Content knowledge was highly correlated to PCK scores, and the correlation increased with teacher expertise. This finding suggests that CK may be a precursor to PCK and that expertise results in more coherent knowledge structures. As noted before, neither PCK nor CK increased with teaching experience in this population. Such research helps clarify the definition of PCK as well as providing initial evidence for how to support its growth.

Summary and recommendations

With limited correlations of traditional measures of teacher knowledge to student achievement, it is important to find alternative measures to understand what teachers know and do. With such knowledge, we have the opportunity to more carefully, effectively, and efficiently support teacher growth and ultimately improve student achievement. While many of the findings discussed are promising, additional research is needed. First, consensus on PCK and CK definitions and measurements is critical to future research. Both in-depth case study measures and standardized tools used for large samples are required to confirm and expand emerging results for both teacher PCK and CK. To attend to this issue, 11 international PCK research teams gathered in 2012 to define PCK and locate it within a broader framework of teacher professional knowledge bases at the PCK Summit I (Gess-Newsome, 2015). Additional work on gaining clarity around the definition of PCK and its application to research occurred at the PCK Summit II in 2016 and will result in a second book explicating the model (Hume, Cooper, & Borowski, in press). Second, research must attend to the links between teacher thinking, teacher practice, and student achievement. While it is appealing to believe that one knowledge type transfers seamlessly to the next, past research has shown that this is not the case. Third, as evidence of PCK mounts, particularly as it affects student achievement, there needs to be a more thoughtful consideration of and research into the effectiveness of teacher preparation and professional development programs. A recent outcome of this research is the growth in content-specific teacher preparation programs, such as the UTeach program developed at the University of Texas at Austin (http://uteach.utexas.edu). This program purposefully blends content knowledge with attention to student learning and powerful instructional strategies. Teacher and student learning results need to be compared to more traditional programs where little time or attention is given to content-specific preparation. Finally, while current evidence is not sufficient to support policy recommendations, further examination of PCK will help identify the nature of the knowledge needed for teaching as well as the methods through which we can assist teachers in translating this knowledge into classroom practices that improve student learning.

References

Barnett, J., & Hodson, D. (2001). Pedagogical context knowledge: Toward a fuller understanding of what good science teachers know. *Science Education, 85,* 426–453.

Baumert, J., Kunter, M., Blum, W., Brunner, M., Voss, T., Jordan, A., . . . Tsai, Y. (2010). Teachers' mathematical knowledge, cognitive action in the classroom, and student progress. *American Educational Research Journal, 47,* 133–180.

Borko, H., & Livingston, C. (1989). Cognition and improvisation: Differences in mathematics instruction by expert and novice teachers. *American Educational Research Journal, 26*(4), 473–498.

Ericsson, K. A., Krampe, R. T., & Tesch-Römer, C. (1993). The role of deliberate practice in the acquisition of expert performance. *Psychological Review, 100,* 363–406.

Ferguson, P., & Womack, S. T. (1993). The impact of subject matter and educational coursework on teaching performance. *Journal of Teacher Education, 44*(1), 55–63.

Gess-Newsome, J. (1999). Secondary teachers' knowledge and beliefs about subject matter and its impact on instruction. In J. Gess-Newsome & N. G. Lederman (Eds.), *Examining pedagogical content knowledge: The construct and its implications for science education* (pp. 51–94). Dordrecht, Netherlands: Kluwer Academic.

Gess-Newsome, J. (2015). A model of teacher professional knowledge and skill including PCK: Results of the thinking from the PCK summit. In A. Berry, P. J. Friedrichsen, & J. Loughran (Eds.), *Re-examining pedagogical content knowledge in science education* (pp. 28–42). New York, NY: Routledge.

Gess-Newsome, J., Taylor, J. A., Carlson, J., Gardner, A. L., Wilson, C. D., & Stuhlsatz, M. A. M. (2017). Teacher pedagogical content knowledge, practice, and student achievement. *International Journal for Science Education.* http://dx.doi.org/10.1080/09500693.2016.1265158.

Gröschner, A., Seidel, T., & Shavelson, R. J. (2013). Methods for studying teacher and teaching effectiveness. In J. Hattie & E. M. Anderman (Eds.), *International guide to student achievement* (pp. 240–242). New York, NY: Routledge/Taylor & Francis Group.

Grossman, P. L. (1990). *The making of a teacher: Teacher knowledge and teacher education.* New York, NY: Teachers College Press.

Hashweh, M. Z. (1987). Effects of subject matter knowledge in the teaching of biology and physics. *Teaching and Teacher Education, 3*(2), 109–120.

Hill, H. C., Rowan, B., & Ball, D. L. (2005). Effects of teachers' mathematics knowledge for teaching on student achievement. *American Educational Research Journal, 42,* 371–406.

Hume, A., Cooper, R., & Borowski, A. (Eds.). (In Press). *Repositioning PCK in teachers' professional knowledge.* Springer.

Krauss, S., Baumert, J., & Blum, W. (2008). Secondary mathematics teachers' pedagogical content knowledge and content knowledge: Validation of the COACTIV constructs. *The International Journal on Mathematics Education, 40*(5), 873–892.

Magnusson, S., Krajcik, J., & Borko, H. (1999). Nature, sources, and development of pedagogical content knowledge for teaching. In J. Gess-Newsome & N. G. Lederman (Eds.), *Examining pedagogical content knowledge: The construct and its implications for science education* (pp. 95–132). Dordrecht, Netherlands: Kluwer Academic.

Shulman, L. S. (1986). Those who understand: Knowledge growth in teaching. *Educational Researcher, 15*(2), 4–14.

Shulman, L. S. (1987). Knowledge and teaching: Foundations of the new reform. *Harvard Educational Review, 57*(1), 1–22.

van Driel, J. H., Verloop, N., & DeVos, W. (1998). Developing science teachers' pedagogical content knowledge. *Journal of Research in Science Teaching, 35,* 673–695.

Wilson, S. M., Shulman, L. S., & Rickert, A. E. (1988). 150 different ways of knowing: Representations of knowledge in teaching. In J. Calderhead (Ed.), *Exploring teacher thinking* (pp. 104–124). Sussex, England: Holt, Rinehart, & Winston.

5.5

Emotion and achievement in the classroom

Thomas Goetz and Nathan C. Hall

Introduction

With the exception of extensive research on test anxiety since the 1950s (Sarason & Mandler, 1952; Zeidner, 2007, 2014) and on emotions in achievement settings based on attribution theory (Weiner, 1985), empirical educational research has largely neglected students' emotions. Over the past 15 years, however, a discernible increase in theoretical and empirical contributions on emotions in education is reflected in numerous special issues, edited volumes and books (Efklides & Volet, 2005; Linnenbrink, 2006; Linnenbrink-Garcia & Pekrun, 2011; Lipnevich & Roberts, 2012; Schutz & Lanehart, 2002; Pekrun, 2014; Pekrun & Linnenbrink-Garcia, 2014; Pekrun, Muis, Frenzel, & Goetz, 2018; Schutz & Pekrun, 2007). Nonetheless, with the exception of research on anxiety/achievement relations (e.g., Hembree, 1988; Ma, 1999; Seipp, 1991; von der Embse, Jester, Roy, & Post, 2018), there exist only scattered empirical findings on relations between other emotions and academic achievement (Pekrun et al., 2018). This lack of emphasis is reflected in a recent PsychINFO search (March 2018) for manuscript titles including "achievement" *and* "anxiety" (612) as compared to "enjoyment" (22), "hope" (35), "pride" (15), "anger" (8), "shame" (12), or "boredom" (7). In contrast to 1,129 titles including "achievement" *and* "self-concept," the relatively small number of publications in the field of emotions as compared to self-concept research is clearly evident.

Research evidence

Strength of emotion/achievement relations

Anxiety – meta-analyses
Concerning the magnitude of emotion/achievement relations, there exist four seminal meta-analyses in which academic anxiety is exclusively evaluated. In

his meta-analysis of 562 North American studies (1952–1986), Hembree (1988) explored the correlates, causes, effects, and remediation of test anxiety. The studies consisted of samples from upper elementary school to high school and included various achievement measures including test scores, course grades, and GPA. Results showed test anxiety to have typically moderate negative relations with achievement: for example, with grades in mathematics (r = -.22), natural sciences (r = .21), and social sciences (r = -.25). Based on this work, von der Embse et al. (2018) published a follow-up meta-analytic review of 238 studies published during the 30 years following Hembree's publication that showed remarkably similar results (e.g., correlation of r = -.24 between test anxiety and grades in undergraduate and graduate students). In Seipp (1991), a meta-analysis of 126 European and North American studies (1975–1988) revealed generally moderate negative relations between anxiety and academic performance, as indicated in a population effect size of -.21 (range = -.36 to -.07). A fourth meta-analysis by Ma (1999) further explored math anxiety and achievement relations across 26 studies of elementary and secondary students, finding once again a modest population correlation of -.27 (range = -.60 to -.12). Taken together, meta-analyses findings consistently demonstrate significant, albeit moderate, negative relations, typically ranging from -.20 to -.25, between anxiety and achievement outcomes.

Discrete emotions – single studies

Empirical findings on relations between discrete emotions and academic achievement are clear with respect to emotion valence: pleasant emotions (e.g., enjoyment, pride) are positively related to achievement, whereas unpleasant emotions (e.g., anxiety, boredom) are negatively related (Pekrun, 2006). Further, cumulative research indicates that emotion/achievement relations are best understood as linear and not curvilinear in nature (e.g., inverted-U relationship as in Yerkes & Dodson, 1908; see Zeidner, 2007, 2014). Concerning the strength of discrete emotions/achievement relations, recent studies indicate differences with respect to emotion type and academic domain. Goetz et al. (2012) (grades 8–11) found the mean and median within-domain relation between discrete classroom-related emotions (enjoyment, pride, anxiety, anger, boredom) and grades in multiple subject domains (mathematics, physics, German, English) to be |.25| (range = .04 to .40; SD = .08). These values are consistent with related studies on emotion/ achievement relations in high school and university students (e.g., Goetz, Cronjaeger, Frenzel, & Lüdtke, 2010; Goetz, Frenzel, Pekrun, Hall, & Lüdtke, 2007; Pekrun, Goetz, Daniels, Stupnisky, & Perry, 2010; Pekrun, Hall, Goetz, & Perry, 2014; Pekrun, Lichtenfeld, Marsh, Murayama, & Goetz, 2017; for a summary of studies on boredom and achievement, see Tze, Daniels, & Klassen, 2016). To summarize, single studies indicate mean discrete emotion/achievement relations of approximately |.25|.

Mediating factors in emotion/achievement relations

There exist few theoretical approaches in which the mechanisms underlying discrete emotion/achievement relations are addressed. Of these models, the most prominent is a comprehensive model outlined by Pekrun (2006; see also Pekrun et al., 2018) that incorporates social-cognitive emotion theories as well as empirical findings concerning discrete emotions in achievement settings. In Pekrun's model, it is assumed that emotion/achievement relations are mediated by cognitive resources, motivation, strategy use, and self-regulated learning, such that specific emotions impact these variables that, in turn, predict achievement outcomes. Further, the effects of emotions on mediating variables and achievement are assumed to be additionally complicated by the emotional dimensions of valence (pleasant versus unpleasant) and activation (activating versus deactivating). Based on these dimensions, four groups of emotions can be distinguished: positive activating emotions (e.g., enjoyment, hope, pride, gratitude), positive deactivating emotions (e.g., relaxation, contentment, relief), negative activating emotions (e.g., anger, frustration, anxiety, shame), and negative deactivating emotions (e.g., boredom, sadness, disappointment, hopelessness). In most conditions, it is assumed that positive activating emotions exert positive effects on achievement, whereas negative deactivating emotions exert negative effects, in contrast to positive deactivating and negative activating emotions, which are assumed to have ambivalent effects on motivation and cognitive processing (Pekrun, 2006). Nevertheless, there exists little research in which these proposed mediation mechanisms are examined, competitively evaluated, or explored with respect to reverse causality (e.g., cognitive resources as mediators of emotion/achievement relations versus emotions as mediators of cognitive resources/achievement relations; Pekrun, Goetz, Titz, & Perry, 2002a; Pekrun et al., 2017; Turner & Waugh, 2007).

Moderators of emotion/achievement relations

Findings on emotion/achievement relations typically show a wide range of relations for both (test) anxiety and other discrete emotions. Moreover, there exist numerous studies in research on anxiety (Zeidner, 2007, 2014) and other discrete emotions (e.g., Pekrun et al., 2002a, 2017; Goetz et al., 2007, 2010) that taken together suggest three primary moderators of emotion/achievement relations:

1. Relations are stronger when emotions and achievement are assessed within a specific domain (e.g., math anxiety and math achievement versus learning anxiety and GPA).
2. Relations are stronger in the math and science domains than in verbal domains.
3. Emotion valence determines relation valence: pleasant emotions are positively related to achievement, and unpleasant emotions are negatively related.

Research on test anxiety and achievement relations suggests additional moderating variables (Zeidner, 2007, 2014), including those that increase these relations (e.g., evaluative settings, negative feedback) and decrease these relations (e.g., structured conditions, social support). Although often cited as a possible moderator, gender has not been found to substantially moderate anxiety/achievement relations (Zeidner, 2007). Empirical findings concerning gender effects on discrete emotion/achievement relations are presently lacking. With respect to causal ordering, it is important to note that reciprocal relations between emotions and achievement are also possible (Pekrun, 2006) and have been observed in recent empirical studies (Pekrun et al., 2014, 2017). More specifically, achievement can impact emotions (e.g., good grades predict enjoyment) directly or via academic self-concept (e.g., good grades predict perceived competence which predicts enjoyment) (Goetz, Frenzel, Hall, & Pekrun, 2008).

Relevance of academic emotions for academic achievement

Studies indicate that emotion/achievement relations are, on average, weak to moderate in magnitude (cf., academic self-concept/achievement: average $r = .50$ to .70) (Marsh & Craven, 2006). However, even relatively weak effects of emotions on academic achievement may have a strong cumulative impact on students' long-term achievement. The findings outlined earlier further suggest considerable variability in emotion/achievement relations as a function of emotion type and academic discipline, highlighting the potential for notably stronger relations for specific emotions in specific academic settings (e.g., anxiety in natural science classes). In addition, whereas academic emotions are of relevance to achievement outcomes, their effects also generalize to salient developmental outcomes including health, subjective well-being, career choice, and lifelong learning (Pekrun et al., 2018). Finally, in light of the dominance of anxiety research, relatively unexplored positive academic emotions have also received recent attention. According to Pekrun et al. (2002b), positive emotions "help to envision goals and challenges, open the mind to thoughts and problem-solving, protect health by fostering resiliency, create attachments to significant others, lay the groundwork for individual self-regulation, and guide the behavior of groups, social systems, and nations" (p. 149).

Summary and recommendations

Given the importance of academic emotions with respect to achievement outcomes as well as student development and accounting for the status quo of research in this field, the following research activities are recommended:

- Research on emotion/achievement relations should focus on discrete emotions, such as enjoyment, hope, pride, gratitude, relaxation, contentment, relief, anger,

frustration, anxiety, shame, boredom, sadness, disappointment, and hopelessness in addition to test anxiety.
- Given the domain specificity of academic emotional experiences and subject domain as a moderator of the strength of emotion/achievement relations, domain-specific investigations are warranted.
- As most research on emotion/achievement relations has focused on testing situations (i.e., anxiety) and the classroom setting, homework-related emotions remain relatively unexplored, and future studies may yield intriguing findings (cf., Dettmers et al., 2011).
- Empirical research examining the assumed causal relations between emotions and achievement is needed (e.g., longitudinal, experimental, intervention designs).
- The continued development of domain- and age-specific instruments for the assessment of discrete emotions other than (test) anxiety is required to adequately explore emotion/achievement relations (e.g., domain-general and domain-specific measures in the Achievement Emotions Questionnaire) (Pekrun, Goetz, Frenzel, Barchfeld, & Perry, 2011).

Concerning implications of research on emotion/achievement relations for teaching and teacher education programs, possible recommendations include the following:

- The impact of academic emotions on learning and achievement should be highlighted in teacher education curricula.
- Antecedents of academic emotions should also be addressed in teacher education curricula to facilitate teachers' understanding of how students' emotions are affected by the mediating and moderating variables outlined earlier.
- Based on knowledge of emotion antecedents, teachers should acknowledge their potential to impact students' emotions and attempt to foster pleasant and reduce negative emotions: for example, by enhancing students' academic self-concept (Goetz et al., 2008), adopting an enthusiastic teaching style (Frenzel, Becker-Kurz, Pekrun, Goetz, & Lüdtke, in press), and fostering students' emotion regulation competencies (e.g., for coping with test anxiety, see Zeidner, 2007; for coping with boredom, see Nett, Goetz, & Hall, 2011; for strategies concerning discrete emotions, see Goetz & Bieg, 2016).
- Teachers should also be aware of their own emotional experiences and attempt to optimize their emotions concerning instruction so as to promote students' emotions and achievement (Frenzel et al., in press; Pekrun et al., 2018).

It is essential that ongoing empirical research on students' emotions be consistently incorporated into teacher education programs and informed by educational practice. In this manner, researchers and educators alike will be better able to identify and develop instructional strategies and intervention programs that optimize students' academic emotional experiences and thereby facilitate not only learning and academic achievement, but also critical developmental outcomes including health and psychological well-being.

References

Dettmers, S., Trautwein, U., Lüdtke, O., Goetz, T., Frenzel, A. C., & Pekrun, R. (2011). Students' emotions during homework in mathematics: Testing a theoretical model of antecedents and achievement outcomes. *Contemporary Educational Psychology, 36*(1), 25–35.

Efklides, A., & Volet, S. (2005). Feelings and emotions in the learning process [Special issue]. *Learning and Instruction, 15*, 377–380.

Frenzel, A. C., Becker-Kurz, B., Pekrun, R., Goetz, T., & Lüdtke, O. (In press). Emotional transmission in the classroom revisited: A reciprocal effects model of teacher and student enjoyment. *Journal of Educational Psychology*.

Goetz, T., & Bieg, M. (2016). Academic emotions and their regulation via emotional intelligence. In A. A. Lipnevich, F. Preckel, & R. D. Roberts (Eds.), *Psychosocial skills and school systems in the 21st century: Theory, research and practice* (pp. 279–298). New York, NY: Springer.

Goetz, T., Cronjaeger, H., Frenzel, A. C., Lüdtke, O., & Hall, N. C. (2010). Academic self-concept and emotion relations: Domain specificity and age effects. *Contemporary Educational Psychology, 35*, 44–58.

Goetz, T., Frenzel, C. A., Hall, N. C., & Pekrun, R. (2008). Antecedents of academic emotions: Testing the internal/external frame of reference model for academic enjoyment. *Contemporary Educational Psychology, 33*, 9–33.

Goetz, T., Frenzel, C. A., Pekrun, R., Hall, N. C., & Lüdtke, O. (2007). Between- and within-domain relations of students' academic emotions. *Journal of Educational Psychology, 99*(4), 715–733.

Goetz, T., Nett, U., Martiny, S., Hall, N. C., Pekrun, R., Dettmers, S., & Trautwein, U. (2012). Students' emotions during homework: Structures, self-concept antecedents, and achievement outcomes. *Learning and Individual Differences, 22*(2), 225–234.

Hembree, R. (1988). Correlates, causes, effects, and treatment of test anxiety. *Review of Educational Research, 58*, 7–77.

Linnenbrink, E. A. (2006). Emotion research in education: Theoretical and methodological perspectives on the integration of affect, motivation, and cognition [Special issue]. *Educational Psychology Review, 18*, 307–314.

Linnenbrink-Garcia, E. A., & Pekrun, R. (2011). Students' emotions and academic engagement [Special issue]. *Contemporary Educational Psychology, 36*(1), 1–3.

Lipnevich, A. A., & Roberts, R. D. (2012). Noncognitive skills in education: Emerging research and applications in a variety of international contexts. *Learning and Individual Differences, 22*(2), 173–177.

Ma, X. (1999). A meta-analysis of the relationship between anxiety toward mathematics and achievement in mathematics. *Journal for Research in Mathematics Education, 30*(5), 520–540.

Marsh, H. W., & Craven, R. G. (2006). Reciprocal effects of self-concept and performance from a multidimensional perspective: Beyond seductive pleasure and unidimensional perspectives. *Perspectives on Psychological Science, 1*(2), 133–163.

Nett, U. E., Goetz, T., & Hall, N. C. (2011). Coping with boredom in school: An experience sampling perspective. *Contemporary Educational Psychology, 36*(1), 49–59.

Pekrun, R. (2006). The control-value theory of achievement emotions: Assumptions, corollaries, and implications for educational research and practice. *Educational Psychology Review, 18,* 315–341.

Pekrun, R. (2014). *Emotions and learning* (Educational Practices Series, Vol. 24). International Academy of Education (IAE) and International Bureau of Education (IBE) of the United Nations Educational, Scientific and Cultural Organization (UNESCO), Geneva, Switzerland.

Pekrun, R., Goetz, T., Daniels, L. M., Stupnisky, R. H., & Perry, R. P. (2010). Boredom in achievement settings: Exploring control-value antecedents and performance outcomes of a neglected emotion. *Journal of Educational Psychology, 102*(3), 531–549.

Pekrun, R., Goetz, T., Frenzel, A. C., Barchfeld, P., & Perry, R. P. (2011). Measuring emotions in students' learning and performance: The achievement emotions questionnaire (AEQ). *Contemporary Educational Psychology, 36*(1), 36–48.

Pekrun, R., Goetz, T., Titz, W., & Perry, R. P. (2002a). Academic emotions in students' self-regulated learning and achievement: A program of qualitative and quantitative research. *Educational Psychologist, 37*(2), 91–105.

Pekrun, R., Goetz, T., Titz, W., & Perry, R. P. (2002b). Positive emotions in education. In E. Frydenberg (Ed.), *Beyond coping: Meeting goals, visions, and challenges* (pp. 149–173). Oxford, England: Oxford University Press.

Pekrun, R., Hall, N. C., Goetz, T., & Perry, R. P. (2014). Boredom and academic achievement: Testing a model of reciprocal causation. *Journal of Educational Psychology, 106*(3), 696–710.

Pekrun, R., Lichtenfeld, S., Marsh, H. W., Murayama, K., & Goetz, T. (2017). Achievement emotions and academic performance: Longitudinal models of reciprocal effects. *Child Development, 88,* 1653–1670.

Pekrun, R., & Linnenbrink-Garcia, L. (Eds.). (2014). *International handbook of emotions in education.* New York, NY: Francis & Taylor/Routledge.

Pekrun, R., Muis, K. R., Frenzel, A. C., & Goetz, T. (2018). *Emotions at school.* New York, NY: Routledge.

Sarason, S. B., & Mandler, G. (1952). Some correlates of test anxiety. *Journal of Abnormal and Social Psychology, 47*(4), 810–817ze.

Schutz, P. A., & Lanehart, S. L. (Eds.). (2002). Emotions in education [Special issue]. *Educational Psychologist, 37*(2).

Schutz, P. A., & Pekrun, R. (Eds.). (2007). *Emotions in education.* San Diego, CA: Elsevier.

Seipp, B. (1991). Anxiety and academic performance: A meta-analysis of findings. *Anxiety Research, 4,* 27–41.

Turner, J. E., & Waugh, R. M. (2007). A dynamical systems perspective regarding students' learning processes: Shame reactions and emergent self-organizations. In P. A. Schutz & R. Pekrun (Eds.), *Emotion in education* (pp. 125–145). San Diego, CA: Academic Press.

Tze, V. M. C., Daniels, L. M., & Klassen, R. M. (2016). Evaluating the effects between boredom and academic outcomes: A meta-analysis. *Educational Psychology Review, 28,* 119–144.

von der Embse, N., Jester, D., Roy, D., & Post, J. (2018). Test anxiety effects, predictors, and correlates: A 30-year meta-analytic review. *Journal of Affective Disorders, 227,* 483–493.

Weiner, B. (1985). An attributional theory of achievement motivation and emotion. *Psychological Review, 92*(4), 548–573.

Yerkes, R. M., & Dodson, J. D. (1908). The relation of strength of stimulus to rapidity of habit-formation. *Journal of Comparative and Neurological Psychology, 18*, 459–489.

Zeidner, M. (2007). Test anxiety: Conceptions, findings, conclusions. In P. A. Schutz & R. Pekrun (Eds.), *Emotion in education* (pp. 165–184). San Diego, CA: Academic Press.

Zeidner, M. (2014). Anxiety in education. In R. Pekrun & L. Linnenbrink-Garcia (Eds.), *International handbook of emotions and education* (pp. 265–288). New York, NY: Taylor & Francis/Routledge.

5.6 Teacher-student relationships

Heather A. Davis and Christopher T. Dague

Introduction

Since the early 1980s, a growing body of literature has documented the important relations of students' perceptions of teacher relationships to their classroom motivation, learning, performance, and school completion (Davis, 2003; Wentzel, 2009). Several meta-analyses have documented moderate to large effects of teacher-relationship quality on social and academic outcomes including participation, satisfaction, self-efficacy, critical thinking, standardized achievement in math and language, increasing attendance, reduction in disruptive behavior, and higher grades. Conversely, findings suggest students' motivation and adjustment to school may be adversely affected when their relationships with teachers are distressed (Cornelius-White, 2008; Quin, 2017; Roorda, Koomen, Split, & Oort, 2011).

Teacher-student relationships have been conceptualized in many ways (Davis, 2003; Wentzel, 2009). The four dominant frameworks in the United States tend to be extensions of parenting styles (Reeve, 2006; Walker, 2008), teachers' beliefs (Woolfolk Hoy & Davis, 2005), attachment theory (Pianta, 1999; Hughes, 2012), and self-system theory (Skinner & Belmont, 1993). Each of these frameworks posits that teachers, like parents, interact with children in ways that are more or less responsive, warm, and controlling. Findings are consistent across studies; when teachers respond to students in ways that are responsive to student needs, are emotionally warm, and provide for student autonomy, students tend not only to feel more motivated in the classroom, but also to achieve at higher rates. Attachment frameworks further add to our understanding of the teacher relationship by arguing that, within the context of the parent relationship, children develop generalized beliefs and feelings of emotional security that they use to interpret their other, non-parental social relationships (Davis, 2003). Findings from attachment studies suggest that students bring to the classroom prior ways of interacting with their teachers that may reflect their previous adult relationships and contribute to the quality of a given teacher-child relationship. In their review of the literature, McGrath and

Bergen (2015) similarly found children who have, in the past, experienced positive relationships with teachers tend to recapitulate supportive relationships with teachers and experience benefits to learning and motivation.

Roorda et al. (2011) developed a logic model that synthesized across these four frameworks. Their meta-analyses revealed that positive and negative elements of teacher-relationship quality make independent contributions to children's engagement and achievement in school. They also discovered specific child attributes (i.e. age of child, gender, and whether the child might be "at risk" for school failure based on low-income status, learning exceptionalities, or status as an ethnic minority) (see also Quin, 2017) and teacher attributes (gender, ethnicity, experience) made independent contributions to predicting relationship quality. Subsequent longitudinal research suggests these two dimensions may develop differently over the course of an academic year (Gelbach, Brinkworth, & Harris, 2012) and throughout a child's academic career (Hughes, 2011; Maulana, Opdenakker, & Bosker, 2013; Spilt & Hughes, 2015).

Understanding dynamics of teacher-child interactions

Research teams outside the United States have tended to take a communications theory approach to examining teacher-student relationships. For over 25 years, Wubbels and colleagues (see Wubbels, Brekelmans, den Brok, & van Tartwijk, 2006 for review) define communication as broadly as possible, to encompass "every behavior that someone displays in the presence of someone else ... [this perspective] assumes that one cannot not communicate ... whatever a person's intentions are, the others will infer meaning from [their] behavior" (p. 1162). Their model is particularly helpful for understanding the process by which teacher actions (and inactions) come to imbue meaning for students independently of a teacher's intent. In their model, interpersonal communication can be described by two dimensions: dominance-submission (or influence) and opposition-cooperation (or proximity). The influence dimension describes who controls the communication. When teachers are directive and in control of the communication, they are said to be displaying dominant behavior. The proximity dimension describes the tone of the communication. When teachers use a tone of patience and understanding, even if they are issuing a directive, they are said to be displaying a cooperative behavior. From these two dimensions Wubbels and colleagues observed eight types of teacher communication behaviors. They argue that each type of communication behavior can play an important role in a teacher's repertoire of interpersonal and relationship building skills: "Teachers can exhibit acceptable behavior in each sector. In the course of a day, or a week, most teachers will encounter classroom situations in which it is appropriate to be dissatisfied, or uncertain, or admonishing ... one of the fundamental ideas ... is that communication behaviors continually change. Communication *styles* [however] emerge only after a great many behaviors have occurred and been observed" (Wubbels, Levy, & Brekelmans, 1997, p. 83).

Wubbels and colleagues have made several important contributions to the field of teacher-student interaction research. Specifically, their research program has identified the critical relation that dominant behaviors play in improving student learning outcomes such as attitude, achievement, and regulation of learning behaviors. The trend in their studies is that the more dominant the teacher, the more her students achieve. With that said, the more cooperative the teacher, the more positive attitudes her students will have. "These results create a dilemma . . . . If teachers want students to be both high-achieving and supportive, they may find themselves pulling in two directions: strictness correlates well with high achievement, while flexibility relates to positive attitudes" (Wubbels et al., 1997 p. 84). The amount of variance explained by the two dimensions, however, tends to vary by teaching context with each dimension making separate but distinctive contributions to both cognitive and motivational outcomes.

As classrooms become increasingly diverse, researchers have become interested in understanding the sources of teachers' differential relationship behaviors: that is, the ways teachers enact nonconscious behaviors when developing relationships with a group of students in their classrooms (Thijs, Westhof, & Koomen, 2012; den Brok, Wubbels, van Tartwijk, & Veldman, 2010; Quin, 2017). These studies suggest students from historically marginalized communities may differentially interpret teachers' displays of influence and proximity. Across several studies, den Brok and colleagues suggest the amount of cultural diversity in the class might also contribute to students' perceptions of teacher-communication style. Levy, Wubbels, Brekelmans, and Morganfield (1997) found "the greater the number of cultural backgrounds in a class, the more dominant and cooperative the perception of the teacher" (p. 45). The greater the percentage of US-born students in the class, the more the students tended to perceive the teacher as submissive; den Brok, Levy, Wubbels, and Roderiguez (2003) also found students' language at home was significantly related to their perceptions of teachers' "understanding" behaviors. Students who spoke primarily Spanish at home tended to perceive more understanding from their teachers than their Asian American or African American peers. Students born outside the United States perceived their teachers to be more admonishing and dissatisfied. Levy, den Brok, Wubbels, and Brekelmans (2002) also found the perception of teacher behavior varied as a function of students' gender and ethnicity, with African American males among the least likely to perceive leadership behaviors and helpful/friendly behaviors from their teachers.

Increasingly, methodological technologies allow researchers to delve deeper into examining how real-time communication exchanges develop over time into a climate of classroom communication (Opdenakker, Maulana, & den Brok, 2012; Pennings at al., 2014; Spilt & Hughes, 2015). Drawing from dynamic systems theory, Pennings and colleagues (2014) were able to observe relationships characterized by a great deal of variability in the kinds of communications between a teacher and students, with others characterized by entropy in relationship quality. Few studies, however, have examined the online decisions teachers make to either modify their communication in ways to improve or to emotionally detach from relationships that are challenging. In 2010, Newberry explored relationship development across an academic year. She identified four distinct phases in relationship development: appraisal, agreement, testing, and planning. These phases represented that emotional work teachers did to get to know their students at the beginning of the year; to establish expectations, routine, and patterns of interactions; to respond to students' attempts to test classroom limits and relational boundaries; and ultimately to reflect throughout the year on the quality of their relationships with each child.

Summary and recommendations

Findings from across these studies suggest *how* teachers exert influence in their classrooms is critically important. Work by Middleton and Midgley (2002) suggests that when teachers adopt the dominant role as an instructional leader, they can exert different types of "press" on their students to engage with academic work. Middleton conceptualizes academic press as the enactment of teacher beliefs, motives, and values regarding their subject matter, teaching, and learning. This concept of the "press" of a context is not new to the field of child development (see also Davis, 2006). Press can be direct through the teacher's interactions with students or indirect through the climate they create around learning in their classrooms. Press communicates not only a type of intensity in the relationship but, depending on the kind of press, can connote the quality of influence displays students perceive from their teachers. They identified three types of academic presses: press for understanding, press for performance, and press for competition. For example, when teachers press their students for understanding, they implicitly communicate to students their confidence in students' abilities to master content and their perception that students can be successful pursuing that type of career. Consistent across the field of motivation are findings that students are more engaged with academic content when they perceive their teachers are focused on understanding.

As teachers, we need to remember the students in our class are all striving to meet their own fundamental needs to belong, to feel competent, and to feel in control. Relationships that support them in meeting these needs tend to complement our overarching educational goals: to engage them and support their learning and achievement. Developing relationships with children can be complicated. They come to our classrooms with relational baggage they brought from their past relationships. While those past relationships are out of our control, this baggage represents a lens for interpreting their interactions with us.

The work by Wubbels and colleagues reminds us, however, that our real-time daily interactions with students are within our control. Their work offers us a lens for evaluating the messages we send to our students. We can begin by evaluating the ways in which we attempt to cultivate a sense of interpersonal warmth with our students. We can monitor our proximity behaviors: are we seeking eye contact, and have we "checked in" with each and every student in the class; are we monitoring the levels of pleasant and unpleasant emotions we express; and do our verbal and nonverbal messages align? We must also evaluate the methods we use to influence students to engage in the tasks we design. When interacting with students, what messages do we send about authority and control? As with proximity behaviors, we can monitor the messages we send that press students toward understanding, performance, or competition. And we can work to send messages that emphasize the importance of mastering material.

Simple measures to videotape our instruction and to journal students' responses to our behavior can provide powerful insights into not only the emotional climate we are creating in our classrooms (via public interactions), but also the differential ways in which we interact with specific children. Newberry's (2010) work also reminds us that relationships are dynamic and can be characterized by different phases of appraisal, reflection, and response, and we need to think of our relationships not only in "real time," but also in "developmental time" (Pennings at al., 2014). How do we bring to consciousness the factors that impede our relationships with specific children? How do we avoid detaching from emotionally challenging relationships? As the language, ethnic, and socioeconomic status of students continues to diverge from the background of many teachers, we can make special efforts to gain the knowledge about our students that allows for mutual respect and appropriate choices in instruction.

References

Cornelius-White, J. (2008). Learner-centered student-teacher relationships are effective: A meta- analysis. *Review of Educational Research, 77,* 113–143.

Davis, H. A. (2003). Conceptualizing the role of student-teacher relationships on children's social and cognitive development. *Educational Psychologist, 38,* 207–234.

Davis, H. A. (2006). Exploring the contexts of relationship quality between middle school students and teachers. *The Elementary School Journal: Special Issue on the Interpersonal Contexts of Motivation and Learning, 106,* 193–223.

den Brok, P., Levy, J., Wubbels, T., & Roderiguez, M. (2003). Cultural influences on students' perceptions of videotaped lessons. *International Journal of Intercultural Relations, 27,* 355–374.

den Brok, P., Wubbels, T., van Tartwijk, J., & Veldman, I. (2010). The differential effect of the teacher-student interpersonal relationship on student outcomes for students with different ethnic backgrounds. *British Journal of Educational Psychology, 80,* 199–221.

Gelbach, H., Brinkworth, M. E., & Harris, A. D. (2012). Changes in teacher-student relationships. *British Journal of Educational Psychology, 82,* 690–704.

Hughes, J. N. (2011). Longitudinal effects of teacher and student perceptions of teacher-student relationship qualities on academic adjustment. *The Elementary School Journal, 112,* 38–60.

Hughes, J. N. (2012). Teacher-student relationships and school adjustment: Progress and remaining challenges. *Attachment & Human Development, 14,* 219–327.

Levy, J., den Brok, P., Wubbels, T., & Brekelmans, M. (2002). Students' perceptions of interpersonal aspects of the learning environment. *Learning Environments Research, 6,* 5–36.

Levy, J., Wubbels, T., Brekelmans, M., & Morganfield, B. (1997). Language and cultural factors in students' perceptions of teacher communication style. *International Journal of Intercultural Relations, 21*, 29–56.

Maulana, R., Opdenakker, M. C., & Bosker, R. (2013). Teacher-student interpersonal relationships do change and affect academic motivation: A multilevel growth curve modeling. *British Journal of Educational Psychology, 84*, 459–482.

McGrath, K. F., & Van Bergen, P. (2015). Who, when, why and to what end? Students at risk of negative student-teacher relationships and their outcomes. *Educational Research Review, 14*, 1–17.

Middleton, M. J., & Midgley, C. (2002). Beyond motivation: Middle school students' perceptions of press for understanding in math. *Contemporary Educational Psychology, 27*, 373–391.

Newberry, M. (2010). Identified phases in the building and maintaining of positive teacher–student relationships. *Teaching and Teacher Education, 26*, 1695–1703.

Opdenakker, M. C., Maulana, R., & den Brok, P. (2012). Teacher-student interpersonal relationships and academic motivation within one school year: Developmental changes and linkage. *School Effectiveness and School Improvement, 23*, 95–119

Pennings, H. J. M. van Tartwick, J, Wubbles, T., Claessens, L. C. A., van der Want, A. C., Brekelmans, M. (2014). Real-time teacher-student interactions: A dynamic systems approach. *Teaching and Teacher Education, 37*, 183–193.

Pianta, R. C. (1999). *Enhancing relationships between children and teachers*. Washington, DC: American Psychological Association.

Quin, D. (2017). Longitudinal and contextual associations between teacher-student relationships and student engagement: A systematic review. *Review of Educational Research, 87*, 345–387.

Reeve, J. (2006). Teachers as facilitators: What autonomy-supportive teachers do and why their students benefit. *Elementary School Journal, 106*, 225–236.

Roorda, D. L., Koomen, H. M. Y., Split, J. L., & Oort, F. J. (2011). The influence of affective teacher-student relationships on students' school engagement and achievement: A meta-analytic approach. *Review of Educational Research, 81*, 493–529.

Skinner, E. A., & Belmont, M. J. (1993). Motivation in the classroom: Reciprocal effects of teacher behavior and student engagement across the school year. *Journal of Educational Psychology, 85*, 571–581.

Spilt, J. L., & Hughes, J. N. (2015). African American children at risk of increasingly conflicted teacher-student relationships in elementary school. *School Psychology Review, 2015, 44*, 306–344.

Thijs, J., Westhof, S., & Koomen, H. (2012). Ethnic incongruence and the student-teacher relationship: The perspective of ethnic majority teachers. *Journal of School Psychology, 50*, 257–273.

Walker, J. (2008). Looking at teacher practices through the lens of parenting style. *Journal of Experimental Education, 76*, 218–240.

Wentzel, K. R. (2009). Students' relationships with teachers as motivational contexts. In K. R. Wentzel & A. Wigfield (Eds.), *Handbook of motivation* (pp. 301–322). New York, NY: Routledge.

Woolfolk Hoy, A. E., & Davis, H. A. (2005). Teacher self-efficacy and its influence on adolescent achievement. In T. Urdan & M. F. Pajares (Eds.), *Adolescence and education: Vol. 5. Self-efficacy beliefs during adolescence* (pp. 117–137). Greenwich, CT: Information Age.

Wubbels, T., Brekelmans, M., den Brok, P., & van Tartwijk, J. (2006). Interpersonal perspective on classroom management in secondary classrooms in the Netherlands. In C. M. Evertson & C. S. Weinstein (Eds.), *Handbook of classroom management: Research, practice, and contemporary issues* (pp. 1161–1191). Mahwah, NJ: Erlbaum.

Wubbels, T., Levy, J., & Brekelmans, M. (1997). Paying attention to relationships. *Educational Leadership, 54*, 82–86.

5.7

Classroom management and student achievement

H. Jerome Freiberg

Introduction

Classroom management is the gatekeeper of learning and is framed by social, cultural, instructional, and organizational contexts. It provides teachers and students with the opportunity to participate and build a positive framework of interpersonal and academic interactions. As teaching, learning, and society in general become more complex, classroom management provides a source to navigate this complexity. The term is often used synonymously with *student behavior* and *discipline* and spans a continuum from compliance and obedience to student reflection and self-discipline. Student achievement may be one result of classroom management because effective management enables the teaching and learning process within the unique educational social context. Achievement outcomes range from high-stakes national, regional, and local testing to end-of-year examinations to course content grades to formal and informal formative and summative assessments. The connection between classroom management and student achievement is undergoing increased global attention as educators, parents, and policy makers seek ways to improve student engagement and academic success.

The study of classroom management has a trend line stretching across multiple decades and nations. In the United States, the idea of classroom management was often discussed during the 20th century. Educators such as Bagley (*Classroom Management*, 1907), Perry (*The Management of a City School*, 1908), and Breed (*Classroom Organization and Management*, 1933) proffered some of the earliest ideas on the ability of classroom management to increase student success, reduce financial costs, and improve test scores. Public opinion polls of education in the United States conducted by the Gallup Organization and reported by *Phi Delta Kappan* have consistently ranked "school discipline" in the top three concerns from the late 1960s until the present; often, it is the primary educational concern for parents and the public.

Research evidence

Studies about the management and organization of classrooms became more specialized in the second half of the 20th century as specific elements of the learning process were analyzed. Behaviorist-based or Skinnerian research in the 1950s and 1960s explored the ability of a rewards and punishment (stimulus/response) system to trigger predictable positive responses. Ecological studies, beginning in the late 1950s, treated classrooms as ecological systems where settings and activities can be altered to create a more conducive environment for learning (as cited by Brophy, 2006). Key areas of research include teacher awareness, "withitness," multitasking, lesson engagement, student engagement, and assignment variability. Process-outcome (product) studies of the 1960s and 1970s examined the relationship between classroom processes and student outcomes, particularly as related to student achievement gains (Emmer & Evertson, 1982).

Wang, Haertel, and Walberg (1993) considered the influence of educational, psychological, and social factors on general learning. Their meta-analysis collected data from over 11,000 unique relations and found that proximal variables such as psychological, instructional, and home influence forces are more impactful than outlier variables such as demographics, policy, and organizational factors. Their analysis identified classroom management as the most important of five factors influencing school learning and student achievement. A meta-analysis of 54 studies (2003–2013) by Korpershoek, Harms, Boer, Kuijk, and Doolaard (2016) had similar findings: effective classroom management programs/strategies significantly increase students' academic achievement and decrease problem behaviors.

Person-centered classroom studies (those that examine teacher/student interpersonal interactions) turned attention toward the direct social and emotional needs of individual students and teachers and how interpersonal relationships can improve student achievement. Cornelius-White (2007) conducted a far-reaching meta-analysis beginning in the 1940s through 2004 and concluded that learner- and person-centered classrooms facilitate higher achievement and positive learning environments (creativity/critical thinking; math/verbal achievement; student participation; student satisfaction/self-esteem; and reduction in absences, disruptive behavior, and dropouts) with stronger teacher-student relationships than teacher-centered or traditional classrooms. Skiba et al.'s 2016 review of the literature continues this trend of findings: sound classroom management is linked to greater on-task behavior, fewer disruptions, and increased student achievement.

Brophy noted in examining the history of classroom management research that a consensus was being reached in the 1980s on interconnectedness between classroom management and student learning and achievement. However, researchers continued exploring unique and particular aspects of student learning (e.g., gender, social-constructivist, sociocultural, and grade-level differences) (Brophy, 2006). By the 1990s, the emphasis on school reform rose to the center of attention and intensified interest in teacher development and student achievement. Researchers at the start of the 21st century revisited the importance of classrooms in the broader milieu. Even though not all agree on the appropriateness or practicality of individual investigations and research findings, studies generally reach a consensus on the significance and potential positive impacts of classroom management. Among those are increased instruction time, increased student achievement, improved learning environments, teacher preparation, and student-teacher connectedness (Freiberg & Oviatt, 2018).

In a series of three studies that spanned two decades, which are described next, strong evidence demonstrates that classroom management (particularly programs or approaches that engage students in the management of the classroom) can produce statistically and educationally significant achievement gains as measured by national and state assessments for students from low-income and minority communities. The implications of matching person-centered (prosocial) management approaches with an active learning curriculum provide a comprehensive view of classroom management's role in student achievement. In the area of student learning, Freiberg, Prokosch, Tresister, and Stein (1990) found that the prosocial management program Consistency Management & Cooperative Discipline (CMCD) improved student performance on the Texas Education Assessment of Minimal Skills (TEAMS) against control schools ($d = 0.51$) and increased passing rates by 17% compared to the 2% decrease in nonprogram schools. Freiberg, Connell, and Lorentz (2001) studied the same prosocial program's impact on mathematics and found greater gains in student achievement than the math-based curriculum implemented singularly with significantly greater achievement gains ($d = 0.33$) against the four comparison schools with the same mathematics curriculum. Freiberg, Huzinec, and Templeton (2009) provided additional evidence of increased student achievement as students in classroom management schools outperformed control students in both reading (64th percentile) and mathematics (67th percentile) assessments in a two-year period compared to control students (50th percentile in both categories). Advances in classroom management can create a significant pathway to student achievement by emphasizing effective and efficient use of instructional time, the building of student self-discipline and student engagement in the operations of the classroom and enabling greater student involvement in more complex academic learning.

Links between classroom management strategies and overall school environment, including student and staff satisfaction, discipline problems, and levels of active learning, are further evidenced by Opuni's (2006) studies of the prosocial CMCD management program over multiple years in different regions. His study revealed improvement in teacher-student relationships (with the majority rising above national mean averages), significant declines in student referrals, and students significantly outperforming comparison cohorts in math and reading standardized test scores. Also crucial was the increase in available instructional time created as a result of decreased attention spent on classroom disruptions. With more instructional time, students showed increased academic performance and greater levels of learning. Student engagement can also be linked to classroom management: teachers who use evidence-based classroom management practices at average to high levels are more likely to have engaged students, increasing the likelihood that students are learning (Gage, Scott, Hirn, & MacSuga-Gage, 2018).

The international applications of classroom management are also gaining increased attention throughout Europe, Asia, and the Middle East. In northern Italy, Chiari (1994) found that classrooms with management systems are more conducive to student learning because students individually assume responsibility for their learning and develop a sense of school connectedness. When students display ownership of the environment, the social, emotional, and learning climates are all improved, resulting in increased higher-order cognitive processes. Harwood (2007) in England continued with this focus, finding that the classroom management program CMCD, implemented in the London Challenge schools, was indeed a powerful tool in transforming, not just managing, both positive and negative student behavior. A decrease in student expulsions coupled with increased academic attainment validated its role in linking classroom management and student achievement. Creemers (1994) conducted educational systems studies that included the Dutch Educational Priority Policy, which sought an increase in effective instruction and effective schools, particularly within lower-income student groups. Findings indicate that effective learning environments are universally most valuable to student achievement and that consistency, achieved in part through classroom management, is a main environmental component. If teachers establish consistent, effective classrooms, students are more apt to demonstrate higher academic attainment.

There is much support for linking student-centered classroom management and increased student achievement, both academically and socially. Lewis, Romi, Katz, and Qui (2008) studied educational institutions in Australia, China, and Israel and identified a connection between student participation in maintaining classroom discipline and a corresponding decrease in distractions and disciplinary issues. Ben-Peretz, Eilam, and Yankelevitch (2006) provided a synthesis of classroom management research undertaken across grade levels in multicultural and heterogeneous classrooms in present-day Israel. Their research highlighted the shift in classroom emphasis toward teacher autonomy and student-oriented teaching. In Turkey, new behavioral teaching programs are impacting perspectives of classroom management – allowing teachers to be successful due to increased interpersonal student interactions (among other factors) (Ari, Tuncer, & Demir, 2016). Previous studies on the impact of classroom learning environments in Asia also exhibit increased attention to classroom environments, including classroom management and the ability to move away from traditional classrooms into more nuanced settings that grant students the ability to become engaged, participatory learners working collaboratively both inside and outside the formal classroom setting (Chionh & Fraser, 2009; Nishioka, 2006).

Summary and recommendations

With the number of international and national studies increasing, classroom management programs for schools have proliferated, offering different approaches to improving classroom cultures. Freiberg and Lapointe (2006) completed a study utilizing the reviews of 14 external groups and organizations that evaluated over 800 discipline, classroom management, and other behavioral intervention programs, identifying "research-based" and "research-tested" programs that prevent or reduce classroom discipline problems as well as improve student achievement. They found few classroom management programs have external, third-party evaluations or longitudinal studies to validate their effectiveness, complicating the already-difficult decision of selecting which program will lead to the greatest post-implementation improvements. However, of all programs, only a few reported gains in student achievement. As countries see the need to educate youth for a more complex society and world, classroom management models that have proved successful at improving student achievement in a range of settings need to be brought to the table of educational transformation. A follow-up of the 2006 study is in progress, with initial trends showing growth in classroom management prevention programs over intervention programs and greater numbers of social emotional learning (SEL) classroom management programs (Freiberg & Oviatt, 2018).

Their exact manifestation will vary, whether ecological, prosocial, or person centered, but it is clear that even the best attempts at curricular improvements will be needlessly hampered without a corresponding plan for managing the day-to-day operations of any school or classroom.

References

Ari, E., Tuncer, B. K., & Demir, M. K. (2016). Primary school teachers' view on constructive classroom management. *International Electronic Journal of Elementary Education, 8*(3), 363–378.

Bagley, W. C. (1907). *Classroom management: Its principles and techniques.* New York, NY: Palgrave Macmillan.

Ben-Peretz, M., Eilam, B., & Yankelevitch, E. (2006). Classroom management in Israel: Multicultural classrooms in an immigrant country. In C. M Evertson & C. S. Weinstein (Eds.), *Handbook of classroom management: Research, practice, and contemporary issues* (pp. 1121–1140). Mahwah, NJ: Erlbaum.

Breed, F. (1933). *Classroom organization and management.* Yonkers-on-Hudson, NY: World Book Co.

Brophy, J. (2006). History of research on classroom management. In C. M. Evertson & C. S. Weinstein (Eds.), *Handbook of classroom management: Research, practice, and contemporary issues* (pp. 17–43). Mahwah, NJ: Erlbaum.

Chiari, G. (1994). *Climi di classe e apprendimento* [Class and learning climates]. Milan, Italy: FrancoAngeli.

Chionh, Y. H., & Fraser, B. J. (2009). Classroom environment, achievement, attitudes and self-esteem in geography and mathematics in Singapore. *International Research in Geographical and Environmental Education, 18*(1), 29–44.

Cornelius-White, J. (2007). Learner-centered teacher-student relationships are effective: A meta-analysis. *Review of Educational Research, 77*(1), 113–143.

Creemers, B. (1994). *The effective classroom*. London: Cassell.

Emmer, E. T., & Evertson, C. M. (1982). Effective classroom management at the beginning of the school year in junior high school classes. *Journal of Educational Psychology, 74*, 485–498.

Freiberg, H. J., Connell, M. L., & Lorentz, J. (2001). Effects of consistency management on student mathematics achievement in seven chapter 1 elementary schools. *Journal of Education for Students Placed at Risk, 6*(3), 249–270.

Freiberg, H. J., Huzinec, C., & Templeton, S. M. (2009). Classroom management: A pathway to student achievement. *Elementary School Journal, 110*(1), 64–80.

Freiberg, H. J., & Lapointe, J. M. (2006). Research-based programs for preventing and solving discipline problems. In C. M. Evertson & C. S. Weinstein (Eds.), *Handbook of classroom management: Research, practice, and contemporary issues* (pp. 735–786). Mahwah, NJ: Erlbaum.

Freiberg, H. J., & Oviatt, D. (2018, April 13). *Classroom management meta-review: Continuation of research-based programs for preventing and solving discipline problems*. Paper presented at American Educational Research Association Annual Meeting, New York, NY.

Freiberg, H. J., Prokosch, N., Tresister, E. S., & Stein, T. (1990). Turning around five at-risk elementary schools. *Journal of School Effectiveness and School Improvement, 1*(1), 5–25.

Gage, N. A., Scott, T., Hirn, R., & MacSuga-Gage, A. S. (2018). The relationship between teachers' implementation of classroom management practices and student behavior in elementary school. *Behavioral Disorders, 43*(2), 302–315.

Harwood, P. (2007). *A review of consistency management & cooperative discipline in the UK*. London Challenge Behaviour Adviser. Unpublished evaluation submitted to the London Challenge, Dept. for Education and Skills, London, England.

Korpershoek, H., Harms, T., Boer, H. D., Kuijk, M. V., & Doolaard, S. (2016). A meta-analysis of the effects of classroom management strategies and classroom management programs on students' academic, behavioral, emotional, and motivational outcomes. *Review of Educational Research, 86*(3), 643–680. doi:10.3102/0034654315626799

Lewis, R., Romi, S., Katz, Y. J., & Qui, X. (2008). Students' reaction to classroom discipline in Australia, Israel, and China. *Teaching and Teacher Education, 24*(3), 715–724.

Nishioka, K. (2006). Classroom management in post-war Japan. In C. M. Evertson & C. S. Weinstein (Eds.), *Handbook of classroom management: Research, practice, and contemporary issues* (pp. 1215–1237). Mahwah, NJ: Lawrence Erlbaum Associates.

Opuni, K. A. (2006). *The effectiveness of the consistency management & cooperative discipline (CMCD) model as a student empowerment and achievement enhancer: The experiences of two K-12 inner-city school systems*. Paper presented at the 4th Annual Hawaii International Conference of Education, Honolulu, Hawaii.

Perry, A. (1908). *The management of a city school*. New York, NY: Palgrave Macmillan.

Skiba, R., Ormiston, H., Martinez, S., & Cummings, J. (2016). Teaching the social curriculum: Classroom management as behavioral instruction. *Theory into Practice, 55*(2), 120–128. doi:10.1080/00405841.2016.1148990

Wang, M. C., Haertel, G. D., & Walberg, H. J. (1993). Toward a knowledge base for school learning. *Review of Educational Research, 63*, 249–294.

5.8

Academic motivation and achievement in classrooms

Lynley H. Anderman and Robin Sayers

Introduction

Motivation is one of the processes that initiates and directs behavior. In the classroom, students' academic motivation explains their willingness and promptness in beginning academic tasks and the amount of effort they put forth (initiation and investment). Motivation also explains students' persistence with academic work in the face of obstacles and distractions and their selection of various tasks or courses of study.

Current research on students' motivation represents a wide range of theoretical perspectives, with many different aspects of motivation studied. Generally, however, research focuses on students' cognitions – perceptions, thoughts, and beliefs – that shape and influence their engagement. These can include, for example, students' perceptions of how interesting (e.g., Ainley, Hidi, & Berndorff, 2002), important, or useful (Eccles, 1983) they find a specific subject or activity; how competent and confident they feel to perform a task satisfactorily (Bandura, 1997; Pajares, 1996); their beliefs about the reasons for their own successes and difficulties (Weiner, 1985); and the degree to which they are focused on the goal of understanding and mastering content versus a focus on the external indicators of success, such as grades and rewards (Ames, 1992). Although all these beliefs and thought processes are linked in some way to students' learning and achievement, the current chapter will discuss three bodies of research in which effects on achievement have been a particular focus of attention: students' expectancies of success and sense of efficacy (e.g., Wigfield, 1994), students' sense of autonomy and perceptions of autonomy support (e.g., Reeve, 2002), and their beliefs about the nature of ability (e.g., Yeager & Dweck, 2012).

Research findings

Students' expectancy beliefs

Of all motivation-related cognitions that have been studied, those related to students' perceptions of their competence, expectancies of success, and sense of efficacy have proven to be particularly robust predictors of achievement. Some researchers examine expectancies of success at the level of a particular class setting (e.g., "How well do you expect to do in your math/English class this year?" Wigfield & Eccles, 2000, p. 70), whereas others focus on much more specific expectancy beliefs (typically referred to as efficacy beliefs) in reference to a particular task or type of task (e.g., Bandura, 1997; Pajares, 1996).

In terms of students' expectancies of success in specific classes, there is considerable evidence from several large-scale studies that students' expectancies are positively related to their course-specific achievement. These studies utilize students' self-reported expectancies of success from large-scale surveys to predict achievement, usually measured by teacher-assigned grades (Eccles, 1983; Wigfield, 1994). Much of this work has focused on understanding students' performance in math classes, although similar findings have also been reported in other academic domains. Although much of the research in this area is cross-sectional in design, these effects also have been demonstrated longitudinally, even over several years of schooling (Wigfield, 1994). For a review of this research, see Wigfield and Eccles (2000). Generally, adolescents' expectancies show stronger associations with their achievement than do those of younger students. This pattern probably reflects older students' increased experience with schooling and greater awareness of their past performance, which lead to more stability in their self-evaluations. Younger children's self-reported expectancies of success tend to be less stable and less reliably associated with later achievement.

In contrast to a general expectation that one will do well in a particular class, the sense of self-efficacy is more narrowly defined. Efficacy refers to an individuals' judgments of their own skills for performing specific actions, solving particular types of problems, or achieving a desired outcome. Students with a strong sense of efficacy have been shown to be more willing to take on and persist with challenging tasks, to expend more effort, and to demonstrate greater academic performance. Furthermore, the positive effects of high efficacy have been demonstrated across a range of age groups and nationalities (e.g., Bong, 2001; Multon, Brown, & Lent, 1991; Pintrich & De Groot, 1990). In a meta-analysis, Multon et al. reported an effect size of .38 for the relation between students' self-efficacy beliefs and academic performance. In other words, across a range of student ages and settings, efficacy beliefs accounted for approximately 14% of the variance in academic performance, most typically measured using tests of basic skills. The effect size was significantly smaller for elementary-aged students than for those in high school or college. Thus, as with the more general expectancy beliefs discussed earlier, young children's self-judgments are less reliable predictors of their achievement than is true for older students.

In the classroom, students' sense of self-efficacy for various tasks and types of problems can be supported through practices that help students recognize their own progress and learning. For example, teaching students to set short-term, achievable goals and to evaluate and record their own progress toward those goals can help build a sense of efficacy. In addition, feedback that links students' successes to a combination of effort and ability (as opposed to other causes, such as good luck or teacher kindness) also has been shown to enhance students' self-efficacy (see Schunk & Zimmerman, 2006, for a review).

Sense of autonomy and autonomy support

A number of studies have investigated the extent to which students experience a sense of autonomy and self-direction while engaging in academic tasks and their successful learning and performance of those tasks. In this research, the focus is not so much on the quantity of students' motivation (i.e., how motivated is this student?) as on the quality or type of motivation students experience. That is, students are assumed to benefit from particular types of motivation – autonomous, self-directed reasons for engaging – rather than motivation based on external incentives, demands, rewards, and constraints (Ryan & Deci, 2000). In this theory, autonomy is defined as "self-governance" and represents a continuum that ranges from having one's behavior regulated completely by external forces to complete self-regulation, where one's behaviors are personally valued and consistent with one's beliefs (Ryan & Deci, 2006, p. 1562). In the classroom, this sense of autonomy would manifest itself in students' sense that they engage in tasks and activities that reflect their personal values and sense of themselves as individuals, rather than because of external influences. In terms of classroom achievement, a particularly important variable is students' perception that their teachers are autonomy supportive: that they emphasize self-direction and the pursuit of interests, rather than emphasizing rewards, punishments, or coercion to promote students' engagement in learning-related behaviors.

Several studies have demonstrated correlational associations between students' perceptions of autonomy support in their classes, often measured using surveys, and indicators of student achievement (see Guay, Ratelle, & Chanal, 2008, for a review). For example, Black and Deci (2000) measured college students' perceptions of autonomy support in a chemistry course. These perceptions were associated with higher exam scores and overall course grades, particularly for those students who reported low levels of self-direction for learning chemistry at the beginning of the course. In addition, a number of studies have demonstrated effects using experimental and quasi-experimental approaches. Grolnick and Ryan (1987) randomly assigned fifth-grade students to different groups for reading instruction in a learning laboratory. Students were tested on their rote and conceptual recall of the story they had read. Students who received noncontrolling instruction (de-emphasizing external contingencies for learning) demonstrated greater interest and conceptual learning than did those who received controlling instruction (i.e., providing an incentive or pressure for learning). This difference was not evident, however, in students' immediate rote recall of the story, although those who received controlling instruction demonstrated greater deterioration in their recall at a one-week follow-up. Thus, these findings suggest that experiencing a greater degree of autonomy in the instructional setting particularly supported students' comprehension and higher-order learning of material more than surface and short-term memorization. A similar pattern of findings has been reported in other studies with a variety of student populations, including college students' performance on analytic reasoning problems (Boggiano, Flink, Shields, Seelbach, & Barrett, 1993), fourth-grade students' solving of anagrams and spatial relationship problems (Flink, Boggiano & Barrett, 1990), and Belgian early adolescents' test scores in a health and nutrition class (Vansteenkiste, Simons, Lens, Soenens, & Matos, 2005).

Given the apparent importance of students' perceptions of autonomy support from teachers, some researchers have focused on the types of instructional practices that promote this perception. Teacher practices such as encouraging students to solve problems in their own way, focusing on the quality of students' performance, acknowledging students' feelings, and spending more time listening than talking have been identified as elements of autonomy-supportive instruction. In contrast, requiring students to solve problems in a particular way, the use of directive and/or commanding statements, and using coercive techniques including rewards and punishments are elements of a controlling teaching style (Black & Deci, 2000; Reeve, 2002).

Students' mind-set beliefs

Recently, there has been an increase in research investigating the impact of students' mind-set beliefs on their motivation, learning, and academic achievement. This research suggests that individuals vary in believing either that intelligence is a fixed, unchangeable trait (an entity theory or fixed mind-set) or that it is malleable and, thus, can be developed (an incremental theory or growth mind-set) (Dweck & Leggett, 1988). Research has examined the impact of students' mind-sets on achievement outcomes, how they form, and what can be done to alter them.

Compared to students with a fixed mind-set, those with a growth mind-set are more likely to see failure as providing an opportunity for growth, persist in the face of challenges, and believe in the importance of effort (e.g., Yeager & Dweck, 2012). Perhaps not surprisingly, then, having a growth mind-set has been shown to predict better academic performance. Blackwell, Trzesniewski, and Dweck (2007) found that as students transitioned to junior high school, their mind-sets were critical in decreasing grade decline and became a significant predictor of math achievement, even after controlling for prior achievement. Another study found that, for students in first and second grade, mind-set views in the fall were predictive of spring math achievement, again while controlling for prior achievement (Park, Gunderson, Tsukayama, Levine, & Beilock, 2016). In other words, across grade levels, students who believed that abilities could improve, and in the importance of effort and persistence, actually did improve more than their peers who saw ability as unchangeable.

Given the importance of these beliefs, more recent research has focused on understanding how a growth mind-set is developed and maintained. In terms of the development of mind-sets, experimental research has begun to show that short-term interventions using in-class instruction or online programs are effective in promoting a growth mind-set in students (Blackwell et al., 2007; Yeager, Schneider, Brien, & Flint, 2016). For example, Blackwell et al. showed that when students participated in a 25-minute session on brain development once a week for eight weeks at the beginning of seventh grade, they were able to eliminate the grade decline commonly seen as students transition to middle school. Additionally, while research has repeatedly shown that teachers' and parents' mind-sets do not directly influence students' beliefs, there is a link between teachers' instructional practices and the mind-sets that students develop. Park et al. (2016) found that, in first- and second-grade math, mastery-oriented instructional practices (i.e., giving a wide range of assignments matched to students' skill level) were linked to students' mind-sets and subsequent math achievement. Additionally, Sun (2015) showed that, in middle school, using process-focused teaching and mixed ability groups, talking about the importance of mistakes, and providing feedback focused on how students engaged in a task rather than the outcome may all be valuable ways to support growth mind-sets.

Summary and recommendations

In summary, students' motivation matters for their academic achievement. Three factors that have been shown to be particularly important in relation to achievement are that students believe they can be successful with the tasks assigned to them, that they perceive some autonomy and self-direction in their activities, and that they believe their abilities can grow and improve. To promote expectancy beliefs in their students, it is important that teachers help students set realistic, appropriately challenging academic goals and monitor their own progress. In terms of supporting students' sense of autonomy, teachers can provide students with choices over things like the topics and procedural aspects of tasks and help students feel ownership of their own learning. This can include supporting students in exploring multiple and unique ways to solve problems and requiring them to defend their strategies and solutions (Stefanou, Perencevich, DiCintio, & Turner, 2004). To promote growth mind-sets, teachers can communicate explicitly to students that improvement stems from effort and practice and that setbacks are an inevitable part of the learning process.

Finally, as noted at the beginning of this chapter, students' expectancies, autonomy, and mind-sets – motivation in general – are not the only or even necessarily the most important influences on achievement outcomes. No combination of positive beliefs will compensate for a lack of necessary skills or content knowledge or for poor-quality instruction. Motivation does, however, have an important role in determining the quantity and quality of students' engagement with learning activities and, thus, indirectly their achievement in classrooms.

References

Ainley, M., Hidi, S., & Berndorff, D. (2002). Interest, learning, and the psychological processes that mediate their relationship. *Journal of Educational Psychology, 94*, 545–561.

Ames, C. (1992). Classrooms: Goals, structures, and student motivation. *Journal of Educational Psychology, 84*, 261–271.

Bandura, A. (1997). *Self-efficacy: The exercise of control*. New York, NY: W. H. Freeman.

Black, A. E., & Deci, E. L. (2000). The effects of instructors' autonomy support and students' autonomous motivation on learning organic chemistry: A self-determination theory perspective. *Science Education, 84*, 740–756.

Blackwell, L. S., Trzesniewski, K. H., & Dweck, C. S. (2007). Implicit theories of intelligence predict achievement across an adolescent transition: A longitudinal study and an intervention. *Child Development, 78*(1), 246–263. https://doi.org/10.1111/j.1467-8624.2007.00995.x

Boggiano, A. K., Flink, C., Shields, A., Seelbach, A., & Barrett, M. (1993). Use of techniques promoting students' self-determination: Effects on students' analytic problem-solving skills. *Motivation and Emotion, 17*, 319–336.

Bong, M. (2001). Role of self-efficacy and task-value in predicting college students' course performance and future enrollment intentions. *Contemporary Educational Psychology, 26*, 553–570.

Dweck, C. S., & Leggett, E. L. (1988). A social cognitive approach to motivation and personality. *Psychological Review, 95*(2), 256–273. https://doi.org/10.1037/0033-295X.95.2.256

Eccles, J. S. (1983). Expectancies, values and academic behaviors. In J. T. Spence (Ed.), *Achievement and achievement motives* (pp. 75–146). San Francisco, CA: Freeman.

Flink, C., Boggiano, A. K., & Barrett, M. (1990). Controlling teaching strategies: Undermining children's self-determination and performance. *Journal of Personality and Social Psychology, 59*, 916–924.

Grolnick, W. S., & Ryan, R. M. (1987). Autonomy in children's learning: An experimental and individual difference investigation. *Journal of Personality and Social Psychology, 52*(5), 890–898.

Guay, F., Ratelle, C. F., & Chanal, J. (2008). Optimal learning in optimal contexts: The role of self-determination in education. *Canadian Psychology, 49*(3), 233–240.

Multon, K. D., Brown, S. D., & Lent, R. W. (1991). Relation of self-efficacy beliefs to academic outcomes: A meta-analytic investigation. *Journal of Counseling Psychology, 38*, 30–38.

Pajares, F. (1996). Self-efficacy beliefs in achievement settings. *Review of Educational Research*, *66*, 543–578.

Park, D., Gunderson, E. A., Tsukayama, E., Levine, S. C., & Beilock, S. L. (2016). Young children's motivational frameworks and math achievement: Relation to teacher-reported instructional practices, but not teacher theory of intelligence. *Journal of Educational Psychology*, *108*, 300–313. https://doi.org/10.1037/edu0000064

Pintrich, P. R., & De Groot, E. V. (1990). Motivational and self-regulated learning components of classroom academic performance. *Journal of Educational Psychology*, *82*, 33–40.

Reeve, J. (2002). Self-determination theory applied to educational settings. In E. L. Deci & R. M. Ryan (Eds.), *Handbook of self-determination research* (pp. 183–203). New York, NY: The University of Rochester Press.

Ryan, R. M., & Deci, E. L. (2000). Self-determination theory and the facilitation of intrinsic motivation, social development, and well-being. *American Psychologist*, *55*, 68–78.

Ryan, R. M., & Deci, E. L. (2006). Self-regulation and the problem of human autonomy: Does psychology need choice, self-determination, and will? *Journal of Personality*, *74*, 1557–1585.

Schunk, D. H., & Zimmerman, B. J. (2006). Competence and control beliefs: Distinguishing the means and ends. In P. A. Alexander & P. H. Winne (Eds.), *Handbook of educational psychology* (2nd ed., pp. 349–367). Mahwah, NJ: Erlbaum.

Stefanou, C. R., Perencevich, K. C., DiCintio, M., & Turner, J. C. (2004). Supporting autonomy in the classroom: Ways teachers encourage student decision making and ownership. *Educational Psychologist*, *39*, 97–110.

Sun, K. L. (2015). *There's no limit: Mathematics teaching for a growth mindset* (Unpublished doctoral dissertation), Stanford University, Stanford, CA.

Vansteenkiste, M., Simons, J., Lens, W., Soenens, B., & Matos, L. (2005). Examining the motivational impact of intrinsic versus extrinsic goal framing and autonomy-supportive versus internally controlling communication style on early adolescents' academic achievement. *Child Development*, *76*, 483–501.

Weiner, B. (1985). An attributional theory of achievement motivation and emotion. *Psychological Review*, *92*, 548–573.

Wigfield, A. (1994). Expectancy-value theory of achievement motivation: A developmental perspective. *Educational Psychology Review*, *6*, 49–78.

Wigfield, A., & Eccles, J. S. (2000). Expectancy-value theory of achievement motivation. *Contemporary Educational Psychology*, *25*, 68–81.

Yeager, D. S., & Dweck, C. S. (2012). Mindsets that promote resilience: When students believe that personal characteristics can be developed. *Educational Psychologist*, *47*(4), 302–314. https://doi.org/10.1080/00461520.2012.722805

Yeager, D. S., Schneider, B., Brien, J. O., & Flint, K. (2016). Using design thinking to improve psychological interventions: The case of the growth mindset during the transition to high school. *Journal of Educational Psychology*, *108*(3), 374–391. https://doi.org/10.1037/edu0000098

5.9 Nontraditional teacher preparation

Belinda G. Gimbert and Ryan Kapa

Introduction

Across the globe, the demand for teachers is rising while the supply continues to wither. In the United States, student enrollments are increasing; pupil-teacher ratios are lowering; and teacher attrition remains high, at 8% annually, with about half of those who leave the teacher workforce having been in the profession for less than five years. Sutcher, Darling-Hammond, and Carver-Thomas (2016) report that a 20% increase in annual teacher demand is probable from 2015 levels, "reaching 316,000 teachers per year by 2025" (p. 2). They claim "two-thirds of leavers depart before retirement age, most because of dissatisfaction with aspects of their teaching conditions" (p. 2). A contributing factor to teacher shortages is the fewer new entrants to teacher preparation programs, a 35% drop in the past decade, which has resulted in fewer newly certified teachers, reported as 23% fewer between 2009 and 2014 (Sutcher et al., 2016). Particularly severe shortfall certification areas include teachers of special education, mathematics, science, and bilingual/English language; these shortages often are located in geographical regions with a disproportionate number of disadvantaged students and challenging teaching conditions.

Demands from the public and practitioners to address chronic shortages in hard-to-staff school districts prompted US legislators to approve policies through statutory provision to diversify options for teacher training routes (Ingersoll, 2004). In response, teacher educators compete to increase the number of program completers through innovative licensure pathways while certifying teachers of quality who can effectively foster the academic achievement of all students. Likewise, in some Western countries (for example, the United Kingdom, Australia, France, Israel, and Germany), shortages of teachers in general or in specific fields impel the growth of teacher training pathways, including alternative or nontraditional routes for teacher certification. In the United States, beginning in the late 1980s, the expansion of alternative (or nontraditional) teacher training continued exponentially into the 21st century. For example, all 50 states and the District of Columbia legislated nontraditional teacher preparation programs (Feistritzer, 2007). These programs are delivered by school districts, educational service agencies, universities, four-year colleges, two-year community colleges, for-profit and nonprofit organizations, and partnerships of these entities. Also included are national programs like Troops to Teachers, which focuses on military personnel moving into teaching positions, and Teach for America (TFA), which recruits new college graduates who did not major in education (Mueller, 2012; Penner, 2013). Alternative teacher training routes prepared 28,846 program completers, which represents 15% of all teacher program completers in AY 2012–2013. As is the case with most educational concepts that become popular over a rather short period, alternate routes to teacher licensure vary markedly from state to state. The proliferation of such programs sustains an age-old controversy surrounding the divergence of training processes required by state and national mandates for traditional teacher preparation. Using student achievement as an outcome measure, researchers studying teacher education programs have aggressively debated the relation between types of teacher training and student performance.

Research evidence

Among those who study teacher education programs and issues related to teacher licensure/certification, the relation between teacher preparation and student performance continues to attract attention. Researchers have applied sophisticated statistical procedures to analyze national and state databases in different countries in order to examine the consequences of teachers' training, whether traditional or alternative, on students' learning outcomes. For example, in the United States, studies have been conducted on the National Assessment of Educational Progress (NAEP), the National Educational Longitudinal Study (NELS), Longitudinal Study of American Youth (LSAY), and Schools and Staffing Surveys (SASS) (Darling-Hammond, Berry, & Thoreson, 2001; Goldhaber & Brewer, 2000; Kane, Rockoff, & Staiger, 2007). More recently, other researchers (Brinkman, 2014; Duke, 2013; Moore, 2012; Mueller, 2012; Ruiz de Castilla, 2018) used state and local school district data to examine the impact of a teacher's preparation pathway on student achievement. Brinkman (2014) reported mixed results of the impact of a teacher's preparation pathway on eighth-grade students' performance in mathematics, reading, science, and social studies. Moore (2012), using data from the Mississippi Subject Area Test (MSAT) scores in Algebra I, Biology I, English II, and US History, found no significant difference in academic outcomes for high school students who were instructed by teachers with traditional and alternate-route certification in the core tested areas of the Mississippi accountability model. Duke (2013) examined the impact of traditional and alternative (non-TFA) certification on student achievement by comparing Virginia Standards of Learning (SOL) end-of-year scores in math and reading for minority students in grades 6 through 8 during 2005–2009. Mathematics scores of minority students taught by alternatively licensed teachers were significantly lower than those of students with traditionally prepared teachers. Further, there was a significant difference in the math scores for gender, where the scores of minority students taught by female teachers with traditional licensure were higher than the scores of students taught by female teachers with alternative licensure. Mueller (2012) assessed how North Carolina's state policies that align with the qualifications of beginning teachers affect achievement by comparing traditionally prepared teachers with alternative-entry teachers, in-state traditionally prepared with out-of-state traditionally prepared teachers, teachers beginning with undergraduate degrees with those beginning with graduate degrees, and teachers prepared at in-state public universities with those prepared at in-state private universities. Using school-fixed effects, Mueller concluded, "Teach For America corps members are more effective than traditionally prepared teachers; other alternative-entry teachers are less effective than traditionally prepared instructors in high school mathematics and science courses; and out-of-state traditionally prepared teachers are less effective than in-state traditionally prepared teachers, especially in elementary subjects where they constitute nearly 40 percent of the workforce" (p. 1). Most recently, Ruiz de Castilla (2018), using data from the Texas state standardized tests, examined the relationships between teacher certification and growth in math and reading achievement and English proficiency among English-learner students. For math, exposure to an alternatively prepared teacher with bilingual certification was associated with the highest growth in grade 4 student achievement. For reading, a teacher with bilingual certification through the traditional route was associated with the highest growth in achievement in grade 4. For English proficiency, a teacher with bilingual certification through the alternative route was associated with the highest growth in English proficiency in grade 5.

International researchers have analyzed data from the French Ministry of Education (Bressoux, 1996) and the Jerusalem Schools Authority, Israel (Angrist & Lavy, 2001) in order to compare the effects of teacher training (traditionally trained and on-the-job training for untrained teachers) on pupil learning with mixed results. On the one hand, trained novice teachers receiving in-service support positively influenced third-grade students mathematics scores, and on the other, on-the-job training for untrained novice teachers resulted in gains in students' reading scores (Angrist & Lavy, 2001; Bressoux, 1996). In England, Allen and Allnutt (2017) examined whether the placement of Teach First's inexperienced new teachers into 168 secondary schools with recruitment difficulties in disadvantaged areas raised or lowered pupil attainment (at the age of 16). They estimated departmental gains of over 5% of a subject grade from placing a Teach First participant in a teaching team of six teachers, concluding the program has "not been damaging to these schools who joined and most likely produced school-wide gains in GCSE results of around one grade in one of the pupils' best eight subjects" (p. 1).

When examined singly, these studies yield contradictory evidence about the relation between the type of teacher certification and student achievement for policy makers, researchers, and practitioners. When analyzed collectively, evidence from large-scale empirical studies points to some consensus. Almost two decades ago, a study of data from the National Educational Longitudinal Study (Goldhaber & Brewer, 2000; National Center for Education Statistics, 1997) examined the relations between twelfth-grade students' performance in mathematics and science and teacher certification (3,786 mathematics students, 2,524 science students, 2,098 mathematics teachers, and 1,371 science teachers). First, students of teachers with mathematics degrees or certification in mathematics achieved better than the students of teachers without subject-matter preparation. Second, student test scores in mathematics were higher when the teacher of record held professional or full state certification relative to the students' scores when taught by a teacher certified out of subject or holding private-school certification. Third, students taught by teachers with bachelor's or master's degrees in mathematics outperformed the students taught by teachers who were not credentialed in the same field. Fourth, students taught by an uncertified science teacher or a science teacher who held a private-school certification showed lower scores. Fifth, measurement of student achievement growth revealed no significant differences between mathematics or science students' test scores for teachers with emergency certification and those traditionally certified. Goldhaber and Brewer postulated that "at the very least," the study's outcomes "cast doubt on the claims of the educational establishment that standard certification should be required of all teachers" (p. 145). In a rejoinder, Darling-Hammond et al. (2001) emphasized that some results for emergency and temporary certification from Goldhaber and Brewer's statistical model emerged from a very small sample and were not statistically significant. In their reanalysis, Darling-Hammond et al. identified that only one-third of the NELS sample teachers who held temporary or emergency licenses were new to teaching with little or no educational background. Further, they demonstrated that many of the 24 science teachers (of 3,469 in Goldhaber and Brewer's study sample) with temporary or emergency certificates had similar years of teaching and subject-matter knowledge to the certified teachers in the sample. High school students taught by the subsample of teachers on temporary or emergency certification and new to teaching attained smaller achievement gains than students taught by those who had attained full state certification through a traditional pathway.

Greenberg, Rhodes, Ye, and Stancavage (2004) analyzed data from the NAEP 2000 grade 8 mathematics assessment to examine how teacher qualifications were related to student achievement in mathematics among students enrolled in US public schools. In this study, four specific teacher qualifications were defined: teacher certification, academic major or minor, highest postsecondary degree, and years of teaching experience. Although relying on cross-sectional NAEP background data for measures of student achievement, they found, independent of other factors and teaching credentials, teacher certification and holding a degree in mathematics were the teacher qualifications associated with higher mathematics achievement among eighth-grade public school students. A second finding pertained to economically disadvantaged eighth-grade students who were less likely to be taught by a mathematics teacher with a degree in mathematics than their more affluent counterparts.

A seminal study conducted by Boyd, Grossman, Lankford, Loeb, and Wyckoff (2006) assessed how changes in entry requirements altered the teacher workforce and affected student achievement. They found that pathways to licensure were of moderate importance. Specifically, for elementary mathematics and English/language arts (ELA), they found that students of nontraditional teachers achieved as well as those of college-recommended pathways by the end of the third year of teaching. Likewise, for middle school mathematics, similar results have indicated that initially, there is no significant difference between pathways of preparation. However, middle school mathematics students of teachers in one particular nontraditional pathway, Teaching Fellows, made significantly greater improvement between their second and third years of teaching, outperforming the students of college-recommended teachers.

Constantine and colleagues (Constantine et al., 2009) studied 87 alternatively certified (AC) teachers and 87 traditionally certified (TC) teachers from 62 schools in 20 districts and seven states. Within each school, students in the same grade were randomly assigned to either an AC teacher or a TC teacher. There were no statistically significant differences between the math and reading performance of students with the TC or AC teachers. The researchers found no correlation between increased teacher training coursework and a teachers' effectiveness in the classroom (see also Gimbert, Cristol, & Sene, 2007).

During the past decade, policy makers, practitioners, and the international educational community have called for evidence about how differing requirements and processes within a teacher training pathway, whether traditional or nontraditional/alternative, influence teacher quality and teaching effectiveness that, in turn, affect student learning outcomes. In response, researchers have compared recruitment and selection processes and characteristics and training experiences of alternatively certified teachers with their traditionally prepared peers. In particular, studies have explored competencies related to content knowledge and pedagogical content knowledge, perceptions of preparedness by candidates and school leaders, initial teaching experiences, and the quality of mentoring afforded to each new teacher. For example, Sass (2011), from the National Center for Analysis of Longitudinal Data in Education Research, reported that alternatively certified science teachers have more coursework in science while in college than traditionally prepared science teachers. However, for math teachers, the hours of college coursework are approximately equal across pathways. Of the three alternative certification pathways studied, teachers who entered through the path requiring no content coursework have substantially less positive impact on student achievement than do either traditionally prepared teachers or alternative training programs that require some formal coursework in education. Thomas and Mockler (2018) recognized previously unrevealed sub-identities in the literature by comparing a cohort of teachers entering the teaching profession through alternative pathways with peers who completed traditional initial teacher education programs. Exposure to different training conditions and constraints generated sub-identities that influence how novice teachers shape their professional identity. Earlier, Kane et al. (2007)

observed that both certified and alternatively certified teachers' effectiveness improves with the first few years of experience. Additional findings suggest that initial classroom performance is a more reliable predictor of teacher effectiveness in the future than certification status of teachers (p. 615). Evans (2011) examined the differences in content knowledge, attitudes toward mathematics, and teacher efficacy among several different types of alternatively certified teachers in a sample from the New York City Teaching Fellows program. He found high school teachers had significantly higher content knowledge than middle school teachers; teachers with strong mathematics backgrounds had significantly higher content knowledge than teachers who did not have strong mathematics backgrounds; and mathematics and science majors had significantly higher content knowledge than other majors. Mathematics content knowledge was not related to attitudes toward mathematics and teacher efficacy since teachers had the same high positive attitudes toward mathematics and same high teacher efficacy, regardless of content ability. Bottoms, Egelsto, Sass, and Uhn (2013) concluded career and technical education (CTE) teachers who enter the profession through alternative routes are more likely to feel confident about their career field knowledge but less confident about their ability to convey that knowledge to students. Further, many alternatively certified CTE teachers expressed concern regarding classroom management, student motivation, and planning instruction for special needs students. Alternatively certified CTE teachers need feedback about their teaching practice, strategies for managing added demands on their time and energy, and resources for planning and teaching. In response to these needs, this field-tested induction model builds the capacity of beginning CTE teachers to offer instruction that is both intellectually demanding and standards-focused and thus more likely to improve CTE students' academic achievement. The model also builds CTE teachers' capacity to design instruction that is actively engaging, using strategies like project-based learning and cooperative learning. Last, Spearman (2017) applied sequential mixed methods to investigate the relationship between the alternate route (AR) teachers' field experiences and years of experience and teachers' effect on student learning. Although no correlation between AR teachers' years of teaching experience and student assessment scores was reported, Spearman found when AR teachers engage in field experiences prior to teaching, their students have higher levels of achievement.

Summary and recommendations

Teaching effectiveness is the most important factor driving student academic success (Goldhaber, Liddle, & Theobald, 2013). While studies around alternative and traditionally certified teachers have attempted to compare teacher quality and teaching effectiveness with student achievement, there is inconclusive evidence that teachers who take alternative pathways into the classroom have any greater or lesser effect on students' academic performance in reading, mathematics, and science. With fewer individuals applying for traditional teacher preparation programs and the growing cadre of teachers entering the teaching profession through alternative routes, policy makers and practitioners call the research community to define the most appropriate training and preparation practices necessary to earn a teaching credential, no matter the pathway that a prospective teacher candidate elects. In the Learning Policy Institute's 2016 report, entitled "A coming crisis in teaching? Teacher supply, demand, and shortages in the U.S," Sutcher et al. (2016) advise those responsible for legislating and implementing evidence-based policies related to teacher training programs to "create competitive, equitable compensation packages for teachers, enhance the supply of qualified teachers for high-need fields and locations; improve retention, especially in hard-to-staff schools; and develop a national teacher supply market" (p. 1). Let's heed that sound advice!

References

Allen, R., & Allnutt, J. (2017). The impact of teach first on pupil attainment at Age 16. *British Educational Research Journal, 43*(4), 627–646. Retrieved from http://discovery.ucl.ac.uk/10052597/

Angrist, J. D., & Lavy, V. (2001). Does teacher training affect pupil learning? Evidence from matched comparison on Jerusalem public schools. *Journal of Labor Economics, 19*(2), 343–369.

Bottoms, G., Egelsto, P., Sass, H., & Uhn, J. (2013). *Improving the quality of career and technical alternative teacher preparation: An induction model of professional development and support.* National Research Center for Career and Technical Education. Retrieved from https://eric-ed-gov.proxy.lib.ohio-state.edu/contentdelivery/servlet/ERICServlet?accno=ED574500

Boyd, D., Grossman, P., Lankford, H., Loeb, S., & Wyckoff, J. (2006, April). *How changes in entry requirements alter the teacher workforce and affect student achievement.* Paper presented at the American Education Research Association annual meeting, San Francisco, CA.

Bressoux, P. (1996). The effects of teachers' training on pupils' achievement: The case of elementary schools in France. *School Effectiveness and School Improvement, 7*(3), 252–279.

Brinkman, B. A. (2014). *The impact of teacher preparation on academic achievement of eighth grade students in a South Texas school district.* Unpublished dissertation Texas A&M University-Corpus Christi, ProQuest Dissertations Publishing. 3619969. Retrieved from https://tamucc-ir.tdl.org/tamucc-ir/bitstream/handle/1969.6/560/Barbara%20Brinkman.pdf?sequence=1

Constantine, J., Player, D., Silva, T., Hallgren, K., Grider, M., & Deke, J. (2009, February). *An evaluation of teachers trained through different routes to certification* (Final report. NCEE 2009–4043). Jessup, MD: National Center for Education Evaluation and Regional Assistance. (ERIC Document Reproduction Service No. ED504313)

Darling-Hammond, L., Berry, B., & Thoreson, A. (2001). Does teaching certification matter? Evaluating the evidence. *Educational Evaluation and Policy Analysis, 23*(1), 57–77.

Duke, R. S. (2013). *The impact of teacher licensure programs on minority student achievement.* ProQuest LLC (Unpublished Dissertation), Old Dominion University. Retrieved from https://eric.ed.gov/?id=ED554654

Evans, B. R. (2011). Secondary mathematics teacher differences: Teacher quality and preparation in a New York City alternative certification program. *Mathematics Educator, 20*(2), 24–32.

Feistritzer, E. (2007). *Building a quality teaching force: Lesson learned from alternative routes*. Upper Saddle River, NJ: Prentice Hall.

Gimbert, B. G., Cristol, D., & Sene, A. M. (2007, September). The impact of teacher preparation on student achievement in algebra in a "hard to staff" urban pre-K-12-university partnership. *School Effectiveness and School Improvement, 18*(3), 245–272.

Goldhaber, D. B., & Brewer, D. (2000). Does teacher certification matter? High school teacher certification and student achievement. *Educational Evaluation and Policy Analysis, 22*(2), 129–145.

Goldhaber, D., Liddle, S., & Theobald, R. (2013). The gateway to the profession: Assessing teacher preparation programs based on student achievement. *Economics of Education Review, 34*, 29–44.

Greenberg, E., Rhodes, D., Ye, X., & Stancavage, F. (2004, April). *Prepared to teach: Teacher preparation and student achievement in eighth-grade mathematics*. Paper presented at the Annual Meeting of the American Educational Research Association, San Diego, CA. Retrieved from www.air.org/news_events/documents/AERA-2004PreparedtoTeach.pdf

Ingersoll, R. (2004). *Why do high-poverty schools have difficulty staffing their classrooms with qualified teachers?* Washington, DC: Center for American Progress.

Kane, T. J., Rockoff, J. E., & Staiger, D. O. (2007). What does certification tell us about teacher effectiveness? Evidence from New York City. *Economics of Education Review, 27*(6), 615–631.

Moore, E. E. (2012). *A study of SATP scores and principals' perceptions for traditional and alternate routes to teacher certification* (Unpublished dissertation), The University of Southern Mississippi (ED548114). Retrieved from https://eric.ed.gov/?id=ED548114

Mueller, C. M (2012). *The impact of teacher certification programs on teacher efficacy, job satisfaction, and teacher performance: A comparison of traditional and alternative certification* (Dissertations). Paper 28. Retrieved from, http://digitalcommons.wku.edu/diss/28

National Center for Education Statistics. (1997). *Digest of educational statistics 1997* (Report No. NCES 98-Ol5). Washington, DC: U.S. Department of Education.

Penner, E. K. (2013). *Society for research on educational effectiveness*. Society for Research on Educational Effectiveness. ED563264. Retrieved from https://eric.ed.gov/?id=ED563264

Ruiz de Castilla, V. (2018). *Teacher certification and academic growth among English learner students in the Houston Independent School District (REL 2018–284)*. Washington, DC: U.S. Department of Education, Institute of Education Sciences, National Center for Education Evaluation and Regional Assistance, Regional Educational Laboratory Southwest. Retrieved from http://ies.ed.gov/ncee/edlabs.

Sass, T. R. (2011). *Certification requirements and teacher quality: A comparison of alternative routes to teaching*. Working paper. National Center for Analysis of Longitudinal Data in Education Research (CALDER). National Center for Analysis of Longitudinal Data in Education Research. Retrieved from https://eric-ed-gov.proxy.lib.ohio-state.edu/contentdelivery/servlet/ERICServlet?accno=ED529179

Spearman, C. F. (2017). *A mixed-methods study of alternate-route teachers' effect on student learning* (Unpublished dissertation), Walden University. Retrieved from https://scholarworks.waldenu.edu/dissertations/4104/

Sutcher, L., Darling-Hammond, L., & Carver-Thomas, D. (2016). *A coming crisis in teaching? Teacher supply, demand, and shortages in the U.S.* Palo Alto, CA: Learning Policy Institute.

Thomas, M. A. M., & Mockler, N. (2018). Alternative routes to teacher professional identity: Exploring the conflated sub-identities of teach for America corps members. *Education Policy Analysis Archives, 26*(6), 1–22.

Summary table: influences from teachers and classrooms

Category	Variable	Considerations
Teachers' Attitudes and Beliefs	Students achieve at higher levels when teachers engage in self-reflection about their personal **attitudes**, **beliefs**, **biases**, and **prejudices**.	*Educators should be encouraged to be reflective practitioners, and to consider, reflect upon, and sometimes change their beliefs, attitudes, and biases. This can be accomplished through small-group discussions, book clubs, professional development opportunities, or a variety of other strategies.*
	Teachers' **epistemological beliefs** (i.e., their beliefs about the nature and acquisition of knowledge) affect achievement. Teachers use more effective instructional practices when they believe that student ability is malleable (as opposed to fixed and unchangeable), that effective learning takes time, and that knowledge is complex (i.e., knowledge consists of more than just memorization of discrete facts).	*New teachers often report that they have sophisticated epistemological beliefs, but sometimes the constraints of schools (e.g., policies, a strong focus on high-stakes testing) lead to teachers with such beliefs using ineffective instructional practices.*
	Teacher efficacy beliefs (i.e., feeling competent and effective at teaching one's students) is related positively to student academic achievement.	*School administrators have a responsibility to work with teachers to ensure that teachers are able to see how specific instructional strategies lead to greater student achievement.*
	Administrative structures and policies that support **teacher motivation** also promote academic achievement.	*School leaders should provide opportunities for teachers to be autonomous, to set and achieve specific goals, and to promote positive relationships with their students. This can be achieved via numerous strategies: for example, (a) by instituting school policies that allow for teachers to have meaningful input into curricular decisions and (b) by encouraging teacher involvement in site-based decision-making committees or parent-teacher organizations.*

(Continued)

Category	Variable	Considerations
Classroom Contexts	The **instructional context** of a classroom is a broad construct that refers to the overall experience that is created for and perceived by students within a classroom. Instructional contexts are composed of numerous aspects of classroom life (e.g., teacher-student-peer relationships, types of instructional practices used, etc.).	*Students in the same classroom may experience instructional contexts differently from each other. Instructional contexts are influenced both by factors within the classroom (e.g., the teachers and students, the nature of instruction), and by factors outside the classroom (e.g., school policies, home environments, school funding). There is no clear conceptual or theoretical model that currently guides research on the effects of instructional contexts on achievement. Students tend to achieve at higher levels when their teachers have demonstrated that they can create effective instructional contexts via advanced professional certifications such as the National Board for Professional Teaching Standards certification.*
	Instructional practices that promote positive motivational beliefs can improve student achievement.	*Students achieve at higher levels when (a) they believe that they can be successful with assigned tasks, (b) they perceive that they have some autonomy, and (c) they have a growth mind-set (i.e., they believe that their abilities can improve). However, positive motivational beliefs will not compensate for a lack of appropriate strategic knowledge or prior knowledge.*
	It is possible to create a classroom context that fosters **creativity** in students, even in an era of high-stakes testing. This often requires a concerted and unified effort among teachers, administrators, parents, and students.	*As teachers, we often focus on producing results on high-stakes tests, at the cost of encouraging our students to be creative. This can be avoided with careful and collaborative planning.*
	Teachers' expressions of **enthusiasm** via expressive behaviors (e.g., maintaining eye contact, varying the tone of one's voice, using effective gestures) create classroom contexts that are related positively to student achievement.	*Schools can provide professional development opportunities to train teachers to be more enthusiastic.*

(Continued)

Category	Variable	Considerations
	When students feel **competent** and **expect** that they can succeed in a particular class, they are more likely to experience academic success in that class. However, holding **high expectations** for all students will only lead to higher achievement if teachers also provide the instructional supports that students need to meet those expectations and if those expectations are communicated in the context of a warm, nurturing classroom. Although teacher expectations do affect achievement, the effects are small.	*Expectations may need to differ by students; high expectations for one student may actually translate to low expectations for another student. Teachers need to provide the appropriate supports so that students can feel competent because of the successes that the students are experiencing. These supports might include helping students set short-term goals through which they can experience success.*
	Classroom contexts that are **autonomy** supportive (i.e., classrooms in which there are opportunities to make meaningful choices) are conducive to higher achievement.	*Provide opportunities for students to make decisions (e.g., what book to read, how to solve a problem, etc.).*
	When students have a **growth mind-set** (i.e., they believe that intelligence is malleable), they are likely to achieve at higher levels.	*Emphasize to students that learning is a result of effort and practice and that occasional difficulties in understanding a topic or completing a task are inevitable parts of how people learn.*
	Students learn more effectively in classrooms that are well **managed** and have **fewer behavioral problems**.	*Teachers can effectively manage behavior if they develop caring relationships with students, focus students on engagement with academic tasks, promote the development of social and self-regulatory skills, reinforce desired behaviors, and use appropriate interventions when needed. Teachers also must acknowledge that behavior management techniques need to be culturally responsive.*
	Teacher-student relationships that are characterized by teachers demonstrating that they care about student learning and by helping students to understand content, are conducive to greater engagement and learning and fewer behavioral infractions.	*Relationships between teachers and students are dynamic; teachers must be aware of their own expectations and biases.*

(Continued)

Category	Variable	Considerations
	Teachers need to attend to the nature of **peer interactions** in their classrooms, because these interactions affect achievement.	*Students who learn in classroom contexts in which they feel accepted by their peers are more likely to participate in class activities and to achieve at higher levels. Students who are victimized and/or experience loneliness may avoid school. Students who are rejected by their peers experience a variety of academic problems; thus, teachers need to do all that they can to prevent and remediate any signs of rejection.*
	Achievement is higher when students experience positive **emotions** in the classroom; negative emotions and anxiety have a moderate negative effect on achievement.	*Teachers should work toward creating classroom contexts that are conducive to positive emotions. Some strategies include providing supports so that students can experience academic success, communicating enthusiasm, and helping students cope with negative emotional experiences (e.g., boredom; test anxiety).*
	Achievement and motivation are enhanced after the **transition from elementary to middle grades schools** when developmentally appropriate instructional practices are used in the middle school context.	*Teachers in middle schools should allow students to express autonomy (make choices), to collaborate with peers, and to pursue personal interests whenever possible. Instructional practices emphasizing ability differences (e.g., excessive grouping of students by ability) should be avoided.*
	The provision of **homework** is related to achievement, but more so for adolescents than for younger children.	*Homework is related to academic achievement for students in middle grades or high schools. Positive effects of homework on achievement are stronger when assignments are of high quality (e.g., interesting and perhaps somewhat challenging), when students put forth appropriate effort, and when students feel confident in their abilities to complete the assignments. Teachers should remember to help students figure out how to manage homework (e.g., how to plan for time to be able to do the assignments).*

(Continued)

Category	Variable	Considerations
	Formative assessment is the process of monitoring students' academic progress and using the data that are acquired to guide further instruction and to provide students with ongoing feedback. The regular use of formative assessments can positively impact student achievement.	*Formative assessments should account for both students' current strengths and their current weaknesses. Appropriate feedback regarding students' current gaps in knowledge/skill need to be clearly and regularly communicated to them.*
	Ability grouping/tracking generally only yields achievement benefits for high-achieving students.	*Tracking practices often lead to an over-representation of low-socioeconomic status and minority students in the lower-ability tracks. If tracking is used, practices should allow for flexibility so that students can change tracks. Moreover, teachers should provide reasonably challenging assignments in the low-ability tracks – lower-ability students should not always get boring "fill-in-the-blank" assignments. Teachers assigned to the lower-ability tracks should have training and experience equivalent to those of teachers assigned to higher-ability tracks.*
	Collaboration between students can enhance achievement, if implemented thoughtfully.	*Although collaboration enhances achievement, this does not occur automatically. Teachers need to (a) ensure that their students understand how to work in a group and have practiced appropriate group communication skills, (b) ensure that low-status students are able to participate equally in group work, (c) structure the collaborative work (e.g., assign roles to students), and (d) monitor groups while they are engaged in collaborative work.*
	High-stakes accountability is not strongly related to either the use of more effective teaching practices or larger, long-term achievement gains. An emphasis on high-stakes accountability as a framework for school reform is not effective.	*School reform efforts aimed at increasing student achievement should be based on adherence to high-quality standards and the use of well-designed assessments that are aligned with those standards.*

(Continued)

Category	Variable	Considerations
Teachers' Preparation and Professional Development	There is little evidence to suggest that teachers prepared through **alternative licensure programs** have either a greater or lesser effect on student achievement than teachers prepared through traditional pathways.	*Alternative licensure programs can increase the size of the teacher workforce; nevertheless, the pathway to licensure is not nearly as important as instructional practices, in terms of effects on achievement.*
	Professional development (PD) for in-service teachers is only going to lead to achievement gains for students if the PD is embedded within teachers' actual jobs and aligned with school policies, practices, and procedures.	*It is often convenient to bring in a guest expert to give a brief PD session on a given topic; such brief sessions (lacking any integration or reinforcement) often are not effective.*
	Teachers who have **pedagogical content knowledge (PCK)** are highly knowledgeable about (a) their area of academic content (e.g., history or chemistry), (b) effective instructional strategies, and (c) how social contexts should be considered during instructional planning. Evidence seems to suggest that higher PCK in teachers is associated with higher achievement in students, although additional research is needed.	*As evidence for the relation of PCK to achievement continues to accrue, an emphasis on PCK should be incorporated into both educator preparation and professional development programs.*

Note: This table summarizes information presented by authors who contributed chapters to sections 5 and 6 of the first edition of The International Guide to Student Achievement, as well as to revised chapters included in the present chapter.

Additional references

Anderman, E. M., & Anderman, L. H. (2014). *Classroom motivation* (2nd ed.). Columbus: Pearson.

Anderman, E. M., & Gray, D. L. (2017). The roles of schools and teachers in fostering competence motivation. In A. J. Elliot, C. S. Dweck, & D. S. Yeager (Eds.), *Handbook of competence and motivation: Theory and application* (2nd ed., pp. 604–619). New York, NY: Guilford Press.

Anderman, E. M., & Mueller, C. (2010). Middle school transitions and adolescent development. In J. Meece & J. S. Eccles (Eds.), *Handbook of research on schools, schooling, and human development* (pp. 198–215). New York: Routledge.

Buehl, M. M., & Beck, L. S. (2015). The relationship between teachers' beliefs and teachers' practices. In H. Fives & M. Gregoire Gill (Eds.), *International handbook of research on teachers' beliefs* (pp. 66–84). New York: Routledge.

Cerasoli, C. P., Nicklin, J. M., & Ford, M. T. (2014). Intrinsic motivation and extrinsic incentives jointly predict performance: A 40-year meta-analysis. *Psychological Bulletin, 140*(4), 980–1008. https://doi-org.proxy.lib.ohio-state.edu/10.1037/a0035661

Cooper, H., Robinson, J. C., & Patall, E. A. (2006). Does homework improve academic achievement? A synthesis of research, 1987–2003. *Review of Educational Research, 76*(1), 1–62.

Dweck, C. S. (2016). *Mindset: The new psychology of success*. New York: Ballantine.

Eccles, J. S., Midgley, C., Wigfield, A., Buchanan, C. M., Reuman, D., Flanagan, C., & Mac Iver, D. (1993). Development during adolescence: The impact of stage-environment fit on young adolescents' experiences in schools and in families. *American Psychologist, 48*(2), 90–101. https://doi-org.proxy.lib.ohio-state.edu/10.1037/0003-066X.48.2.90

Eccles, J. S., & Roeser, R. W. (2009). Schools, academic motivation, and stage-environment fit. In R. M. Lerner & L. Steinberg (Eds.), *Handbook of adolescent psychology: Individual bases of adolescent development, Vol. 1, 3rd ed.* (pp. 404–434). Hoboken, NJ: John Wiley & Sons Inc. https://doi-org.proxy.lib.ohio-state.edu/10.1002/9780470479193.adlpsy001013

Goe, L. (2013). Quality of teaching. In J. Hattie & E. M. Anderman (Eds.), *International guide to student achievement* (pp. 237–239). New York, NY: Routledge/Taylor & Francis Group.

Gregory, A., & Jones, J. R. (2013). Secondary classroom management. In J. Hattie & E. M. Anderman (Eds.), *International guide to student achievement* (pp. 196–198). New York, NY: Routledge/Taylor & Francis Group.

Jussim, L. (2013). Teachers' expectations. In J. Hattie & E. M. Anderman (Eds.), *International guide to student achievement* (pp. 243–246). New York, NY: Routledge/Taylor & Francis Group.

Keller, M., Neumann, K., & Fischer, H. E. (2013). Teacher enthusiasm and student learning. In J. Hattie & E. M. Anderman (Eds.), *International guide to student achievement* (pp. 247–249). New York, NY: Routledge/Taylor & Francis Group.

Klassen, R. M., & Tze, V. M. C. (2014). Teachers' self-efficacy, personality, and teaching effectiveness: A meta-analysis. *Educational Research Review, 12*, 59–76. https://doi-org.proxy.lib.ohio-state.edu/10.1016/j.edurev.2014.06.001

Ladd, G. W. (2013). Peer influences in elementary school. In J. Hattie & E. M. Anderman (Eds.), *International guide to student achievement* (pp. 205–208). New York, NY: Routledge/Taylor & Francis Group.

Levin, B. B. (2015). The development of teachers' beliefs and practices. In H. Fives & M. Gregoire Gill (Eds.), *International handbook of research on teachers' beliefs* (pp. 48–65). New York: Routledge.

Meyer, D. K. (2013). Classroom instructional contexts. In J. Hattie & E. M. Anderman (Eds.), *International guide to student achievement* (pp. 181–184). New York, NY: Routledge/Taylor & Francis Group.

Ross, J. A. (2013). Teacher efficacy. In J. Hattie & E. M. Anderman (Eds.), *International guide to student achievement* (pp. 266–267). New York, NY: Routledge/Taylor & Francis Group.

Roth, G., & Weinstock, M. (2013). Teachers' epistemological beliefs as an antecedent of autonomy-supportive teaching. *Motivation & Emotion, 37*(3), 402–412.

Schofield, J. W. (2013). Ability grouping. In J. Hattie & E. M. Anderman (Eds.), *International guide to student achievement* (pp. 212–214). New York, NY: Routledge/Taylor & Francis Group.

Schraw, G., Brownlee, J., & Olafson, L. (2013). Teachers' epistemological beliefs and achievement. In J. Hattie & E. M. Anderman (Eds.), *International guide to student achievement* (pp. 268–270). New York, NY: Routledge/Taylor & Francis Group.

Schraw, G., & Olafson, L. (2002). Teachers' epistemological world views and educational practices. *Issues in Education, 8*(2), 99.

Valli, L., & Finkelstein, C. (2013). School reform. In J. Hattie & E. M. Anderman (Eds.), *International guide to student achievement* (pp. 263–265). New York, NY: Routledge/Taylor & Francis Group.

Vandenbroucke, L., Spilt, J., Verschueren, K., Piccinin, C., & Baeyens, D. (2018). The classroom as a developmental context for cognitive development: A meta-analysis on the importance of teacher–student interactions for children's executive functions. *Review of Educational Research, 88*(1), 125–164. https://doi-org.proxy.lib.ohio-state.edu/10.3102/0034654317743200

Watt, H. M. G., & Richardson, P. W. (2013). Teacher motivation and student achievement outcomes. In J. Hattie & E. M. Anderman (Eds.), *International guide to student achievement* (pp. 271–273). New York, NY: Routledge/Taylor & Francis Group.

Wentzel, K. R. (2017). Peer relationships, motivation, and academic performance at school. In A. J. Elliot, C. S. Dweck, & D. S. Yeager (Eds.), *Handbook of competence and motivation: Theory and application* (2nd ed., pp. 586–603). New York, NY: Guilford Press.

Wigfield, A., Rosenzweig, E. Q., & Eccles, J. S. (2017). Achievement values: Interactions, interventions, and future directions. In A. J. Elliot, C. S. Dweck, & D. S. Yeager (Eds.), *Handbook of competence and motivation: Theory and application* (2nd ed., pp. 116–134). New York, NY: Guilford Press.

Yoon, K. S., Duncan, T., Lee, S. W.-Y., Scarloss, B., & Shapley, K. L. (2007). *Reviewing the evidence on how teacher professional development affects student achievement* (Issues & Answers. REL 2007-No. 033). Regional Educational Laboratory Southwest.

CHAPTER 6

Influences from the curriculum

The curriculum that is used to guide instruction is crucial and is strongly related to student learning outcomes. Nevertheless, many educators probably take curriculum for granted. When a teacher is hired for a teaching position in a particular school, the teacher is often provided with curricular materials that are used by the personnel in that school, district, or region. Whereas some educators can select from a range of curricular materials, many are limited to curricula that have been preselected by educators or administrators.

So how does a teacher know if the curriculum that is being used is actually effective? Some curricula have been evaluated and have a strong research base to support their use, whereas others may not have a strong evidence base. Some curricula may have been subjected to rigorous randomized control trials, whereas other curricula are deemed effective based on little substantive evidence. Moreover, curricula that *are* effective at producing achievement gains generally are only effective if the curricula are implemented with fidelity. In this chapter, we review some of the research-based qualities of curricula that have been demonstrated to be related to achievement.

In the original *Guide*, we invited authors to comment on the relations of a wide range of curricular topics to academic achievement. That section, which was edited by Rayne Sperling (Pennsylvania State University), included the entries and authors listed below (entries marked with an asterisk have been updated for this edition):

Values Education Programs
  Terence Lovat

Activity-Based Learning Strategies
  Kira J. Carbonneau and Scott C. Marley

Bilingual Education Programs and Student Achievement★
  Jill Fitzgerald and Jackie Eunjung Relyea-Kim

Intelligent Tutors – Strategy Types
Bonnie J. F. Meyer

Creativity and Creativity Programs
Heather L. Hammond, Lauren E. Skidmore, Amanda Wilcox-Herzog, and James C. Kaufman

Outdoor Education
Justin Dillon

Role of Discussion in Reading Comprehension*
Ian A. G. Wilkinson and Kathryn Nelson

The Impact of Calculators on Student Achievement in the K–12 Mathematics Classroom
Aimee J. Ellington

Second Language Vocabulary
Yongqi Gu

Language Teaching Curricula*
Eli Hinkel

Measurement of History Achievement in the United States and Europe
Mark Smith, Joel Breakstone, and Sam Wineburg

Reading: Phonics Instruction
William E. Tunmer and Alison W. Arrow

Repeated Reading
William J. Therrien and Sarah J. Watt

Reading: Sentence Combining: Grammar Programs
Bruce Saddler and Nicole Bak

Extracurricular Activities in Secondary Schools
Boaz Shulruf and Grace Ying Wang

Improving Academic Achievement with Social Skills
Frank M. Gresham, Michael J. Vance, and Jeffrey Chenier

Visual Perception Programs
Barbara Hanna Wasik, Adrienne N. Villagomez, Sheena Berry, and Sandra B. Evarrs

Reading: Vocabulary Programs

   A. Wilson, R. Jesson, and S. McNaughton

Achievement in Adolescent Health Education★

   Megan Sanders, Rashea Hamilton, and Eric M. Anderman

Writing Achievement★

   Mark Torrance and Raquel Fidalgo

Reading: Comprehension Programs

   Janice F. Almasi and Barbara Martin Palmer

Response to Intervention and Multi-Tiered Systems of Support★

   Paul J. Riccomini and Gregory W. Smith

(Note: *This chapter has been reconceptualized in the new edition to focus on multitiered systems of support*)

Successful Mathematics Achievement Is Attainable★

   Patti Brosnan, Aaron Schmidlin, and Melva R. Grant

We next present an overview of some of the major takeaway points from the research on the relations between curriculum and achievement. We have organized our discussion into three categories: general/overarching curricular influences, language, and math/science.

General/overarching curricular influences

There are some general curricular principles related to academic achievement that are fairly generalizable across grade levels and subject domains. These curricular principles tend to reflect the ways in which curricula are implemented in classrooms by teachers. Nevertheless, many educators assume that some aspects of curricula are unquestionably related to achievement gains, although some of those assumptions are not necessarily true (Berliner & Glass, 2014).

For example, some curricula are touted as being effective because they provide hands-on activities. Such activities may include manipulating various objects or performing experiments. However, there actually is little consistent research suggesting best practices for incorporating hands-on activities into curricula. Whereas benefits may accrue through the use of specific curricula where such effects have been demonstrated, there is no universal evidence suggesting that merely using curricula that provide hands-on learning opportunities for students will lead to achievement gains.

Another common assumption is that curricula that provide opportunities for creativity will yield achievement benefits. Research to date is inconclusive at best. Part of the problem is the use of generic terms such as *creativity*; terms of this nature are broad in scope and definition. For example, some may operationalize creativity in terms of curricula that allow for participation in the arts; yet research to date does not suggest strong direct effects on achievement for creative opportunities of this nature (e.g., Jindal-Snape et al., 2018). There is some evidence that play-based programs that allow for creative expression do yield achievement benefits for young children. Thus, creativity quite likely leads to cognitive benefits that may indirectly affect achievement, but sweeping generalizations are not warranted. Moreover, curricula that emphasize creativity must ensure that there is a balance between curricula that emphasize (i.e., teach) creativity, as compared to curricula that allow for students to be creative with regard to specific academic content.

Broad assumptions about other beneficial aspects of curricula also are not always appropriate. For example, although bilingual education can be extraordinarily helpful for students who need to learn a non-native language in order to succeed at school, research to date does not overwhelmingly suggest that bilingual programs are universally more effective than other types of programs (e.g., language immersion). As another example, some educators promote the use of curricula that require students to engage in educational activities in the outdoors. Outdoor education programs can promote achievement, but only when the programs are well aligned with instructional goals, occur over a substantial period of time, and are supported with follow-up instruction from the teacher.

Finally, there is evidence that curricula that focus on some specific cognitive and noncognitive aspects of learning can support achievement. For example, many curricula build on the successes of socioemotional learning interventions by including the teaching of a variety of social skills (e.g., Corcoran, Cheung, Kim, & Xie, 2018). Instruction in social skills is effective, although effects on learning are most likely due to reductions in aggressive and externalizing behaviors in youth; when students are less likely to misbehave and act out, they are better able to engage with their academic work and thus are more likely to experience achievement gains. Other curricula have built on the successes of response-to-intervention initiatives and now incorporate multitiered systems of support (MTSS). MTSS-infused curricula can improve achievement when implemented with fidelity and over ample time.

Language

Many curricula also address aspects of language (e.g., reading, writing, etc.). Whereas some curricula are designed to directly improve students' language/verbal skills, others incorporate specific aspects of language usage (e.g., extensive writing assignments) into curricula that focus on content areas (e.g., history or astronomy). An example of a type of curriculum that was developed to address language skills is phonics curricula. Phonics curricula are designed to improve students' facility with language across any and all subject domains; phonics curricula may be particularly effective with students who are struggling to learn how to read. Other curricula specific to the development of language skills may include activities and tasks that build verbal skills through curricular innovations such as the repeated reading of texts, vocabulary instruction, or instruction in self-regulatory strategies (e.g., summarizing texts; asking oneself comprehension questions). The inclusion of instruction in these skills in curricula of this nature can improve reading and writing achievement, provided that they are implemented by teachers who have been trained in the effective use of these techniques.

In contrast, some curricula that focus on a specific topic or content area (e.g., a history curriculum focusing on modern European history) may include activities and tasks that incorporate the use of language/verbal skills but focus on learning in the content area. In curricula of this nature, language is used as a tool that enhances learning of the content area materials being studied (e.g., modern European history). For example, curricula that encourage the discussion of texts (e.g., discussions of articles about various aspects of modern European history) may foster small but meaningful gains in comprehension of texts, which ultimately lead to gains in achievement (i.e., increased achievement in the study of European history).

Finally, many (if not most) curricula include assignments that involve writing. Curricula of this nature can lead to both enhanced learning of academic content and improved writing skills. Some curricula focus on the technical aspects of writing (e.g., grammar), whereas other curricula focus on more complex aspects of writing (e.g., writing a persuasive essay).

Math and science

There are many types of curricula and instructional methods available for the teaching of mathematics. Given the international emphasis on enhancing students' interest in science, technology, engineering, and math (STEM) careers, there is extraordinary growth in the availability of instructional materials. In general, math curricula are most likely to yield achievement gains when teachers are cognizant of individual differences among learners; math curricula must be adapted as appropriate, both for individual students and for entire classes.

Given the availability of instantaneous technology via smartphones, tablets, and the internet, students have unprecedented access to calculators; this has led to renewed debate about the potential achievement benefits of allowing students to use calculators during math instruction. Researchers generally agree that calculators are a part of the modern world in which we live. Research suggests that the use of calculators in math instruction should be limited during the early grades and increased as students develop basic math skills and move on to more complex types of mathematics (e.g., algebra or calculus).

Similar to the case of math, there also are many diverse science curricula available across all domains of science (e.g., biology, chemistry, physics, geology, etc.). Science curricula are particularly effective when teachers are well-organized and students engage in meaningful laboratory experiences that encourage higher-order thinking. One aspect of science education that is required of most students but is discussed less often is health education. Whereas curricula aimed at teaching more traditional science (e.g., biology and chemistry) are often implemented through a combination of laboratory experiences and in-class lessons, achievement in health needs to be considered from a different vantage point. Specifically, health is a domain in which knowledge may be necessary but not sufficient in and of itself. For example, students certainly benefit from learning about the dangers of opioids, but effective health education curricula focus in particular on teaching students the skills that they need to know (and to utilize) in order to resist the temptation to use opioids (or to engage in other risky behaviors); it isn't sufficient to simply have knowledge about the dangers of opioids – students must learn and become efficacious at utilizing strategies to resist the temptation of using opioids.

6.1 Successful mathematics achievement is attainable

Patti Brosnan, Aaron Schmidlin, and Melva R. Grant

Introduction

Success in mathematics achievement is a goal shared by nations worldwide. Understanding how educational systems can best help students succeed is a central challenge facing education policy makers, school administrators, and teachers today. Herein we will provide readers with research indicating how early studies focused on predictors of successful mathematics achievement, and then we will review some of the current and future directions of research related to this topic and provide policy makers with concrete recommendations for improving student mathematics performance. Whereas the data do not allow causal inference, the results of international studies highlight key differences between mathematics education systems that perform well and those that do not. It is hoped that continued examination of these results would serve as a catalyst for conversations among educational researchers worldwide as a means to define venues for improving mathematical achievement among learners.

We acknowledge that achievement in mathematics might be interpreted in a variety of ways, drawing from various data sources based on one's own paradigm and stance. For the purpose of this section, we define mathematical achievement to correspond with the current views suggested by various international organizations. These views include, but are not limited to, success in meeting both mastery of basic skills and the command of thinking tools and problem-solving skills that assure success in navigating the subject area, including mathematical problem solving, mathematical meaning making depicted through appropriate use of tools when solving novel problems, and the ability to use mathematics in unfamiliar contexts.

Research findings

Scholars had initially defined predictors of mathematics achievement as those factors that organized students into categories according to variables such as sex, race, and socioeconomic status (Gonzales et al., 2008). Accordingly, studies were reported on student success on various measures of achievement according to these criteria. In brief, the difference scores between males and females have decreased dramatically over time, with males having a small gain over females in the highest-performing countries. Cheema and Galluzzo (2013) further stipulated that the gender gap evaporates when analyses control for self-efficacy and anxiety, which are also predictors of mathematics achievement.

Differences between racial/ethnic groups have shown little improvement with the minority populations scoring lower. Socioeconomic status remains the greatest challenge as the difference scores remained consistently lower for students living in poverty. Over time, other predictors such as background knowledge, immigrant student language development, students with disabilities, parental income, and parental education, as well as community type, home background, and motivation were included in studies as a means to expand analysis of factors contributing to mathematics achievement among various groups (Gonzales et al., 2008; Organisation for Economic Co-operation and Development (OECD), 2010a, 2010b, 2016). Collectively, the focus on student characteristics and their influence on achievement did produce results that showed performance gaps among student groups. For instance, disproportionate numbers of poor and racial minority students consistently provided evidence of low performance on high-stakes tests of mathematical competency (Cheema and Galluzzo, 2013; National Action Committee for Minorities in Engineering, 1997; Reardon, 2011).

It has been recognized that the reliance on high-stakes testing and achievement-gap analyses for making instructional and policy decisions regarding mathematics is not without its limitations (Lubienski & Gutiérrez, 2008). For example, Shepard (2001) reviewed the effects of high-stakes accountability pressures. Her findings contend that these measures mostly focus on mathematics skills resulting in "(a) inflated test score gains, (b) curriculum distortion, and (c) loss of intrinsic motivation to learn" (p. 1). Given the pressures of high-stakes testing, many teachers feel that they must focus on skills-based mathematics instruction and therefore fail to provide students with access to the quality of learning that expands their capacity to think and problem solve.

Furthermore, Stipek's (1996) research on motivation and instruction in mathematics concludes that when teachers emphasize preparation for high-stakes testing, there is a corresponding decrease in students' intrinsic motivation toward and interest in learning mathematics. When students are faced with this kind of pressure, they become less engaged in learning tasks and are much less likely to persist in solving difficult problems. These data seem to indicate that the way teachers and administrators go about meeting the mathematics achievement standards before them can be determinant in student success.

According to Schoenfeld (2002), meeting the goal of securing higher levels of student achievement in mathematics, education professionals must commit to delivering a high-quality curriculum; securing a stable, knowledgeable, and professional teaching community; using high-quality assessment that is aligned with curricular goals; and establishing stability and mechanisms for the evolution of curricula, assessment, and professional learning. Current research indicates that there is hope for mathematics educators who are seeking to improve their students' performance. Large-scale reform-oriented research projects have shown that the ability to diminish gaps in performance experienced by minorities and other underrepresented groups (Schoenfeld, 2002), as well as the importance of and students' positive perception of their opportunity to learn mathematics influenced mathematics achievement (Barnard-Brak, Lan, & Yang, 2018).

Learning mathematics

Dewey (1938) stated that "the principle that development of experience comes about through interaction means that education is essentially a social process" (p. 58). Therefore, the social environment plays a crucial role in learning. He also believed that "education begins with the curiosity of the learner" (Savery, 2006, p. 11), thus setting a foundation for the scientific inquiry movement. In this process, a relationship exists between designing experiences and various aspects of learning and cognition (Honey, Pearson, & Schweingruber, 2014). This indicates that acquisition and application of content knowledge and skill must accompany knowledge of how students learn and the instructional strategies for implementing mathematics instruction related to theories of learning.

The learning process through constructing not memorizing is emphasized, and teaching is not simply a process of transferring knowledge to the students (Berns & Erickson, 2001). Contextual learning occurs only when students process new information or knowledge in such a way that it makes sense to them in their own frames of reference. The mind naturally seeks meaning in context by searching for relationships that make sense and appear useful. Instruction should include the basic practices of asking questions or defining problems, brainstorming, planning a design, creating and testing a design, and improving the design of tasks (Engineering is Elementary, 2017; NASA, 2016).

Characteristics of high-achieving programs

International mathematics assessments indicate that high-performing mathematics education programs include curricula that focus on developing higher-order thinking skills, empowered and competent classroom-based professionals, and effective accountability systems that hold schools and administrators responsible for student performance (OECD, 2010b). Under this model, an empowered staff has the freedom to make decisions about mathematics curriculum and instruction and is provided with the support necessary to implement the curriculum effectively (OECD, 2010b). Senk and Thompson (2003) confirm that a focus on instructional practices that aim to advance students' mathematical thinking, instead of mastery of skills, leads to higher performance on measures of achievement on all levels. Additionally, data indicate that when mathematics standards, assessment, curriculum, and professional development are appropriately aligned, historically low-performing groups manage to outperform other groups on all measures of achievement.

Curricula

Educational theorists argue that researchers and policy makers must seek to implement curricula for students that are robust in mathematics content and a pedagogy that is student-centered and challenging and utilize assessment that is formative and summative. To do so, mathematics educators need to develop a deep knowledge of subject matter, child development, learning theories, curriculum trajectory, and teaching methods (Darling-Hammond, 1999). Decades of research and thought have been directed toward developing successful curricula for school mathematics.

High-performing mathematics education programs empower classroom-based professionals and administrators to make decisions about curriculum and instruction for effective implementation and should serve to inform policy makers and educational leaders seeking to implement successful educational programs (OECD, 2010b). A top-down model of reform and implementation wherein policy makers and educational leaders make all curricular decisions has long proven futile in assuring success in nurturing growth among teachers or students. Consensus exists that grounding teacher growth and development in knowledge about student thinking can result in more effective mathematics practice that, in turn, produces higher student mathematics achievement at all levels (Fennema et al., 1996; Franke & Kazemi, 2001).

A mathematics instructional model that has shown much promise is the cognitively guided instruction (CGI) program. In various forms, a CGI model operates on the theory that if teachers understand how students think and learn mathematics, they can better predict what their students need and match their instruction accordingly. Research has shown consistently that students in CGI classrooms demonstrated higher-level problem-solving abilities and greater recall of number facts, while CGI teachers more often emphasized problem-solving skills, listened to students, and had greater knowledge of students' thinking when compared to control-group students and teachers (Carpenter, Fennema, Peterson, Chiang, & Loef, 1989).

While programs like CGI empower teachers to be more successful in the mathematics classroom, sustained support is needed to effectively navigate the demands of student-centered curriculum and instruction. International assessments indicate that student mathematics performance can be negatively impacted when teachers are not adequately prepared, supported, or accountable when making curricular decisions for their students (OECD, 2010b). Clearly, any attempt to implement an effective mathematics education program must include staff capable of providing it.

Prerequisite support for implementation

International assessment results and their associated inquiries indicate that high-performing mathematics education programs include teaching professionals that are sufficiently supported to implement the curriculum effectively (OECD, 2010b). One characteristic of nations that are high achieving in mathematics is commitment to professional learning for teachers, and the research literature supports the effectiveness of these practices. This suggests a connection among opportunities for teacher learning, quality of teaching, and student learning of mathematics. This characteristic focus on supporting teachers should not be surprising. In their systematic review of 1,300 studies on the effectiveness of teachers' in-service professional learning, Yoon and colleagues (Yoon, Duncan, Lee, Scarloss, & Shapley, 2007) analyzed the findings from six studies that offered substantial contact hours of professional learning in mathematics education (ranging from thirty to one hundred hours in total) spread out over 6 to 12 months showed a positive and significant effect on student mathematics achievement gains by approximately 21 percentile points (Polly et al., 2014).

While qualitative studies have sought to examine how professional communities in mathematics are formed and how they operate, a number of large-scale studies have illustrated how collaborative, classroom-embedded professional learning that is focused on student performance has resulted in changed practices and improved student mathematics achievement (Calkins, Guenther, Belfore, & Lash, 2007; Goddard, Goddard, & Tschannen-Moran, 2007; ndunda, Van Sickle, Perry, & Capelloni, 2017).

One strategy that features classroom-embedded professional learning is school-based coaching. Coaching is grounded in the notion of building capacity for positive change in teaching practice and having highly trained practitioners working with their colleagues to promote learning and improve practice (Becker, 2001). Coaching models recognize that if professional learning is to take root in teachers' practice, ongoing and specific follow-up is necessary to help teachers incorporate new knowledge and skills into mathematics classroom practice (Killion, 2017; Campbell & Malkus, 2011; Garet, Porter, Desimone, Birman, & Yoon, 2001; Guskey, 2000).

Summary and recommendations

Understanding how educational systems can best help students succeed in mathematics is a central challenge facing education policy makers, school administrators, and teachers today. Older research in the field of mathematics education sought to categorize and track students to understand why certain groups of students were more likely to succeed or fail. International research indicates that this focus on students as the problem may be misguided. As internationally successful mathematics programs continue to show lower differences in student performance than is observed in less-successful programs, it is becoming clearer that the presence or absence of this gap in student mathematics performance seems to be dependent upon the educational system in which students happen to find themselves (OECD, 2010b). This indicates that the problem is not the result of individual student deficiencies but rather the result of deficiencies in the system they attend. Recognizing this possibility is a good first step to improving student mathematics performance in any educational system.

Recommendations, on the basis of international research, suggest that increasing student mathematics achievement cannot be accomplished in the absence of robust educational programs for teacher development. Primarily, in order for our educational systems to be successful in mathematics, teachers need to be able to respond to students' needs. This cannot occur unless teachers are allowed to adjust curriculum in response to the needs of their students; are able to understand student-learning needs; and are provided the time, peer support, and classroom-embedded training necessary to perform these functions well. When mathematics teachers are well supported in teaching for understanding and have good curricular materials to use, children really do learn mathematics problem-solving skills, and racial and SES differences in performance diminish. Given this, the policy issue that needs to be addressed is what kinds of systemic support structures will promote the successful implementation of mathematics curricula and their progressive refinement over time?

Critical-thinking skills can be acquired through nonroutine problem solving, using reasoning to link evidence to explanation and application of knowledge to other situations (Bybee, 2013). Research highlights three significant social processes involved in learning: learner participation, teacher guidance, and the nature and meaning of the learning activities. An important factor is the design of the instruction and related experiences that support productive and successful cognitive and social interactions within the learning community that will ultimately affect learning outcomes (Honey et al., 2014). Studies of engineering design and practices assert that "failure plays a prominent role and provides unique opportunities for learning and improving design" (Madhavan, 2015).

Further research needs to be conducted into how teachers and students may be assisted in establishing a platform for success in ways that both groups contribute to and benefit from quality mathematics education. While mathematics may be a civil rights issue, clearly educational programs cannot succeed unless they account for the needs of their participants (Schoenfeld, 2002).

References

Barnard-Brak, L., Lan, W. Y., & Yang, Z. (2018). Differences in mathematics achievement according to opportunity to learn: A 4pL item response theory examination. *Studies in Educational Evaluation, 56*, 1–7.

Becker, J. R. (2001). Classroom coaching: An emergent method of professional development. In R. Speiser, C. A. Maher, & C. N. Walter (Eds.), *Proceedings of the twenty third meeting of the psychology of mathematics education – NA XXIII* (pp. 751–760). Snowbird, UT: Psychology of Mathematics Education.

Berns, R. G., & Erickson, P. (2001). Contextual teaching and learning: Preparing students for the new economy. *The Highlight Zone: Research @ Work, 5*, 2–9.

Bybee, R. W. (2013). *The case for STEM education challenges and opportunities.* Arlington, VA: National Science Teachers Association.

Calkins, A., Guenther, W., Belfore, G., & Lash, D. (2007). *The turnaround challenge: Why America's best opportunity to dramatically improve student achievement lies in our worst performing schools.* Boston, MA: Mass Insight Education & Research Institute.

Campbell, P., & Malkus, N. N. (2011). The impact of elementary mathematics coaches on student achievement. *The Elementary School Journal, 111*(March), 430–454.

Carpenter, T. P., Fennema, E., Peterson, P. L., Chiang, C. P., & Loef, M. (1989). Using knowledge of children's mathematics thinking in classroom teaching: An experimental study. *American Educational Research Journal, 26*(4), 499–531.

Cheema, J. R., & Galluzzo, G. (2013). Analyzing the gender gap in math achievement: Evidence from a large-scale US sample. *Research in Education, 90*, 98–112.

Darling-Hammond, L. (1999). *Teacher quality and student achievement: A review of state policy evidence.* Seattle, WA: Center for the Study of Teaching and Policy, University of Washington.

Dewey, J. (1938). *Experience and education.* New York: Simon and Schuster.

Engineering is Elementary. (2017). *The engineering design process.* Retrieved from http://www.eie.org/overview/engineering-design-process

Fennema, E., Carpenter, T., Franke, M., Levi, L., Jacobs, V., & Empson, S. (1996). A longitudinal study of learning to use children's thinking in mathematics instruction. *Journal for Research in Mathematics Education, 27*(4), 403–434.

Franke, M., & Kazemi, E. (2001). Learning to teach mathematics: Focus on student thinking. *Theory into Practice, 40*(2), 102–109.

Garet, M., Porter, A., Desimone, L., Birman, B., & Yoon, K. S. (2001). What makes professional development effective? Results from a national sample of teachers. *American Educational Research Journal, 38*(4), 915–945.

Goddard, Y. L., Goddard, R. D., & Tschannen-Moran, M. (2007). Theoretical and empirical investigation of teacher collaboration for school improvement and student achievement in public elementary schools. *Teachers College Record, 109*(4), 877–896.

Gonzales, P., Williams, T., Jocelyn, L., Roey, S., Kastberg, D., & Brenwald, S. (2008). *Highlights from TIMSS 2007: Mathematics and science achievement of U.S. fourth- and eighth-grade students in an international context.* Jessup, MD: National Center for Education Statistics.

Guskey, T. G. (2000). *Evaluating professional development.* Thousand Oaks, CA: Corwin Press.

Honey, M., Pearson, G., & Schweingruber, H. (Eds.). (2014). *STEM integration in K-12 education: Status, prospects, and an agenda for research.* Washington, DC: Committee on Integrated STEM Education; National Academy of Engineering; National Research Council.

Killion, J. (2017). Meta-analysis reveals coaching's positive impact on instruction and achievement. *The Learning Professional, 38*(2), 20–23.

Lubienski, S. T., & Gutiérrez, R. (2008). Bridging the "gaps" in perspectives on equity in mathematics education. *Journal for Research in Mathematics Education, 39*(4), 365–371.

Madhavan, G. (2015). *Applied minds: How engineers think.* New York, NY: W. W. Norton & Company, Incorporated.

NASA. (2016). *NASA's BEST – The engineering design process*. Retrieved from https://www.nasa.gov/audience/foreducators/best/edp.html

National Action Committee for Minorities in Engineering. (1997). *Engineering and affirmative action: Crisis in the making*. New York, NY: Author.

ndunda, M., Van Sickle, M., Perry, L., & Capelloni, A. (2017). University–urban high school partnership: Math and science professional learning communities. *School Science and Mathematics, 117*, 137–145. doi:10.1111/ssm.12215

Organisation for Economic Co-operation and Development (OECD). (2010a). *PISA 2009 results: Overcoming social background – Equity in learning opportunities and outcomes* (Vol. 2). http://dx.doi.org/10.1787/9789264091504-en

Organisation of Economic Co-operation and Development (OECD). (2010b). *PISA 2009 results: Learning to learn – Student engagement, strategies and practices* (Vol. 3). http://dx.doi.org/10.1787/9789264083943-en

Organisation for Economic Co-operation and Development (OECD). (2016). *PISA 2015 results: Collaborative problem solving* (Vol. 5). http://dx.doi.org/10.1787/9789264091504-en

Polly, D., Wang, C., McGee, J. R., Lambert, R. G., Martin, C. S., & Pugalee, D. K. (2014). Examining the influence of a curriculum-based elementary mathematics professional development program. *Journal of Research in Childhood Education, 28*, 327–343. doi:10.1080/02568543.2014.913276

Reardon, S. F. (2011). The widening academic achievement gap between the rich and the poor: New evidence and possible explanations. In R. Murnane & G. Duncan (Eds.), *Whither opportunity? Rising inequality and the uncertain life chances of low-income children*. New York, NY: Russell Sage Foundation.

Savery, J. R. (2006). Overview of problem-based learning: Definitions and distinctions. *Interdisciplinary Journal of Problem-Based Learning, 1*(1), 9–20.

Schoenfeld, A. (2002). Making mathematics work for all children: Issues of standards, testing, and equity. *Educational Researcher, 31*(1), 13–25.

Senk, S., & Thompson, D. (Eds.). (2003). *Standards-oriented school mathematics curricula: What does the research say about student outcomes?* Mahwah, NJ: Erlbaum.

Shepard, L. (2001). *Protecting learning from the harmful effects of high-stakes testing*. Paper presented at the annual meeting of the American Educational Research Association, Seattle, WA.

Stipek, D. J. (1996). Motivation and instruction. In D. C. Berliner & R. C. Calfee (Eds.), *Handbook of educational psychology* (pp. 85–113). New York, NY: Palgrave Macmillan.

Yoon, K. S., Duncan, T., Lee, S. W-Y., Scarloss, B., & Shapley, K. (2007). *Reviewing the evidence on how teacher professional development affects student achievement* (Issues & Answers Report, REL 2007 – No. 033). Retrieved from http://ies.ed.gov/ncee/edlabs/regions/southwest/pdf/REL_2007033.pdf

6.2 Bilingual education programs and student achievement

Jill Fitzgerald and Jackie Eunjung Relyea

Introduction

The term *bilingual education program* refers to school-based instruction in which students' first language and another language, sometimes the societal language, are used. There are many forms and labels for bilingual education programs, including dual-language, one- or two-way dual-language, bilingual immersion education, developmental bilingual education, and transitional bilingual education. Program labels typically depend on the timing of instructional introduction and cessation of either native or new language and on the extent to which each language is emphasized.

Over 7,000 languages are spoken in the world (Simons & Fenning, 2018), and more than half the world's population is bilingual (Bialystok, 2017). Reasons for bilingual education vary and depend on factors such as the linguistic heterogeneity of a country, the desire to promote national identity or cultural heritage, and the political will for national participation in global citizenship. In many parts of the world, bilingualism has been a culturally important standard for thousands of years. The literature is replete with support for the important personal and societal benefits of bilingualism. For example, bilingual children may outperform monolinguals on cognitive and metalinguistic tasks (e.g., Bialystok & Martin, 2004). However, bilingual education in many parts of the world is not without critics. For instance, where language-minority children represent a fast-growing segment of the school-age population, use of minority language in schooling and bilingual education programs is controversial (Cummins & Swain, 2014).

Sound bilingual education program implementation and policy depend in part on data-based studies. However, situational factors surrounding bilingual education program implementation, as well as challenges in accomplishing bilingual education research, make attribution of outcome effects to program characteristics and synthesis across studies difficult. Unfortunately, the challenges are not well addressed in much of the current research literature on bilingual education effectiveness. The most salient research design challenges to address include the following: (a) studying effectiveness of potentially contributory variables within "packages" of instructional delivery; (b) conducting true experiments with random assignment; (c) documenting student growth over reasonably long periods of time; (d) including researcher-designed and curriculum-based measures which may provide additional insight into students' progress; (e) demonstrating group equivalence before intervention or providing statistical control for pre-intervention group differences; (f) including sample sizes sufficient to ensure reasonable power to reveal significant differences where they exist; and (g) assuring that competing explanations for results are controlled, for instance, assuring that content, delivery, and quality are similar across groups. Additional challenges for research syntheses include researcher failure to report (a) comparison program description and implementation fidelity; (b) description of societal, political, and cultural contexts that might impact students' language-learning motivation identity formation, or academic performance – a particular challenge when trying to synthesize across nations (e.g., English-as-a foreign-language learning situations tend to be quite different from English learning as a second language when the national language is English) (e.g., Marsh, Hau, & Kong, 2000); (c) extensive descriptions of student variables such as length of time living in the country or level of native- and new-language oracy and literacy; and (d) clear and complete description of outcome measures, especially information about test score reliability and validity.

Research evidence

Three large-scale, longitudinal, quasi-experimental US studies that were published by federally funded agencies or a private company resulted in comparable conclusions and are frequently cited in the literature. Ramírez and colleagues (Ramírez, Yuen, Ramey, & Pasta, 1991) and Thomas and Collier (1997) reported that young students learning English as a new language who were in earlier-exit bilingual programs, on average, made similar or greater progress in English reading, English language arts, and mathematics as compared to counterparts in English-immersion programs or to norms reported for standardized tests. However, after third grade (through sixth or twelfth, respectively), students who were enrolled in earlier-exit programs demonstrated decelerated rates of performance while those in maintenance, late-exit, or dual-language programs made more positive academic strides on average. Thomas and Collier (2002) later reported similar findings and cautioned that students with low levels of English proficiency should only be placed in long-term dual-language or maintenance programs.

In addition to the three large-scale studies, a handful of narrative or quantitative meta-analytic research syntheses on the topic of bilingual education program achievement effects in the United States are also widely cited by researchers, practitioners, and policy makers (e.g., Baker & de Kanter, 1981; Greene, 1998; Krashen & McField, 2005; Rolstad, Mahoney, & Glass, 2005, 2008; Rossell & Baker, 1996; Slavin & Cheung, 2003; Willig, 1985). Conclusions across the research syntheses are mixed. For example, Willig (1985) and Greene (1998) conducted meta-analyses using strict criteria for study inclusion, and Rolstad et al (2005) conducted a meta-analysis using broad criteria for inclusion, resulting in reviews of 23, 11, and 17 studies, respectively. All three sets of researchers concluded that bilingual education was more advantageous for English-language learners' academic and language learning when compared to various other programs. The authors of the only located meta-analysis of European studies of bilingual education similarly reported a small positive effect for bilingual education over submersion programs for reading in five studies (Reljić, Ferring, & Martin, 2015).

On the other hand, conclusions from three often-cited narrative research syntheses were mixed. Baker and de Kanter (1981), Rossell and Baker (1996), and Slavin and Cheung (2003) each used relatively strict criteria for study inclusion, resulting in reviews of 28, 72, and 16 studies of English-language learners, respectively. Only one set of researchers, Slavin and Cheung (2003), concluded that, on the whole, the evidence favored bilingual approaches, especially dual-language programs. Baker and de Kanter (1981) reported mixed results. Students in transitional bilingual education sometimes outperformed counterparts in other types of programs, but sometimes students in English-as-a-second-language pullout programs outperformed those in other programs. Rossell and Baker (1996) updated the Baker and de Kanter (1981) study and concluded there was no consistent research support for transitional bilingual education as a superior instructional program for students learning English.

In addition to the meta-analyses and syntheses, over the last three decades, many studies have investigated bilingual education in the United States and internationally. In a previous search of the literature, we employed a minimum standard for quasi-experimental and experimental design rigor (cf. August & Shanahan, 2006) for peer-reviewed studies published between 1985 and 2010, and we included and reported on 14 studies that met the minimum criteria (Fitzgerald & Relyea-Kim, 2013). For the present review, we included studies from 1985 to 2018 and increased the criteria for rigor in an effort to discern the most dependable results. Among the new requirements, assessment of pre-intervention group equivalence on the outcome(s) had to be accomplished, or the pretested dependent variable(s) had to be used as a covariate(s), and acceptable reliability estimates for measures had to be reported. Only nine studies (one international study examining secondary students and eight US studies examining preschool through second grade) met the criteria for close analysis. Although the number was very small and highly focused on preschool and primary grades, identification of findings from the selected most rigorously designed studies has the potential to provide at least some valuable information for the field.

The following main findings emerged:

(a) For growth in English and Spanish language, literacy, and mathematics measures, there was a tendency for bilingual education students to perform similarly to counterparts in English-only or no-preschool settings. For English (as new language) outcomes, among the five studies in which some form of bilingual education was compared to either English (as new language) immersion or to no preschool, for 23 of 26 assessed outcomes, there were no comparative group differences (Admiraal, Westhoff, & de Bot, 2006; Barnett, Yarosz, Thomas, Jung, & Blanco, 2007; Durán, Roseth, & Hoffman, 2010; Rodríguez, Díaz, Duran, & Espinosa, 1995; Winsler, Díaz, Espinosa, & Rodríguez, 1999). In only two studies, bilingual preschool education favored no preschool (Rodríguez et al., 1995; Winsler et al., 1999).

Similarly, when Spanish (native-language) outcomes were measured in four studies, the preponderance of evidence indicated no difference in growth between comparative groups (Barnett et al., 2007; Durán et al., 2010; Rodríguez et al., 1995; Winsler et al., 1999). For only 6 of the 21 outcomes that were measured, some form of bilingual education advantaged end-of-year achievement or growth on selected language and/or literacy outcomes.

(b) When comparing two forms of bilingual education for kindergarten through grade 2 few differences between groups were reported for English outcomes. In each study, some form of bilingual education was associated with more growth in one or more languages or literacy outcomes as compared to another form of bilingual education. For example, students who received enhanced transitional bilingual education that had more oral English instruction (Tong, Lara-Alecio, Irby, Mathes, & Kwok, 2008) or more structured English instruction (Tong, Lara-Alecio et al., 2008; Tong, Irby, Lara-Alecio, & Mathes, 2008) outperformed counterparts on selected outcomes. However, for 12 of the 19 assessed outcomes across the studies, no differences between groups were found.

(c) When two forms of bilingual education involving Spanish and English for preschool or for kindergarten through first or second grade were compared, there was a trend favoring inclusion of more Spanish instruction (Durán, Roseth, Hoffman, & Robertshaw, 2013; Durán, Roseth, & Hoffman, 2015; Tong, Irby et al., 2008).

(d) Finally, a pressing policy issue in some countries is related to whether any advantages witnessed in new-language learning in bilingual situations simultaneously negatively affect maintenance of native language. In no case was student growth on any measure of native language diminished, as compared to peers'.

Summary and recommendations

In part because of great variability in program definition and in research design, conclusions from research and research syntheses are mixed. Rather than address the "Does bilingual education work?" question, perhaps more will be learned by asking "What desirable learning outcomes are achieved under which kinds of conditions and for which kinds of students?" To accomplish such research, however, there is a great need to give more attention to at least three factors. First, researchers must attend to theoretical reasoning and hypothesizing about potential factors and critical mechanisms at play in studies. Such attention might provide an important scaffold for both research design and interpretation of results (cf. Marsh et al., 2000). For instance, researchers could address potential aptitude-by-treatment interactions under conditions where student outcomes may be functions of student characteristics such as language background and motivation, sociocultural factors, and educational program characteristics (e.g., Cummins, 1996). Second, mixed-methods studies might lead to better understanding of program results in relation to program, sociocultural, and student characteristics. Third, increased research activity worldwide, especially with regard to both native- and new-language program emphases and outcomes, could greatly enhance our understanding of program impact on student achievement in varying social contexts.

References

Admiraal, W., Westhoff, G., & de Bot, K. (2006). Evaluation of bilingual secondary education in the Netherlands: Students' language proficiency in English. *Educational Research and Evaluation, 12*, 75–93.

August, D., & Shanahan, T. (2006). *Developing literacy in second-language learners: Report of the national literacy panel on language minority children and youth.* Mahwah, NJ: Erlbaum.

Baker, K., & de Kanter, A. A. (1981). *Effectiveness of bilingual education: A review of the literature* (Final draft report). Washington, DC: Department of Education, Office of Planning, Budget, and Evaluation.

Barnett, W. S., Yarosz, D. J., Thomas, J., Jung, K., & Blanco, D. (2007). Two-way and monolingual English immersion in preschool education: An experimental comparison. *Early Childhood Research Quarterly, 22*, 277–293.

Bialystok, E. (2017). The bilingual adaptation: How minds accommodate experience. *Psychological Bulletin, 143*(3), 233–262.

Bialystok, E., & Martin, M. M. (2004). Attention and inhibition in bilingual children: Evidence from the dimensional change card sort task. *Developmental Science, 7*, 325–339.

Cummins, J. (1996). Bilingual education: What does the research say? In J. Cummins (Ed.), *Negotiating identities: Education for empowerment in a diverse society* (pp. 97–133). Los Angeles, CA: California Association for Bilingual Education.

Cummins, J., & Swain, M. (2014). *Bilingualism in education: Aspects of theory, research and practice.* New York, NY: Routledge.

Durán, L. K., Roseth, C., & Hoffman, P. (2010). An experimental study comparing English-only and transitional bilingual education on Spanish-speaking preschoolers' early literacy development. *Early Childhood Research Quarterly, 25*, 207–217.

Durán, L. K., Roseth, C., & Hoffman, P. (2015). Effects of transitional bilingual education on Spanish-speaking preschoolers' literacy and language development: Year 2 results. *Applied Psycholinguistics, 36*, 921–951.

Durán, L. K., Roseth, C., Hoffman, P., & Robertshaw, M. B. (2013). Spanish-speaking preschoolers' early literacy development: A longitudinal experimental comparison of predominantly English and transitional bilingual education. *Bilingual Research Journal, 36*, 6–34.

Fitzgerald, J., & Relyea-Kim, E. J. (2013). Bilingual education programs and student achievement. In J. Hattie & E. Anderman (Eds.), *International handbook of student achievement* (pp. 285–288). London and New York, NY: Routledge.

Greene, J. P. (1998). *A meta-analysis of the effectiveness of bilingual education*. Claremont, CA: Thomas Rivera Policy Institute.

Krashen, S., & McField, G. (2005). What works? Reviewing the latest evidence on bilingual education. *Language Learner, 1*(2), 7–10.

Marsh, H. W., Hau, K. T., & Kong, C. W. (2000). Late immersion and language of instruction in Hong Kong high schools: Achievement growth in language and non-language subjects. *Harvard Educational Review, 70*, 302–346.

Ramírez, D. J., Yuen, S. D., Ramey, D. R., & Pasta, D. J. (1991). *Final report: National longitudinal study of structured English immersion strategy, early-exit and late-exit transitional bilingual education programs for language-minority children* (Vols. 1–2). San Mateo, CA: Aguirre International.

Reljić, G., Ferring, D., & Martin, R. (2015). A meta-analysis on the effectiveness of bilingual programs in Europe. *Review of Educational Research, 85*, 92–128.

Rodríguez, J. L., Díaz, R. M., Duran, D., & Espinosa, L. (1995). The impact of bilingual preschool education on the language development of Spanish-speaking children. *Early Childhood Research Quarterly, 10*, 475–490.

Rolstad, K., Mahoney, K., & Glass, G. (2008). The big picture in bilingual education: A meta-analysis corrected for Gersten's coding error. *Journal of Educational Research & Policy Studies, 8*(2), 1–15.

Rolstad, K., Mahoney, K., & Glass, G. V. (2005). The big picture: A meta-analysis of program effectiveness research on English language learners. *Educational Policy, 19*(4), 572–594.

Rossell, C. H., & Baker, K. (1996). The educational effectiveness of bilingual education. *Research in the Teaching of English, 30*(1), 7–74.

Simons, G. F., & Fenning, C. D. (2018). *Ethnologue: Languages of the world, twenty-first edition*. Dallas, TX: SIL International.

Slavin, R. E., & Cheung, A. (2003). *Effective reading programs for English language learners: A best-evidence synthesis*. Baltimore, MD: Johns Hopkins University Center for Research on the Education of Students Placed at Risk (CRESPAR).

Thomas, W. P., & Collier, V. (1997). *School effectiveness for language minority students*. Washington, DC: National Clearinghouse for Bilingual Education.

Thomas, W. P., & Collier, V. (2002). *A national study of school effectiveness for language minority students' long-term academic achievement: Final report*. Washington, DC: Center for Research on Education, Diversity & Excellence.

Tong, F., Irby, B. J., Lara-Alecio, R., & Mathes, P. G. (2008). English and Spanish acquisition by Hispanic second graders in developmental bilingual programs: A 3-year longitudinal randomized study. *Hispanic Journal of Behavioral Science, 30*, 500–529.

Tong, F., Lara-Alecio, R., Irby, B., Mathes, P., & Kwok, O. (2008). Accelerating early academic oral English development in transitional bilingual and structured English immersion programs. *American Educational Research Journal, 45*, 1011–1044.

Willig, A. C. (1985). A meta-analysis of selected studies on the effectiveness of bilingual education. *Review of Educational Research, 5*(3), 269–318.

Winsler, A., Díaz, R. M., Espinosa, L., & Rodríguez, J. L. (1999). When learning a second language does not mean losing the first: Bilingual language development in low-income, Spanish-speaking children attending bilingual preschool. *Child Development, 70*, 349–362.

6.3

Language teaching curricula

Eli Hinkel

Introduction

English-language learners (ELLs) represent a large majority of those who set out to learn a language other than their mother tongue in school systems in English-speaking countries. These students work to acquire English as a second language (ESL) in the process of their schooling. According to the National Center for Educational Statistics, in 2018, more than 30% of all students in US schools were ELLs who were speakers of over 500 languages, with Spanish being the most common and spoken by 71% of ELLs. In practically all school systems in various world regions, such as Australia, Canada, New Zealand, and the United Kingdom, ELLs come from a wide variety of backgrounds. These students can be recent immigrants, children of guest workers, children of employees of multinational companies, or other types of sojourners, as well as individuals raised in families or communities where English is not used for communication. In regions where English is the primary language of schooling, extensive resources are dedicated to providing ELLs with the essential proficiencies that are fundamental to their schooling (e.g., listening comprehension, speaking, reading, and writing). These resources include supplementary instruction in language and skill development; teacher preparation, education, and special training; curricula; textbooks; language testing and assessment instruments; and the teaching materials, time, and financial means to utilize these resources. Due to the fact that the number of ELLs in school systems in various countries is expected to grow, extensive and intensive efforts have been undertaken to meet their language-learning needs.

Research evidence

To date, an enormous amount of data has established that a dramatic divide persists in the academic achievement of ELLs and other groups of students (e.g.,

Darling-Hammond, 2015; Espinoza-Herold & Gonzalez-Carriedo, 2017; Thomas & Collier, 2002). Data consist of test and examination scores, graduation rates, a broad range of language proficiency measures, and a vast body of research. A key reason for the prominent and persistent achievement divide stems from the fact that ELLs need to develop their language proficiencies while simultaneously attaining and demonstrating knowledge of content in school subjects, such as social studies, history, and math. Currently, there is no empirical validation of the effectiveness of curriculum designs developed specifically for ELLs (e.g., Espinoza-Herold & Gonzalez-Carriedo, 2017; Hinkel, 2017; What Works Clearinghouse, 2013). For this reason, the remainder of this overview will take a brief look at the two most predominant and widely adopted curricular models for teaching ELLs language and content simultaneously.

At present, two different types of curricula that seek to combine instruction in both language and school subjects are prevalent in various world regions. Content-based language and subject-matter instruction is commonly adopted in US and Canadian school curricula, whereas genre-based language teaching predominates in the UK, Australia, and New Zealand. Since 2014 and 2015, a far less prevalent curricular model that corresponds to North American content-based instruction has emerged in various European regions under the umbrella term of content and language integrated learning.

The main principles of *content-based curricula* consist of integrating second-language reading, writing, and language instruction with subject-matter content, such as history or math (e.g., Snow, 2017; Snow & Brinton, 2017). For example, integrated instruction in content and language can pivot on thematically selected readings or writing tasks, with the attendant language teaching that focuses on the uses of grammar and contextualized vocabulary. In some cases, content-based instruction can also have supplementary foci on other academic skills, such as critical thinking, library research, or information gathering (Hinkel, 2015).

Content-based teaching in the form of sheltered instruction observation protocol (SIOP) has been widely adopted in US schools that enroll large numbers of ELLs. The SIOP model in effect represents a framework for teaching school subjects and language in mainstream classes. To this end, SIOP also deals with various classroom strategies and techniques for teachers who work with ELLs in their schools (e.g., Echevarría, Vogt, & Short, 2016). Under the auspices of the US Department of Education, the What Works Clearinghouse (WWC) has examined 32 studies of SIOP effectiveness that were published or released between 1983 and 2012. According to this review (What Works Clearinghouse, 2013, p. 1), 7 of the empirical studies of SIOP effectiveness do not meet "evidence standards," 22 do not have "an eligible study design" because they "do not use a comparison group" or present only meta-analyses and literature reviews, and the remaining 3 include student samples with "less than 50%" ELLs. Thus, "the lack of studies meeting WWC evidence standards means that" no conclusions can be made "based on research about the effectiveness or ineffectiveness of SIOP on English language learners" (p. 1).

Outside the United States as well, several important and practical concerns have been widely noted regarding content-based instruction and the teaching of language at the same time. One of these, for instance, pertains to the level of expertise in matters of content and language expected of mainstream or language teachers who work within content-based curricular models. Many empirical reports indicate that language teachers are trained to deal with language pedagogy but are far less trained in the areas of content and school subjects (e.g., Lightbown, 2014; Snow, 2017). On the other hand, in the context of language-centered curricula, it may be difficult to determine what content should be included for the purposes of language development. Additionally, in content-based instruction, research has not yet established what content needs to be taught in order to advance students' language skills (e.g., Dalton-Puffer, 2011). In light of the fact that a great deal of preparation and work is required for teaching content to ELLs, in many cases, the teaching of the language – for example, grammar and writing – is often neglected. As an outcome, a vast majority of instructional materials on content-based teaching consistently emphasize the need for intensive and focused language instruction (e.g., Hinkel, 2020; Snow, 2017).

In the UK, New Zealand, and Australia in particular, *genre-based curricular models and approaches* predominate among methodological schools of thought on language and subject-matter instruction. Genre-based curricula, similar to content-based teaching, also seek to integrate the teaching of language with instruction in reading and writing. The genre-based approach and teaching techniques draw on the foundations of systemic functional linguistics and genre theory. These analytical approaches serve as the basis for teaching the language required of ELLs in school subjects. To this end, genre-based language instruction centers on the features of language employed in a diverse range of spoken and written genres, such as school textbooks, academic speaking and writing, or subject matter assignments that require both reading and writing. This curricular model addresses a broad array of genres from news reports to textbooks and formal written prose. The overarching objective of genre-based pedagogy is to enable ELLs to analyze school discourse while reading and writing in order to produce written prose typically expected in the context of schooling (e.g., Christie, 2012).

In genre-based curricula, language teaching endeavors to address the features of discourse and text in the social and practical contexts where the written prose is produced and the purposes which it is expected to meet. To achieve this goal, teaching activities may represent an analysis of written prose in such genres as textbooks in social sciences or history or math story problems. Classroom teaching is designed to increase students' awareness of particular grammar and vocabulary elements found in school texts or other contexts (e.g., Gibbons, 2014).

However, as with the content-based curricular design, the effectiveness of genre-based curricula and teaching methods has not been established empirically. Many experts in the teaching and learning of language and second language contend that genres and their linguistic features may be subjective, culture bound, vaguely defined, or even irrelevant to diverse types of ELLs (Hinkel, 2011; Leki, 2007). For example, Henry Widdowson, one of the prominent world-class authorities on language teaching (Widdowson, 2003, p. 69) states that "the conception of genres as stable entities is only a convenient fiction: they are in reality sociocultural processes, continually in flux." According to Widdowson (Widdowson, 2013), the findings of genre analyses represent impressionistic judgments about their distinctiveness, and therefore, such findings simply have limited validity. Thus, given that genres are far from well defined, the pedagogic viability of genre-based curricula and the attendant teaching of genre-defined discourse and language features is, in fact, "limited" (Widdowson, 2003, p. 70).

Summary and recommendations

In the practical matters of teaching, several important issues have been noted in connection with content- and genre-based instruction and ELL curricula. At present, practically all pedagogical materials on content and curricula across the school grades explicitly direct teachers to focus intensively on ELLs' needs for developing academic language.

Research has also demonstrated that, in many cases, crucial factors that confound L2 teaching and learning have to do with early childhood language proficiencies that considerably disadvantage L2 learners' school readiness and performance. In recent years, a number of measures have been implemented to address ELLs' academic progress and achievement, including full-day kindergarten mandated in close to 20 states, as well as prekindergarten programs with a focus on oral skills and vocabulary. The findings of numerous research reports emphasize, however, that, for ELLs at practically all levels of schooling and education, academic language proficiency and skills take years to attain.

In school instruction and curriculum, it is often assumed that ELLs' language proficiencies can increase with L2 exposure and that academic language demands can be met in the context of learning. It is a fact, however, that the languages of science, mathematics, and history – vocabulary, grammar, and concepts – is not encountered in routine daily tasks and social interactions simply because it does not occur there. A fundamental and foundational goal of schooling and learning the academic language is to determine what the language-learning needs are and to design a curriculum of study that can enable ELLs to meet the demands of schooling and education. That is, first and foremost, to build a curriculum, it is essential to determine what content is needed and in what sequence, what the teaching needs are, and how these needs can be met.

The large amount of evidence on L2 teaching and learning supports a clear conclusion that academic vocabulary and grammar (e.g. to meet the demands of listening, speaking, reading, and writing) have to be explicitly and persistently taught. Explicit instruction relies on teachers' professional preparation, direct and deliberate attention to the language of academic tasks, and assessments to make the content accessible to ELLs and for their proficiencies to grow. A well-designed and careful curriculum is of the essence.

Valid research takes a top priority in identifying language skills and teaching methodologies to help bridge the unmistakable achievement divide between ELLs and other cohorts of students. Specifically, to improve language capacities and raise academic achievements, new investigations and insights are called for in the areas of ELLs' immediate and long-term learning needs, educational objectives, effective school curricula, instructional strategies, and professional teacher preparation. In the final count, the overarching objective of empirically grounded and principled curricular designs is to provide ELLs with access to educational opportunities and to enable these students to communicate effectively in a broad range of educational and social contexts.

References

Christie, F. (2012). *Language education throughout the school years: A functional perspective*. West Sussex: Wiley-Blackwell.

Dalton-Puffer, C. (2011). Content-and-language integrated learning: From practice to principles? *Annual Review of Applied Linguistics, 31*, 182–204.

Darling-Hammond, L. (2015). *The flat world and education: How America's commitment to equity will determine our future*. New York: Teachers College Press.

Echevarría, J., Vogt, M., & Short, D. (2016). *Making content comprehensible for English learners: The SIOP model* (5th ed.). Boston, MA: Pearson.

Espinoza-Herold, M., & Gonzalez-Carriedo, R. (2017). *Issues in Latino education: Race, school culture, and the politics of academic success*. New York, NY: Taylor & Francis.

Gibbons, P. (2014). *Scaffolding language, scaffolding learning: Teaching English language learners in the mainstream classroom* (2nd ed.). Portsmouth: Heinemann.

Hinkel, E. (2011). What research on second language writing tells us and what it doesn't. In E. Hinkel (Ed.), *Handbook of research in second language teaching and learning* (Vol. 2, pp. 523–538), New York, NY: Routledge.

Hinkel, E. (2015). *Effective curriculum for teaching L2 writing: Principles and techniques*. New York, NY: Routledge.

Hinkel, E. (Ed.). (2017). *Handbook of research in second language teaching and learning* (Vol. 3). New York, NY: Routledge.

Hinkel, E. (2020). *Teaching academic L2 writing: Practical techniques in vocabulary and grammar* (2nd ed.). New York, NY: Routledge.

Leki, I. (2007). *Undergraduates in a second language: Challenges and complexities of academic literacy development*. New York, NY: Routledge.

Lightbown, P. (2014). *Focus on content-based language teaching*. Oxford: Oxford University Press.

Snow, M. (2017). Content-based language teaching and academic language development. In E. Hinkel (Ed.), *Handbook of research in second language teaching and learning* (Vol. 3, pp. 153–172). New York, NY: Routledge.

Snow, M., & Brinton, D. (2017). *The content-based classroom: New perspectives on integrating language and content* (2nd ed.). Ann Arbor, MI: University of Michigan Press.

Thomas, W., & Collier, V. (2002). *A national study of school effectiveness for language minority students' long-term academic achievement: Final report.* Santa Cruz, CA: Center for Research on Education, Diversity & Excellence.

What Works Clearinghouse. (2013). *WWC intervention report: Sheltered instruction observation protocol (SIOP).* Washington, DC: Institute of Education Sciences, U.S. Department of Education.

Widdowson, H. (2003). *Defining issues in English language teaching.* Oxford: Oxford University Press.

Widdowson, H. G. (2013). On the applicability of empirical findings. *European Journal of Applied Linguistics, 1*(1), 4–21.

6.4

Response to intervention and multitiered systems of supports

Paul J. Riccomini and Gregory W. Smith

Introduction

Pertaining to the education of students with disabilities, the international trend of Western countries has been influenced by rights-based principles inherent in the reports, declarations, and treaties of the United Nations (UN), the United Nations Educational, Scientific and Cultural Organization (UNESCO), and the Organization for Economic Cooperation and Development (OECD) (O'Brien, Shevlin, O'Keefe, Fitzgerald, Curtis, & Kenny, 2009). By putting into place systems of compensatory education, remedial education, and special education, many countries around the world have responded to the issue of difficulties in learning and achievement (van Kraayenoord, 2010).

In 2004 the Individuals with Disabilities Education Improvement Act (IDEIA) allowed for the first time the use of a response to intervention (RTI) process in the context of the identification of individuals with learning disabilities in the United States. RTI models were focused on the use of scientifically validated reading interventions for use with children at risk for reading disabilities and the monitoring of their progress before a decision on eligibility was made. This was a significant change in the learning disability identification process previously mandated because the focus was on early intervention, scientifically validated interventions, and progress monitoring (Riccomini & Witzel, 2010). As states, districts, and schools implemented RTI models under the IDEIA, the results were met with both criticism and acclamation from stakeholders involved in the process.

On December 10, 2015, US president Barack Obama signed the Every Student Succeeds Act (ESSA) into law. This piece of legislation reauthorizes the 50-year-old Elementary and Secondary Education Act and replaces the often criticized No Child Left Behind Act. The ESSA represents the nation's commitment to equal educational opportunities for all students (regardless of ethnicity, race, disability, income, or English proficiency) and authorizes federal funding for public K–12 schools (Young,

Winn, & Reedy, 2017). By allowing states and school districts greater flexibility in the use of federal funding (Coppes, 2016), the ESSA hopes to achieve one primary goal: to fully prepare all students for success in college and their careers (Darrow, 2016)

In order to achieve this goal (and in addition to other requirements), the ESSA, similar to IDEIA, forces districts to take into account all aspects of children's learning and development by (a) addressing the need for expanded access to explicit evidence-based academic instruction, (b) incorporating strategies to improve positive behavior and social/emotional learning skill development, and (c) providing comprehensive school psychological services (Gayl, 2018; NASP, 2017). Additionally, the ESSA allows for school districts to provide these services within a multitiered system of support (MTSS), a comparable but much broader framework than RTI models.

School districts can use an MTSS model to "design a comprehensive continuum of evidence-based, systemic practices to support a rapid response to students' needs, with regular observation to facilitate data-based instructional decision making" (ESSA, 2015). The essential components of MTSS (similar to RTI) are (a) screening, (b) progress monitoring, (c) multilevel prevention system, and (d) data-based decision-making (Fuchs & Jenkins, 2018; National Center on Response to Intervention, 2010). By following an MTSS model, districts should clearly identify how the needs of at-risk children will be met using evidence-based instructional strategies to strengthen academic programs; school districts can also use federal funds to provide professional development to increase teachers' ability to effectively teach children with disabilities and English learners, which may include the use of multitiered systems of support (Mandlawitz, 2016).

Even though many educational systems use the acronyms RTI and MTSS interchangeably, MTSS is more comprehensive than RTI. While RTI focuses primarily on the academic development of struggling learners, MTSS emphasizes the need for social, emotional, and behavioral support for all students and staff (Cunningham, 2018). In this sense, RTI can be used as part of an MTSS approach to provide a catalyst for overall positive school advancement.

For students with LD, a lack of academic ability in reading and mathematics reflects inefficiencies in intellectual processes that have far-reaching implications across cognitive domains; the need for effective interventions based on specially designed instruction to support such students is paramount (Fuchs, Fuchs, & Malone, 2017; Riccomini, Morano, & Hughes, 2017). For children experiencing difficulties in learning, early identification is essential for the implementation of a timely and effective intervention (Koegel, Koegel, Ashbaugh, & Bradshaw, 2014; Leung, Lindsay, & Loc, 2007). Historically (and across disciplines), target setting, progress monitoring, and program evaluation are identified as crucial components for cultivating improvement in student learning outcomes (Davies et al., 1999). MTSS offers a comprehensive system to guide educators in their efforts to seamlessly blend these crucial components to improve the educational outcomes (both social and performance) of all students including students with learning disabilities.

Due to the change in language (RTI to MTSS), the research base is still primarily framed in an RTI model, and therefore, RTI is the focus for the following review.

A typical model of RTI is represented by a multilevel intervention system that increases in intensity across the tiers (Hallahan, Kaufman, & Pullen, 2009). The primary goal of RTI is twofold: (a) to provide interventions that struggling students require to become successful in the general education curriculum and (b) if the interventions are not successful, to provide school districts with enough progress monitoring data to make a well-informed decision to either implement different interventions or initiate a referral for special education eligibility testing (Martinez & Young, 2011). In order for an intervention program to be sustainable, it needs to be cost effective and beneficial to all participants (Dawkins, Ritz, & Louden, 2009). RTI serves as a bridge to link evidenced-based practice with a practical and efficient decision-making process for determining special education eligibility; by doing so, RTI and now MTSS models remain efficient, practical, and sustainable.

Research evidence

As educational systems struggle with the challenges of educating a rapidly growing student population composed of varied educational needs, educators seek research-based instructional models and programs. With the growing emphasis now moving toward MTSS with the passing of ESSA (at least in the United States), educators and researchers are looking for evidence to support the overall effectiveness of MTSS through the research base on RTI models. However, there remain many unanswered questions and conflicting opinions regarding the overall effectiveness and research support of RTI models for academic achievement and identification of students with learning disabilities (Balu et al., 2015; Fuchs & Fuchs, 2017). We provide a brief overview of research on RTI related to academic achievement and eligibility decisions for students with learning disabilities.

In a review of field studies employing RTI models, Hughes and Dexter (2011) reviewed and synthesized the findings of 16 studies (www.rtinetwork.com). Broadly speaking, their conclusions are that "we characterize the research base for establishing the impact of various models of approaches to RTI as emerging..." (p. 10). This description of "emerging" by Hughes and Dexter is still appropriate today.

Specifically, four main conclusions were ascertained from their review. First, "emerging evidence" from the studies suggests that academic gains are possible within an RTI model; however, this finding is limited in that there are significant concerns regarding the research designs and procedures used. Second, improving mathematics performance through an RTI model has "tentative" support in the research because of the limited number of studies and small sample sizes used. Third, there is "emerging data" that suggest the number of placements in special education can be reduced; however, the studies that demonstrated these findings have limitations with specific aspects of how students who did not respond were identified and procedures used to establish eligibility. Finally, common themes emerged across all 16 studies reviewed regarding the various system factors that are essential to the efficacy of RTI models and included (a) high quality and continuous professional development, (b) system- and building-level administrative support, (c) teacher acceptance and adjustment to different instructional roles, (d) full participation of all school staff, and (e) appropriate time for meeting (Fuchs & Fuchs, 2017; Hughes & Dexter, 2011).

In contrast, a meta-analysis conducted by Burns, Appleton, and Stehouwer (2005) found the use of RTI models reduced the number of referrals to special education and increased overall reading scores. Interestingly, one of the authors of the meta-analysis (Burns, 2010), cautions against "summative" statements regarding the effectiveness of RTI models given that research is currently continuing to evolve. More specifically, Burns stressed his cautionary point by stating "because of the nature of RTI as a school wide initiative there are no studies that examine the model in its entirety using a randomized design" (p. 1). Additionally, a meta-analysis conducted on RTI literature by Tran, Sanchez, Arellano, and Swanson (2011) reported strong and encouraging effect sizes in important reading skills; however, the results also demonstrated that RTI conditions were not effective in the mitigation of learner characteristics related to pretest conditions (Tran et al., 2011).

Continuing to add conflicting results, a report by the National Center for Education Evaluation and Regional Assistance in 2017 called into question the effectiveness of RTI in literacy. The authors of the evaluation found students who received intervention continued to perform poorly even after receiving the interventions (Balu et al., 2015), thus concluding that RTI is not effective. Criticism of the evaluation centered on the evaluation's focus and weaknesses in the evaluation design (Fuchs & Fuchs, 2017). Additionally, serious questions were raised pertaining to whether or not essential elements supported by research were implemented (Fuchs & Fuchs, 2017). Nonetheless, many questions remain unanswered (as is often the case in education-related research) as educators continue to implement RTI models in the new context of MTSS models to improve student performance.

As the RTI research evolves and incorporates the broader elements of MTSS, a clearer picture of effective and less effective models should become more apparent. Given the conflicting conclusions and limitations of the past and current research on RTI and the lack of research on MTSS models, it is obvious that much more work with carefully controlled research is warranted to fully examine the many variables involved with the process of response to intervention.

Summary and recommendations

The process of RTI and now MTSS is the combination of well-established educational practices that together form a systematic and effective approach to improving the instructional programs for all students as well as possibly a more complete manner in which to diagnose students with learning disabilities. Although largely a US-led initiative, the components are grounded in educational practices that occur across international educational systems. Scholars around the world have initiated research to examine how best to intervene with students at risk for learning disabilities within a comprehensive framework of RTI and MTSS. Additional future research, however, is necessary to explicate components of effective MTSS.

References

Balu, R., Pei, Z., Doolittle, F., Schiller, E., Jenkins, J., & Gersten, R. (2015). *Evaluation of response to intervention practices for elementary school reading* (NCEE 2016–4000). Washington, DC: National Center for Education Evaluation and Regional Assistance, Institute of Education Sciences, U.S. Department of Education.

Burns, M. K. (2010). *Response-to-intervention research: Is the sum of the parts as great as the whole?* Retrieved from www.rtinetwork.org/learn/research/response-to-intervention-research-is-the-sum-of-the-parts-as-great-as-the-whole

Burns, M. K., Appleton, J. J., & Stehouwer, J. D. (2005). Meta-analysis of response-to-intervention research: Examining field-based and research-implemented models. *Journal of Psychoeducational Assessment, 23*, 381–394.

Coppes, M. (2016). New opportunities for CTE in the Every Student Succeeds Act. *Techniques: Connecting Education & Careers, 91*(5), 24–27.

Cunningham, B. (2018). *What's the difference between RTI and MTSS?* Retrieved from www.understood.org/en/school-learning/special-services/rti/whats-the-difference-between-rti-and-mtss

Darrow, A. (2016). The Every Student Succeeds Act (ESSA). *General Music Today, 30*(1), 41–44. doi:10.1177/1048371316658327

Davies, D. D., Lee, J., Postlethwaite, K., Tarr, J., Thomas, G., & Yee, W. C. (1999). After inspection and special schools: Action planning and making progress. *British Journal of Special Education, 26*(3), 130–135.

Dawkins, S., Ritz, M. E., & Louden, W. (2009). Evaluating the practicability and sustainability of a reading intervention programme, using preservice teachers as trained volunteers. *Australian Journal of Language and Literacy, 32*(2), 136–147.

ESSA. (2015). Every Student Succeeds Act of 2015, Pub. L. No. 114-95 § 114 Stat. 1177 (2015–2016).

Fuchs, D., & Fuchs, L. S. (2017). Critique of the national evaluation of response to intervention: A case for simpler frameworks. *Exceptional Children, 83*(7), 255–268.

Fuchs, L. S., Fuchs, D., & Malone, A. S. (2017). Taxonomy of intervention intensity. *Teaching Exceptional Children, 50*(1), 35–43.

Fuchs, L., & Jenkins, J. (2018). *MTSS, RTI, special education . . . OH My! gaining an understanding of MTSS and RTI.* Retrieved from https://intensiveintervention.org/resource/mtss-rti-special-educationoh-my-gaining-understanding-mtss-and-rti-drs-lynn-fuchs-and-joe

Gayl, C. L. (2018). Student academic, social, and emotional learning. *Education Digest, 83*(5), 17–24.

Hallahan, D. P., Kauffman, J. M., & Pullen, P. C. (2009). *Exceptional learners: An introduction to special education.* Boston, MA: Allyn & Bacon.

Hughes, C. A., & Dexter, D. D. (2011). *Field studies of RTI programs, revised.* Retrieved from www.rtinetwork.org/learn/research/field-studies-rti-programs.

Koegel, L. K., Koegel, R. L., Ashbaugh, K., & Bradshaw, J. (2014). The importance of early identification and intervention for children with or at-risk for autism spectrum disorders. *International Journal of Speed-Language Pathology, 16*(1), 50–56.

Leung, C., Lindsay, G., & Loc, S. K. (2007). Early identification of primary school students with learning difficulties in Hong Kong: The development of a checklist. *European Journal of Special Needs Education, 22*(3), 327–339.

Mandlawitz, M. R. (2016). *Every student succeeds act: Summary of key provisions.* Retrieved from www.casecec.org.

Martinez, H., & Young, A. (2011). Response to intervention: How is it practiced and perceived? *International Journal of Special Education, 26*(1), 44–52.

National Association of School Psychologists. (2017, September). *National Association of School Psychologists strategic plan: 2017–2022.* Bethesda, MD: Author. Retrieved from http://www.nasponline.org/utility/about-nasp/vision-core-purpose-core-values-and-strategic-goals

National Center on Response to Intervention. (2010). *Essential components of RTI: A closer look at response to intervention.* Washington, DC: Author. Retrieved from www.rti4success.org/resource/essential-components-rti-closer-look-response-intervention

O'Brien, P., Shevlin, M., O'Keefe, M., Fitzgerald, S., Curtis, S., & Kenny, M. (2009). Opening up a whole new world for students with intellectual disabilities within a third level setting. *British Journal of Learning Disabilities, 37*(4), 285–292.

Riccomini, P. J., Morano, S., & Hughes, C. (2017). Big ideas in special education: Specially designed instruction, high leverage practices, explicit instruction, and intensive instruction. *Teaching Exceptional Children, 50*(1), 22–27.

Riccomini, P. J., & Witzel, B. S. (2010). *Response to intervention in Mathematics.* Thousand Oaks, CA: Corwin Press.

Tran, L., Sanchez, T., Arellano, B., & Swanson, H. L. (2011). A meta-analysis of RTI literature for children at risk for reading disabilities. *Journal of Learning Disabilities, 44*(3), 285–295. doi:10.1177/0022219410378447

van Kraayenoord, C. E. (2010). Response to intervention: New ways and wariness. *Reading Research Quarterly, 45*(3), 363–376.

Young, M. D., Winn, K. M., & Reedy, M. A. (2017). The Every Student Succeeds Act: Strengthening the focus on educational leadership. *Educational Administration Quarterly, 53*(5), 705–726. doi:10.1177/0013161X17735871

6.5 Writing instruction

Mark Torrance and Raquel Fidalgo

Introduction

Achievement in writing, in educational contexts at least, is marked by the ability to produce text that extends across a number of paragraphs, that coheres – sentences and paragraphs are tied into a meaningful whole – and that accommodates the needs of potential readers. Achieving writers will be able to do this in a number of different textual genres (stories, persuasive letters, expository essays, etc.) and for a range of audiences. They will be able to write accurately – with minimal grammatical and spelling errors – and fluently, producing text within a reasonable timescale. Learning to write, in this sense, occurs almost exclusively within school, through instruction. This is in contrast to learning to communicate in speech, which is rarely a focus of formal education.

Achieving writing competence requires development of a number of component skills that interact in complex ways that are not yet well understood. Some of these skills are imported from speech: beginning writers bring with them knowledge of vocabulary and morphology that can be applied directly to writing. Children suffering from general language impairment will therefore also tend to be struggling writers (Dockrell, Lindsay, & Connelly, 2009; Dockrell & Connelly, 2015). They are also likely to bring implicit knowledge of typical content and structure of simple narratives. There is some evidence that being read to at home has positive effects on students' writing in school (Sylva, Scott, Totsika, Ereky-Stevens, & Crook, 2008). Beginning writers also require sufficiently well-developed motor skills and hand-eye coordination to make handwriting possible. (It remains the case that nearly all early writing within schools is by hand rather than by keyboard.)

All other component skills need to be taught. Initially, and most obviously, beginning writers need to learn how to form letters and how to spell. However, mastering these low-level skills is not sufficient for writing achievement. Students also need to move beyond communication skills that have developed in the context of spoken interaction and learn to communicate in the absence of an immediate and present audience. This involves the ability to monitor the possible communicational effect of what is being written (e.g., "Will my readers know what I'm talking about? Will this entertain them?") without the instant feedback that is available in conversation. Writers also need to have their own strategies for generating content for their text. Writing, particularly in educational contexts, rarely starts with the writer having specific ideas to communicate. In conversation the other speaker's utterances provide an ongoing source of cues to support the retrieval of appropriate things to say. This is absent in writing. Writers therefore need not only to decide how to structure their ideas within the text, but also to determine what these ideas should be.

Novice writing (and expert writing in some contexts) is characterized by "knowledge telling" (Scardamalia & Bereiter, 1991). This involves allowing either the text just produced or knowledge of prototypical text schemas (genre knowledge) to cue what to say next. Students at this stage of development might, for example, write stories with a very linear structure: "She did this, then she did that, then she . . ." and so forth. If asked to think aloud while writing, nearly everything that they say will appear as text. There is little or no evidence of reflection. Sophisticated and complex "knowledge-transforming" strategies are used by expert writers for determining content. These involve consideration of audience needs and of the characteristics of the genre of the text that is being produced. In Scardamalia and Bereiter's terms, decisions about what to say derive from a dialectic between content space (what the writer knows that is relevant to the topic) and discourse space (rhetorical knowledge relevant to how this content might be expressed). Expert writers' think-aloud protocols, therefore, typically include considerable evaluation of possible content options and reflection about how these might best be expressed. In a reverse of novice practice, most of what is thought does not appear on the page.

Writing achievement therefore involves development of both low-level transcription and formulation skills necessary for making grammatically correct sentences appear on the page and higher-level metacognitive skills associated with determining content and structure necessary to create effective text that communicates the writer's ideas. Developing competence typically takes at least the duration of formal schooling, and expertise is probably not achieved by the majority of students. Arguably, one of the reasons for this is that the various different decisions and processes associated with producing good text, such as forming letters, spelling, planning syntax, determining content, word choice, determining macrostructure, and considering audience response, potentially converge within the writer's mind at the same (or approximately the same) time. Students' minds, and particularly young students' minds, do not have the resources to cope with these multiple demands. Several researchers have identified limitations in cognitive processing capacity (often labeled loosely as "working memory capacity") as a dominant reason for writing being both difficult to learn and, even for experts, difficult to do. Writing achievement is therefore partly dependent (a) on the processing resources that the student brings to the task, (b) on the extent to which the student has automatized writing's component processes, and (c) on whether or not the student can sequence or schedule the writing process in such a way as to avoid cognitive overload (Torrance & Galbraith, 2006). As children develop, there is a general cross-domain increase in the ability to maintain information in working memory. With practice and instruction, spelling and handwriting move from requiring explicit and conscious processing ("I must carefully form my letters"; "Now how do I spell that word?") to being implicit and automatic. This liberates processing resources which can then be allocated to higher-level processes and particularly those associated with evaluating and developing the text's rhetorical impact. However, anecdotally at least, even older writers with well-developed basic literacy still run the risk of overload. Writing achievement, therefore, may require the use of explicit strategies for separating out thinking about what to write from the lower-level demands of putting words on the page. There is some evidence, for example, that instructing adult writers to produce a plan in advance of producing full texts tends to result in a better final product (e.g., Kellogg, 1990, but see Johnson, Mercado, & Acevedo, 2012).

So, in broad terms, becoming a competent writer requires (a) mastery of spelling and handwriting, (b) possessing appropriate discourse knowledge so that text can be tailored to reader needs, and (c) possessing appropriate metacognitive control strategies to schedule the writing process in such a way that content and rhetorical decisions interact while at the same time avoiding cognitive overload. In addition to these, writers obviously also require (d) motivation to apply these strategies to their own writing, independently of teacher prompts. This strategy-plus-motivation combination is captured in the concept of "writing self-regulation."

Research evidence

Very early (preschool and first grade) writing ability is predicted by both literacy (reading and spelling) and more general oral-language and cognitive (memory and attention) abilities (Kent, Wanzek, Petscher, Al Otaiba, & Kim, 2014). By second grade, in English first-language students, oral-language skills become relatively unimportant as predictors of writing performance, compared to writing-specific (spelling, handwriting) skills (Dockrell & Connelly, 2016). Most other languages have more regular spelling patterns than English, however, and then oral-language ability may predict writing performance into later grades (Arfé, Dockrell, & De Bernardi, 2016).

There is, as might be expected, correlation between independent measures of handwriting and spelling ability and children's ability to produce text. Graham, Berninger, Abbott, Abbott, and Whitaker (1997) estimated that in a sample of first- to sixth-grade students, between 25% and 41% of variance in composition quality and a higher proportion of variance in writing fluency was predicted by spelling and handwriting ability. There is some evidence from longitudinal studies of a decline in the influence of handwriting (Abbott, Berninger, & Fayol, 2010) and spelling (Juel, 1988) on writing fluency and quality as children get older. However, although recent meta-analyses confirm a moderate effect of handwriting and spelling skills on the quality of students' text, they have not found evidence that this effect weakens with age (Feng, Lindner, Ji, & Joshi, 2017; Kent & Wanzek, 2016).

Training in both spelling and handwriting has benefits for writing fluency and quality (meta-analyses by Graham & Santangelo, 2014, for handwriting, and Santangelo & Graham, 2016, for spelling). Directly teaching handwriting – teaching children to shape letters – shows benefits not just for the legibility of students' handwriting, but also for handwriting fluency (words copied per minute). More general motor or multisensory training does not appear to have these effects. A smaller number of studies has explored effects on text composition, as opposed to copying tasks. These indicate quite substantial benefits of handwriting training both for composition fluency and for text quality. Formal spelling instruction results in substantially greater improvements in students' spelling compared to general literacy instruction without a formal spelling component. Again, fewer studies have explored effects on text composition. These suggest that formal spelling instruction generalizes to spelling accuracy during composition but, spelling accuracy aside, does not significantly improve text quality. Therefore, evidence is mixed for the impact of training in low-level skills on the tendency of students to include in their text those higher-level composition skills that are captured in text-quality scores. This provides only partial support for the theory that automaticity in spelling and handwriting is necessary to liberate cognitive resources that can then be used for determining content and rhetoric.

Classroom interventions that focus specifically on composition skills can, broadly, take one of two forms. Some interventions are designed to scaffold production and, therefore, to have immediate positive effects on students' performance of a specific writing task. For example, several studies have compared the quality of texts written with and without students first writing an outline. Other interventions were aimed at developing writing skills in students that they then apply to their writing, independently and with prompting from their teacher. Interventions of this form are successful if, after instruction, students spontaneously apply the new skill or skills to whenever they complete a writing task, with a resulting general increase in text quality. There is a relatively large body of research evaluating both scaffolding and skill-development interventions. These studies have, again, been usefully summarized in recent meta-analyses: Gillespie and Graham (2014), Graham and Perin (2007), Graham, McKeown, Kiuhara, and Harris (2012), and Koster, Tribushinina, de Jong, and van den Bergh (2015), for, respectively, struggling school-age writers, secondary students, all primary ages, and upper-primary students.

A number of scaffolding strategies appear effective. For both primary and secondary students, both asking students to set specific goals for the finished text ("My text should include the following features . . .") and collaborative or peer-supported writing give relatively strong positive effects. Smaller but still significant benefits result from requiring that students engage in specific prewriting activities (e.g., producing a structured outline before composing the full text). Fewer studies have focused on struggling writers. Evidence suggests benefits for goal setting but is inconclusive for the effects of prewriting and peer collaboration. Clearly these forms of scaffolding are not mutually exclusive, and it is possible that greater gains in writing quality could be achieved if they are sensibly combined.

Simply changing the conditions under which a particular writing task is performed does not, however, really result in writing achievement: achieving writers should be able to produce good text independently of teacher scaffolding. Research exploring training in specific sentence-level skills does not indicate benefits for formal grammar instruction on the overall quality of students text but does suggest benefits for teaching sentence combining (training with tasks that involve taking two or more short sentences and using them to create a single, grammatically more sophisticated sentence [e.g., Saddler & Graham, 2005]). These findings hold true for both primary and secondary students. Interventions of this form have not been systematically evaluated in struggling writers.

Other writing interventions adopt more holistic approaches, aiming to train students in a range of writing skills, particularly skills necessary for structuring text above the sentence level. One group of interventions might loosely be described as the *process approach* to writing instruction (overview by Pritchard & Honeycutt, 2006). Process approach teaching emphasizes the production of meaningful composition with specified audiences and communicational goals. Classes are taken through several draft-review-edit cycles, with considerable peer and teacher interaction and feedback. There is considerable diversity across classes adopting this approach. However, there is a tendency toward learning by doing and avoiding teaching formal procedures or rules for what constitutes good text. This contrasts with *strategy-focused* writing instruction (e.g., De La Paz & Graham, 2002). Strategy-focused interventions deliver a package of instruction aimed at students' learning explicit procedures for controlling their writing processes (e.g., strategies for generating and organizing ideas, considering audience, and reviewing and revising what they write). Strategy-focused intervention shares with the process approach a focus on producing full and meaningful texts but, through a combination of direct instruction and teacher modeling, prescribes how text should be produced. A third general approach to teaching written composition is to teach *text structure*. Through various activities students learn, explicitly, the textual features that are found in well-written examples of a specific genre (e.g., stories).

Evidence summarized in the meta-analyses referenced above suggest that both process and strategy-focused approaches benefit students. This is true for primary, secondary, and struggling writers. Research supports teaching text structure in primary school but not in secondary school and has been the focus of too few studies to draw conclusions about benefits for struggling writers. The benefits of strategy-focused instruction appear to be substantially greater than the benefits afforded by the process approach and by teaching text structure.

Finally, some interventions specifically target students' self-efficacy and motivation and students' ability to self-regulate (i.e., to take deliberate executive control over their own behavior). A small number of studies have evaluated interventions that directly target motivation by, for example, providing students with appropriately encouraging feedback. These suggest large positive effects. Adding teaching specifically aimed at developing self-regulation – students monitoring, evaluating, and correcting their own writing behavior – to strategy-focused training provides moderate additional gains, over and above those provided by teaching strategy alone.

Summary and recommendations

Unlike speech, writing is late developing and requires protracted instruction and practice. Achievement in writing is partly dependent on home environment and particularly how much the child reads. However, writing achievement, we've argued, results first and foremost from effective writing instruction, and the form of the instruction that students receive probably plays an important role in predicting their success.

Students require explicit and direct instruction focused on handwriting and spelling. However, mastering spelling and handwriting is not enough to develop students' writing competence. Students also require instruction that focuses specifically on developing content and structure for their text. We have provided a superficial overview of what is now a relatively large body of research aimed at determining the relative merits of various forms that this instruction might take.

However, our summary and, to a certain extent, the meta-analyses on which it is based, gloss over detail that requires attention before findings can be put into practice. We offer three examples. First, drawing firm conclusions across different studies is made difficult by the fact that choice of control condition varies and is not independent of the type of intervention being evaluated. Sentence combining has typically (though not always) been contrasted with traditional grammar instruction, whereas teaching text structure has typically been contrasted with instruction based around reading. Second, approach to delivery varies systematically across type of intervention. For example, potential end users of findings from these studies should establish whether studies that show positive effects evaluate training delivered to whole classes over a fixed time period or whether training was paced to accommodate the learning needs and rates of individual students. Third, successful interventions – particularly those based in the strategy-focused and process approaches – typically comprise a package of different components. It is often unclear whether all or just some of these are contributing to the intervention's success. Taking an example from our own work, we found evidence of large and sustained benefits of a program of strategy-focused instruction for sixth-grade Spanish students (Fidalgo, Torrance, & García, 2008; Torrance, Fidalgo, & García, 2007). Our intervention comprised a package of activities focused on developing in students both an explicit understanding of the features of good text and specific planning, drafting, and revising procedures ("process strategies"). This was delivered through a combination of direct instruction, teacher modeling, and collaborative practice. In a subsequent study, we contrasted this intervention with instruction that retained the product-focused component but did not teach process strategies (Torrance, Fidalgo, & Robledo, 2015). We found similar gains in both conditions.

In a third study we found no significant gains from direct (formal) teaching of strategy-focused instruction over and above students simply observing and discussing a model that was using these strategies (Fidalgo, Torrance, Rijlaarsdam, van den Bergh, & Álvarez, 2015).

With these caveats, we believe that existing research points toward the following general conclusions: (1) Instruction that focuses on the mechanics of writing – spelling, handwriting, grammar – and ignores higher-level composition processes will not result in achieving writers. Successful instruction needs to give students the knowledge and strategies necessary for generating higher-level text structure – the content and rhetorical features that turn text into coherent communication. There is some evidence that teaching these features has substantial benefits even at the start of schooling, when children are still learning to handwrite and spell (Arrimada, Torrance, & Fidalgo, in press). (2) Instructional approaches that teach students explicit writing strategies are likely to result in greater gains than approaches that immerse students in the written composition process but do not make writing strategies explicit.

References

Abbott, R. D., Berninger, V. W., & Fayol, M. (2010). Longitudinal relationships of levels of language in writing and between writing and reading in grades 1 to 7. *Journal of Educational Psychology, 102*(2), 281–298. https://doi.org/10.1037/a0019318

Arfé, B., Dockrell, J. E., & De Bernardi, B. (2016). The effect of language specific factors on early written composition: The role of spelling, oral language and text generation skills in a shallow orthography. *Reading and Writing.* https://doi.org/10.1007/s11145-015-9617-5

Arrimada, M., Torrance, M., & Fidalgo, R. (in press). Effects of teaching planning strategies to first-grade writers. *British Journal of Educational Psychology.* https://doi.org/10.1111/bjep.12251

De La Paz, S., & Graham, S. (2002). Explicitly teaching strategies, skills, and knowledge: Writing instruction in middle school classrooms. *Journal of Educational Psychology, 94*(4), 687–698. https://doi.org/10.1037//0022-0663.94.4.687

Dockrell, J. E., & Connelly, V. (2015). The role of oral language in underpinning the text generation difficulties in children with specific language impairment. *Journal of Research in Reading, 38*(1), 18–34. https://doi.org/10.1111/j.1467-9817.2012.01550.x

Dockrell, J. E., & Connelly, V. (2016). The relationships between oral and written sentence generation in English speaking children: The role of language and literacy skills. In J. Perera, M. Aparici, E. Rosado, & N. Salas (Eds.), *Written and spoken language development across the lifespan: Literacy studies (Perspectives from cognitive neurosciences, linguistics, psychology and education)* (pp. 161–177). Champaign, IL: Springer. https://doi.org/10.1007/978-3-319-21136-7_11

Dockrell, J. E., Lindsay, G., & Connelly, V. (2009). The impact of specific language impairment on adolescents' written text. *Exceptional Children, 75*(4), 427–446.

Feng, L., Lindner, A., Ji, X. R., & Malatesha Joshi, R. (2017). The roles of handwriting and keyboarding in writing: A meta-analytic review. *Reading and Writing.* https://doi.org/10.1007/s11145-017-9749-x

Fidalgo, R., Torrance, M., & García, J-N. (2008). The long-term effects of strategy-focussed writing instruction for grade six students. *Contemporary Educational Psychology, 33*(4), 672–693. https://doi.org/10.1016/j.cedpsych.2007.09.001

Fidalgo, R., Torrance, M., Rijlaarsdam, G., van den Bergh, H., & Lourdes Álvarez, M. (2015). Strategy-focused writing instruction: Just observing and reflecting on a model benefits 6th grade students. *Contemporary Educational Psychology, 41*, 37–50. https://doi.org/10.1016/j.cedpsych.2014.11.004

Gillespie, A., & Graham, S. (2014). A meta-analysis of writing interventions for students with learning disabilities. *Exceptional Children, 80*(4), 454–473. https://doi.org/10.1177/0014402914527238

Graham, S., Berninger, V. W., Abbott, R. D., Abbott, S. P., & Whitaker, D. (1997, March). Role of mechanics in composing of elementary school students: A new methodological approach. *Journal of Educational Psychology.* https://doi.org/10.1037/0022-0663.89.1.170

Graham, S., McKeown, D., Kiuhara, S., & Harris, K. R. (2012). A meta-analysis of writing instruction for students in the elementary grades. *Journal of Educational Psychology, 104*(4), 879–896. https://doi.org/10.1037/a0029185

Graham, S., & Perin, D. (2007). A meta-analysis of writing instruction for adolescent students. *Journal of Educational Psychology, 99*(3), 445–476.

Graham, S., & Santangelo, T. (2014). Does spelling instruction make students better spellers, readers, and writers? A meta-analytic review. *Reading and Writing, 27*(9), 1703–1743. https://doi.org/10.1007/s11145-014-9517-0

Johnson, M. D., Mercado, L., & Acevedo, A. (2012). The effect of planning sub-processes on L2 writing fluency, grammatical complexity, and lexical complexity. *Journal of Second Language Writing, 21*(3), 264–282. https://doi.org/10.1016/j.jslw.2012.05.011

Juel, C. (1988). Learning to read and write: A longitudinal study of 54 children from first through fourth grades. *Journal of Educational Psychology, 80*(4), 437–447. https://doi.org/10.1037/0022-0663.80.4.437

Kellogg, R. T. (1990). Effectiveness of prewriting strategies as a function of task demands. *American Journal of Psychology, 103*(3), 327–342.

Kent, S. C., & Wanzek, J. (2016). The relationship between component skills and writing quality and production across developmental levels: A meta-analysis of the last 25 years. *Review of Educational Research, 86*(2), 1–32. https://doi.org/10.3102/0034654315619491

Kent, S., Wanzek, J., Petscher, Y., Al Otaiba, S., & Kim, Y-S. (2014). Writing fluency and quality in kindergarten and first grade: The role of attention, reading, transcription, and oral language. *Reading and Writing, 27*(7), 1163–1188. https://doi.org/10.1007/s11145-013-9480-1

Koster, M., Tribushinina, E., de Jong, P. F., & van den Bergh, H. (2015). Teaching children to write: A meta-analysis of writing intervention research. *Journal of Writing Research, 7*(2), 249–274. https://doi.org/10.17239/jowr-2015.07.02.2

Pritchard, R., & Honeycutt, R. (2006). The process approach to writing instruction: Examining its effectiveness. In C. MacArthur, S. Graham, & J. Fitzgerald (Eds.), *Handbook of Writing Research* (pp. 275–290). New York, NY: Guilford Publications.

Saddler, B., & Graham, S. (2005). The effects of peer-assisted sentence-combining instruction on the writing performance of more and less skilled young writers. *Journal of Educational Psychology, 97*(1), 43–54. https://doi.org/10.1037/0022-0663.97.1.43

Santangelo, T., & Graham, S. (2016). A comprehensive meta-analysis of handwriting instruction. *Educational Psychology Review, 28.* https://doi.org/10.1007/s10648-015-9335-1

Scardamalia, M., & Bereiter, C. (1991). Literate expertise. In K. A. Ericsson & J. Smith (Eds.), *Toward a general theory of expertise: Prospects and limits* (pp. 172–194). Cambridge: Cambridge University Press.

Sylva, K., Scott, S., Totsika, V., Ereky-Stevens, K., & Crook, C. (2008). Training parents to help their children read: A randomized control trial. *British Journal of Educational Psychology*, *78*(3), 435–455. https://doi.org/10.1348/000709907X255718

Torrance, M., & Galbraith, D. (2006). The processing demands of writing. In C. MacArthur, S. Graham, & J. Fitzgerald (Eds.), *Handbook of writing research* (pp. 67–82). New York, NY: Guilford Publications.

Torrance, M., Fidalgo, R., & García, J-N. (2007). The teachability and effectiveness of cognitive self-regulation in sixth-grade writers. *Learning and Instruction*, *17*(3), 265–285. https://doi.org/10.1016/j.learninstruc.2007.02.003

Torrance, M., Fidalgo, R., & Robledo, P. (2015). Do sixth-grade writers need process strategies? *British Journal of Educational Psychology*, *85*(1), 91–112. https://doi.org/10.1111/bjep.12065

6.6

Role of discussion in reading comprehension

Ian A. G. Wilkinson and Kathryn Nelson

Introduction

Classroom discussions about texts are thought to provide a powerful vehicle for deepening students' understanding of texts they read and for fostering their general comprehension abilities. Martin Nystrand (2002), one of the leading proponents of discussion as a means of enhancing reading comprehension, defined discussion as the "free exchange of information among students and/or between at least three participants that lasts longer than 30 seconds" (p. 30). However, discussion can be defined more generally as the open-ended, collaborative exchange of ideas among a teacher and students or among students for the purpose of furthering students' thinking, understanding, learning, or appreciation of text (Wilkinson, 2009). Participants present multiple points of view on the topic, respond to the ideas of others, and reflect on each other's ideas in an effort to build their knowledge, understanding, or interpretation of the text. Engaging students in discussion about texts provides an alternative or additional means of developing students' reading comprehension abilities beyond the explicit teaching of comprehension strategies (Wilkinson & Son, 2011).

To illustrate, the following excerpt is taken from a discussion between a teacher and a small group of fourth-grade students about a story called "Victor," by James Howe. The story is about a young boy named Cody, who is incapacitated, lying in a coma in a hospital bed. Cody creates an imaginary world ("The Land Above"), inspired by the ceiling tiles in the hospital, to help him get through the illness. During his stay in hospital, a mysterious man named Victor visits Cody and tells Cody stories about what his life will be like when he grows up. The teacher and students are trying to understand who Victor is:

Michelle: I think Victor's an angel.
Teacher: You think Victor's an angel? Can you tell me why you think so?

Michelle: Because he, well, maybe he comes from, like, the land above, and that's where he's talking to him. And that's why maybe Cody can't see Victor 'cause he's from the land above, and he's talking to him from up there.

Nancy: Maybe's he's just a figure, but he always has this thing on his face that he doesn't have—

Matt: But he, Cody kept saying "three tiles up, two to the left."

Teacher: That was interesting

Andrew: You mean "three tiles down, two to the left."

Nancy: Yeah, he was talking about the ceiling.

Sam: He thought it was a real place where people lived and stuff, but he said the funny thing about it was he never gave them a name.

Andrew: And also, the reason why I don't think Victor was in the land above, well, how could he be talking from the land above because remember when Cody said he could hear him, hear the screeching on the floor from when Victor was pulling up a chair to keep Cody company.

Teacher: So that's— Are you saying that's evidence?

Andrew: Yeah.

Teacher: Interesting.

Andrew: So how could he be from the land above? I mean, he could be from the land above, but how could he be talking from the land above?

Matt: But how do you know people can't travel from and to [the] land above?

Nancy: This isn't realistic. This isn't like nonfiction, so anything can happen.

Note that the students had considerable responsibility for constructing their understanding and interpretation of the story. Michelle stated her opinion, and the teacher asked a question that probed for the reason for her opinion ("Can you tell me why you think so?"), which elicited a variety of responses. Most of the contributions came from students, and there were several consecutive exchanges among students with only brief, occasional comments from the teacher. The students appear to have been genuinely interested in exploring the issue of who Victor is, they asked questions that built on each other's responses, and they challenged each other's views, often using evidence from the text, in a collective effort to make sense of the story. This kind of exchange stands in contrast to the traditional recitation model or I-R-E (Mehan, 1979) pattern of classroom discourse in which the teacher *initiates* a question (e.g., "What does he see in the nest?"), a student *responds* (e.g., "Eagles"), and the teacher *evaluates* the response (e.g., "He actually sees eaglets"). In a recitation model, the teacher controls the direction of the discussion and is responsible for determining the correctness of students' answers. Students take a passive role as the teacher shapes and guides the students' learning.

Research evidence

The origins of discussion as a teaching method can be traced back to Socrates and Plato, though research on discussion about text as a means of enhancing students' abilities and learning has a shorter history. One of the first empirical studies on the topic was a doctoral dissertation by Casper (1964) on the effects of the Junior Great Books discussion program (Great Books Foundation, 1987) with gifted fifth-grade students, as measured by a test of intellectual operation based on the work of J. B. Guilford. The 1980s and 1990s saw a proliferation of approaches to conducting high-quality discussion about text. There are now a large number of discourse-intensive pedagogies that serve to disrupt the traditional I-R-E pattern of classroom discourse in favor of more open-ended, collaborative exchanges of ideas among participants for the purpose of improving students' comprehension of text (e.g., Beck & McKeown, 2006; Billings & Fitzgerald, 2002). Many of these approaches are now framed under the general pedagogical model of dialogic teaching (Alexander, 2017).

Several major studies have shed light on the incidence of discussion about text in teaching of language arts. Commeyras and DeGroff (1998) surveyed the teaching practices of a random sample of 1,519 K–12 US literacy teachers and related professionals and found that only 33% of respondents reported that they frequently or very frequently had students meet in small groups to discuss literature in their classrooms. Commeyras and DeGroff also found that discussions were more common in elementary and middle school classes than they were in high school classes. In a large observational study of eighth-grade and ninth-grade language arts and English classes in eight Midwestern communities in the United States, Nystrand (1997) found that open-ended, whole-class discussion averaged only 52 seconds per class in eighth grade and only 14 seconds per class in ninth grade. Similarly, in an observational study of 64 middle and high school English classrooms in five US states, Applebee, Langer, Nystrand, and Gamoran (2003) found that the amount of time spent on open discussions averaged only 68 seconds per class. Discussions also seem to be relatively uncommon in UK classrooms (Alexander, 2017). Thus, despite educators' recognition that discussion has potential value, "true" discussions about text are quite rare.

What does research show about the effects of discussion on reading comprehension? There have been several major reviews of the role of discussion in shaping students' reading comprehension. Nystrand (2006) provided a broad, narrative review of the role of discussion in promoting reading comprehension. Murphy, Wilkinson, Soter, Hennessey, and Alexander (2009) conducted a meta-analysis of 42 studies of the effects of nine approaches to conducting text-based discussions on measures of teacher and student talk and individual student comprehension and learning outcomes. Wilkinson, Murphy, and Binici (2015) and Murphy, Wilkinson, Soter, and Firetto (2016) have also conducted reviews of the literature on the role of discussion in enhancing students' comprehension. Collectively, these reviews show that the effects of discussion vary depending on the nature of the discussion and the type of study. Many approaches to discussion are effective at promoting students' literal and inferential comprehension, producing effects as large as 3.0 standard deviations for single-group design studies and 0.8 standard deviations for multiple-group studies. Some approaches are effective at promoting students' critical thinking, reasoning, and argumentation about text, producing effects as large as 2.5 standard deviations for single-group studies and 0.4 standard deviations for multiple-group studies.

The effects of discussion also vary by type of outcome measure. The effects of discussion have been assessed on measures of teacher and student talk; researcher-developed measures, including complex writing tasks (e.g., persuasive essays); and commercial standardized tests of reading comprehension. By and large, the effects are greatest on measures of student and teacher talk – student talk increases and teacher talk decreases. They are smaller on researcher-developed measures of comprehension, and they are smaller still on commercial standardized assessments of comprehension. Studies involving measures of the effects of discussion that are independent of the texts discussed suggest there is some evidence that the effects transfer to new texts and tasks, with some studies showing effects on the order of 0.4 standard deviations and above (Wilkinson et al., 2015). However, the effects are variable and, because most studies are quasi-experimental, it is difficult to separate effects of discussion from factors associated with the schools, classes, or groups of students particular to the studies.

A number of other factors seem to moderate the effects of discussion on reading comprehension. One factor is the kind of talk. Increases in student talk do not necessarily result in concomitant increases in student comprehension; rather, it seems that a particular kind of talk is necessary to promote comprehension (cf. Wells, 1989). As we have indicated, productive discussions are structured and focused yet not dominated by the teacher. Students hold the floor for extended periods of time, and they are prompted, either by the teacher or by other students, to discuss texts through open-ended and authentic questions. In productive discussions, there is a high degree of uptake where the teacher or students incorporate the ideas of others into their questions and build on each other's ideas. Another moderating factor is students' reading ability. The benefits of discussion seem to be more potent for students of below-average ability than for students of average or above-average ability, presumably because students of higher ability levels already possess the skills needed to comprehend stories.

Why does discussion seem to benefit students' reading comprehension? As reviews of the research suggest, the key agent is the talk in the discussion. But what does the talk accomplish? The views of scholars who do research on discussion differ on this issue. Some scholars argue that the talk in discussion fosters greater student engagement in making sense of the text (e.g., McKeown, Beck, & Blake, 2009). They contend that the talk serves as a tool to help students organize their thoughts, make inferences, reason, and reflect on the meaning of the text. Some scholars take a more social view of learning and argue that the talk makes students' thinking public, enabling them to learn how others think about the text and prompting them to come to terms with different points of view (e.g., Almasi, 1994). Some scholars take an even more social view of learning and argue that the talk enables students to co-construct knowledge and understandings together (e.g., Wells, 2007). According to this view, the talk functions as a vehicle that enables students to combine their intellectual resources to collectively make sense of the text – a process Mercer (2000) calls "inter-thinking." Some argue that the dynamic interplay among different perspectives and competing voices helps students make meaning from the text (e.g., Nystrand, 2006).

Regardless of which perspective is taken, there is increasing realization that talk in discussions seems to be especially productive when students are encouraged to consider others' perspectives and to explain, elaborate, and defend their positions: that is, to argue constructively about the issues raised by the text. Students come away from such discussions knowing not only how to think critically and reflectively about the text they have discussed, but also, it is hoped, how to apply these ways of thinking to other texts in other reading situations (Reznitskaya, Hsu, & Anderson, 2015).

Summary and recommendations

Taken together, the level of evidence on the effects of discussion on reading comprehension might best be described as moderate (Kamil et al., 2008; Shanahan et al., 2010). Although current studies suggest that discussion improves reading comprehension, producing some medium to large effect sizes, more experimental and quasi-experimental studies of the topic are needed, especially with younger students (kindergarten through third grade). Much of the research consists of single-group pretest/post-test design studies or multiple-group studies with criterion measures that afford little confidence in the veracity of the outcomes. It is particularly important to establish evidence of the effects of discussion beyond measures of the effects on learning and comprehension of texts that were the subject of the discussion – measures of students' abilities to comprehend new, unfamiliar texts and to perform novel comprehension-related tasks. It stands to reason that enabling students to engage in discussions about texts should improve their comprehension of those same texts. The more interesting and important question is whether the discussion enables students to acquire the habits of mind to transfer their comprehension abilities to new texts and novel tasks (Wilkinson et al., 2015).

For teachers, learning to facilitate productive discussions about texts can be a challenging undertaking (Alvermann & Hayes, 1989). Although there is good understanding of what productive talk sounds like and the frameworks for achieving such talk, it is difficult to prescribe teacher moves that can be applied with all texts and all topics; the moves needed are contingent on the quality of talk in the discussion. Moreover, for most teachers, implementing productive discussions about text requires a substantial shift in their knowledge and beliefs about their role as a teacher and about the role of talk in learning and its potential benefit for students' comprehension. It also requires a deep conceptual understanding of what constitutes productive talk about text.

There at least two schools of thought on how best to support teachers in facilitating productive discussion. One approach might be to identify a small number of high leverage discussion practices that teachers can learn to implement readily with a high likelihood of success (Grossman, Hammerness, & McDonald, 2009). This would enable teachers to approximate good practice in a relatively short amount of time. Another approach, of course, is to develop effective programs that provide intensive and sustained professional development in how to scaffold students' talk (Wilkinson et al., 2017). Much work remains to be done in the area of teacher education and professional development if educators are to confront the challenge of implementing such dialogic pedagogies at scale (Osborne, 2015).

References

Alexander, R. (2017). *Towards dialogic teaching: Rethinking classroom talk* (5th ed.). Cambridge: Dialogos.

Almasi, J. F. (1994). The nature of fourth graders' sociocognitive conflicts in peer-led and teacher-led discussions of literature. *Reading Research Quarterly, 30*(3), 314–351.

Alvermann, D. E., & Hayes, D. A. (1989). Classroom discussion of content area reading assignments: An intervention study. *Reading Research Quarterly, 24*, 305–335.

Applebee, A. N., Langer, J. A., Nystrand, M., & Gamoran, A. (2003). Discussion-based approaches to developing understanding: Classroom instruction and student performance in middle and high school English. *American Education Research Journal, 40*(3), 685–730.

Beck, I. L., & McKeown, M. G. (2006). *Improving comprehension with questioning the author: A fresh and expanded view of a powerful approach*. New York, NY: Scholastic.

Billings, L., & Fitzgerald, J. (2002). Dialogic discussion and the Paideia seminar. *American Educational Research Journal, 39*(4), 907–941.

Casper, T. P. (1964). Effects of the junior great books program at the fifth grade level on four intellectual operations and certain of their component factors as defined by J. P. Guilford (Unpublished doctoral dissertation), Saint Louis University, St. Louis.

Commeyras, M., & DeGroff, L. (1998). Literacy professionals' perspectives on professional development and pedagogy: A national survey. *Reading Research Quarterly, 33*, 434–472.

Great Books Foundation. (1987). *An introduction to shared inquiry*. Chicago: Author.

Grossman, P., Hammerness, K., & McDonald, M. (2009). Redefining teaching, re-imagining teacher education. *Teachers and Teaching: Theory and Practice, 15*(2), 273–289.

Kamil, M. L., Borman, G. D., Dole, J., Kral, C. C., Salinger, T., & Torgesen, J. (2008). *Improving adolescent literacy: Effective classroom and intervention practices: A practice guide* (NCEE #2008–4027). Washington, DC: National Center for Education Evaluation and Regional Assistance, Institute of Education Sciences, U.S. Department of Education.

McKeown, M. G., Beck, I. L., & Blake, R. G. K. (2009). Rethinking reading comprehension instruction: A comparison of instruction for strategies and content approaches. *Reading Research Quarterly, 44*(3), 218–253.

Mehan, H. (1979). *Learning lessons: Social organization in the classroom*. Cambridge, MA: Harvard University Press.

Mercer, N. (2000). *Words and minds: How we use language to think together*. London: Routledge.

Murphy, P. K., Wilkinson, I. A. G., Soter, A. O., & Firetto, C. M. (2016). Instruction based on discussion. In R. E. Mayer & P. A. Alexander (Eds.), *Handbook of research on learning and instruction* (2nd ed.). New York, NY: Routledge.

Murphy, P. K., Wilkinson, I. A. G., Soter, A. O., Hennessey, M. N., & Alexander, J. F. (2009). Examining the effects of classroom discussion on students' high-level comprehension of text: A meta-analysis. *Journal of Educational Psychology, 101*, 740–764.

Nystrand, M. (1997). *Opening dialogue: Understanding the dynamics of language and learning in the English classroom*. New York, NY: Teachers College Press.

Nystrand, M. (2002). *CLASS 4.0 User's manual: A Windows laptop computer system for the in-class analysis of classroom discourse*. Madison, WI: Wisconsin Center for Education Research.

Nystrand, M. (2006). Research on the role of classroom discourse as it affects reading comprehension. *Research in the Teaching of English, 40*(4), 392–412.

Osborne, J. (2015). The challenge of scale. In L. Resnick, C. Asterhan, & S. N. Clarke (Eds.), *Socializing intelligence through academic talk and dialogue* (pp. 403–414). Washington, DC: American Educational Research Association.

Reznitskaya, A., Hsu, J. Y., & Anderson, R. C. (2015). Using inquiry dialogue to promote the development of argument skills: Possibilities, challenges, and new directions. In S. R. Parris & K. Headley (Eds.), *Comprehension instruction: Research-based best practices* (3rd ed., pp. 29–44). New York, NY: Guilford.

Shanahan, T., Callison, K., Carriere, C., Duke, N. K., Pearson, P. D., Schatschneider, C., & Torgesen, J. (2010). *Improving reading comprehension in kindergarten through 3rd grade: A practice guide* (NCEE 2010–4038). Washington, DC: National Center for Education Evaluation and Regional Assistance, Institute of Education Sciences, U.S. Department of Education.

Wells, G. (1989). Language in the classroom: Literacy and collaborative talk. *Language and Education, 3*, 251–273.

Wells, G. (2007). Semiotic mediation, dialogue and the construction of knowledge. *Human Development, 50*(5), 244–274.

Wilkinson, I. A. G. (2009). Discussion methods. In E. M. Anderman & L. H. Anderman (Eds.), *Psychology of classroom learning: An encyclopedia* (pp. 330–336). Detroit, MI: Gale/Cengage.

Wilkinson, I. A. G., Murphy, P. K., & Binici, S. (2015). Dialogue-intensive pedagogies for promoting reading comprehension: What we know, what we need to know. In L. B. Resnick, C. A. Asterhan, & S. N. Clarke (Eds.), *Socializing intelligence through academic talk and dialogue* (pp. 35–48). Washington, DC: American Educational Research Association.

Wilkinson, I. A. G., Reznitskaya, A., Reninger, K., Oyler, J., Glina, M., Drewry, R., . . . Nelson, K. (2017). Toward a more dialogic pedagogy: Changing teachers' beliefs and practices through professional development in language arts classrooms. *Language and Education, 31*(1), 65–82.

Wilkinson, I. A. G., & Son, E. H. (2011). A dialogic turn in research on learning and teaching to comprehend. In M. L. Kamil, P. D. Pearson, E. Moje, & P. Afflerbach (Eds.), *Handbook of reading research* (Vol. 4, pp. 359–387). New York, NY: Routledge.

6.7

Achievement in adolescent health education

Megan Sanders, Rashea Hamilton, and Eric M. Anderman

Introduction

The area of health education is unique: whereas performance on standardized examinations is used to evaluate success in most academic domains, demonstrating factual knowledge often does not subsequently correspond to the desired outcomes of health education. For example, many adolescents and adults know that it is important to eat healthy foods and to exercise but nevertheless continue to engage in unhealthy behaviors (e.g., eating unhealthy foods) despite having this knowledge. Similarly, smokers often fail to quit the habit, even though most have heard reports about the risks and dangers of smoking. Although these individuals possess factual knowledge about how to live healthier lives, that knowledge often does not translate to a change in attitudes and behavior.

Thus, given this inconsistent relation between knowledge and behavior, "achievement" within health education needs to be assessed and evaluated somewhat differently than the way it is measured in most other academic domains. Specifically, in addition to factual knowledge, other important outcome variables must be considered. These other outcomes include enhanced efficacy to engage in safe behaviors and to refuse to participate in dangerous or risky activities, improved attitudes and motivation to avoid dangerous and unhealthy situations, increased intentions to engage in healthful behaviors, and actual engagement in healthy and nonrisky activities. Health education programs may be effective to the extent that they encourage achievement in terms of such outcomes.

Therefore, in the present entry, we review some of the characteristics of effective health education and make recommendations for health educators based on these characteristics. In our review, we focus in particular on adolescents because adolescence represents a period of development in which individuals are particularly likely to engage in risky activities and to develop unhealthy habits (e.g., smoking, poor nutrition, lack of exercise, and alcohol and drug use) that may persist into adulthood and lead to serious long-term health risks (Rew, 2005).

Research evidence

Before exploring the characteristics of effective health education programs, it is first important to note that achievement is represented by various outcome variables across different domains of health. For example, in studies of pregnancy prevention, outcome variables can include sexual activity, contraceptive use, pregnancy rates, and childbirth (Franklin, Grant, Corcoran, Miller, & Bultman, 1997). In studies of HIV prevention, outcomes may include sexual intentions, knowledge, attitudes, behaviors, and motivation (Anderman, Lane, Zimmerman, Cupp, & Phebus, 2009). Thus, examinations of achievement in health education must be sensitive to the fact that outcome measures vary greatly based on the focus of the program and the types of measures that were employed within studies. Despite the variability in outcome measures, effective health education programs have many features in common. One area of commonality is that most of these programs are focused on prevention (e.g., prevention of engagement in risky behaviors) and are designed to prevent the initiation of unhealthy behaviors. In a review of effective prevention programs (i.e., programs that lead to achievement), Nation et al. (2003) identified five characteristics demonstrated by effective prevention programs across four different domains of health education: substance abuse, risky sexual behavior, school failure, and delinquency. Specifically, effective programs (a) are comprehensive in nature (i.e., they incorporate multiple interventions that occur across multiple settings), (b) incorporate a variety of teaching methods (e.g., interactive instruction and opportunities to practice newly learned skills), (c) are delivered with sufficient dosage (i.e., participants are exposed to sufficient amounts of the program), (d) are informed by theory, and (e) promote positive relationships (e.g., between participants and their peers) (see also Dusenbury & Falco, 1995; Kirby et al., 1994).

Research has also cited the timing in which students are exposed to programming as influencing effectiveness. Somers and Surmann (2005) reported that later and decreased exposure to sex education was predictive of more sexual activity. Similarly, Mueller, Gavin, and Kulkarni (2008) reported that sex education may be more effective if provided prior to initiation of sexual activity. Other researchers support this argument, noting that students that are younger and not active sexually may be easier to influence (Franklin & Corcoran, 2000).

There is also a research base that notes the importance of peers in enhancing program effectiveness. Mellanby, Newcombe, Rees, and Tripp (2001) reported that, although peers may not be as effective as adults in imparting information to students, peers are more effective in helping establish norms and attitudes related to sex. In previous studies, peers were seen as better models of behavior than teachers (Walcott, Meyers, & Landau, 2008). Additionally, peer leaders have been demonstrated to enhance acceptability of health-related information, promote more accurate self-reports, and encourage attitude change (Valente, Unger, Ritt-Olson, Cen, & Johnson, 2006; Vuttanont, Greenhalgh, Griffin, & Boynton, 2006; Walcott et al., 2008).

Effective programs also utilize a theory-based approach to changing student behavior and attitudes. In their exploration of school-based health promotion programs, Peters, Kok, Ten Dam, Buijs, and Paulussen (2009) reported that theory-based programs were more effective across the three domains of substance abuse, sexual behavior, and nutrition than were non-theory-based programs. Franklin and Corcoran (2000) found similar results in their review of programs' effectiveness in preventing pregnancy. Both these reviews specifically cite curriculum based on social-cognitive theory as being particularly effective in impacting outcome variables.

Other research has also highlighted the relevance of program content as an important characteristic of effective health education programs. For example, research suggests that programs (e.g., HIV prevention programs) are particularly effective when they are designed or adjusted to be relevant to the culture in which the program is being implemented (Gewin & Hoffman, 2016; Halperin et al., 2004; Nation et al., 2003). Similarly, programs that are fitted to participants' developmental stages (Nation et al., 2003) and that address the concerns of that particular age group (Dusenbury & Falco, 1995) are also particularly effective. Thus, a health program that is effective in one culture or with one developmental group may not necessarily be equally effective in another context.

Another key characteristic of effective programs that lead to achievement is the mode of presentation of health-related information, which is an important predictor of acquiring health-related knowledge (Donohew, Lorch, & Palmgreen, 1998). One of the practices that most strongly distinguishes effective from ineffective health education programs is the use of interactive techniques to communicate information (Dusenbury & Falco, 1995; Herbert & Lohrmann, 2010). More specifically, a review of ten effective health curricula used with adolescent populations indicated that five communication strategies were common across many of these programs, including the use of role playing, group activities, interactive technologies (e.g., websites), team games, and small-group discussions (Herbert & Lohrmann, 2010). Instructional approaches that utilize diverse presentation techniques are likely to be particularly effective (Nation et al., 2003; Park, 2006; Vuttanont et al., 2006; Walcott et al., 2008). Health education also at times is integrated into other academic subjects, particularly when scheduling precludes offering separate health education classes; research suggests that integrating health education into other content areas yields small positive effects on the reduction of substance abuse (Melendez-Torres et al., 2018).

Finally, effective health education programs are also distinct in their implementation. Research suggests that well-trained teachers are integral to effective programs (Nation et al., 2003; Peters et al., 2009; Vuttanont et al., 2006) and that teaching educators how to use interactive techniques may be a particularly important component of this training (Dusenbury & Falco, 1995). However, initial training is not enough; effective programs also provide continuing support for teachers (Dusenbury & Falco, 1995). One way that programs provide this support is through feedback to instructors; such feedback helps educators evaluate and improve the program effectiveness (Nation at al., 2003).

Summary and recommendations

Achievement in health education needs to be defined broadly to include behavioral and attitudinal/motivational outcomes, in addition to factual knowledge. We briefly reviewed the program characteristics that are related to this expanded understanding of achievement. Research suggests that effective programs are comprehensive in nature, attempt to intervene with youth as early as possible, incorporate peers in the implementation of programming, are driven by theory, are culturally and developmentally relevant to the participants, are interactive in nature, and are applied in appropriate dosages. Additionally, sufficient training and support for educators are also important factors for the success of these programs.

The implications of these conclusions for the professional development of health educators are particularly important. As we suggested, teaching that encourages achievement in broader terms is different from teaching that frames achievement more narrowly as demonstrating factual knowledge. In light of these conclusions, it is clear that health educators need to consider the perspectives and concerns of the participating students in order for programs to be maximally effective. Furthermore, health educators must also acknowledge that the ways in which they communicate and reinforce health-related information to these adolescent populations can have effects on health-related outcomes. Simply presenting information and asking students to memorize it for a test is less effective in health education than techniques that allow students to come to deeply understand and value the information and skills that are being acquired (Anderman et al., 2011). Future research that examines differential effects of preventive health education programs (e.g., by gender or socioeconomic status) are warranted (Das, Salam, Arshad, Finkelstein, & Bhutta (2016).

References

Anderman, E. M., Cupp, P. K., Lane, D. R., Zimmerman, R., Gray, D., & O'Connell, A. (2011). Classroom goal structures and HIV/pregnancy prevention education in rural high school health classrooms. *Journal of Research on Adolescence, 21*, 904–922.

Anderman, E. M., Lane, D. R., Zimmerman, R., Cupp, P. K., & Phebus, V. (2009). Comparing the efficacy of permanent classroom teachers to temporary health educators for pregnancy and HIV prevention. *Health Promotion Practice, 10*, 597–605.

Das, J. K., Salam, R. A., Arshad, A., Finkelstein, Y., & Bhutta, Z. A. (2016). Interventions for adolescent substance abuse: An overview of systematic reviews. *Journal of Adolescent Health, 59*(4, Suppl), S61–S75. https://doi-org.proxy.lib.ohio-state.edu/10.1016/j.jadohealth.2016.06.021

Donohew, L., Lorch, E. P., & Palmgreen, P. (1998). Applications of a theoretic model of information exposure to health interventions. *Human Communication Research, 24*, 454–468.

Dusenbury, L., & Falco, M. (1995). Eleven components of effective drug abuse prevention curricula. *Journal of School Health, 65*, 420–425.

Franklin, C., & Corcoran, J. (2000). Preventing adolescent pregnancy: A review of programs and practices. *Social Work*, *45*(1), 40–52.

Franklin, C., Grant, D., Corcoran, J., Miller, P. O. D., & Bultman, L. (1997). Effectiveness of prevention programs for adolescent pregnancy: A meta-analysis. *Journal of Marriage and the Family*, *59*, 551–567.

Gewin, A. M., & Hoffman, B. (2016). Introducing the cultural variables in school-based substance abuse prevention. *Drugs: Education, Prevention & Policy*, *23*(1), 1–14. https://doi-org.proxy.lib.ohio-state.edu/10.3109/09687637.2015.1071781

Halperin, D. T., Steiner, J. J., Cassell, M. M., Green, E. C., Hearst, N., Kirby, D., . . . Cates, W. (2004). The time has come for common ground on preventing sexual transmission of HIV. *The Lancet*, *364*, 1913–1915.

Herbert, P. C., & Lohrmann, D. K. (2010). It's all in the delivery! An analysis of instructional strategies from effective health education curricula. *Journal of School Health*, *81*, 258–264.

Kirby, D., Short, L., Collins, J., Rugg, D., Kolbe, L., Howard, M., . . . Zabin, L. S. (1994). School-based programs to reduce sexual risk behaviors: A review of effectiveness. *Public Health Reports*, *109*, 339–360.

Melendez, T. G. J., Tancred, T., Fletcher, A., Thomas, J., Campbell, R., & Bonell, C. (2018). Does integrated academic and health education prevent substance use? Systematic review and meta-analyses. *Child: Care, Health and Development*, *44*(4), 516–530. https://doi-org.proxy.lib.ohio-state.edu/10.1111/cch.12558

Mellanby, A. R., Newcombe, R. G., Rees, J., & Tripp, J. H. (2001). A comparative study of peer-led and adult-led school sex education. *Health Education Research*, *16*(4), 481–492.

Mueller, T. E., Gavin, L. E., & Kulkarni, A. (2008). The association between sex education and youth's engagement in sexual intercourse, age at first intercourse, and birth control use at first sex. *Journal of Adolescent Health*, *42*(1), 89–96.

Nation, M., Crusto, C., Wandersman, A., Kumpfer, K. L., Seybolt, D., Morrissey-Kane, E., & Davino, K. (2003). What works in prevention: Principles of effective prevention programs. *American Psychologist*, *58*, 449–456.

Park, E. (2006). School-based smoking prevention programs for adolescents in South Korea: A systematic review. *Health Education Research Theory and Practice*, *21*(3), 407–415.

Peters, L. W. H., Kok, G., Ten Dam, G. T. M., Buijs, G. J., & Paulussen, T. G. W. M. (2009). Effective elements of school health promotion across behavioral domains: A systematic review of reviews. *Biomedical Public Health*, *9*(182), 1–14.

Rew, L. (2005). *Adolescent health: A multidisciplinary approach to theory, research, and intervention*. Thousand Oaks, CA: Sage.

Somers, C. L., & Surmann, A. T. (2005). Sources and timing of sex education: Relations with American adolescents' sexual attitudes and behavior. *Educational Review*, *57*(1), 37–54.

Valente, T. W., Unger, J. B., Ritt-Olson, A., Cen, S. Y., & Johnson, A. (2006). The interaction of curriculum type and implementation method on 1-year smoking outcomes in a school-based prevention program. *Health Education Research Theory and Practice*, *21*(3), 315–324.

Vuttanont, U., Greenhalgh, T., Griffin, M., & Boynton, P. (2006). "Smart boys" and "sweet girls" – Sex education needs in Thai teenagers: A mixed-method study. *Lancet*, *368*, 2068–2080.

Walcott, C. M., Meyers, A. B., & Landau, S. (2008). Adolescent sexual risk behaviors and school-based sexually transmitted infection/HIV prevention. *Psychology in the Schools*, *45*(1), 39–51.

Summary table: influences from the curriculum

Category	Variable	Considerations
General/ Overarching Curricular Influences	Research on the effects of the use of **hands-on activities** (involving the use of manipulative objects) is inconclusive.	*The use of hands-on activities within a curriculum may enhance achievement, but research on best practices is inconclusive.*
	Achievement can be enhanced by encouraging students to be **creative**.	*Students can be encouraged to be creative within a variety of curricula. Play-based curricula are more effective than direct instruction at fostering creativity and achievement. Avoid evaluating creativity and focusing on the production of a final product. Provide positive feedback and encouragement for creativity.*
	Outdoor education can be incorporated into curricula and can enhance achievement.	*To be effective within curricula, outdoor education should involve a substantial amount of time and should include follow-up discussion/instruction. Adventure programs are particularly effective because students' learning opportunities are structured and have clear outcomes and extensive feedback is given throughout.*
	The **teaching of social skills** is related to improved social behaviors, particularly for students who exhibit or are at risk for emotional and behavioral disorders.	*Social skills instruction leads to reduced aggression and externalizing behaviors. These changes may foster greater engagement and concentration in students, which can lead to enhanced achievement. Effects on achievement are small but positive.*
	Research on the effects of **bilingual education** on achievement are mixed.	*Although bilingual programs are related to achievement gains, research to date does not clearly indicate that bilingual education programs universally lead to higher achievement than other programs (e.g., English-immersion programs). The implementation of bilingual education programs must be considered in light of resources, quality of program, ages of students, and training of teachers.*

(Continued)

Category	Variable	Considerations
	Response to Intervention (RTI), as well as **multitiered systems of support (MTSS)**, can enhance student achievement when (a) educators receive appropriate professional development; (b) it is supported by teachers, schools, and the district; and (c) educators are provided with sufficient time to meet and plan for students' needs.	*Research on MTSS is somewhat limited at this time. Some studies suggest that the effectiveness of MTSS may vary by subject domain.*
Language	**Discussion of texts** with students is related to improved reading comprehension.	*Effects of discussion on comprehension are moderate. Discussions should be both structured and focused; students should talk more than the teacher does in such discussions. Use interesting, engaging questions to stimulate discussions. Discussions are most beneficial when students are encouraged to consider their classmates' opinions and also to explain and defend their own opinions.*
	Phonics instruction helps children learn to read.	*Instruction in phonics is essential in the development of reading skills. Supplemental phonics instruction focusing on recognition of orthographic patterns and on word identification strategies is particularly helpful for struggling readers. The acquisition of phonics skills varies across many dimensions; thus, not all children will acquire these skills and be able to apply them at the same pace. Training of teachers in research-based phonics instructional techniques could be stronger.*
	Repeated reading of the same texts can benefit young children who are struggling readers.	*Repeated reading is most effective when (a) students are provided with feedback on specific words that they do not read correctly, (b) students are encouraged to reread texts until they reach a prespecified success rate (e.g., reading a certain number of words per minute accurately), and (c) students are encouraged to set and reach specific goals.*

(Continued)

Category	Variable	Considerations
	The most effective programs for teaching **vocabulary** are comprehensive and long term and utilize a variety of instructional strategies.	*Strategies may include providing students with materials that include new vocabulary, teaching strategies that students can use to figure out the meanings of new words independently, and vocabulary instruction along with opportunities to practice newly learned words.*
	Effective **reading comprehension** instruction focuses on teaching students to both monitor their comprehension and self-regulate while reading.	*Students need to be taught to use specific comprehension monitoring and self-regulatory strategies and be given the opportunity to practice and apply those strategies. Examples of these strategies include summarizing text, visualization, asking oneself questions, relating texts to prior knowledge, predicting future events that will occur in a text, and recognizing various types of text. Reading comprehension programs can also yield small gains in vocabulary knowledge.*
	Effective **writing** instruction focuses both on technical aspects of writing (e.g., spelling, grammar, and handwriting), and on specific strategies that support the development of higher-level aspects of composition (e.g., structure of an argument).	*A key component in developing effective writers is the instruction in specific writing strategies. Some strategies include setting short-term goals and working collaboratively with peers on drafts and revisions.*
	Research on the effects of various types of **curricula on emerging language skills of English-Language learners** is mixed.	*There is a large achievement gap between English-language learners (ELLs) and native speakers of English. There are two main types of curricula that are used to teach English to ELLs. Content-based curricula incorporate both language instruction and instruction in content areas simultaneously; in contrast, genre-based curricular models focus on language, reading, and writing. Research to date has not clearly established that one type is more effective than the other.*

(Continued)

Category	Variable	Considerations
Math and Science	Math achievement can be enhanced when students are allowed to use **calculators** in some circumstances.	*Calculators have a small positive effect on math achievement. Nevertheless, the use of calculators does not eliminate the need for students to learn how to solve problems by hand, how to understand numbers ("number sense"), and how to make mental calculations. Calculators should be used for basic computation; calculator usage should be limited during the early grades; use of calculators should increase as students progress into higher grades.*
	Student **achievement in math** is enhanced when teachers are provided with high-quality math curricula and are trained to adapt math instruction to meet individual students' needs.	*Teachers should not take a "one size fits all" approach to math instruction. Teachers need to be carefully trained to be able to adjust lessons and approaches as appropriate.*
	Effective health education programs aimed at the prevention of risky behaviors generally are characterized by multiple lessons taught in a variety of ways. Effective programs allow students to practice newly learned preventive strategies numerous times.	*Factual knowledge is only one outcome of health education, and it is limited in importance. Successful achievement in health education is demonstrated when students' health-related behaviors and intentions to engage in preventive behaviors are increased.*

Note: This table summarizes information presented by authors who contributed chapters to section 7 of the first edition of The International Guide to Student Achievement, as well as to revised chapters included in the present chapter.

Additional references

Berliner, D. C., & Glass, G. V. (2014). *Fifty myths and lies that threaten America's public schools: The real crisis in education.* New York, NY: Teachers College Press.

Corcoran, R. P., Cheung, A. C. K., Kim, E., & Xie, C. (2018). Effective universal school-based social and emotional learning programs for improving academic achievement: A systematic review and meta-analysis of 50 years of research. *Educational Research Review, 25,* 56–72. https://doi-org.proxy.lib.ohio-state.edu/10.1016/j.edurev.2017.12.001

Jindal-Snape, D., Davies, D., Scott, R., Robb, A., Murray, C., & Harkins, C. (2018). Impact of arts participation on children's achievement: A systematic literature review. *Thinking Skills & Creativity, 29,* 59–70. https://doi-org.proxy.lib.ohio-state.edu/10.1016/j.tsc.2018.06.003

CHAPTER 7

Influences from teaching strategies

Students regularly use many strategies when they are learning. The term "strategy" is a broad term that can refer to any cognitive or noncognitive approach that students utilize while working on academic tasks. Over the past few decades, research has clearly demonstrated that students achieve at higher levels when they use specific, evidence-based cognitive and self-regulatory strategies (e.g., Ergen & Kanadli, 2017; Richardson, Abraham, & Bond, 2012). Whereas many strategies are very effective (e.g., the ones that are reviewed in this chapter), others (e.g., trying to memorize a large amount of information the night before a test) are ineffective. Nevertheless, students generally do not simply learn the effective strategies on their own; students need to be taught how to choose the appropriate strategies for a given academic task and then to appropriately apply the strategies (Pressley & Harris, 2008). In this chapter, our contributors have identified some of the most effective strategies and best practices in terms of how to support students' use of those strategies.

In the original *Guide*, we invited authors to comment on the relations of a wide range of teaching strategies to academic achievement. That section, which was edited by Christine Rubie-Davies (University of Auckland), included the entries and authors listed below (entries marked with an asterisk have been updated for this edition):

Goal Orientation★

Andrew J. Martin

Goal Setting and Personal Best Goals

Andrew J. Martin

Keller's Personalized System of Instruction

Eric J. Fox

Concept Mapping
  Joseph D. Novak

Direct Instruction*
  Gregory Arief D. Liem and Andrew J. Martin

Reciprocal Teaching*
  Annemarie Sullivan Palincsar

Cooperative, Competitive, and Individualistic Learning Environments
  David W. Johnson and Roger T. Johnson

Peer Tutoring School-Age Children
  Dilara Deniz Can and Marika Ginsburg-Block

Problem Solving*
  R. Taconis

Problem-Based Learning*
  David Gijbels, Piet Van den Bossche, and Sofie Loyens

The Search for the Key for Individualized Instruction
  Catherine Scott

Instructional Simulations
  Jennifer J. Vogel-Walcutt, Naomi Malone, and Sae Schatz

Programmed Instruction
  Deborah V. Svoboda, Andrea L. Jones, Kimberly van Vulpen, and Donna Harrington

Multimedia Learning*
  Richard E. Mayer

Technology-Supported Learning and Academic Achievement*
  Peter Reimann and Anindito Aditomo

Feedback
  Helen Timperley

Individualized Instruction
  Hersh C. Waxman, Beverly L. Alford, and Danielle B. Brown

Worked Examples
  Paul Ayres and John Sweller

Spaced and Massed Practice
>   *Dominic A. Simon*

Questioning★
>   *Scotty D. Craig*

Effects of Testing
>   *Jaekyung Lee and Young-Sun Lee*

Metacognitive Strategies★
>   *Linda Baker*

Mentoring
>   *Brian Hansford and Lisa Catherine Ehrich*

Teacher Immediacy★
>   *Ann Bainbridge Frymier*

The Impact of Teaching Assistants on Pupils
>   *Rob Webster and Peter Blatchford*

Time on Task
>   *Tamara van Gog*

Study Skills★
>   *Dale H. Schunk and Carol A. Mullen*

Matching Style of Learning
>   *Steve Higgins*

Two Types of Perceived Control over Learning: Perceived Efficacy and Perceived Autonomy
>   *Nir Madjar and Avi Assor*

Distance Education
>   *Yong Zhao and Jing Lei*

Home School Programs
>   *Andrea Clements*

Evidence-Based Reading Comprehension Programs for Students with Learning Disabilities
>   *H. Lee Swanson and Michael Orosco*

We first present a brief overview of some of the major takeaway points from the research on the relations of teaching strategies to achievement. We have organized the strategies into three categories: cognitive/motivational strategies, instructional strategies, and technology-infused strategies.

Cognitive/motivational strategies

Some of the contributors described the importance of cognitive and motivational strategies. Whereas these strategies are often discussed in terms of the student (i.e., almost as a characteristic or trait of the student), it is important to recognize that students do not learn how to use these strategies on their own. Whereas teachers may assume that students simply know how to use and adapt various cognitive and motivational strategies across tasks and subject areas, this is not necessarily the case – students must be taught when and how to effectively use all strategies.

The three exemplars of cognitive/motivational strategies that our authors identified are (a) metacognitive strategies, (b) goal orientations, and (c) goal setting. Metacognitive strategies include a wide range of strategies that learners can use in order to work on academic tasks effectively. The use of metacognitive strategies is related positively to academic achievement, although these relations vary somewhat by subject area and grade in school (Dent & Koenka, 2016). Some examples of metacognitive strategies include monitoring one's progress, planning the steps in completing a task, asking oneself questions, and evaluating both the process of working on the task and the products that are produced. Thus, if a student is presented with an academic task (e.g., to write a persuasive essay), the student would hopefully employ appropriate metacognitive strategies in order to make decisions about the more specific approaches that he or she would use (i.e., the more specific cognitive strategies) to write the essay (e.g., making an outline, gathering appropriate reference material, etc.).

Goal orientations represent students' beliefs about why they do their academic work. Some students approach academic tasks because they truly have the goal of learning the material ("I want to really learn and understand why water turns to ice when put in a freezer"), but others sometimes have different types of goals – for example, some students may simply have the goal of not appearing incompetent or "dumb" when engaged with specific tasks ("I just don't want to look like I don't know what I'm doing if the teacher asks me to explain how I solved the algebra problem"). Goal orientations vary across subject areas and even across specific tasks or assignments. Thus, a student might have a goal of truly learning and understanding the material in a French language class, but that same student might have the goal of not appearing "dumb" in math class. Moreover, goal orientations are often adopted by students based on the ways that teachers organize instruction. If instructional practices allow students to make mistakes and try something again if they don't initially succeed, students are likely to adopt mastery goals; in contrast, if instructional practices focus on completing an assignment as quickly as possible, then students may adopt performance goals. As you'll see in the chapter on this topic, the types of goals that students adopt affects what and how they learn.

Another strategy that is discussed is goal setting. Sometimes teachers set goals for their students, but often students are asked to set their own goals. The types of goals that students set for themselves can have profound effects on their achievement. If students set high-level, complex goals, they may become frustrated if they do not feel that they are making adequate progress toward the goal ("My goal is to learn how to speak Spanish"); in contrast, if students set short-term goals and they receive appropriate support and feedback in reaching those goals, they are likely to persist and ultimately to learn more ("My goal is to learn how to count to ten in Spanish by the end of the week").

Instructional strategies

Our contributors also identified several types of instructional strategies that teachers can use in their daily practice. One of the most important takeaway messages is that in order to positively affect achievement, these strategies *must be implemented by teachers with fidelity and according to research-based recommendations*. If they are implemented in a piecemeal manner, students are unlikely to benefit.

Some of the strategies that are discussed focus on broad instructional strategies that can either be implemented with a whole class or with smaller groups of students. For example, although educators often organize students into small cooperative groups or have students work on projects, direct instruction by the teacher is a strategy that can still yield significant achievement benefits. Moreover, the amount of time that teachers allocate for a given task is an important determinant of achievement, as long as teachers realize that some students may need more (or less) time than others.

Other strategies focus on teacher-student interactions. For example, although teachers' nonverbal interactions with students (e.g., making eye contact, smiling) may seem trivial, they are related to achievement – students learn more from teachers who smile and look students in the eye, quite likely because these teacher behaviors invoke positive affect among students. Moreover, the ways that teachers ask questions also can enhance or hinder learning; generally, questions that require students to both recall and then apply knowledge yield greater long-term achievement gains than do questions that simply require the student to recall basic facts. And the type of feedback that teachers provide to their students also matters – to affect achievement, feedback needs to be specific and offer clear suggestions for remediation and improvement.

Technology and strategies

Finally, some strategy instruction can occur via technology. There is enormous growth in the application of technology to strategy instruction, and this will only increase in the coming years. Nevertheless, there is some research that clearly suggests best practices for developing and implementing technological innovations.

There are numerous applications, simulations, and multimedia lessons available for use in virtually any academic domain, for virtually any age group. But the mere use of technological teaching tools does not automatically lead to achievement gains – what matters is how the technology is used. For example, although digital simulations are widely popular among educators, they tend to be the most effective in producing achievement gains when classroom teachers are engaged and involved with their students while the students are working on the simulations; when teachers just "turn on the computer" and let the students work with software, achievement gains will not be as strong. Moreover, although many curricula are available in digital format and offer enticing features, the most effective multimedia curricula have been designed not to overwhelm the students with huge amounts of text and many distracting pictures and videos; rather, the most effective ones emphasize the essential points and are presented clearly and without distractions.

We next present updated versions of eleven of the chapters that appeared in the original *Guide*. The chapter then concludes with a table that summarizes the main takeaway points.

7.1

Metacognitive strategies

Linda Baker

Introduction

A primary goal of education is to help students become independent, autonomous, and effective learners. Fostering students' metacognitive knowledge and control is a means toward this goal. Metacognitive knowledge includes knowledge about the skills, strategies, and resources that are needed to perform a task effectively, and metacognitive control is the use of strategies to ensure successful task completion, such as planning, monitoring, and evaluating.

Research on metacognition has its roots in the 1970s work of cognitive developmental psychologists John Flavell and Ann Brown, whose interests in memory development led them to ask what children know about their memory and how they learn to control it. Researchers soon turned to investigations of metacognition in relation to student achievement, and today, this topic is a significant area of inquiry across the globe.

One reason metacognition has received so much attention is that younger and less successful students do not use metacognitive strategies effectively, if at all, and they have limited knowledge of when, where, and why to use those strategies. A second and more compelling reason is that these strategies can be taught, and doing so leads to increases in achievement. Much contemporary research on metacognition is framed within the broader context of self-regulated learning, which acknowledges the inextricable connections among cognitive and metacognitive strategies, affect, and motivation.

The distinction between cognitive and metacognitive strategies is not always explicitly articulated in research and practice, but one way of thinking about the distinction is that cognitive strategies enable us to make progress on a given task, whereas metacognitive strategies enable us to control progress. For example, cognitive strategies for learning include rehearsal (e.g., underlining), elaboration (e.g., summarizing), and organization (e.g., creating a concept map). Metacognitive strategies include planning (e.g., allocating resources), monitoring (e.g., self-testing to check understanding), and evaluating (e.g., making judgments about the effectiveness of one's efforts).

Metacognitive strategies can be applied productively in any content domain. Before beginning a task, students set goals and develop an action plan. Then, during the task, they monitor their cognitive activities and adjust them as needed to make adequate progress. After finishing the task, they evaluate the adequacy and reasonableness of outcomes and revise accordingly, if necessary.

Research evidence

The body of research on metacognitive strategies continues to expand, reflecting the ongoing interest in the topic as well as its practical importance. Literature syntheses are available in scholarly texts (e.g., Desoete & Veenman, 2006; Hacker, Dunlosky, & Graesser, 2009; Israel, Block, Bauserman, & Kinnucan-Welsch, 2005) and journals (e.g., *Metacognition and Learning*). A wide variety of print and online sources offer teachers evidence-based recommendations for metacognitively oriented instruction (e.g., McGuire, 2015; Wilson & Conyers, 2016).

One source of evidence that metacognition is important to student achievement comes from correlational studies. Although correlation does not mean causation, there is such an abundance of research with large samples, carefully selected covariates, and strong analytic designs that one can have confidence that the correlations are educationally meaningful. Given the strength of the existing evidence, the 2009 Program for Student Assessment (PISA), which was administered to 470,000 15-year-olds in 65 countries/economies, included assessments of metacognition in relation to reading (OECD, 2010). Students completed a self-report rating of behaviors such as *When I study, I start by figuring out what exactly I need to learn* and *When I study, I try to figure out which concepts I still haven't really understood*. Students also responded to scenarios in which they were asked what would be the best strategy to use for successful completion of the task. Results showed that, in all the tested countries, better-performing readers had higher metacognition scores. Moreover, knowledge of effective strategies was a stronger predictor of performance than self-reported strategy use.

Recent correlational research has been synthesized in a meta-analysis comparing effects of metacognitive and cognitive processes in relation to academic achievement (Dent & Koenka, 2016). Correlations were stronger for metacognitive strategies than cognitive strategies, indicating that one cannot rely on cognitive strategies alone while attempting to learn and remember information but that one must also use metacognitive strategies to ensure that efforts are successful. Also examined in the meta-analysis was whether particular metacognitive strategies are more important than others. What students did while they were engaged in the task (monitoring and control) was more strongly related to achievement than what they did beforehand (planning) or afterward (evaluation). Although planning was also strongly related to achievement, evaluation was not.

A second source of evidence that metacognition is important to student achievement comes from classroom intervention research. Most interventions include instruction of multiple strategies that have been well validated as effective. They typically have both teacher-led and student-centered components, such as explicit explanation of how, when, and why to use metacognitive strategies, modeling, guided practice, and peer collaboration. The typical sequence is for teacher-led explicit instruction to be followed by a gradual release of responsibility to the students themselves. Research has shown that students who are taught to use a variety of cognitive and metacognitive strategies have greater gains in metacognitive awareness and academic achievement than comparison groups of students who do not receive the training. Successful outcomes have been obtained in reading, writing, mathematics, and science, from early primary grades to secondary and tertiary education levels.

The number of well-designed and well-executed studies that include metacognitive strategies instruction has increased dramatically in the 21st century, and their results have been synthesized in recent meta-analyses (de Boer, Donker, Kostons, & van der Werf, 2018; Dignath & Buttner, 2008; Donker-Bergstra, De Boer, Kostos, Dignath-van Ewijk, & van der Werf, 2014). These meta-analyses compare effects in different content domains (reading, writing, math, and science), at different grade levels (primary, secondary), with different instructional components (cognitive strategies, metacognitive strategies, metacognitive knowledge/reflection, and motivation), with different durations, and with different student characteristics (ability level, income level). Following are some of the key findings.

Two of the meta-analyses focused more broadly on self-regulated learning and so included not only metacognitive strategies and metacognitive knowledge, but also cognitive strategies, management strategies, and motivational aspects. Overall, intervention effects were stronger when cognitive strategies and metacognitive strategies were the joint focus of instruction (Dignath & Buttner, 2008). Instruction in each of the three metacognitive strategies (planning, monitoring, and evaluation) had strong effects on achievement, as did instruction designed to foster metacognitive knowledge. Of particular interest was which specific strategies, among all the self-regulated learning strategies considered, had the greatest effect on academic performance. Metacognitive knowledge, planning, and task value (a motivational aspect) were the three strongest (Donker-Bergstra et al., 2014).

Individual studies typically focus on one academic domain, but because meta-analyses synthesize effects across studies, they allow for comparisons across subject areas. In the correlational meta-analysis, metacognitive strategy use was more strongly related to achievement in social studies than in English/language arts (Dent & Koenka, 2016). The difference in effects may reflect the increased strategic demands of reading for remembering in addition to reading for understanding in social studies. In the intervention meta-analyses, metacognitive strategies instruction, and attention to metacognitive knowledge had significant effects in all domains, with the greatest effect on writing and the smallest effect on reading (Donker-Bergstra et al., 2014). The smaller effect on reading may reflect an important change in educational practice since the studies included in the meta-analysis were published. Intervention effectiveness in reading had already been documented by the turn of the century, leading the National Reading Panel to recommend that teachers incorporate metacognitive strategies instruction in the classroom. It may be that students in the intervention and comparison conditions alike already possessed metacognitive knowledge of reading (Baker, DeWyngaert, & Zeliger-Kandasamy, 2015).

The meta-analyses also allow us to see whether metacognitive strategies have as large an impact on student achievement in the primary grades as in the secondary grades, an advantage over individual studies that typically focus on more limited age ranges. Correlations between metacognitive strategies and achievement were stronger in secondary school than in primary school (Dent & Koenka, 2016), most likely because younger children are not yet using self-regulatory strategies effectively if at all. Relatedly, metacognitive strategy instruction yielded greater benefits for older students (Dignath & Buttner, 2008). Older students likely have already acquired some metacognitive knowledge from their more extensive schooling history and so are better able to build on prior experiences. The developmental difference may also be due to adolescent maturation of the prefrontal cortex, which is involved in higher-order cognitive processes and executive control (Baker, 2017). Intervention effects at the secondary level, but not the primary level, were stronger when metacognitive reflection was included in the training (Dignath & Buttner, 2008). It is not enough to instruct metacognitive strategies; students also need feedback about their strategy use, knowledge about effective strategies, and conditions under which they are most useful. Developmentally, adolescents are more proficient at abstract thinking, including thinking about their own thought processes.

Classroom-based intervention programs vary in length considerably, ranging from a few weeks up to six months or more. Programs are more effective the longer they are implemented (Dignath & Buttner, 2008). Learning to use metacognitive strategies effectively does not happen quickly. Students need ample time to practice the strategies, to receive feedback on their use, and to take on full responsibility for their application. The likelihood of transfer of strategies to new contexts also increases with more instructional time.

The ultimate goal of teaching students to use metacognitive strategies is to help them become self-regulated learners, able to use appropriate strategies when and where they are needed, without external prompting. It is, therefore, important to determine whether what students learn during an intervention remains with them after the intervention has ended. A recent meta-analysis showed large effects of metacognitive strategies instruction both immediately and after a delay, with effect sizes even stronger on the delayed assessment (de Boer et al., 2018). The follow-up effect was of similar magnitude, regardless of which metacognitive strategies had been included in the intervention.

An important question for policy and practice is whether all students can benefit from instruction in metacognitive strategies, regardless of ability level or socio-economic status. In contrast to earlier syntheses, it now appears that intervention effectiveness does not differ by student ability level or socioeconomic status (Donker-Bergstra et al., 2014). Moreover, students from low-SES backgrounds showed the strongest increase in achievement over time in the long-term follow-up studies (de Boer et al., 2018). These results are encouraging in their potential for decreasing academic disparities.

Summary and recommendations

The research summarized in this entry has shown that metacognitive strategies enhance achievement across core subject areas and that these strategies can be successfully taught. Fostering students' metacognitive knowledge appears to be the most powerful intervention of all. Research converges on the following instructional practices:

- Explicit teaching and modeling of metacognitive strategies;
- Gradual transition from external regulation (by the teacher/tutor) to self-regulation (by the students);
- Informative feedback on strategy implementation;
- Opportunities for students to reflect on the approaches they used to reach their goals;
- Instruction that explicitly links the quality of performance with the strategies used so that students see the value of using strategies;
- Opportunities for students to transfer their metacognitive knowledge across areas of the curriculum; and
- Discussions with students about what strategies they find helpful and unhelpful.

Metacognitive strategies instruction is beginning to be observed in the classroom, but it is still not common practice, and interviews with teachers continue to reveal limited knowledge about metacognition and how to foster it (Baker et al., 2015). Teachers would benefit from enhanced professional development to give them the knowledge and skills to foster metacognition as part of their regular instructional practice. Increasing teachers' own metacognitive awareness is an important first step in preparing them to increase students' awareness. Providing opportunities for teachers to talk with one another about their own thinking can be helpful in fostering such understandings. Practical resources for teachers are increasingly available that focus specifically on metacognitive strategies for K–12 (e.g., Wilson & Conyers, 2016) and higher education (e.g., McGuire, 2015).

Worldwide, educational policy makers now recommend attention to metacognition in the classroom (e.g., OECD, 2009). Nationally adopted educational standards in numerous countries call for students to be taught effective metacognitive strategies in literacy, math, and science. The evidence that metacognitive strategies impact academic achievement is too strong to ignore.

References

Baker, L. (2017). The development of metacognitive knowledge and control of comprehension: Contributors and consequences. In K. Mokhtari (Ed.), *Improving reading comprehension through metacognitive reading instruction* (pp. 1–31). Lanham, MD: Roman and Littlefield.

Baker, L., DeWyngaert, L. U., & Zeliger-Kandasamy, A. (2015). Metacognition in comprehension instruction: New directions. In S. R. Parris & K. Headley (Eds.), *Comprehension instruction: Research-based best practices* (3rd ed.). New York, NY: Guilford.

de Boer, H., Donker, A. S., Kostons, D., van der Werf, G. (2018). Long-term effects of metacognitive strategy instruction on student academic performance: A meta-analysis. *Educational Research Review, 24*, 98–115.

Dent, A. L., & Koenka, A. C. (2016). The relation between self-regulated learning and academic achievement across childhood and adolescence: A meta-analysis. *Educational Psychology Review, 28*, 425–474.

Desoete, A., & Veenman, M. (Eds.). (2006). *Metacognition in mathematics education.* Hauppauge, NY: Nova Science.

Dignath, C., & Buttner, G. (2008). Components of fostering self-regulated learning among students. A meta-analysis on intervention studies at primary and secondary school level. *Metacognition and Learning, 3*, 231–264.

Donker-Bergstra, A., De Boer, H., Kostons, D., Dignath-van Ewijk, C., & van der Werf, G. (2014). Effectiveness of learning strategy instruction on academic performance: A meta-analysis. *Educational Research Review, 11*, 1–26.

Hacker, D. J., Dunlosky, J., & Graesser, A. (2009). *Handbook of meta-cognition in education.* New York, NY: Routledge.

Israel, S. E., Block, C. C., Bauserman, K. L., & Kinnucan-Welsch, K. (Eds.). (2005). *Metacognition in literacy learning: Theory, assessment, instruction, and professional development.* New York, NY: Erlbaum.

McGuire, S.Y. (2015). *Teach students how to learn: Strategies you can incorporate into any course to improve student metacognition, study skills, and motivation.* Sterling, VA: Stylus Publishing, LLC.

OECD. (2010). *PISA 2009 results: Learning to learn – Student engagement, strategies and practices* (Vol. III). http://dx.doi.org/10.1787/9789264083943-en

Wilson, D., & Conyers, M. (2016). *Teaching students to drive their brains: Metacognitive strategies, activities, and lesson ideas.* Alexandria, VA: Association for Supervision and Curriculum Development.

7.2 The role of questions in academic achievement

Scotty D. Craig

Introduction

Successful learning attempts often start with some form of a question. In fact, researchers have claimed that questioning is one of the processing components that underlies comprehension (Collins, Brown, & Larkin, 1980), problem solving (Reisbeck, 1988), reasoning (Graesser, Baggett, & Williams, 1996), creativity (Sternberg, 1987), and learning (McDermott, 2006; Pashler et al., 2007), making questions a primary component of academic achievement (Roscoe & Chi, 2007).

Rosenshine, Meister, and Chapman (1996) provided a comprehensive analysis of the impact of question generation on learning in a meta-analysis of 26 empirical studies that compared conditions in which students were trained to ask questions during learning with appropriate controls. Outcome measures included standardized tests, multiple-choice questions prepared by the experimenters, and text summaries. The median effect size was 0.36 for the standardized tests, 0.87 for the experimenter-generated tests, and 0.85 for text summaries.

Research evidence

What allows questions to facilitate a learner's achievement?

Questions perform two guiding functions in the learning process. First, they serve as a prompt to encourage active processing of material, thus increasing the likelihood that discrepancies will be detected. Second, they serve to focus the learner's processing by providing activation to the learner's larger network of knowledge.

When the question is presented to the learner, it sets up expectations based on their previous knowledge by facilitating schema activation. When a schema is activated, it attempts to interpret the current experience. If this interpretation fails, schema modification occurs: that is, the activated schemas are reconstituted in ways that incorporate the new experience and new evidence (Derry, 1996).

When a question is initially presented, it activates the learner's existing schemas. When the subsequent content is interpreted, the learner uses the activated schemas to attempt to interpret the new information. If there are no inconsistencies between the active mental representation and the information, then no learning occurs (i.e., the content is already known); if there are inconsistencies, new learning can occur.

Questions are important when discrepancies are present because the questions encourage attempts to understand the new information in the face of expectation violations (Schank, 1986), cognitive disequilibrium (Graesser, Lu, Olde, Cooper-Pye, & Whitten, 2005), or other types of events that cause confusion (Bjork & Bjork, 2006) or curiosity (Zillmann & Cantor, 1973). Without the question, the learner is less prone to bothering to rectify the conceptual violations (Eakin, 2005). When discrepancies are detected, there is a need for explanation, which results in a modification to the learner's mental model and a deeper comprehension of the material. The learner detects discrepancies between schemas and the new content; they have the opportunity to recompose existing schemas and bring them into correspondence with that content (Chi, 2000).

Are some questions more effective than others?

Questions must encourage sufficient processing of the information for discrepancies to be identified. Presenting a statement, while it might activate the underlying schema, would not always encourage learning. Likewise, simple or shallow questions that to not require much processing may also not increase learning.

Researchers have investigated the impact of deep questions on learning in recent years (Wisher & Graesser, 2007). A deep question is a question integrated with content that builds links between understanding and the mechanisms and components described in the materials to be learned. These questions are aligned with the higher levels of Bloom's taxonomy (1956) and the long-answer question categories in the question taxonomy proposed by Graesser and Person (1994). In order to illustrate the difference between deep questions and shallow questions, consider an example of each. An example of a shallow question, according to Graesser and Person (1994), would be a verification question (e.g., "Can I just kind of trace this?"), in which the student is referring to a diagram of the heart. The purpose of categorizing this type of question as shallow is that it does not take much intrinsic thought on the student's part. It is a simple yes or no question. In contrast, an example of a deep-reasoning question would be a casual antecedent question (e.g., "Why is it that your arteries clog based on your cholesterol level but your veins don't?"). The reason for categorizing this question as "deep" is because the student must take the knowledge he or she has about the circulatory system, make a connection, and compare the differences between the two.

Driscoll and colleagues (2003) provided evidence for this distinction. In a laboratory experiment with college students, they demonstrated that only participants who observed dialogues with deep-level questions showed improved learning over a simple presentation of the information. Presentation of a simple statement or a shallow question on the same content at the same point in the presentations did not improve learning. This effect has been shown to hold across a wide range of academic levels and STEM topics (Gholson, Coles, & Craig, 2010).

Summary and recommendations

How can you get students to ask good questions?

It is easy to implement strategies that elicit deep questions from middle school students (Davey & McBride, 1986; King, 1994) and college students (Craig, Gholson, Ventura, Graesser, & the Tutoring Research Group, 2000). The training procedures used to induce question generation among middle school children were usually quite explicit, conducted as part of classroom activity, and required multiple training sessions. Both methods involved exposing students to question stems that included appropriate question words used to create good questions. The Davey and McBride (1986) study taught students to generate these stems themselves; whereas, the King (1994) study provided students with stems for them to develop their own questions. Both studies revealed improved question asking from students.

Craig et al. (2000) used vicarious learning procedures to induce good question asking by having participants view a model of a good question asking. Participants viewed either a 30-minute video of a student agent asking deep questions of their tutor or a video of a session where the student was passively tutored. When participants were tutored on a new transfer topic, the question-condition participants asked significantly more as well as deep questions whereas the few questions the participants in the no-question conditions tended to be shallow questions.

Do the teacher's questions impact the classroom?

Implementation of questions by teachers can be equally important to the learning process as student generations of questions. Question-answer dialogues are an effective method by which teachers can identify student knowledge deficits (Silliman & Wilkinson, 1994) and improve teachers' explanations to the students (Aguiar, Mortimer, & Scott, 2010). However, questioning strategies are rarely implemented, with only 16.3% knowing about them and only 1.9% reportedly implemented them due to difficulty (Henderson & Dancy, 2009). In a controlled classroom experiment, deep question-answer dialogues led by a teacher have shown to improve students' learning on classroom tests by a letter grade (Gholson, Graesser, & Craig, 2009).

Questions can play an important role in the learning process by activating previous knowledge and guiding the integration of new knowledge. During this process, deep questions are more effective for facilitating knowledge acquisition. Deep questions have been effectively used during learning by inducing question asking by students via questions stems or observational models and by good question explanation dialogues led by teachers.

References

Aguiar, O. G., Mortimer, E. F., & Scott, P. (2010). Learning from and responding to students' questions: The authoritative and dialogic tension. *Journal of Research in Science Teaching*, 47, 174–193.

Bjork, R. A., & Bjork, E. L. (2006). Optimizing treatment and instruction: Implications of a new theory of disuse. In L-G. Nilsson & N. Ohta (Eds.), *Memory and society: Psychological perspectives* (pp. 116–140). New York, NY: Psychology Press.

Bloom, B. S. (1956). *Taxonomy of educational objectives. Vol. 1: Cognitive domain*. New York: McKay.

Chi, M. T. H. (2000). Self-explaining expository texts: The dual processes of generating inferences and repairing mental models. In R. Glaser (Ed.), *Advances in instructional psychology* (pp. 161–238). Hillsdale, NJ: Erlbaum.

Collins, A., Brown, J. S., & Larkin, K. M. (1980). Inference in text understanding. In R. J. Spiro, B. C. Bruce, & W. F. Brewer (Eds.), *Theoretical issues in reading comprehension* (pp. 385–410). London: Routledge.

Craig, S., D., Gholson, B., Ventura, M., Graesser, A. C., & The Tutoring Research Group. (2000). Overhearing dialogues and monologues in virtual tutoring sessions: Effects on questioning and vicarious learning. *International Journal of Artificial Intelligence in Education*, 11, 242–253.

Davey, B., & McBride, S. (1986). Effects of question generating training on reading comprehension. *Journal of Educational Psychology*, 78, 256–262.

Derry, S. J. (1996). Cognitive schema theory in the constructivist debate. *Educational Psychologist*, 31(3–4), 163–174.

Driscoll, D., Craig, S. D., Gholson, B., Ventura, M., Hu, X., & Graesser, A. (2003). Vicarious learning: Effects of overhearing dialog and monolog-like discourse in a virtual tutoring session. *Journal of Educational Computing Research*, 29, 431–450.

Eakin, D. K. (2005). Illusions of knowing: Metamemory and memory under conditions of retroactive interference. *Journal of Memory and Language*, 52, 526–534.

Gholson, B., Coles, R., & Craig, S. D. (2010). Features of computerized multimedia environments that support vicarious learning processes. In M. S. Khine & I. M. Saleh (Eds.), *New science of learning: Cognition, computers and collaboration in education* (pp. 53–78). New York, NY: Springer.

Gholson, B., Graesser, A. C., & Craig, S. D. (2009, June). *IDRIVE project summary: An overview of our randomized classroom experiments in the Memphis city Schools*. Poster presented at the 4th Annual Institute of Educational Sciences Research Conference, Washington, DC.

Graesser, A. C., Baggett, W., & Williams, K. (1996). Question-driven explanatory reasoning. *Applied Cognitive Psychology*, 10, S17–S32.

Graesser, A. C., Lu, S., Olde, B. A., Cooper-Pye, E., & Whitten, S. (2005). Question asking and eye tracking during cognitive disequilibrium: Comprehending illustrated texts on devices when the devices break down. *Memory & Cognition, 33,* 1235–1247.

Graesser, A. C, & Person, N. (1994). Question asking during tutoring. *American Educational Research Journal, 31,* 104–137.

Henderson, C., & Dancy, M. H. (2009). Impact of physics education research on the teaching of introductory quantitative physics in the United States. *Physical Review Physics Educational Research, 5,* 1–9. https://doi.org/10.1103/PhysRevSTPER.5.020107

King, A. (1994). Guiding knowledge construction in the classroom: Effect of teaching children how to question and explain. *American Educational Research Journal, 31,* 338–368.

McDermott, L. C. (2006). Preparing K-12 teachers in physics: Insights from history, experience, and research. *American Journal of Physics, 74,* 758–762.

Pashler, H., Bain, P., Bottge, B., Graesser, A., Koedinger, K., McDaniel, M., & Metcalf, J. (2007). *Organizing Instruction and Study to Improve Student Learning* (NCER 2007–2004). Washington, DC: National Center for Education Research, Institute of Education Sciences, U.S. Department of Education. Retrieved from http://ncer.ed.gov

Reisbeck, C. K. (1988). Are questions just function calls? *Questing Exchange, 2,* 17–24.

Roscoe, R. D., & Chi, M. T. (2007). Understanding tutor learning: Knowledge-building and knowledge-telling in peer tutors' explanations and questions. *Review of Educational Research, 77,* 534–574.

Rosenshine, B., Meister, C., & Chapman, S. (1996). Teaching students to generate questions: A review of the intervention studies. *Review of Education Research, 66,* 188–221.

Schank, R. C. (1986). *Explanation patterns: Understanding mechanically and creatively.* Hillsdale, NJ: Lawrence Erlbaum.

Silliman, E. R., & Wilkinson, L. C. (1994). Discourse scaffolds for classroom intervention. In G. P. Wallach & K. G. Butler (Eds.), *Language learning disabilities in school-aged children and adolescents* (2nd., pp. 27–52). Boston, MA: Allyn & Bacon.

Sternberg, R. J. (1987). Questioning and intelligence. *Questing Exchange, 1,* 11–13.

Wisher, R. A., & Graesser, A. C. (2007). Question asking in advanced distributed learning environments. In S. M. Fiore & E. Salas (Eds.), *Toward a science of distributed learning and training.* Washington, DC: American Psychological Association.

Zillmann, D., & Cantor, J. R. (1973). Induction of curiosity via rhetorical questions and its effect on the learning of factual materials. *British Journal of Educational Psychology, 43,* 172–180.

7.3

Teacher immediacy

Ann Bainbridge Frymier

Introduction

The concept of immediacy was introduced by psychologist Albert Mehrabian (1971) and refers to the degree of perceived physical or psychological closeness between people in a relationship. He defined the immediacy principle in terms of the implicit messages that people use to signal approach and avoidance. Specifically, "people are drawn toward persons and things they like, evaluate highly, and prefer; and they avoid or move away from things they dislike, evaluate negatively, or do not prefer" (Mehrabian, 1971, p. 1). While immediacy is a perception, it has been operationalized primarily by a set of nonverbal behaviors and, to a lesser extent, verbal behaviors. Communication behaviors that have been shown to enhance perceptions of immediacy include, but are not limited to, closer distances; increased eye contact; smiling; vocal variety; more direct body orientation; more open, relaxed, and accessible postures; forward leans; and decreased occurrences of arms akimbo. These nonverbal behaviors reflect liking and are perceived as being warm, active, inviting, approachable, dynamic, and engaging.

Research evidence

Andersen (1979) conducted the first research examining the relationship between teacher immediacy and student achievement. She hypothesized that students would learn more from high than low immediate teachers. Anderson found a positive relationship between teacher immediacy and affective learning; that is, students reported liking and valuing the content and the teacher more when the teacher engaged in more immediacy behaviors. However, she did not find a relationship with cognitive learning, which was measured with a typical content exam. Much was made about the lack of relationship between immediacy and cognitive learning. Critics characterized immediacy as simply a means for teachers to win popularity contests. Later research using experimental designs with recall tests (Bolkan, Goodboy, & Myers, 2017; Comstock, Rowell, & Bowers, 1995; Frymier & Houser, 1998) and self-report measures of cognitive learning (Frymier & Houser, 1999; Richmond, McCroskey, Kearney, & Plax, 1987) provided stronger evidence that immediacy had a positive effect on cognitive learning, as well as affective learning.

Using meta-analysis, Witt, Wheeless, and Allen (2004) examined the relationship between nonverbal and affective learning (55 studies), self-reported cognitive learning (44 studies), and recall (11 studies). Teacher nonverbal immediacy had the strongest relationship with self-reported cognitive learning ($r = .51$), a similar relationship with affective learning ($r = .49$), and the weakest relationship with recall ($r = .17$) (Witt et al., 2004). Additional experimental studies have confirmed the positive relationship between teacher nonverbal immediacy and test scores (Bolkan et al., 2017) and motivation (Houser, Cowan, & West, 2007). In addition to learning and motivation, instructor nonverbal immediacy has been positively associated with students' oral participation and nonverbal attentiveness (Frymier & Houser, 2016), student perceptions of teacher credibility (Schrodt & Witt, 2006), and students' intent to persist in college (Witt, Schrodt, Wheeless, & Bryand, 2014). The research evidence is clear that teacher use of nonverbal immediacy has a positive impact on students. Understanding *why* the relationship exists has been more challenging.

Several studies have sought to understand why teacher nonverbal immediacy affects student learning. Early on, motivation was proposed as mediating the relationship between immediacy and learning and received substantial support (Christophel, 1990). Frymier (1994) confirmed the motivation explanation using longitudinal data and path analysis. However, issues with measuring motivation and learning hampered support for this model (Rodriguez, Plax, & Kearney, 1996). Recently, Goldman, Goodboy, and Weber (2017) resolved some of the measurement issues with the development of a measure of intrinsic motivation aligned with self-determination theory (Deci & Ryan, 2000) and providing initial support for a motivation explanation for the benefits on effective teacher communication.

Communication scholars have embraced self-determination theory, and it provides the best explanation for understanding the importance of teacher nonverbal immediacy. Self-determination theory proposes students' basic psychological needs for autonomy, competence, and relatedness must be satisfied for intrinsic motivation to develop (Deci & Ryan, 2000). In a review of literature, Frymier (2016) proposed that instructor communication behavior such as nonverbal immediacy helps satisfy student needs, which enhances intrinsic motivation and, in turn, affects learning. Teacher nonverbal immediacy most likely helps satisfy students' relatedness need by creating a positive and supportive connection between the teacher and the student. Witt et al. (2014) provided support for this explanation. They found that teacher nonverbal immediacy mitigated the negative effects of student anxiety on learning. Goldman et al. (2017) provided additional support by demonstrating that student needs mediated the relationship between teacher interpersonal competence (a construct similar to immediacy) and intrinsic motivation.

Teacher nonverbal immediacy is clearly an important part of effective teaching; however, it is not sufficient by itself. Nonverbal immediacy behaviors must accompany other teacher behaviors that facilitate learning such as clear teaching (see Bolkan, 2017) and strong content. Immediacy helps satisfy student needs and increases motivation, setting the stage for learning.

Summary and recommendations

On the surface, advising teachers to smile, use vocal variety, make eye contact, and use positive gestures with students seems rather insubstantial. Most people who lack formal training in communication respond to such advice by rolling their eyes. However, the research that has been reviewed in this entry clearly indicates that these nonverbal behaviors consistently have a positive impact on students. So how is it that such seemingly mundane behaviors are so important?

First, communication is made up of both verbal and nonverbal messages that stimulate meaning in other people. Verbal messages involve words, which can be oral or written. Nonverbal messages, in contrast, encompass all the behaviors that we use to communicate that do not involve words, such as vocal characteristics, facial expressions, hand gestures, head movements, posture, attire and appearance, eye contact, touch, physical distance, and the use of space. We use nonverbal messages in a variety of ways in conjunction with verbal messages. For instance. we might emphasize a word by snapping our fingers, or to prevent someone from interrupting we might increase our volume and speak faster. When we like someone, we often move a little closer (but not too close), and when we dislike someone we often move a little farther away. When we are farther away from someone than we'd like to be, we often make more eye contact as a way of reducing the distance between ourselves and the receiver: that is, we use nonverbal messages to help our verbal messages make sense to others. A verbal message without nonverbal messages is confusing at best. Oral communication without nonverbal messages (which is impossible) is like written communication with no spaces or punctuation.

The nonverbal messages that convey immediacy enhance the meaning of the verbal messages they accompany. We use a speaker's nonverbal messages to help us understand the verbal message and to judge its value. If the speaker sounds bored and uninterested (conveyed by nonverbal behaviors), we are apt to believe that about the content. When a teacher uses nonverbal immediacy behaviors, he or she is communicating that the content is interesting and exciting and also conveying that the teacher likes the students. Classrooms are by definition evaluative environments. Being liked by the person who is evaluating us almost always makes us feel more at ease and more willing to take risks and do things like ask questions. Therefore, these seemingly mundane nonverbal behaviors communicate powerful messages that accompany the content a teacher is sharing with students.

For most of us, when we are excited and interested about our topic and like the people with whom we are talking, we naturally use nonverbal immediacy behaviors as this conveys our enthusiasm and liking. There are a number of reasons why teachers may not feel excited about or interested in what they are teaching, and there is a similar list of reasons why teachers may not like their students. When this is the case, teachers are unlikely to exhibit nonverbal immediacy. So what do you do if you don't like your students or are bored with what you are teaching? Can you fake immediacy? Most of us can fake immediacy at least a little, but very few of us can fake it convincingly for any extended period of time. So what can you do? First, you can make changes in your lessons or teaching assignment so that you can be excited about what you are teaching and the students you are teaching. We may have limited control over these things, and if you really do not like students, you should probably find a different profession. The second answer lies in your awareness of your own communication behaviors and the extent to which your behaviors match the message you're intending to send. While it can be uncomfortable, video recording yourself teaching is the best way to assess your communication behaviors. You may discover that you do not smile nearly as much as you think you do or that your voice is much shriller than you thought. After videotaping yourself, view the video and look for the following immediacy behaviors:

- Gesturing while talking to the class
- Using vocal variety when talking to the class
- Looking at the class while talking
- Smiling at the class while talking
- A relaxed body position while talking
- Moving around the classroom while teaching
- Moving closer to students while talking
- Smiling at individual students in class

How frequently do you use each behavior? How often do you use the opposite of each behavior such as having a tense body position or using a monotone voice? Are the behaviors you are using conveying the feelings you want to convey? Sometimes we have to make a conscious effort to "turn up the volume" on our nonverbal behaviors so that they have the desired impact. This is particularly true in large classes where the physical distance between the teacher and the students is great or when we are tired. At other times we may need to "psych ourselves up" before we teach so that we feel the necessary enthusiasm for the content and the class. This may be particularly important when our teaching assignment is difficult.

When reviewing your video of yourself teaching, really listen and look for what messages you are communicating. Some teachers may be afraid of their students or nervous that their students will know more than they do. Like all emotions, fear is communicated primarily through nonverbal behaviors. You may lack immediacy because of the fear or anxiety you feel about teaching. In this case, you need to tackle the cause of the fear or anxiety. Most of us cannot display a relaxed posture until we feel relaxed.

To conclude, nonverbal immediacy is a set of related nonverbal behaviors that accompany verbal messages. In the teaching context, teachers often focus exclusively on the content of their lesson and neglect the subtle nonverbal behaviors used to communicate that content. However, the nonverbal behaviors help teachers accomplish their teaching goals by communicating approach to students. While we can learn in negative environments, it is easier and more fun to learn from teachers who we believe like us. We are more apt to reciprocate the teacher's approach behaviors and approach the teaching and the content ourselves.

References

Andersen, J. F. (1979). Teacher immediacy as a predictor of teaching effectiveness. In D. Nimmo (Ed.), *Communication yearbook* (Vol. 3, pp. 543–559). New Brunswick, NJ: Transaction.

Bolkan, S. (2017). Development and validation of the clarity indicators scale. *Communication Education, 66*, 19–36.

Bolkan, S., Goodboy, A. K., & Myers, S. A. (2017). Conditional processes of effective instructor communication and increases in students' cognitive learning. *Communication Education, 66*, 129–147. doi:10.1080/03634523.2016.1241889

Christophel, D. M. (1990). The relationship among teacher immediacy behaviors, student motivation and learning. *Communication Education, 39*, 323–340.

Comstock, J., Rowell, E., & Bowers, J. (1995). Food for thought: Teacher nonverbal immediacy, student learning, and curvilinearity. *Communication Education, 44*, 251–266.

Deci, E. L., & Ryan, R. M. (2000). The "what" and "why" of goal pursuits: Human needs and the self-determination of behavior. *Psychological Inquiry, 11*, 227–268. doi:10.1207/S15327965PLI1104_01

Frymier, A. B. (1994). A model of immediacy in the classroom. *Communication Quarterly, 42*, 133–144.

Frymier, A. B. (2016). Students' motivation to learn. In P. L. Witt (Ed.), *Handbooks of communication science: Vol. 16. Communication and learning* (pp. 377–396). Berlin, Germany: DeGruyter Mouton.

Frymier, A. B., & Houser, M. L. (1998). Does making content relevant make a difference in learning? *Communication Research Reports, 15*, 121–129.

Frymier, A. B., & Houser, M. L. (1999). The revised learning indicators scale. *Communication Studies, 50*, 1–12.

Frymier, A. B., & Houser, M. L. (2016). The role of oral participation in student engagement. *Communication Education, 65*, 83–104. doi:10.1080/03634523.2015.1066019

Goldman, Z. W., Goodboy, A. K., & Weber, K. (2017). College students' psychological needs and intrinsic motivation to learn: An examination of self-determination theory. *Communication Quarterly, 65*, 167–191.

Houser, M. L., Cowan, R. L., & West, D. A. (2007). Investigating a new education frontier: Instructor communication behavior in cd-rom texts – Do traditionally positive behaviors translate into this new environment? *Communication Quarterly, 55*, 19–38. doi:10.1080/01463370600998319

Mehrabian, A. (1971). *Silent messages*. Belmont, CA: Wadsworth.

Richmond, V. P., McCroskey, J. C., Kearney, P., & Plax, T. G. (1987). Power in the classroom VII: Linking behavior alteration techniques to cognitive learning. *Communications Education*, *36*(1), 1–12.

Rodriguez, J. I., Plax, T. G., & Kearney, P. (1996). Clarifying the relationship between teacher nonverbal immediacy and student cognitive learning: Affective learning as the central causal mediator. *Communication Education*, *45*, 293–305.

Schrodt, P., & Witt, P. L. (2006). Students' attributions of instructor credibility as a function of students' expectations of instructional technology use and nonverbal immediacy. *Communication Education*, *55*, 1–20. doi:10.1080/03634520500343335

Witt, P. L., Schrodt, P., Wheeless, V. E., & Bryand, M. C. (2014). Students' intent to persist in college: Moderating the negative effects of receiver apprehension with instructor credibility and nonverbal immediacy. *Communication Studies*, *65*, 330–352. doi:10.1080/10510974.2013.811428

Witt, P. L., Wheeless, L. R., & Allen, M. (2004). A meta-analytical review of the relationship between teacher immediacy and student learning. *Communication Monographs*, *71*, 184–207.

7.4

Problem-based learning

David Gijbels, Piet Van den Bossche, and Sofie Loyens

Introduction

Originally developed for medical training in Canada at McMaster University, the orthodox version of problem-based learning (PBL) has been modified and applied globally in many disciplines. Many curricula or parts thereof are modeled on the basis of problem-based learning. Nowadays, PBL can be considered as "one of the few curriculum-wide educational innovations surviving since the sixties" (Schmidt, van der Molen, Winkel, & Wijnen, 2009, p. 2). In the literature, PBL has been defined and described in different ways. Based on the original method as developed at McMaster University, Barrows (1996) described six core characteristics of PBL. The first characteristic is that learning needs to be student centered. Second, learning has to occur in small student groups under the guidance of a tutor. The third characteristic refers to the tutor as a facilitator or guide. Fourth, authentic problems are primarily encountered in the learning sequence before any preparation or study has occurred. Fifth, the problems are used as a trigger for students' prior knowledge, which leads to the discovery of knowledge gaps. Finally, these knowledge gaps are overcome through self-directed learning.

The aim of schools and colleges implementing PBL is to educate students so that they are able to understand and solve complex problems in a changing world (Gijbels, Dochy, Van den Bossche, & Segers, 2005). Therefore, if one ponders the implementation of PBL, a major question is "Do students using PBL reach these goals in a more effective way than students who receive conventional instruction?" Albanese and Mitchell (1993, p. 56) pose this question as follows: "Stated bluntly, if problem-based learning is simply another route to achieving the same product, why bother with the expense and effort of undertaking a painful curriculum revision?" The interest in this question has produced, until now at least, seventeen systematic reviews of the effects of problem-based learning. Three of these were published in the same year and in the same journal (Albanese & Mitchell, 1993; Berkson, 1993; Vernon & Blake, 1993). Colliver (2000) and Smits, Verbeek, and

Buisonje (2002) undertook a systematic review, each from a different point of view. Dochy, Segers, Van den Bossche, and Gijbels (2003) and Gijbels et al. (2005) looked to students' achievement in problem-based learning and how the effects of PBL are moderated. Walker and Leary (2009) have built on the latter two meta-analyses in a more recent systematic review on problem-based learning in which they looked at differences across problem types, disciplines, and assessment models. Recently, reviews have focused on the effects of PBL in specific countries (Ding et al., 2014; Huang, Zheng, Li, Li, and Yu, 2013; Schmidt et al., 2009; Schmidt, Muijtjens, Van der Vleuten, and Norman, 2012; Zhang et al., 2015) or specific disciplines other than medical education (Galvao, Silva, Neiva, Ribeiro, & Pereira, 2014; Kong, Qin, Zhou, Mou, & Gao, 2014; Shin & Kim, 2013). Finally, Dolmans and colleagues (2016) focused on the effect of PBL on students' approaches to learning.

Research evidence

The review by Albanese and Mitchell (1993) is probably the most widely known. The core question in this review, "What are the effects of problem-based learning?" is investigated by means of five sub-questions: (a) what are the costs compared with lecture-based instruction? (b) Do PBL students develop the cognitive scaffolding necessary to easily assimilate new basic sciences information? (c) To what extent are PBL students exposed to an adequate range of content? (d) Do PBL students become overly dependent on a small-group environment? (e) Do faculty dislike PBL because of the concentrated time commitment required? The study categorizes and lists the qualitative results of studies in medical education from 1972 to 1993. The results are presented in a review that reports effect sizes and p-values with the institutions as the units of analysis. The main results from this review are that PBL is more nurturing and enjoyable and that PBL graduates perform as well, and sometimes better, on clinical examinations and faculty evaluations than students in more conventional instruction. However, PBL students score lower on basic science examinations and view themselves as less well prepared in the basic sciences in comparison to their conventionally trained counterparts. Further, PBL graduates tend to engage in backward reasoning rather than the forward reasoning experts engage in. Finally, the costs of PBL are high when class sizes are larger than 100.

At the same time, Vernon and Blake (1993) synthesized all available research from 1970 through 1992 comparing PBL with more conventional methods of medical education. Five separate statistical meta-analyses resulted in the following main results: PBL was found to be significantly superior with respect to students' attitudes and opinions about their programs and measures of students' clinical performance. Contrary to the previous reviews' findings, the results of PBL students did not significantly differ from conventionally taught students on miscellaneous tests of factual knowledge and tests of clinical knowledge. However, students from conventional education performed significantly better than their PBL counterparts on the National Board of Medical Examiners (NBME), a standardized test administered to medical students in the United States.

Berkson (1993) also searched for evidence of the effectiveness of PBL in the medical PBL literature up until 1992. Six topics on the effectiveness of PBL compared to conventional curricula underlie this narrative meta-analysis in the medical domain: problem solving, the imparting of knowledge, students' motivation to learn medical science, the promotion of self-directed learning skills, student and faculty satisfaction, and financial costs. The results showed no distinction between graduates from PBL and conventional instruction but found that PBL can be stressful for both students and faculty, and a PBL curriculum may be unreasonably expensive. Subsequently, Colliver (2000) questioned the educational superiority of PBL relative to standard approaches. Colliver focused on the credibility of the claims about the ties between PBL and educational outcomes and the magnitude of the effects. He conducted a review of medical education literature, starting with the three reviews published in 1993 and moving on to research published from 1992 through 1998 in the primary sources for research in medical education. For each study, a summary was written, which included the study design, outcomes measures, and effect sizes, as well as further information relevant to the research conclusion. Colliver concluded that there was no convincing evidence that PBL improves the student's knowledge base and clinical performance, at least not of the magnitude that would be expected given the resources required for a PBL curriculum. Nevertheless, PBL may provide a more challenging, motivating, and enjoyable approach to medical education.

A later review by Smits et al. (2002) is limited to the effectiveness of PBL in continuing medical education. This review only included controlled evaluation studies in continuing medical education from 1974 to 2000. In short, Smits and colleagues concluded that there was limited evidence for PBL to increase participants' knowledge and performance and patients' health. However, there was only moderate evidence that doctors were more satisfied with PBL.

The review by Dochy et al. (2003) was the first review searching for studies beyond the domain of medical education. The main question was similar but much more itemized than the other reviews: What are the main effects of PBL on students' knowledge and knowledge application, and what are the potential moderators of the effect of PBL? The results of this meta-analysis suggested that PBL has statistically and practically significant positive effects on students' knowledge application. The effects of PBL on students' knowledge base tended to be negative. However, this effect was found to be strongly influenced by outliers, and the moderator analysis suggested that students in a PBL environment could rely on a more structured knowledge base.

In order to further investigate the moderating effect of the method of assessment on the effects of PBL, a second meta-analysis was set up (Gijbels et al., 2005). In this meta-analysis, the influence of assessment was the main independent variable. The goal of this study was to describe the effects of PBL from the angle of the underlying focal constructs being measured with the assessment. Using

Sugrue's model (1995) as a frame of reference, the research questions were: What are the effects of PBL when the assessment of its main goals focuses on, respectively, (a) the understanding of concepts, (b) the understanding of the principles that link concepts, and (c) the linking of concepts and principles to conditions and procedures for application? In order to be congruent with its educational goals and resulting instructional principles and practices, the assessment of the application of knowledge when working with authentic problems is at the heart of the matter in PBL. Therefore, it was expected that students in PBL would perform better at the third level when compared to students in more traditional learning environments. The results of the meta-analysis showed a difference in the reported effects of PBL between each of the three levels. However, contrary to expectations that the effects of PBL would be larger when the method of assessment was more capable of evaluating complex levels, the effect size for the third level of the knowledge structure was smaller than the effect size of the second level and not statistically significant. Moreover, in only 8 of the 40 studies included in the meta-analysis was the assessment focused at the third level. Most studies (n = 31) assessed at the level of understanding of concepts. PBL had the most positive effects when focal constructs being assessed were at the second level, understanding the principles that link concepts. These results imply an implicit challenge for PBL to pay more attention to the third level of the knowledge structure, during both the learning activities that take place and students' assessment.

A meta-analysis by Walker and Leary (2009) builds upon the studies by Dochy et al. (2003) and Gijbels et al. (2005). They performed a meta-analysis that crossed disciplines and categorized the types of problems used, the PBL approach employed, and the level of assessment. Across 82 studies and 201 outcomes, their findings favored PBL ($d = 0.13$) with sufficient heterogeneity to warrant a closer examination of moderating factors.

Schmidt and colleagues (2009) conducted a meta-analysis of curricular comparisons, using a single PBL medical school in the Netherlands. This school was compared with traditional medical schools in the Netherlands. Medical knowledge was one of the outcome variables in this meta-analysis and was measured by medical students' scores on the so-called progress test consisting of 200 to 300 questions dealing with medicine as a whole. The overall weighted effect size averaged over the 90 comparisons involving the PBL curriculum under study and various Dutch medical schools was $d = .07$. This implies a small positive effect. However, it has been argued that curriculum comparison studies are, at best, quasi-experimental, so they are prone to forms of selection bias. To address this issue, Schmidt et al. (2012) reanalyzed the data from the Schmidt et al. study of 2009 and controlled for two potential biases: differential student attrition (because graduation rates are often higher in PBL compared to traditional curricula) and differential exposure (because, in general, study duration is shorter in PBL than in traditional curricula). The reanalysis demonstrated medium-level effect sizes favoring PBL curricula. After corrections for attrition and study duration, the mean effect size for knowledge acquisition was 0.31 and for diagnostic reasoning was 0.51 (Schmidt et al., 2012).

The meta-analysis by Zhang and colleagues (2015) focused on randomized and nonrandomized controlled trial studies on PBL use in undergraduate medical education in China. Based on 31 studies, they concluded that students in PBL yielded higher course examination pass rates, excellence rates, and examination scores but also that the course type was a significant confounding factor in explaining the results of the examination scores. They concluded that PBL can increase course examination excellence rates and scores in the Chinese medical system but that it is more effective when applied to laboratory courses than to theory-based courses.

PBL is also increasingly popular among preventive medicine educators in China, according to Ding and colleagues (2014). They selected 15 studies in this area and conducted a pooled analysis to obtain an overall estimate of the effectiveness of PBL on learning outcomes of preventive medicine students. Overall, PBL was associated with a significant increase in students' theoretical examination scores compared to lecture-based learning. For the skills-based outcomes, the pooled PBL effects were also significant for problem solving skills, self-directed learning skills, and collaborative learning skills.

While widespread in preventive medicine in China, PBL is still in its infancy in Chinese dental education. A meta-analysis by Huang et al. (2013) included 11 articles in which PBL was compared to traditional teaching methods. Theoretical/knowledge scores, practical/skills scores, and pass rates were investigated. Results showed positive effects in favor of PBL for knowledge and skills scores. However, the pooled result did not show any positive effect on higher pass rates for PBL.

The aim of Shin and Kim (2013) was to conduct a meta-analysis on the available literature in the field of nursing education in order to synthesize the effects of PBL. They reported a medium-to-large effect size of PBL in nursing education and also positive effects on the outcome domains of satisfaction with training, clinical education, and skill course.

A systematic review and meta-analysis including nine articles was performed by Kong and colleagues specifically for nursing students' critical thinking skills in PBL (Kong et al., 2014). The pooled effect size showed problem-based learning was able to improve nursing students' critical thinking compared with traditional lectures. However, differences in the measurement instruments could be observed, with some instruments (e.g., Bloom's taxonomy) favoring PBL, while others were inconclusive (e.g., California Critical Thinking Skills Test).

Galvao and colleagues (2014) conducted a meta-analysis to assess the effects of PBL on the learning achievements of students in pharmaceutical education. They concluded that PBL students performed better on midterm examinations and final examinations than students in the traditional learning groups.

Finally, the systematic review by Dolmans and colleagues (2016) investigated the effects of PBL on students' deep and surface approaches to learning and whether and why these effects differ across the context of the learning environment and study quality. Their results indicated that PBL has a small positive effect on the development of deep approaches to learning but no effect on students' use of surface approaches to learning. The results could not be explained by study quality, but they concluded that a curriculum-wide implementation had a more positive impact on fostering a deep approach to learning than the implementation of PBL in a single course.

Summary and recommendations

Considering the numerous reviews of research on PBL, we can concur with the two tendencies that were noted earlier by Strobel and Van Barneveld (2009, p. 53). The first is that traditional learning approaches tended to produce better outcomes on assessment of basic science knowledge; however, this was not always the case. A second trend noted was that a PBL approach tended to produce better outcomes for clinical knowledge and skills. This suggests that PBL fosters an accessible and connected knowledge base.

We would like to highlight that, although PBL is implemented in a large variety of disciplines, the research evidence discussed is still dominated by research in the field of health sciences education because other research is not available or does not meet the quality criteria used in meta-analyses (Hallinger & Bridges, 2016). Future research on the effects of PBL would therefore benefit from taking a more cross-disciplinary focus. Another important finding is that the more recent meta-analyses point to the important role of several mediating variables, such as the implementation level, the type of problem tasks, or the level of assessment in explaining the effects of PBL. When implementing or investigating PBL, much more attention needs to be paid to the conditions under which the effects of PBL can be maximized in a wide range of disciplines.

References

Albanese, M. A., & Mitchell, S. (1993). Problem-based learning: A review of literature on its outcomes and implementation issues. *Academic Medicine, 68*, 52–81.

Barrows, H. S. (1996). Problem-based learning in medicine and beyond. In L. Wilkerson & W. H. Gijselaers (Eds.), *Bringing problem-based learning to higher education: Theory and practice* (pp. 3–13) (New Directions for Teaching and Learning, No. 68). San Francisco, CA: Jossey-Bass.

Berkson, L. (1993). Problem-based learning: Have the expectations been met? *Academic Medicine, 68*(10), S79–S88.

Colliver, J. A. (2000). Effectiveness of problem-based learning curricula: Research and theory. *Academic Medicine, 75*(3), 259–266.

Ding, X., Zhao, L., Chu, H., Tong, N., Ni, C., Hu, Z., Zhang, Z., & Wang, M. (2014). Assessing the effectiveness of problem-based learning of preventive medicine education in China. *Scientific Reports, 30*, 1–5. doi:10.1038/srep05126

Dochy, F., Segers, M., Van den Bossche, P., & Gijbels, D. (2003). Effects of problem-based learning: A meta-analysis. *Learning and Instruction, 13*, 533–568.

Dolmans, H. J. M., Loyens, S. M. M., Marcq, H., & Gijbels, D. (2016). Deep and surface learning in problem-based learning: A review of the literature. *Advances in Health Sciences Education, 21*, 1087–1112.

Galvao, T. F., Silva, M. T., Neiva, C. S., Ribeiro, L. M., & Pereira, M. G. (2014). Problem-based learning in pharmaceutical education: A systematic review and meta-analysis, *The Scientific World Journal, 2014*, ID 578382.

Gijbels, D., Dochy, F., Van den Bossche, P., & Segers, M. (2005). Effects of problem-based learning: A meta-analysis from the angle of assessment. *Review of Educational Research, 75*(1), 27–61.

Hallinger, P., & Bridges, E. M. (2016). A systematic review of research on the use of problem-based learning in the preparation and development of school leaders. *Educational Administration Quarterly, 5*(2), 255–288.

Huang, B., Zheng, L., Li, C., Li, L., & Yu, H. (2013). Effectiveness of problem-based learning in Chinese dental education: A meta-analysis. *Journal of Dental Education, 77*, 377–383.

Kong, L.-N., Qin, B., Zhou, Y.-Q., Mou, S.-Y., & Gao, H.-M. (2014). The effectiveness of problem-based learning on development of nursing students' critical thinking: A systematic review and meta-analysis. *International Journal of Nursing Studies, 51*, 458–469.

Schmidt, H. G., Muijtjens, A. M. M., Van der Vleuten, C. P. M., & Norman, G. R. (2012). Differential student attrition and differential exposure mask effects of problem-based learning in curriculum comparison studies. *Academic Medicine, 87*, 463–475. doi:10.1097/ACM.0b013e318249591a

Schmidt, H. G., Van der Molen, H. T., Winkel, W. W. R., & Wijnen, W. H. F. W. (2009). Constructivist, problem-based learning does work: A meta-analysis of curricular comparisons involving a single medical school. *Educational Psychologist, 44*, 1–23.

Shin, I. S., & Kim, J. H. (2013). The effect of problem-based learning in nursing education: A meta-analysis. *Advances in Health Sciences Education, 18*(5), 1103–1120. doi:10.1007/s10459-012-9436-2

Smits, P. B. A., Verbeek, J. H. A. M., & De Buisonje, C. D. (2002). Problem based learning in continuing medical education: A review of controlled evaluation studies. *British Medical Journal, 321*, 153–156

Strobel, J., & Van Barneveld, A. (2009). When is PBL more effective? A meta-synthesis of meta-analyses comparing PBL to conventional classrooms. *Interdisciplinary Journal of Problem-Based Learning, 3*, 44–58.

Sugrue, B. (1995). A theory-based framework for assessing domain-specific problem solving ability. *Educational Measurement: Issues and Practice, 14*(3), 29–36.

Vernon, D. T. A., & Blake, R. L. (1993). Does problem-based learning work? A meta-analysis of evaluative research. *Academic Medicine, 68*, 550–563.

Walker, A., & Leary, H. (2009). A problem based learning meta-analysis: Differences across problem types, implementation types, disciplines, and assessment levels. *Interdisciplinary Journal of Problem-Based Learning, 3*(1), 12–43.

Zhang, Y., Zhou, L., Liu, X., Liu, L., Wu, Y., Zhao, Z., . . . Yi, D. (2015). The effectiveness of the problem-based learning teaching model for use in introductory Chinese undergraduate medical courses: A systematic review and meta-analysis. *Plos ONE, 10*(3), e0120884

7.5 Direct instruction

Gregory Arief D. Liem and Andrew J. Martin

Introduction

Direct instruction (DI), which originated in the work of Engelmann and colleagues in the 1960s, is a systematic model of teaching that focuses on a sequenced and incremental mastery of curriculum-based competence (Adams & Engelmann, 1996). DI is implemented through carefully planned lessons in which students are provided with substantial and yet gradually reduced guidance (i.e., mediated scaffolding). Key features of DI lie in the clear and explicit teacher-scripted instruction and all students having multiple and relatively equal opportunities to respond – more so than the more limited opportunities available to individual students in traditional classes (Adams & Engelmann, 1996). To ensure high-quality instruction for students of all skill levels, DI involves careful and flexible differentiation of lessons that are appropriate to students' learning needs. Hence, DI is appropriate for all students, including those in at-risk groups. Indeed, a growing number of studies have shown the effectiveness of DI in improving achievement of students with learning difficulties (e.g., see Datchuk, 2017; Wieber et al., 2017).

DI is underpinned by the basic assumptions that all students are teachable and have the potential to improve academically, lower-performing and less advantaged students should be taught at an accelerated pace to catch up with their higher-performing peers, all teachers can be trained to conduct DI, and the implementation of DI has to be controlled and standardized in order to minimize student misinterpretation and maximize instructional effects (Barbash, 2011; Engelmann & Carnine, 1991). As reviewed by Hattie (2009), DI implementation involves seven carefully organized major steps, including to (a) communicate learning goals and orient students to learn; (b) examine if students possess the knowledge and skills needed to understand the new lesson; (c) present key principles of the new lesson through clear instruction; (d) check student mastery and understanding by posing questions, providing examples, and correcting misconceptions; (e) provide opportunities for guided practice; (f) assess performance and provide feedback on the guided practice; and (g) provide opportunities for independent practice through group or individual work in class or homework. Thus, guided intensive learning, in the forms of deliberate practice and worked examples, is at the heart of DI. As our review below suggests, DI is regarded as a highly effective instructional model that brings about significant improvements in student academic achievement and also positive changes in student affective and behavioral outcomes. This review is focused on DI and its principal components (e.g., guided practice, worked examples) and what research evidence says about their links to academic achievement. More detailed information about this instructional method can be found on the National Institute for Direct Instruction (NIFDI) website (www.nifdi.org). Readers may specifically refer to a recent DI bibliography that provides a comprehensive list of DI-related studies, meta-analyses and reviews, technical reports, dissertations, and books (NIFDI, 2017).

Research evidence

Evidence for the yields of DI on academic achievement is seen in the specific empirical studies and meta-analyses demonstrating the effectiveness of various DI programs relative to other programs. In this line of research, investigators typically compare the academic performance of students in a DI program with that of students in control or other intervention groups or measure achievement scores gained by students before and after exposure to a DI program. Evidence of the effectiveness of DI can also be seen in studies showing the yields of various components, strategies, and techniques emphasized in DI practices (e.g., spaced practice, worked examples). Adams and Engelmann (1996) provided one of the first comprehensive and systematic reports on DI. Their report focused on the implementation of Project Follow Through, a national project considered to be the largest experimental study conducted in a naturalistic setting, involving 72,000 early childhood students over ten years (1965–1975). The project aimed to examine the effectiveness of nine major educational approaches, including DI, on a myriad of key educational outcomes. The findings showed that DI was the only program with consistently positive effects (with effect sizes or $d > .25$) on basic skills (e.g., word recognition, spelling, math computation), cognitive skills (e.g., reading comprehension, math problem solving), and affective outcomes (e.g., self-concept, attributions to success). In a follow-up study of participants in the project, Meyer (1984) found that, compared to students in non-DI control schools, students in DI schools reported higher rates of graduation and acceptance to college, lower rates of dropping out, and higher ninth-grade scores on reading ($d = 0.43$) and math ($d = 0.28$).

Adams and Engelmann (1996) reported on meta-analysis based on 37 DI studies. They found DI had large effect sizes for various groups of students, including regular ($d = 1.27$) and special education students ($d = 0.76$) and younger ($d = .087$) and older students ($d = 1.50$), and across different academic domains, including reading ($d = 0.69$), social studies ($d = 0.97$), math ($d = 1.11$), spelling ($d = 1.33$), and science ($d = 2.44$). In support of this range of findings, a meta-analysis conducted by Haas (2005) suggested that, compared with other instructional methods (e.g., problem-based teaching), the most effective method of teaching algebra is DI ($d = 0.55$). He attributed this finding to the fact that DI focuses on desired learning outcomes, gradual improvement, appropriate pacing, curriculum-based competence, and mastery for all students. Moreover, a great amount of opportunities for students to practice that are emphasized in DI – both guided and independent practice – seem to be effective in optimizing student mastery of the curriculum. Indeed, as a meta-analysis conducted by Donovan and Radosevich (1998) showed, students in spaced or distributed practice conditions performed better than those in massed practice conditions ($d = 0.46$) because spaced practice provides students with time to reorganize their knowledge (i.e., integrating, adjusting, correcting).

In one of the most ambitious reviews, Borman and colleagues (Borman, Hewes, Overman, & Brown, 2003) conducted a meta-analysis of the effectiveness of 29 school reform programs. They concluded that DI, with an average effect size of $d = 0.21$, is the instructional program with the strongest systematic evidence of effectiveness (based on 49 DI studies and 182 effect sizes) – outperforming all the other programs including Success for All ($d = 0.18$) and School Development Program ($d = 0.15$).

DI has also been found to be effective in optimizing learning and achievement in special education settings. Forness and colleagues (Forness, Kavale, Blum, & Lloyd, 1997) conducted a mega-analysis of prior meta-analyses and demonstrated that DI was the only one of seven intervention programs for special education students with convincing effect sizes for both reading ($d = 0.85$) and math ($d = 0.50$). In a similar vein, a comprehensive analysis of interventions for learning disabled students by Swanson (2000) indicated that while an emphasis on DI alone generated a large effect ($d = 0.72$), programs that integrate DI with learning strategies enhancement were even more effective in maximizing student achievement ($d = 0.84$).

A recent DI application in promoting metacognitive skills provided further evidence for the benefits of this pedagogical instruction not only for learning and achievement, but also for motivational outcomes. In a randomized controlled trial study, Zepeda, Richey, Ronevich, and Nokes-Malach (2015) found that students in the intervention group who received a DI-guided metacognitive training and a relatively limited number of problem-solving practices, performed better on a conceptual physics test ($d = 0.64$) and a novel self-guided learning activity ($d = 0.87$) and showed higher task values ($d = 0.87$), self-efficacy ($d = 0.85$), mastery-approach goals ($d = 0.83$), and growth mind-set ($d = 0.77$) than students in the control group who received extensive problem-solving practices. This finding provides an empirical ground for harnessing DI philosophies, principles, and practices in developing academic motivational beliefs, cognitive strategies, and metacognitive skills – important correlates of student achievement relatively less studied in the context of DI.

Notwithstanding its documented benefits for learning and achievement, it is worthwhile to note that the use of DI in general and special education settings is not without challenges. As reviewed by McMullen and Madelaine (2014, pp. 143–146), the resistance toward its adoption as a pedagogical instruction is mainly due to the beliefs that "DI is only suitable for some children," "DI is just rote learning and only suitable for learning basic skills," "DI is too teacher directed and encourages students to be passive," "Teachers feel that DI does not allow them to be creative," "DI relegates teachers to being technicians rather than professionals," or "DI is not the best way to teach; there are more effective ways." Contrary to these, Hattie (2009) noted that DI should not be confused with didactic teaching relying on one-way teacher-directed instruction or transmission teaching characterized by acquisition of knowledge through mere repetition or rote learning. Indeed, on the basis of his synthesis of four meta-analyses involving over 42,000 students across 304 DI studies and 597 effects, Hattie (2009) found an average effect size of $d = 0.59$, which ranked DI at 26th out of 138 effects on achievement. Given this finding, Hattie concluded, "the very successful DI method . . . and the underlying principles of DI place it among the most successful outcomes" (pp. 204–205).

Ongoing debates (see, e.g., Kirschner, Sweller, & Clark, 2006; Mayer, 2004; Tobias & Duffy, 2009) have contrasted the achievement yield of DI and its various procedural components with that of minimally guided instructional approaches, including discovery learning, problem-based learning, and enquiry-based learning. The preponderance of empirical findings apparently points to effectiveness of DI methods relative to the other approaches. A meta-analysis by Alfieri and colleagues (Alfieri, Brooks, Aldrich, & Tenenbaum, 2011), for example, showed that explicit instruction, of which DI is one form, was more beneficial for student achievement than unassisted discovery ($d = 0.38$). They also found that the effectiveness of explicit instruction differed across academic subjects, with a significantly larger average effect size for verbal and social skills ($d = 0.95$) than for problem solving ($d = 0.48$), science ($d = 0.39$), or math ($d = 0.16$). The relative advantage of explicit instruction over unassisted discovery-based instructions was also moderated by age, with the mean effect size for adolescents ($d = 0.53$) significantly greater than that for adults ($d = 0.26$). Furthermore, the benefits of explicit instruction differed as a function of the outcomes considered, with a mean effect size for acquisition scores ($d = 0.95$) relatively larger than those for post-test scores ($d = 0.35$) and solution time ($d = 0.21$). Interestingly, the specific instructional techniques emphasized in DI also moderated the findings, with participants provided with worked examples ($d = 0.63$), feedback ($d = 0.46$), direct teaching ($d = 0.29$), and explanations ($d = 0.28$) performing better than those in pure discovery groups.

Considering this, our current review supports the view that instructional methods that allow teachers to be activators of student learning (e.g., reciprocal teaching, explicit instruction, $d = 0.60$) (Hattie, 2009) have an overall effect size that is larger than that of instructional methods in which teachers predominantly serve as facilitators of student learning (e.g., inquiry-based teaching, problem-based learning,

$d = 0.17$) (Hattie, 2009). This is possible as the intensive guidance provided in DI alleviates cognitive demands and allows working memory and executive functioning to more effectively process the presented information using higher-order thinking skills (e.g., reorganizing, inferring, integrating) (see Alfieri et al., 2011; Kirschner et al., 2006). Indeed, Martin (2016) recently proposed the load-reduction instruction (LRI) approach as "instruction that appropriately reduces or manages the cognitive load on the student in the learning process" (p. 6). This instructional approach is specifically based on five key principles closely grounded in DI, including (a) reducing the difficulty of a task during initial learning (e.g., think-aloud strategies, showcasing good practices, segmenting learning), (b) instructional support and scaffolding through the task (e.g., signaling, organizing information thematically), (c) ample structured practice (e.g., deliberate, mental, and guided practices), (d) appropriate provision of instructional feedback (e.g., providing feedback and feedforward), and (e) independent practice and guided autonomy (e.g., providing opportunities for independent practice and guided discovery learning). Importantly, Martin and Evans (2018) recently demonstrated that the extent to which students perceived that each of these principles is put into practice in the classroom setting was linked to their heightened positive motivation (e.g., task valuing, self-efficacy), positive engagement (e.g., planning, monitoring), academic buoyancy, and achievement and to their lower negative engagement (e.g., self-handicapping, disengagement) and perceived difficulty and complexity associated with learning topics (intrinsic cognitive load) and those associated with the way in which information is presented (extraneous cognitive load). Thus, LRI is a novel DI-based instructional approach likely to promote motivation, engagement, and achievement through the reduction of cognitive burden on students as they learn. Importantly, it encompasses both explicit instructional techniques – principles (a) through (d) – and, at the appropriate point in the learning process, guided independent learning – principle (e).

Summary and recommendations

A consistent pattern identified in our reviews points to the effectiveness of direct instruction (DI), a specific teaching program, and of specific explicit instructional practices underpinning the program (e.g., deliberate practice, worked examples) in maximizing student academic achievement. Collectively, studies, reviews, and encompassing meta-analyses (e.g., Hattie, 2009; NIFDI, 2017) show that DI has significantly large effects on achievement. Although these effects may vary as a function of various moderating factors (e.g., academic subjects, types of performance outcome, specific instructional practices, age groups, expertise levels), the bulk of the evidence supports the benefits of DI and its key instructional practices relative to minimally guided or unassisted instructions. However, this is not to dismiss the constructivist view of learning – which is often believed to be supported by minimally guided instructions – because DI principles and practices are indeed useful to promote the process of knowledge construction, especially by reducing cognitive burdens on novice students when they learn. Importantly, though, it seems constructivist approaches are better assisted by direct and structured input from the teacher that systematically and unambiguously builds the knowledge and skills needed to subsequently engage in meaningful discovery and problem-based and inquiry-based learning. If we may, the horse must be well and truly before the cart when it comes to effective instruction and learning. Indeed, Martin and Evans (2018) showed that direct instruction strategies and guided independent learning are not mutually exclusive; guided independent learning is optimally effective when the student is first explicitly taught to become sufficiently skilled and knowledgable in the subject matter at hand. According to them, the success of one is dependent on the success of the other.

Research evidence into the links between DI and academic achievement has also pointed to relevant educational implications and recommendations. As a general point, teachers can be encouraged to follow DI steps in their lessons. Specifically, this can be done by meeting each of the following conditions and implementing its more specific facilitating strategies. First, teachers ought to ensure that students see that the task to be learned is achievable and manageable. This can be done by stating the lesson goals explicitly, separating the task into smaller subtasks, and communicating optimism to the class. Second, teachers can carefully prepare, plan, and sequence lessons that comprise appropriately scripted/well-thought-through instructions. Third, teachers can look to better ensure student understanding of the lesson by posing questions and modeling the use of procedures and strategies effective to solve problems. Fourth, teachers can provide students with opportunities to deliberately and purposefully practice the skills and knowledge they are to learn. This can be done by assigning students an adequate amount of assisted practice (e.g., worked examples) and then allowing for appropriately monitored independent practice (e.g., homework). Fifth, teachers should continually assess student mastery of lessons and subject matter by evaluating how they perform during practice and providing immediate feedback. Finally, direct and explicit remediation is needed when vital skills and knowledge have not been learned. Taken together, these evidence-based applications of DI research hold important educational implications in optimizing student achievement.

References

Adams, G., & Engelmann, S. (1996). *Research on direct instruction: 25 years beyond DISTAR*. Seattle, WA: Educational Achievement Systems.

Alfieri, L., Brooks, P. J., Aldrich, N. J., & Tenenbaum, H. R. (2011). Does discovery-based instruction enhance learning? *Journal of Educational Psychology, 103*, 1–18. http://dx.doi.org/10.1037/a0021017

Barbash, S. (2011). *Clear teaching: With direct instruction, Siegfried Engelmann discovered a better way of teaching*. Arlington, VA: Education Consumers Foundation.

Borman, G. D., Hewes, G. M., Overman, L. T., & Brown, S. (2003). Comprehensive school reform and achievement: A meta-analysis. *Review of Educational Research, 73*, 125–230. http://dx.doi.org/10.3102/00346543073002125

Datchuk, S. (2017). A direct instruction and precision teaching intervention to improve the sentence construction of middle school students with writing difficulties. *The Journal of Special Education, 51*(2), 62–71. http://dx.doi.org/10.1177/0022466916665588

Donovan, J. J., & Radosevich, D. J. (1998). A meta-analytic review of the distribution of practice effect: Now you see it, now you don't. *Journal of Applied Psychology, 84*, 795–805. http://dx.doi.org/10.1037/0021-9010.84.5.795

Engelmann, S., & Carnine, D. (1991). *Theory of instruction: Principles and applications.* Eugene, OR: ADI Press.

Forness, S. R., Kavale, K. A., Blum, I. M., & Lloyd, J. W. (1997). Mega-analysis of meta-analyses: What works in special education. *Teaching Exceptional Children, 29*, 4–9. https://doi.org/10.1177/004005999702900601

Haas, M. (2005). Teaching methods for secondary algebra: A meta-analysis of findings. *NASSP Bulletin, 89*, 24–46. https://doi.org/10.1177/019263650508964204

Hattie, J. (2009). *Visible learning: A synthesis of over 800 meta-analyses relating to achievement.* New York, NY: Routledge.

Kirschner, P. A., Sweller, J., & Clark, R. E. (2006). Why minimal guidance during instruction does not work: An analysis of the failure of constructivist, discovery, problem-based, experiential, and inquiry-based teaching. *Educational Psychologist, 41*, 75–86. https://doi.org/10.1207/s15326985ep4102_1

Martin, A. J. (2016). *Using Load Reduction Instruction (LRI) to boost motivation and engagement.* Leicester, UK: British Psychological Society.

Martin, A. J., & Evans, P. (2018). Load reduction instruction: Exploring a framework that assesses explicit instruction through to independent learning. *Teaching and Teacher Education, 73*, 203–214. https://doi.org/10.1016/j.tate.2018.03.018

Mayer, R. E. (2004). Should there be a three-strikes rule against pure discovery learning? The case for guided methods of instruction. *American Psychologist, 59*, 14–19. http://dx.doi.org/10.1037/0003-066X.59.1.14

McMullen, F., & Madelaine, A. (2014). Why is there so much resistance to direct instruction. *Australian Journal of Learning Difficulties, 19*(2), 137–151. https://doi.org/10.1080/19404158.2014.962065

Meyer, L. A. (1984). Long-term effects of the direct instruction project follow through. *Elementary School Journal, 84*, 380–394. http://dx.doi.org/10.1086/461371

National Institute of Direct Instruction (NIFDI). (2017). *Writings on direct instruction: A bibliography.* Eugene, Oregon: Author. Retrieved from www.nifdi.org/docman/research/bibliography/205-di-bibliography-reference-list/file

Swanson, H. L. (2000). What instruction works for students with learning disabilities? Summarizing the results of a meta-analysis of interventions studies. In R. M. Gersten, E. P. Schiller, & S. Vaughn (Eds.), *Contemporary special education research: Syntheses of the knowledge base on critical instructional issues* (pp. 1–30). Mahwah, NJ: Erlbaum.

Tobias, S., & Duffy, T. M. (Eds.). (2009). *Constructivist instruction: Success or failure?* New York, NY: Routledge.

Wieber, A. E., Evoy, K., McLaughlin, T. F., Derby, K. M., Kellogg, E., Williams, R. L., & Peterson, S. M. (2017). The effects of a modified direct instruction procedure on time telling for a third grade student with learning disabilities with a brief comparison of interesting and boring formats. *Learning Disabilities: A Contemporary Journal, 15*(2), 239–248.

Zepeda, C. D., Richey, J. E., Ronevich, P., & Nokes-Malach, T. J. (2015). Direct instruction of metacognition benefits adolescent science learning, transfer, and motivation: An in vivo study. *Journal of Educational Psychology, 107*(4), 954–970. http://dx.doi.org/10.1037/edu0000022

7.6 Goal orientation

Andrew J. Martin

Introduction

This discussion examines the link between academic goals and academic achievement (operationalized through indices such as course grades, class achievement, standardized test scores, literacy, and numeracy proficiency). Different types of goal constructs have been implemented in psychoeducational research including goal setting, goal orientations, and goal structures (Anderman & Wolters, 2006; Grant & Dweck, 2003; Maehr & Zusho, 2009). Goal orientation generally refers to the reasons *why* students do what they do. Goal setting tends to be concerned with *what* students are aiming for. Goal structures refer to the goal-related messages made salient in the classroom, including motivation climates (Anderman & Wolters, 2006; Maehr & Zusho, 2009). This discussion is focused on goal orientation and what evidence says about its links to academic achievement.

The classic (or normative) goal orientation perspective focuses on mastery and performance goals, positing that mastery goals are adaptive for achievement outcomes whereas performance goals tend to be inimical to achievement. More recent work has suggested a revised or multiple goals perspective that incorporates avoidance and approach dimensions, positing that some types of performance goals can assist learning and achievement and seeking to articulate the conditions and ways this occurs (see Anderman & Wolters, 2006; Elliot, 2005; Maehr & Zusho, 2009; Martin, Marsh, Debus, & Malmberg, 2008 for summaries and reviews).

Mastery orientation is focused on factors and processes such as effort, self-improvement, skill development, learning, and focus on the task at hand. Performance orientation is focused more on demonstrating relative ability, social comparisons, and outperforming others (Martin et al., 2008). When integrated with approach-avoidance dimensions (thus, a 2 × 2 goal orientation model), mastery approach is focused on learning, improving, and understanding; mastery avoidance is focused on avoiding misunderstanding and not being able to learn; performance approach is focused on outperforming others and appearing competent;

and performance avoidance is focused on avoiding appearing incompetent (Elliot, 2005). Thus, there are three salient models: the classic two-goal model (mastery and performance) and the subsequent three-goal (mastery, performance approach, and performance avoidance) and four-goal (mastery approach, mastery avoidance, performance approach, and performance avoidance) models. Subsequently, other research has extended to a 3 × 2 model that includes self-based goals. According to Elliot, Murayama, and Pekrun (2011), "self-based goals use one's own intra-personal trajectory as the evaluative referent" (p. 633; see also Elliot, Murayama, Kobeisy, & Lichtendfeld, 2015). Thus, whereas mastery goals refer to mastery of the task, self-based goals are more focused on mastery or improvement of the self. In addition to considering self-based goals under a 3 × 2 framework, research has also operationalized self-based goals via personal best (PB) goals, finding that PB goals are significantly associated with achievement, motivation, and engagement (e.g., Martin & Elliot, 2016a, 2016b). However, the two- and three-goal "classic" models remain the most frequently investigated (Maehr & Zusho, 2009) and are the focus of the present discussion.

Research evidence

The link between mastery orientation and most academic factors and processes is generally quite clear: it is positively related to persistence, interest, choice, effort, self-regulation, and deep processing; it is negatively related to maladaptive factors such as self-handicapping, avoidance, and disengagement (Anderman & Wolters, 2006; Huang, 2011). In terms of achievement, however, the evidence is mixed, with some research finding no significant connection to achievement (see Anderman & Wolters, 2006, for a summary), and other research suggesting greater effects but under particular conditions such as in experimental settings (Linnenbrink-Garcia, Tyson, & Patall, 2008). Moreover, although correlational analyses show significant associations with achievement (Linnenbrink-Garcia et al., 2008), when prior achievement is taken into account, regression analyses suggest no major role for mastery orientation in achievement outcomes (Church, Elliot, & Gable, 2001).

In explaining these findings, some have suggested it is inappropriate to expect mastery orientation to directly map onto achievement in noteworthy ways because that is not what mastery is about; mastery is about learning, not about normative grading standards and performance (Maehr & Zusho, 2009). Moreover, recent meta-analysis has suggested that the specific content and focus of mastery goals may also be influential in affecting achievement. Hulleman and colleagues (Hulleman, Schrager, Bodmann, & Harackiewicz, 2010), for example, found that mastery goals with a goal-relevant focus evinced a negative relationship with performance (course grades, exam scores), whereas mastery goals without a goal focus were positively associated with performance.

Other meta-analyses have demonstrated positive achievement effects for mastery goals but also suggest moderating factors. For example, Utman (1997) found that adaptive effects for mastery goals may be stronger for relatively complex tasks and relatively limited in the achievement of young children. Assessing factors in the three-goal model, meta-analysis by Payne, Youngcourt, and Beaubien (2007) found the strongest effect for mastery goals.

In wrestling with the sometimes inconsistent link between mastery and achievement, it has been recognized that mastery goals may need "something more or different" (Brophy, 2005, p. 172) to more directly and powerfully predict performance outcomes. According to Brophy, this may entail rote learning, drill, deliberate practice, last-minute cramming, and even some shallow processing strategies that are aligned with test conditions and demands. As noted earlier, more recent work has built on the task-based mastery goals to propose self-based goals (Elliot et al., 2011, 2015) and PB goals (Martin, 2006, 2011; Martin & Elliot, 2016a, 2016b; Martin & Liem, 2010) that seek to explain mastery and improvement of self.

Performance orientation

Particularly in relation to achievement, researchers have emphasized the need to differentiate performance approach and avoidance goals. Performance avoidance goals are quite consistently negatively associated with achievement (e.g., Anderman & Wolters, 2006; Elliot, 2005; Maehr & Zusho, 2009; Payne et al., 2007). Interestingly, when considering performance approach goals, research has more consistently (relative to performance avoidance) found positive links to achievement. The extent to which performance approach goals positively link to achievement, however, can depend on the context or the individual. In terms of context, Harackiewicz and colleagues find that, in highly competitive circumstances, performance approach is associated with academic achievement (Harackiewicz, Barron, Pintrich, Elliot, & Thrash, 2002). In terms of individual factors, performance approach goals are associated with achievement for students high in self-efficacy and for students also high in mastery goals (Midgley, Kaplan, & Middleton, 2001).

As noted earlier, meta-analysis has suggested that the specific content and focus of goals may also be influential in affecting achievement. Hulleman et al. (2010) found that normative performance approach goals (e.g., comparisons with others; outperforming others) were positively associated with performance (course grades), whereas performance goals with an appearance or evaluative component (e.g., wanting to appear smart) were negatively associated with performance. This is consistent with earlier work by Grant and Dweck (2003), who suggested that resolving some of the ongoing controversies in goal orientation research may require clearly and consistently distinguishing between goals with a comparison component and goals with a content component. Perhaps reflecting the counterbalancing of different performance goal content, Payne et al.'s (2007) meta-analysis found a null relationship between performance approach goals and achievement. Similarly, Utman's (1997) meta-analysis found no compelling link between performance approach and achievement, particularly under experimental conditions. Another view suggests that students with a performance approach are more likely to have a history of positive achievement, and it is this that is associated with subsequent achievement, not the performance goal (Brophy, 2005).

Brophy (2005) raised other concerns with performance goals. For example, a focus on peer comparisons and competition distracts students from attending to what is needed to achieve on assessment tasks. He also suggested that performance approach goals render the student at risk of shifts to performance avoidance goals, which are known to negatively impact achievement. This shift is more likely when performance approach students do not perform well or are under disproportionate pressure of weighty and difficult schoolwork because then there is a risk that performance avoidance will ensue. For these reasons, Brophy (2005) suggests teachers should abandon performance goals that involve peer comparisons and instead promote performance goals directed to actual achievement.

Summary and recommendations

Probably the most consistent aspect of achievement effects under goal orientation is the size of the associations. Irrespective of whether mastery and performance goals do or do not positively or negatively associate with achievement, the effects are generally small. Specific studies, reviews, and encompassing meta-analyses generally yield absolute correlations of up to approximately $r = .20$ (e.g., see Brophy, 2005; Hulleman et al., 2010; Payne et al., 2007). Hence, although the debate as to the relative advantages and drawbacks of performance orientation in the context of a mastery orientation is ongoing (see Brophy, 2005; Harackiewicz et al., 2002; Kaplan & Middleton, 2002), there can be little vigorous debate as to the overarching aggregate range of absolute effects. This is not to dismiss the more powerful role of goal orientations for other valued educational processes and factors (e.g., effort, interest, persistence, valuing), but it is perhaps prudent to have appropriate perspective in relation to actual achievement effects.

Research into the link between goal orientation and achievement has also identified issues relevant to educational practice. In the main, it appears educational advice would lean toward mastery more than performance approaches (Van Yperen, Blaga, & Postmes, 2015). The promising findings of PB goals for achievement, motivation, and engagement (Martin & Elliot, 2016a, 2016b; Martin & Liem, 2010) suggest that these, too, might be a focus for intervention. Furthermore, research has identified important nuances relevant to all goal types that are of potential use for educators. First, it is important that educators be clear about the effects of goal orientation: for example, as a result of promoting mastery, expecting gains in motivation and engagement is perhaps more feasible than expecting gains in achievement. Second, understanding the role of goal orientation in simple and complex tasks is important. For example, mastery may be more appropriate for complex tasks. Third, there may be a need to alert students to times when non-mastery strategies are needed – such as rote learning, cramming, and drill leading up to a test. Fourth, in terms of performance goals, it is evident that some performance goals are not inimical to performance whereas others that have a heavy evaluative component may be. Fifth, performance goals directed to achievement itself more than the comparative aspects of achievement may have their place. Sixth, goal orientation might be moderated by achievement domain. For example, meta-analysis by Van Yperen, Blaga, and Postmes (2014) found that, in school and work domains (but not so much the sporting domain), approach goals (both mastery and performance) were positively associated with performance, whereas avoidance goals were negatively associated with performance (see also Lochbaum & Gottardy, 2015, for meta-analytic work showing goal orientation differences across education and sport). Finally, the recent research into self-based and PB goals suggests a potentially important and useful goal-based expansion from task and performance dimensions to dimensions relevant to self and self-improvement. Taken together, a vast volume of research has been conducted in this area and provided considerable insight into the precise nature of goal orientation, its effects, and its implications for educators.

References

Anderman, E. M., & Wolters, C. A. (2006). Goals, values, and affect: Influences on student motivation. In P. A. Alexander & P. Winne (Eds.), *Handbook of educational psychology* (pp. 369–389). Mahwah, NJ: Erlbaum.

Brophy, J. (2005). Goal theorists should move on from performance goals. *Educational Psychologist, 40,* 167–176. https://doi.org/10.1207/s15326985ep4003_3

Church, M. A., Elliot, A. J., & Gable, S. L. (2001). Perceptions of classroom environment, achievement goals, and achievement outcomes. Journal of *Educational Psychology, 93,* 43–54. https://doi.org/10.1037/0022-0663.93.1.43

Elliot, A. J. (2005). A conceptual history of the achievement goal construct. In A. J. Elliot & C. S. Dweck (Eds.), *Handbook of competence and motivation* (pp. 52–72). New York, NY: Guilford.

Elliot, A., Murayama, K., Kobeisy, A., & Lichtenfeld, S. (2015). Potential-based achievement goals. *British Journal of Educational Psychology, 85,* 192–206. https://doi.org/10.1111/bjep.12051

Elliot, A. J., Murayama, K., & Pekrun, R. (2011). A 3 × 2 achievement goal model. *Journal of Educational Psychology, 103,* 632–648. https://doi.org/10.1037/a0023952

Grant, H., & Dweck, C. (2003). Clarifying achievement goals and their impact. *Journal of Personality and Social Psychology, 85,* 541–553. https://doi.org/10.1037/0022-3514.85.3.541

Harackiewicz, J., Barron, K., Pintrich, P., Elliot, A., & Thrash, T. (2002). Revision of achievement goal theory: Necessary and illuminating. *Journal of Educational Psychology, 94,* 638–645. https://doi.org/10.1037/0022-0663.94.3.638

Huang, C. (2011). Achievement goals and achievement emotions: A meta-analysis. *Educational Psychology Review, 23,* 359–388. https://doi.org/10.1007/s10648-011-9155-x

Hulleman, C. S., Schrager, S. M., Bodmann, S. M., & Harackiewicz, J. M. (2010). A meta-analytic review of achievement goal measures: Different labels for the same constructs or different constructs with similar labels? *Psychological Bulletin, 136,* 422–449. https://doi.org/10.1037/a0018947

Kaplan, A., & Middleton, M. (2002). Should childhood be a journey or a race? Response to Harackiewicz et al. (Eds.). *Journal of Educational Psychology, 94*, 646–648. https://doi.org/10.1037/0022-0663.94.3.646

Linnenbrink-Garcia, L., Tyson, D. F., & Patall, E. A. (2008). When are achievement goal orientations beneficial for academic achievement? A closer look at moderating factors. *International Review of Social Psychology, 21*, 19–70.

Lochbaum, M., & Gottardy, J. (2015). A meta-analytic review of the approach-avoidance achievement goals and performance relationships in the sport psychology literature. *Journal of Sport and Health Science, 4*, 164–173. https://doi.org/10.1016/j.jshs.2013.12.004

Maehr, M. L., & Zusho, A. (2009). Achievement goal theory: The past, present, and future. In K. R. Wentzel & A. Wigfield (Eds.), *Handbook of motivation at school* (pp. 77–104). New York, NY: Routledge.

Martin, A. J. (2006). Personal bests (PBs): A proposed multidimensional model and empirical analysis. *British Journal of Educational Psychology, 76*, 803–825. https://doi.org/10.1348/000709905X55389

Martin, A. J. (2011). Personal best (PB) approaches to academic development: Implications for motivation and assessment. *Educational Practice and Theory, 33*, 93–99. https://doi.org/10.7459/ept/33.1.06

Martin, A. J., & Elliot, A. J. (2016a). The role of personal best (PB) and dichotomous achievement goals in students' academic motivation and engagement: A longitudinal investigation. *Educational Psychology, 36*, 1285–1302. https://doi.org/10.1080/01443410.2015.1093606

Martin, A. J., & Elliot, A. J. (2016b). The role of personal best (PB) goal setting in students' academic achievement gains. *Learning and Individual Differences, 45*, 222–227. https://doi.org/10.1016/j.lindif.2015.12.014

Martin, A. J., & Liem, G. A. (2010). Academic personal bests (PBs), engagement, and achievement: A cross-lagged panel analysis. *Learning and Individual Differences, 20*, 265–270. https://doi.org/10.1016/j.lindif.2010.01.001

Martin, A. J., Marsh, H. W., Debus, R. L., & Malmberg, L-E. (2008). Performance and mastery orientation of high school and university/ college students: A Rasch perspective. *Educational and Psychological Measurement, 68*, 464–487. https://doi.org/10.1177/0013164407308478

Midgley, C., Kaplan, A., & Middleton, M. (2001). Performance-approach goals: Good for what, for whom, under what circumstances, and at what costs? *Journal of Educational Psychology, 93*, 77–86. https://doi.org/10.1037/0022-0663.93.1.77

Payne, S. C., Youngcourt, S. S., & Beaubien, J. M. (2007). A meta-analytic examination of the goal orientation nomological net. *Journal of Applied Psychology, 92*, 128–150. https://doi.org/10.1037/0021-9010.92.1.128

Utman, C. H. (1997). Performance effects of motivational state: A meta-analysis. *Personality and Social Psychology Review, 1*, 170–182. https://doi.org/10.1207/s15327957pspr0102_4

Van Yperen, N. W., Blaga, M., & Postmes, T. (2014). A meta-analysis of self-reported achievement goals and nonself-report performance across three achievement domains (work, sports, and education). *PloS one, 9*, e93594. https://doi.org/10.1371/journal.pone.0093594

Van Yperen, N. W., Blaga, M., & Postmes, T. (2015). A meta-analysis of the impact of situationally induced achievement goals on task performance. *Human Performance, 28*, 165–182. https://doi.org/10.1080/08959285.2015.1006772

7.7

Multimedia learning

Richard E. Mayer

Introduction

What is multimedia learning?

Multimedia learning refers to learning with words and pictures (Mayer, 2009, 2014a). The words may be spoken (delivered live or via speakers) or printed (delivered on a page, board, or screen); the pictures may be static graphics (such as illustrations, charts, maps, or photos delivered on a page or screen) or dynamic graphics (such as animation or video delivered on a screen). Examples of multimedia instruction include a narrated animation, an instructional video, a digital educational game or simulation, a PowerPoint presentation, or an illustrated textbook. Figure 7.1 shows frames and spoken words from a narrated animation on how a pump works.

For hundreds of years, the primary vehicle for instruction has been words, such as lectures or textbooks. Advances in computer and communication technologies now allow instructors to supplement verbal modes of instruction with visual modes of instruction, including dazzling graphics that students can interact with. Research on multimedia learning provides encouraging evidence that, under appropriate circumstances, students learn better from words and pictures than from words alone, with a median effect size of $d = 1.39$ based on transfer tests in 11 experimental comparisons (Mayer, 2009, 2014a). These findings constitute the *multimedia principle*, which has been recognized as a fundamental principle of instructional design (Butler, 2014; Clark & Mayer, 2016).

What is the historical context of multimedia learning?

More than 350 years ago in 1658, John Amos Comenius published the world's first and most popular illustrated textbook for children, *Orbis Pictus* ("The World in Pictures"). Each page contained a line drawing (such as a tailor's shop, the parts of a house, or the planets) with each part labeled with a name and description both in the reader's first language and in Latin (Comenius, 1887 [1658]). As the first book to combine

Influences from teaching strategies

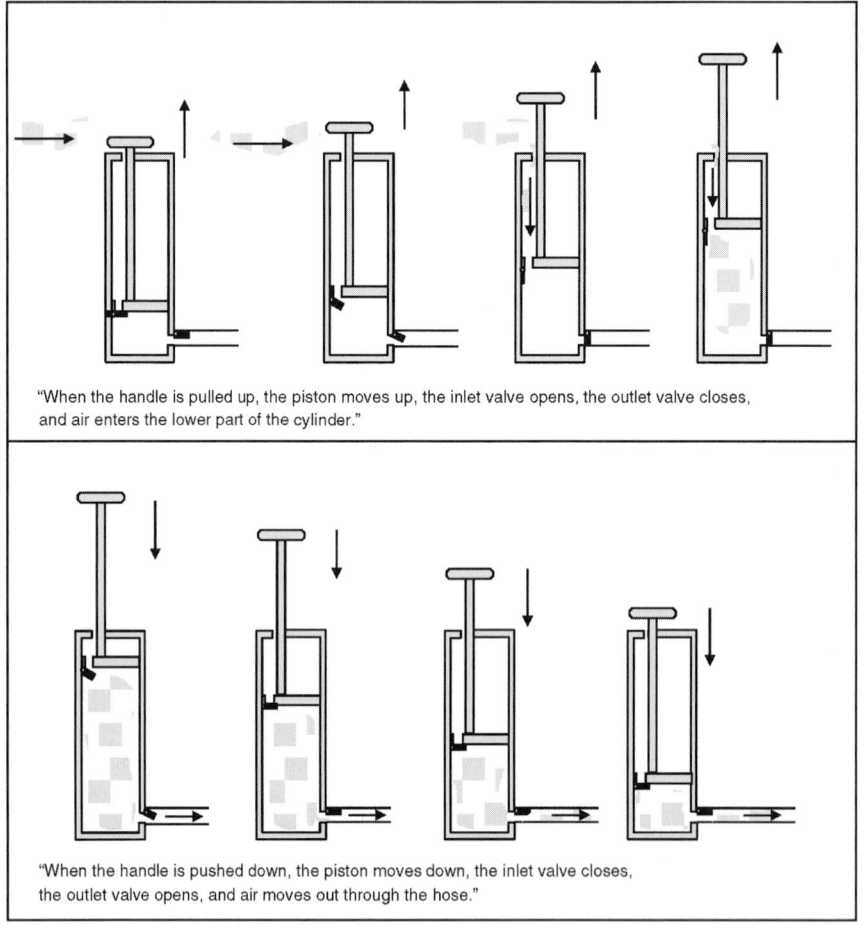

Figure 7.1 Frames from a narrated animation on how a pump works

words and pictures in order to promote learning, *Orbis Pictus* is a forerunner of today's illustrated textbooks and multimedia instruction in general. Other technological milestones in the evolution of multimedia learning include the initial educational use of motion pictures in the early 1920s, television in the 1950s, personal computers in the 1980s, the internet in the 1990s, and virtual reality in the 2000s.

Research evidence

How does multimedia learning work?

The *cognitive theory of multimedia learning* is based on three principles of how people learn within the human information processing system: *dual channels* – humans have separate information processing channels for words and pictures

(Paivio, 1986); *limited capacity* – within each channel people can engage in only a small amount of cognitive processing at one time (Plass, Moreno, & Brunken, 2010; Sweller, Ayres, & Kalyuga, 2011); and *active processing* – meaningful learning depends on the learner's cognitive processing during learning, including attending to relevant incoming verbal and pictorial information, mentally organizing it into a coherent verbal or pictorial representation, and integrating them with each other and with knowledge activated from long-term memory (Fiorella & Mayer, 2015; Mayer, 2009, 2014a). Three kinds of cognitive processing during learning are *extraneous processing* – cognitive processing that does not support the instructional objective and is caused by poor instructional design; *essential processing* – cognitive processing that is required to mentally represent the presented words and pictures and is caused by the complexity of the essential material; and *generative processing* – cognitive processing that involves mentally organizing and integrating the material for deep understanding and depends on the motivation of the learner to exert effort. Given the limits on information processing capacity, three important goals of instructional design are to reduce extraneous processing, manage essential processing, and foster generative processing.

What are the effects of multimedia instruction on student achievement?

Researchers have identified evidence-based principles for how to design effective multimedia instruction that are consistent with cognitive theories of how people learn from words and pictures. Techniques intended to reduce extraneous processing include the coherence principle, signaling principle, redundancy principle, spatial contiguity principle, and temporal contiguity principle (Mayer & Fiorella, 2014). The *coherence principle* is that people learn better when extraneous words, sounds, and pictures are excluded from a multimedia lesson. In a meta-analysis based on 23 experimental comparisons, Mayer and Fiorella (2014) reported a median effect size of $d = 0.86$. The *signaling principle* – also called the *cueing principle* (van Gog, 2014) – is that people learn better from a multimedia lesson when cues highlight the essential material. In a meta-analysis based on 28 experimental comparisons, Mayer and Fiorella (2014) reported a median effect size of $d = 0.41$. The *redundancy principle* is that people learn better from graphics and narration than from graphics, narration, and onscreen text. In a meta-analysis based on 16 experimental comparisons, Mayer and Fiorella (2014) reported a median effect size of $d = 0.86$. The *spatial contiguity principle* is that people learn better when corresponding printed words and pictures are presented near each other on the screen or page. In meta-analyses, Mayer and Fiorella (2014) reported a median effect size of $d = 1.10$ based on 22 experimental comparisons, and Ginns (2006) reported a weighted mean effect size of $d = 0.72$ based on 37 experimental comparisons. The *temporal contiguity principle* is that people learn better when corresponding words and pictures are presented at the same time. In meta-analyses, Mayer and Fiorella (2014) reported a median effect size of $d = 1.22$ based on 9 experimental comparisons, and Ginns (2006) reported a weighted mean effect size of $d = 0.72$ based on 13 experimental comparisons.

Techniques aimed at managing essential processing are the segmenting principle, the pretraining principle, and the modality principle (Mayer & Pilegard, 2014). The *segmenting principle* is that people learn better when a multimedia lesson is presented in user-paced segments rather than as a continuous presentation. In a meta-analysis involving 10 experimental comparisons, Mayer and Pilegard (2014) reported a median effect size of $d = 0.79$. The *pretraining principle* is that people learn better from a multimedia lesson when they receive pretraining in the names and characteristics of the main concepts. In a meta-analysis involving 16 experimental comparisons, Mayer and Pilegard (2014) reported a median effect size of $d = 0.75$. The *modality principle* is that people learn better from graphics and narration than from animation and onscreen text. In a meta-analysis involving 61 experimental comparisons, Mayer and Pilegard (2014) reported a median effect size of $d = 0.76$, whereas Ginns (2005) reported a weighted mean effect size of $d = 0.93$ based on 31 experimental comparisons with system-paced presentation.

Techniques for fostering generative processing include the personalization, voice, and embodiment principles (Mayer, 2014b). The *personalization principle* is that people learn better from a multimedia lesson when the words are in conversational style rather than formal style. In a meta-analysis involving 17 experimental comparisons, Mayer (2014b) reported a median effect size of $d = 0.79$. The *voice principle* is that people learn better from a multimedia lesson when the words are spoken in an appealing human voice rather than a machine voice (Mayer, 2014b). In a meta-analysis based on 6 experimental comparisons, the median effect size was $d = 0.74$ (Mayer, 2014b). The *embodiment principle* is that people learn better from a multimedia lesson when an onscreen agent engages in humanlike gestures, facial expressions, movements, and eye contact. In a meta-analysis involving 11 experimental comparisons, Mayer (2014b) reported a median effect size of $d = 0.36$.

Finally, techniques that do not appear to improve multimedia learning include increasing the visual realism of the graphics and adding a static image of the instructor or the instructor's face on the screen (Clark & Mayer, 2016; Lowe & Ploetzner, 2017; Mayer, 2014b).

Summary and recommendations

Overall, there are important boundary conditions for some of the principles, including evidence that some principles apply more strongly for learners with low prior knowledge than for learners with high prior knowledge, for tests of transfer rather than retention, and when the material is unfamiliar and presented at a fast pace (Clark & Mayer, 2016; Kalyuga, 2014; Mayer, 2014a). For example, Kalyuga (2014) reported evidence for the *expertise reversal effect* in which some multimedia instructional design principles that are effective for novices are not effective for experts and may even be detrimental.

Most of the studies on multimedia learning involve short lessons with immediate tests in laboratory contexts. It would be useful to determine the extent to which multimedia design principles apply to more authentic learning environments (e.g., Issa et al., 2013) and to continue to pinpoint the boundary conditions under which the principles are most effective in improving student achievement.

The primary practical recommendation for improving student achievement is that people can understand material better when it is presented with words and pictures rather than with words alone. However, all graphics are not equally effective in promoting student achievement. In creating multimedia lessons that promote student achievement, instructors should be guided by evidence-based principles of multimedia design.

References

Butler, K. B. (2014). The multimedia principle. In R. E. Mayer (Ed.), *The Cambridge handbook of multimedia learning* (2nd ed., pp. 174–205). New York, NY: Cambridge University Press.

Clark, R. C., & Mayer, R. E. (2016). *e-Learning and the science of instruction* (4th ed.). San Francisco, CA: Pfeiffer.

Comenius, J. A. (1887). *The Orbis Pictus*. Syracuse, NY: C. W. Bardeen. (Original work published 1658).

Fiorella, L., & Mayer, R. E. (2015). *Learning as a generative activity*. New York, NY: Cambridge University Press.

Ginns, P. (2005). Meta-analysis of the modality effect. *Learning and Instruction, 15*, 313–332.

Ginns, P. (2006). Integrating information: A meta-analysis of spatial contiguity and temporal contiguity effects. *Learning and Instruction, 16*, 511–525.

Issa, N., Mayer, R. E., Schuller, M., Wang, E., Shapiro, M., & DaRosa, D. A. (2013). Teaching for understanding in medical classrooms using multimedia design principles. *Medical Education, 47*, 388–396.

Kalyuga, S. (2014). The expertise reversal principle in multimedia learning. In R. E. Mayer (Ed.), *The Cambridge handbook of multimedia learning* (pp. 576–597). New York, NY: Cambridge University Press.

Lowe, R., & Ploetzner, R. (Eds.). (2017). *Learning from dynamic visualization*. New York, NY: Springer.

Mayer, R. E. (2009). *Multimedia learning* (2nd ed.). New York, NY: Cambridge University Press.

Mayer, R. E. (Ed.). (2014a). *The Cambridge handbook of multimedia learning* (2nd ed.). New York, NY: Cambridge University Press.

Mayer, R. E. (2014b). Principles based on social cues in multimedia learning: Personalization, voice, images, and embodiment. In R. E. Mayer (Ed.), *The Cambridge handbook of multimedia learning* (2nd ed., pp. 345–368). New York, NY: Cambridge University Press.

Mayer, R. E., & Fiorella, L. (2014). Principles for reducing extraneous processing in multimedia learning: Coherence, signaling, redundancy, spatial contiguity, and temporal contiguity principles. In R. E. Mayer (Ed.), *The Cambridge handbook of multimedia learning* (2nd ed., pp. 279–315). New York, NY: Cambridge University Press.

Mayer, R. E., & Pilegard, C. (2014). Principles for managing essential processing in multimedia learning: Segmenting, pre-training, and modality principles. In R. E. Mayer (Ed.), *The Cambridge handbook of multimedia learning* (2nd ed., pp. 316–344). New York, NY: Cambridge University Press.

Paivio, A. (1986). *Mental representations: A dual-coding approach*. Oxford, England: Oxford University Press.

Plass, J. L., Moreno, R., & Brunken, R. (Eds.). (2010). *Cognitive load theory*. New York, NY: Cambridge University Press.

Sweller, J., Ayres, P., & Kalyuga, S. (2011). *Cognitive load theory*. New York, NY: Springer.

van Gog, T. (2014). The signaling (or cueing) principle in multimedia learning. In R. E. Mayer (Ed.), *The Cambridge handbook of multimedia learning* (2nd ed., pp. 263–278). New York, NY: Cambridge University Press.

7.8 Reciprocal teaching

Annemarie Sullivan Palincsar

Introduction

Reciprocal teaching (RT) is an instructional procedure designed to enhance students' reading comprehension. The procedure typically engages teachers and students in a dialogue, the purpose of which is to jointly construct the meaning of the text. The dialogue is supported with the use of four strategies: question generating, summarizing, clarifying, and predicting. When students are initially introduced to RT, the teacher models the application of these strategies for both actively bringing meaning to the text and monitoring one's own thinking and learning from text. Over the course of time, the students assume increased responsibility for leading the dialogues. By focusing on the processes requisite to successful comprehension, RT provides students with tools for learning from text independently.

Reciprocal teaching has a long history; it was Palincsar's dissertation study (1982), conducted in the early 1980s at the Center for the Study of Reading (University of Illinois, Urbana-Champaign) and was the focus of a number of studies by Palincsar and Brown over several decades. In addition, as the references suggest, there have been numerous replications of RT with diverse groups of students.

Research evidence

The majority of research regarding RT has been conducted in reading and listening comprehension by general, remedial, and special educators. Approximately 300 middle school students and 400 primary-grade students participated in the research conducted by Palincsar and Brown on RT. In the research, designed especially for students who were at risk for academic difficulty or who were already identified as remedial or special education students, participants typically scored below the 40th percentile on norm-referenced measures of reading achievement. To evaluate the success of the intervention, criterion-referenced measures of text comprehension were administered as one of several assessments of student learning. These assessments were designed to evaluate students' ability to recall information, draw inferences, identify the gist of the passage, and apply information presented in the text to a novel situation. The criterion level of performance was defined as the ability to score 75% to 85% on four out of five consecutive assessments. Prior to instruction, students typically scored approximately 30% on these criterion-referenced measures of text comprehension (averaging 3 of 10 questions correct). However, at the conclusion of instruction (typically 20 days). approximately 80% of both the primary and middle school students achieved the criterion level of performance. Furthermore, participants demonstrated maintenance of these gains for up to six months to a year following instruction (Palincsar & Brown, 1984).

Rosenshine and Meister (1994) completed a meta-analysis of 16 studies of RT, conducted with students from age seven to adulthood, in which RT was compared with traditional basal reading instruction, explicit instruction in reading comprehension, and reading and answering questions. They determined that, when standardized measures were used to assess comprehension, the median effect size, favoring RT, was .32. When experimenter-developed comprehension tests were used, the median effect size was .88. Furthermore, the researchers found no significant relationship between the effects and the number of sessions (which ranged from 6 to 25) or for the size of the instructional group (which ranged from 2 to 23). In addition, reciprocal teaching has been found effective in teaching children with mild disabilities in resource room programs (Marston, 1995) and in inclusion classrooms (Lederer, 2000), with deaf and hard-of-hearing students (Al-Hilawani, 2003), with high school students (Alfassi, 1998; Westera & Moore, 1995), with bilingual students (Padron, 1992) and English-language learners (Navaie, 2018), and with English learners in countries other than the United States (Fung, Wilkinson, & Moore, 2002). Some researchers are now integrating RT into online learning environments (e.g., Huang & Yang, 2015; Tseng & Yeh, 2018), although this research is nascent. Whereas most research with RT has been conducted in the domain of reading, researchers have adapted RT for use in other domains, including mathematics (e.g., Darsono, 2015) and science (e.g., Takagaki & Tahara, 2005).

The causal mechanisms

There are at least two categories of mechanisms: (a) the role of the strategies in promoting comprehension and comprehension monitoring and (b) the affordances of the participation structure for both the teacher and children. There are four RT strategies: summarizing, questioning, clarifying, and predicting. Recent research suggests that teachers' fidelity to the use of these strategies is essential for RT to be effective (Okkinga, van Steensel, van Gelderen, & Sleegers, 2018). When students first begin RT dialogues, they are encouraged to use the strategies with each segment of text; later, as the students become more familiar with the strategies and the purposes for each, the strategies are used opportunistically.

- *Summarizing*: Summarizing engages students in identifying, paraphrasing, and integrating important information in the text. Students ask themselves: "What is the gist of the text? What is the most important information? Why did the author write this part?" The reader then puts the answers to these questions into their own words.
- *Questioning*: Students can be taught to generate and ask questions about the text at many levels. For example, questions can be raised that recall details in the text; others engage the students in drawing inferences from the text or in applying information in the text to a novel problem or situation (questions that may or may not have a single, agreed-upon answer).
- *Clarifying*: Clarifying is particularly useful when working with students who may believe that the purpose of reading is merely to correctly identify the words, not necessarily to make sense of them. Clarifying engages students in attending to the many reasons why text may be difficult to understand (e.g., unfamiliar vocabulary, challenging concepts, awkward structure, unclear referent words, idiomatic expressions). Students are taught to be alert to such situations and, most importantly, to take some measures to restore meaning when the text is unclear (e.g., rereading, reading ahead, asking for help).
- *Predicting*: Predicting requires students to hypothesize about what the author might discuss next in the text. There are several approaches that students can take to predicting. One is to think about what one already knows about the topic; another is to attend to text features (e.g., headings, embedded questions) or text structure: that is, how the text is organized (e.g., as a chronology, in terms of problems and solutions or causes and effects). Students make predictions and then read for the purpose of confirming or disproving their hypotheses.

Using the strategies in RT dialogues. A typical discussion might follow this pattern: The group reads a section of text silently or reading along as someone in the group reads orally (depending on the decoding skills of the students). The discussion leader (a teacher or student) generates a question to which the other members respond. Other members of the group are invited to ask questions they thought of while reading the text. The leader then summarizes the text and asks the group if they would like to elaborate upon or revise the summary. Necessary clarifications may be discussed throughout the dialogue or all at once. Finally, in preparation for moving on to the next segment of text, the group makes predictions.

In summary, in the context of RT, strategies are being taught in meaningful contexts: that is, while reading extended text, rather than in isolation using artificial tasks (e.g., "underline the main idea"). In addition, students are encouraged to use the strategies flexibly and opportunistically; in other words, students learn to use the strategies as opportunities arise in which they will assist comprehension, rather than routinely applying the strategies. Finally, the strategies are taught as a means for enhancing comprehension, rather than as an end in themselves.

The learning principles underlying the use of RT and how these relate to the participant structure

Underlying the model of RT is the notion that expert-led social interactions play an important role in learning and can provide a major impetus to cognitive development. This idea, found in the writings of Vygotsky, Dewey, and Piaget, emphasizes the role of guided practice in the context of social interaction as a key to developmental change. Dialogue is a critical element of socially mediated instruction, since it provides the means by which experts provide and adjust support to novice learners, and novice learners have the opportunity to "try out" the use of the tools they are learning about (in this case, the strategies and the dialogue).

Socially mediated instruction is sometimes referred to as scaffolded instruction to the extent that a scaffold provides support that is both temporary and adjustable. In the initial phase of RT, teachers provide considerable support to students as they learn the strategies and their application to understanding text. Scaffolding may take the form of the teacher's explaining, modeling through the use of think aloud, or prompting (e.g., supplying an appropriate interrogative with which to start a question). Over the course of instruction, there is a conscious effort on the part of the teacher to gradually decrease the amount of support provided to students so that, eventually, teachers provide minimal support and act more in the role of coach, providing feedback and prompting only as necessary. This approach encourages the teacher to differentiate scaffolding; some students may need more sustained assistance than others.

Metacognitive strategy instruction has also informed RT. Metacognition refers to (a) the knowledge we have about ourselves as learners, the demands of learning tasks, and the strategies we employ to achieve tasks successfully and (b) the ability to monitor and regulate learning. Metacognitive knowledge is developmental in nature since it is acquired over time and is influenced by our experiences in the same way that we acquire and use any kind of knowledge. As students participate in RT dialogues, they acquire more awareness about themselves as readers and how they interact with texts that have different demands.

Finally, RT takes into consideration the influence of motivation on student learning and the kinds of attributions that students who have a history of academic difficulty typically make. Students who are anxious and feel helpless in school are inclined to attribute success with a task to "luck," while attributing failure with a task to their own lack of ability. Students making these kinds of attributions need to make connections between engaging in strategic activity and the outcomes of this activity. Reciprocal teaching enhances motivation by increasing student awareness of the kinds of factors that influence learning outcomes; furthermore, as students become experienced with RT dialogues, they come to appreciate the relationship between their activity as readers and the outcomes of this activity. RT also enhances motivation since students typically enjoy interacting with their peers and collaborating with their teachers.

Summary and recommendations

Comparative studies have been conducted to determine the essential features of RT. Specifically, the studies were designed to evaluate the role of dialogue in teaching students to be self-regulated learners and to determine whether all four strategies were needed to improve students' comprehension of text. To compare RT with other kinds of instruction that focused on teaching the same set of strategies, not in dialogic manner, students were randomly assigned to one of four conditions: (a) modeling, in which the teacher demonstrated how to use the strategies while reading text, and the students observed and responded to the teacher's questions; (b) isolated skills practice, in which students were taught the RT strategies using worksheet activities with extensive teacher feedback regarding their performance; (c) RT/independent practice, in which students were taught RT for only four days, followed by eight days of independently applying the strategies in writing while reading text; and (d) traditional RT. Only the traditional RT procedure that incorporated dialogic instruction was effective in bringing about large and reliable changes in student performance (Brown & Palincsar, 1987). A second comparative study was conducted to determine if all four strategies were needed to improve students' comprehension abilities or whether a subset would suffice. The performance of students who were taught ten days of reciprocal questioning alone and students who were taught ten days of reciprocal summarizing alone were compared with ten days of the traditional RT procedure, in which students were taught all four strategies concurrently. Neither of the individual strategy conditions was as effective as the full set of strategies (Brown & Palincsar, 1987).

Results of these and other studies suggest that RT, when implemented with fidelity, can improve learners' comprehension of text. Given the importance of reading comprehension in all types of academic learning, the beneficial effects of RT on comprehension have the potential to enhance achievement across multiple academic domains.

References

Alfassi, M. (1998). Reading for meaning: The efficacy of reciprocal teaching in fostering reading comprehension in high school students in remedial reading classes. *American Educational Research Journal, 35*(2), 309–332.

Al-Hilawani, Y. A. (2003). Clinical examination of three methods of teaching reading comprehension to deaf and hard-of-hearing students: From research to classroom applications. *Journal of Deaf Studies and Deaf Education, 8*(2), 146–156.

Brown, A. L., & Palincsar, A. (1987). Reciprocal teaching of comprehension strategies: A natural history of one program for enhancing learning. In J. Day & J. Borkowski (Eds.), *Intelligence and exceptionality: New directions for theory, assessment, and instructional practices* (pp 81–131). Norwood, NJ: Ablex.

Darsono. (2015). The application of reciprocal teaching on the subject of straight line equation in second grade of junior high school. *Journal of Education and Practice, 6*(5), 73–78.

Fung, I. Y. Y., Wilkinson, I. A. G., & Moore, D. W. (2002). L-1-assisted reciprocal teaching to improve ESL students' comprehension of English expository text. *Learning and Instruction, 13*(1), 1–31.

Huang, C-T., & Yang, S. C. (2015). Effects of online reciprocal teaching on reading strategies, comprehension, self-efficacy, and motivation. *Journal of Educational Computing Research, 52*(3), 381–407.

Lederer, J. M. (2000). Reciprocal teaching of social studies in inclusive elementary classrooms. *Journal of Learning Disabilities, 33*(1), 91–106.

Marston, D. (1995). Comparison of reading intervention approaches for students with mild disabilities. *Exceptional Children, 62*(1), 20–37.

Navaie, L. A. (2018). The effects of reciprocal teaching on reading comprehension of Iranian EFL learners. *Advances in Language and Literary Studies, 9*(4), 26–30.

Okkinga, M., van Steensel, R., van Gelderen, A. J. S., & Sleegers, P. J. C. (2018). Effects of reciprocal teaching on reading comprehension of low-achieving adolescents: The importance of specific teacher skills. *Journal of Research in Reading, 41*(1), 20–41.

Padron, Y. N. (1992). The effect of strategy instruction on bilingual students' cognitive strategy use in reading. *Bilingual Research Journal, 16*(3–4), 35–51.

Palincsar, A. S. (2003). Collaborative approaches to comprehension instruction. In A. S. Sweet & C. E. Snow (Eds.), *Rethinking reading comprehension* (pp. 99–114). New York, NY: Guilford.

Palincsar, A. S., & Brown, A. (1984). Reciprocal teaching of comprehension-fostering and comprehension-monitoring activities. *Cognition and Instruction, 1*(2), 117–175.

Rosenshine, B., & Meister, C. (1994). Reciprocal teaching: A review of the research. *Review of Educational Research, 64*(4), 479–530.

Takagaki, M., & Tahara, H. (2005). Using a modified reciprocal teaching strategy to induce conceptual change: Elementary school science lessons. *Japanese Journal of Educational Psychology, 53*(4), 551–564.

Tseng, S-S., & Yeh, H-C. (2018). Integrating reciprocal teaching in an online environment with an annotation feature to enhance low-achieving students' English reading comprehension. *Interactive Learning Environments, 26*(6), 789–802.

Westera, J., & Moore, D. W. (1995). Reciprocal teaching of reading comprehension in a New Zealand high school. *Psychology in the Schools, 32*(3), 225–232.

7.9 Technology-supported learning and academic achievement

Peter Reimann and Anindito Aditomo

Introduction

Computer technologies have been introduced into schools since about 1960, with large-scale deployment starting in the 1980s once personal computers became widely available and affordable. A second wave of deployment saw the networking of computers, first in the form of classroom-based local-area networks (LAN), and more recently the connection to the internet. More recent trends include such developments as the introduction of interactive whiteboards into classrooms and the establishment of 1:1 computing (one digital device per student) in some systems. However, the major meta-analyses available at this time do not address these more recent developments – one might also add the increasing interest in mobile and cloud computing among them – but focus on the classic question: Do students in classes where computers are used profit from this compared to students in classes where no computers are used?

Concerning our question of whether technologies make a difference for education, more than 60 meta-analyses have appeared since 1980, covering thousands of individual comparative studies. Most of the meta-analyses have focused on questions specific to certain types of technologies, subject matter, or grade level. However, a secondary meta-analysis has been published (Tamim, Bernard, Borokhosvski, Abrami, & Schmid, 2011) that aggregates the data from 25 meta-analyses. We will use Tamim et al. (2011) to answer the general question; we complement this by drawing from more recent meta-analyses, most of them not covered in Tamim et al. (2011), to address more specific questions regarding the effects on important learning areas (mathematics, reading, writing, language learning). Notably absent from the literature are meta-analyses of technology use for science learning.

Although space does not permit us to report on the effectiveness of specific types of educational technology, it is worth mentioning what types are typically included in the label "computer technology" (CT). What is covered in these studies are CT applications that can be categorized fairly well into five types (Li & Ma,

2010): (a) tutorials: programs that directly teach by providing information, demonstration, and opportunities for (drill and) practice; (b) communication media, such as email, web browsers, and videoconferencing tools that provide access to information and opportunities for communication, including student-to-student communication; (c) exploratory environments, including simulations, hypermedia environments, and web quests; (d) tools, in particular productivity tools (word processors, presentations tools); media manipulation software, such as for digital imaging and music, and (data) analysis tools, such as spreadsheet programs; and (e) programming languages, ranging from general purpose ones (e.g., Java, Prolog) to those with a didactic function (e.g., Logo). It is important to keep this variety of meanings of CT in mind when looking at the field through the lens of meta-analyses.

Research evidence

The most comprehensive review currently available is provided by Tamim and colleagues (2011). They employed a second-order meta-analysis procedure to summarize 25 meta-analyses, which together cover 1,055 primary studies and more than 100,000 students. This represents 40 years of research activity addressing the question of whether students in face-to-face classrooms that use CT obtained higher achievement than those in classrooms without technology. The study found that technology had a positive but relatively small effect ($d = 0.35$) on student achievement. The effect was larger for K–12 ($d = 0.40$) than for postsecondary classrooms ($d = 0.29$). Another recent meta-analysis (Schmid et al., 2009), not included in Tamim et al.'s review, found a very similar effect size ($d = 0.28$) for postsecondary classrooms. A further moderating variable identified by Tamim et al. was related to *how* technology is used: it had a larger effect when used to support instruction ($d = 0.42$) than when used to deliver content ($d = 0.31$). Again, this was consistent with the findings of Schmid et al., which showed that technology for cognitive support ($d = 0.41$) was more beneficial than technology for presentation support ($d = 0.10$). To go beyond this broad picture, we now review evidence for specific content areas.

Li and Ma (2010) performed a meta-analysis of 85 independent effect sizes extracted from 46 primary studies involving a total of 36,793 learners that indicated statistically significant positive effects of CT on *mathematics* achievement ($d = 0.28$). In addition, several characteristics of primary studies were identified as having effects. For example, CT showed advantage in promoting the mathematics achievement of elementary over secondary school students. As well, CT showed larger effects on the mathematics achievement of special needs students than that of general education students. The positive effect of CT was greater when combined with a constructivist approach to teaching than with a traditional approach to teaching, and studies that used nonstandardized tests as measures of mathematics achievement reported larger effects of CT than studies that used standardized tests.

Another meta-analysis on the effect of computers on mathematics was reported by Cheung and Slavin (2013). The total sample size was 56,886 students at both the elementary (n = 31,555) and secondary (n = 25,331) levels. Technology had a positive but small effect (0.15 standard deviations) on students' scores on standardized math tests. In terms of other variables that moderated the effect, Cheung and Slavin found that computers had a larger effect when used more than 30 minutes per week. The effect also varied depending on the type of intervention, with supplemental computer-assisted instruction having larger impacts than "comprehensive models" and "computer-managed learning." Furthermore, the authors also reported that larger effects were more often found in quasi-experiments ($d = 0.19$) than in randomized experiments ($d = 0.10$) and in smaller sample studies ($d = 0.26$) compared to larger sample studies ($d = 0.12$).

More recently, Higgins, D'Angelo, and Crawford (2017) reported a meta-analysis of technology use in mathematics examined not only achievement, but also motivation and attitude. Their meta-analysis covered 29 studies published between 1985 and 2013 on kindergarten through grade 8 mathematics classrooms. Overall, the between-group effect sizes ranged from $d = 0.30$ for motivation to $d = 0.59$ for attitude and $d = 0.68$ for achievement. The larger effect size for achievement (compared to other meta-analysis findings) is possibly related to the inclusion of studies using nonexperimental designs. With regards to moderating variables, technology use had larger effects on achievement for the content domains of geometry and numbers and operations, compared to algebra. Another interesting finding was that achievement, motivation, and attitude were impacted to a larger extent for shorter (one to five sessions) than longer interventions (six to ten sessions), suggesting that technology's influence partly depends on its novelty. Whether technology was used in a personalized manner did not influence the effect size for any of the three dependent variables.

A meta-analysis focusing on dynamic geometry software (DGS) in mathematics classrooms was reported by Chan and Leung (2014). DGS refers to computer-based environments which enable users to digitally construct, manipulate, measure, and test geometric figures. Based on their analysis of nine quasi-experimental studies of primary and secondary students published between 1990 and 2013, the authors found that instruction using DGS had a large effect size on achievement scores ($d = 1.02$). A number of moderating variables were identified, with the use of DGS being more effective for primary than secondary students, when the intervention was shorter (less than two weeks), when teachers served as facilitators rather than instructors, when students worked in pairs rather than individually, and when the achievement test included open-ended questions compared to only selected-response ones. Chan and Leung (2014) also found larger effect sizes for studies with larger sample sizes than for smaller ones.

A meta-analysis reported by Cheung and Slavin (2012) reviewed 85 studies on the effect of various CTs on *reading* achievement. This included students at the kindergarten (n = 2,068), elementary (n = 34,200), and secondary (n = 24,453) levels. They found an average effect size of $d = 0.16$, indicating a small positive impact on reading achievement. This effect varied depending on how technology was used. When technology was used just to supplement traditional classroom instruction, the effect was only $d = 0.11$. But when technology was used in a more integrated manner, the effect increased to $d = 0.28$. Technology's impact was also greater for low ability ($d = 0.37$) than for high ability ($d = 0.08$) students and for secondary ($d = 0.31$) than for elementary students ($d = 0.10$). In addition, the authors found that some methodological features influenced the effect size, with large-scale randomized experiments finding smaller effects of technology than smaller-scale quasi-experiments did.

Archer et al. (2014) reanalyzed 38 empirical studies included in three previous meta-analyses on technology use in reading classrooms (Slavin, Cheung, Groff, & Lake, 2008; Slavin, Lake, Chambers, Cheung, & Davis, 2009; Torgerson & Zhu, 2003), to focus on the potential moderating effects of variables related to the implementation of an intervention. The overall effect size was positive but small ($d = 0.18$). Analysis of the moderating variables indicated that effect sizes were larger in five studies that mentioned the availability of training and support for teachers to implement an intervention ($d = 0.57$). Implementation fidelity and who delivered the intervention did not moderate the effects. It is important to note, however, that the moderating variables examined by Archer et al. (2014) refer to whether or not the authors of the empirical articles provided information regarding those variables. In other words, an article coded "0" on the implementation fidelity variable, for instance, does not mean that the study's intervention was implemented poorly. It just means that the study did not measure the fidelity of its intervention. Further research would need to examine the quality of support/training and implementation fidelity as moderators in the effects of technology use on reading/literacy.

The meta-analysis reported by Goldberg, Russell, and Cook (2003) examined the question of whether word processing software positively impacted K–12 students' *writing*. Included were 26 independent studies published between 1992 and 2002 (sample sizes were not reported). On writing quantity, the analysis found an average effect size of 0.54, indicating a moderate positive impact of word processing technology on the length of students' writing. The study also looked into writing quality, which was measured using various indicators such as coherence, organization, tone, voice, and creativity. On measures of quality, word processors also had a positive effect ($d = 0.40$) on students' writing. The effects on both quantity and quality were stable across students with varying prior computer experience and prior achievement. In addition, the availability of writing support (keyboard training, technical assistance, teacher feedback, and peer editing) made little difference to the effect of computers on students' writing.

Goldberg and colleagues also examined studies that provided information on students' writing processes. Six studies found that students made more changes between drafts when using word processors. Other studies showed that when using computers, students' writing became more collaborative, with more peer editing and discussions. Furthermore, a study found that students' writing when using paper and pencil followed a linear process from brainstorming, outlining, and drafting to revising. When using computers, however, this process became less linear, with students iterating between producing and revising their texts.

Zhao (2003) reported a meta-analysis of nine studies on technology-supported (second) *language learning* in postsecondary classrooms. These studies covered 419 students and a variety of target languages (English, German, Spanish, French, and Arabic). The analysis found a large average effect size of $d = 1.12$. Unfortunately, probably because of the limited number of studies examined, the analysis did not examine potential moderating variables that may influence the effect.

The last study we include sheds light on a tendency reported in various of the meta-analyses described earlier: that the pedagogy employed along with CT use in classrooms plays an important role. Rosen and Salomon (2007) made this the focus of their meta-analysis by comparing studies along the dimension constructivist pedagogy versus traditional pedagogy. By analyzing 32 studies that varied on this dimension – all of them in mathematics education – they found that, while the mean effect size across all studies was medium ($d = 0.46$), it rose to 0.90 in favor of constructivist learning environments when constructivist-appropriate measures were used (i.e., those that assess creativity and collaboration, as opposed to just computation fluency). But even in cases where traditional pedagogy was used and assessed only with traditional learning measures for math achievement, traditional education yielded poorer or similar outcomes when compared with constructivist use of CT.

Summary and recommendations

Table 7.1 summarizes the findings from the meta-analyses included in this chapter by learning area. It seems safe to conclude that, most of the time, ICT does have a positive, albeit often relatively small, impact on students' achievement across many content areas. Thus, claims that any particular technology in and of itself will bring large, radical, or revolutionary impact on achievement should be met with skepticism. But, at the very least, these findings show that technology does not have detrimental effects on learning.

The key pedagogical message resulting from the research reviewed is that CT use in classrooms will more likely be supporting learning if it is employed for the purpose of students interacting with content and interacting with peers rather than solely distributing and presenting content. There are quantitative variations across different content areas, with the effects on writing seemingly the strongest. But it is particularly difficult to discern with meta-analyses the extent to which this can be attributed to a general effect of text processing technology (that usually includes spell checkers and basic grammar checking), as different from (additional) effects on editing, revising, organizing text, and other deep features of writing.

The rapid development of technology will mean that there will always be new gadgets to be trialed in the classroom, ever tempting researchers and educators to

Table 7.1 Summary of studies by learning area

Content area	Effect size	Use of technology	Implementation feature	Education level	Methodological features
Overall	0.35	Support instruction > Deliver content	Not examined	K-12 > Post-secondary	Not examined
Mathematics	0.15–1.02	Constructivist, collaborative learning > Traditional pedagogy	Shorter > longer interventions	Elementary > Secondary	a) Randomized exp. > Quasi-experiment b) Open-ended > closed-ended measure of achievement
Reading	0.16	Integrated > Traditional pedagogy	Training and support > no teacher training/support	Secondary > Elementary	a) Randomized exp. > Quasi-experiment b) Small sample > Large sample
Writing	0.54 (quantity) 0.40 (quality)	Not examined	Not examined	Not examined	Not examined
Second language	1.12	Not examined	Not examined	Not examined	Not examined

conduct yet again another technology/nontechnology study. But we argue that it's time to end technology versus nontechnology studies because (a) it is unlikely that there are students left who do not use ICT (outside the classroom at least), and (b) there is strong evidence, some of which is summarized earlier, showing that what matters more is *how* rather than *whether* technology is used in the classroom. The second aspect has been argued famously by Richard E. Clark (1983), who considered CT to no-CT comparisons meaningless (for learning with media) because it makes little sense to look at a tool/medium without considering how the tool is used, what messages are conveyed, and what the use context is. While we do not want to end on so skeptical a note, it needs to be considered to what extent it continues to make sense to ask the CT versus no-CT question in its most general variant. To us, at least, it seems more appropriate for future meta-analytical work to look at the *differential* effects of different types of technologies, given the vast differences between CT use for communication and collaboration compared to problem solving or media construction, for instance.

References

Archer, K., Savage, R., Sanghera-Sidhu, S., Wood, E., Gottardo, A., & Chen, V. (2014). Examining the effectiveness of technology use in classrooms: A tertiary meta-analysis. *Computers & Education, 78*, 140–149.

Chan, K. K., & Leung, S. W. (2014). Dynamic geometry software improves mathematical achievement: Systematic review and meta-analysis. *Journal of Educational Computing Research, 51*(3), 311–325.

Cheung, A., & Slavin, R. E. (2012). *The effectiveness of educational technology applications for enhancing reading achievement in K-12 classrooms: A meta-analysis*. Baltimore, MD: Johns Hopkins University, Center for Research and Reform in Education, Retrieved from www.bestevidence.org/word/tech_read_Apr_25_2012.pdf

Cheung, A., & Slavin, R. E. (2013). The effectiveness of educational technology applications for enhancing mathematics achievement in K-12 classrooms: A meta-analysis. *Educational Research Review, 9*, 88–113.

Clark, R. E. (1983). Reconsidering research on learning from media. *Review of Educational Research, 53*, 445–449.

Goldberg, A., Russell, M., & Cook, A. (2003). The effect of computers on student writing: A meta-analysis of studies from 1992–2002. *Journal of Technology, Learning, and Assessment, 2*, 3–51.

Higgins, K., D'Angelo, J. H., & Crawford, L. (2017). Effects of technology in mathematics on achievement, motivation, and attitude: A meta-analysis. *Journal of Educational Computing Research*. doi:10.1177/0735633117748416

Li, Q., & Ma, X. (2010). A meta-analysis of the effects of computer technology on school students' mathematics learning. *Educational Psychology Review, 22*(3), 215–243.

Rosen, Y., & Salomon, G. (2007). The differential learning achievements of constructivist technology-intensive learning environments as compared with traditional ones: A meta-analysis. *Journal of Educational Computing Research, 36*, 1–14.

Schmid, R. F., Bernard, R. M., Borokhovski, E., Tamim, R., Abrami, P.C., Anne Wade, C. . . . Lowerison, G. (2009). Technology's effect on achievement in higher education: A stage I meta-analysis of classroom applications. *Journal of Computing in Higher Education, 21*, 95–109.

Slavin, R. E., Cheung, A., Groff, C., & Lake, C. (2008). Effective reading programs for middle and high schools: A best-evidence synthesis. *Reading Research Quarterly, 43*(3), 290–322. https://doi.org/10.1598/RRQ.43.3.4

Slavin, R. E., Lake, C., Chambers, B., Cheung, A., & Davis, S. (2009). Effective reading programs for the elementary grades: A best-evidence synthesis. *Review of Educational Research, 79*(4), 1391–1466. https://doi.org/10.3102/0034654309341374

Tamim, R. M., Bernard, R. M., Borokhovski, E., Abrami, P. C., & Schmid, R. F. (2011). What forty years of research says about the impact of technology on learning: A second-order meta-analysis and validation study. *Review of Educational Research, 81*(1), 4–28.

Torgerson, C., & Zhu, D. (2003). *A systematic review and meta-analysis of the effectiveness of ICT on literacy learning in English, 5-16*. EPPI-Centre, Social Science Research Unit, Institute of Education, University of London.

Zhao, Y. (2003). Recent developments in technology and language learning: A literature review and meta-analysis. *CALICO Journal, 21*(10), 7–27. Retrieved from www.calico.org/html/article_279.pdf

7.10 Study skills

Dale H. Schunk and Carol A. Mullen

Introduction

Tonya and Kim are high school students in the same English class. Their homework is to study three chapters in Charles Dickens's *Great Expectations* for discussion and a quiz the next day. After dinner, each retreats to study. Tonya turns off her cell phone, laptop, and social network web page and assembles her e-reader and class notebook. She flips through her book, estimating about two hours for task completion. She asks herself questions about the text before starting to read, a process that activates prior knowledge about the subject. While highlighting relevant text and jotting points in her tablet, she pauses periodically, asking herself questions to prompt understanding of the content. Visualizing the context ensures better understanding, something she enjoys doing. After an hour, she is more than halfway done and feels confident about her grasp of the material. She takes a short break but finishes early, continuing to ask herself questions about the content. In contrast, Kim does not turn off electronic devices. While watching videos on her laptop, she occasionally highlights text and does not take notes. She text-messages friends and hums along to tunes on her cell phone. After an hour, she is not halfway done but quickly skims the remaining pages. She lacks confidence about doing well on the assigned work and has not generated any questions before, during, or after the reading.

These vignettes illustrate differences in students' approaches to study skills and strategies used to learn information (Crespi & Bieu, 2005). Whereas Tonya effectively applies numerous research-supported skills, Kim – except for some text highlighting – does not. One can surmise that Tonya – the more skillful reader – will perform better in the class, on tests, and in future reading situations.

Research evidence

Study skills are strategies applied to learning and remembering new knowledge and skills (Dembo & Seli, 2016). Not only essential for obtaining good grades, these skills also are useful for lifelong learning (Gettinger & Seibert, 2002). There are different types of study skills: *Cognitive/metacognitive skills* include planning, organizing, rehearsing (e.g., memorizing, underlining), elaborating (e.g., note taking, summarizing), monitoring comprehension, self-questioning, and technological skills (e.g., internet search strategies). *Environmental/contextual skills* involve establishing a productive work environment, managing time, minimizing distractions, and seeking help when needed. *Motivational/affective skills* include setting goals, monitoring goal progress, feeling efficacious about learning, maintaining interest, making desirable attributions (i.e., perceived causes) for outcomes, and maintaining a positive attitude about learning. A *learning strategy* is a collection of skills that students use to attain a goal. Use of study skills is a central feature of *self-regulation*, which refers to self-generated thoughts, feelings, and actions directed toward reaching academic goals (Zimmerman, 1998).

For years, study skills have been emphasized in education, as in the case of the well-known SQ4R (survey-question-read-recite-record-review) method for reading comprehension. Interest in study skills accelerated in the 1980s and continues today. Researchers and practitioners are concerned about which study skills promote learning and how to teach them and encourage their use in real-world situations.

Various outcome measures have been investigated. At a basic level, researchers determine what skills students use by observing them study and analyzing their work samples and questionnaire responses (e.g., Learning and Study Strategies Inventory [LASSI]) (Weinstein, Palmer, & Schulte, 1987). Researchers also compare students' use of study skills to their academic performances to determine how skill use relates to performance and whether some skills are more effective for learning particular content (Purdie & Hattie, 1999).

Reviews of the research generally show that use of study skills relates to better academic performance (Dembo & Seli, 2016). Weinstein and Mayer (1986) found benefits for rehearsing, elaborating, organizing, monitoring comprehension, and maintaining a positive affective climate. Zimmerman (1998) obtained positive effects for cognitive/metacognitive skills, motivational/affective skills (e.g., goal setting, attributions, self-efficacy), and environmental/contextual skills (e.g., help seeking, time management). Purdie and Hattie (1999) found that students who used multiple study skills demonstrated higher performances, as did those who activated skills (e.g., organizing, note taking, elaborating) to process information at a deeper level.

These benefits of study skills to performance are consistent with predictions of cognitive and motivational theories. Information processing theories postulate that learning involves *encoding* or entering new information in the processing system and preparing it for storage (Radvansky & Ashcraft, 2014; Weinstein & Mayer, 1986). Encoding includes selection (attending to relevant information and transferring it to short-term memory), acquisition (transferring information from short- to long-term memory); construction (making connections between information in short-term memory), and integration (creating connections between information in short- and long-term memory). Study skills deal with these processes. Thus, rehearsing (e.g., repeating, underlining) addresses selection and acquisition, and elaborating (e.g., rephrasing, summarizing) involves construction and integration. Monitoring comprehension may address all four processes.

Motivational researchers postulate that students enter learning situations with goals and *self-efficacy* (perceived competence) for attaining them (Schunk, 2012), especially when they understand how to use study skills. While working, they periodically assess their goal progress. Perceptions of progress strengthen self-efficacy and motivation. Learners who attribute their successes to effectively using study skills experience higher self-efficacy and motivation. Motivation may be involved in all mental encoding processes.

Developmental, sociocultural, and individual difference variables can moderate the influence of study skills on academic performances. Children's capabilities of processing information improve with development (Radvansky & Ashcraft, 2014) as they are better able to predict content, sustain attention, encode, link, and retrieve information in memory and monitor their comprehension. Younger children may learn study skills but not know when to use them. This *utilization deficiency* tends to diminish as cognitive capacities develop (Matlin, 2009).

Sociocultural variables such as peers, family members, and socioeconomic status (SES) influence students' use of study skills. Peers and family members are important models for students (Schunk, 2012). Students benefit when their peers value learning and demonstrate good study skills. Also important are family members who model study skills while reading and using technology (e.g., watching educational videos with children). SES includes social status (position, rank) and economic indicators (wealth, education). Higher SES families are more resource enriched with books, technology, games, travel, cultural experiences, and social networks. Greater access to resources and positive models can improve students' use of study skills, whereas lower SES families have fewer resources, some of which are not educational per se (e.g., entertainment on TV). A study of at-home use of electronic devices suggests that "media saturated" youth often use printed texts infrequently and have poor concentration when working with materials of substance and low parental regulation (Rideout, Foehr, & Roberts, 2010).

Individual differences in abilities and learning strategies can affect how well students use study skills. Developmental disabilities can influence how effectively students process information (Matlin, 2009). Learners' preferred learning modalities (e.g., auditory, visual), which vary across cultures (McInerney, 2008), also may affect their motivation and information processing.

Summary and recommendations

Reviews of instructional programs suggest that students can be taught to use study skills and improve their performances beyond information learning of rules or procedures (Dembo & Seli, 2016; Hattie, Biggs, & Purdie, 1996). For low-level learning (e.g., facts, procedures), rehearsal and *mnemonics* (e.g., HOMES for the five Great Lakes) are useful. More complex skills such as summarizing and self-questioning are better when higher-order learning is necessary. Examples involving analysis and synthesis of two or more concepts include constructing maps and writing case reports.

To facilitate the transfer of skills beyond the training setting, it has been recommended that study skills instruction occurs where learning is taking place rather than as a separate process (Hattie et al., 1996). Transfer is enhanced when students learn skills (e.g., metacognitive awareness) in conditions that are conducive to learning and when they have instructional support for using the requisite skills. Students should learn how to establish a productive work environment (Lens & Vansteenkiste, 2008). Pressley, Harris, and Marks (1992) recommended that teachers introduce a few skills at a time, stress the value of study skills, model skills, personalize feedback, individualize teaching, use a distributed practice technique (producing many study sessions short in duration), provide opportunities for transfer, sustain motivation, and encourage reflection and planning.

Other issues involve differentiating instruction and time costs. Students differ in their capacity to self-regulate. Some – especially those with learning problems – may benefit from explicit study skills instruction. Because using study skills takes time, learners who do not notice any learning improvements may feel discouraged. Given the pressures of standardized testing, teachers may not have time to cover study skills. But teaching effective study skills helps students perform better, particularly when integrated with academic content.

References

Crespi, T. D., & Bieu, R. P. (2005). Study skills. In S. W. Lee (Ed.), *Encyclopedia of school psychology* (pp. 539–543). Thousand Oaks, CA: Sage.

Dembo, M. H., & Seli, H. (2016). *Motivation and learning strategies for college success: A focus on self-regulated learning*. New York, NY: Routledge.

Gettinger, M., & Seibert, J. K. (2002). Contributions of study skills to academic competence. *School Psychology Review, 31*, 350–365.

Hattie, J., Biggs, J., & Purdie, N. (1996). Effects of learning skills interventions on student learning: A meta-analysis. *Review of Educational Research, 66*, 99–136.

Lens, W., & Vansteenkiste, M. (2008). Promoting self-regulated learning: A motivational analysis. In D. H. Schunk & B. J. Zimmerman (Eds.), *Motivation and self-regulated learning: Theory, research, and applications* (pp. 141–168). New York, NY: Taylor & Francis.

Matlin, M. W. (2009). *Cognition* (7th ed.). Hoboken, NJ: Wiley.

McInerney, D. M. (2008). The motivational roles of cultural differences and cultural identity in self-regulated learning. In D. H. Schunk & B. J. Zimmerman (Eds.), *Motivation and self-regulated learning: Theory, research, and applications* (pp. 369–400). New York, NY: Taylor & Francis.

Pressley, M., Harris, K. R., & Marks, M. B. (1992). But good strategy instructors are constructivists! *Educational Psychology Review, 4*, 3–31.

Purdie, N., & Hattie, J. (1999). The relationship between study skills and learning outcomes: A meta-analysis. *Australian Journal of Education, 43*, 72–86.

Radvansky, G. A., & Ashcraft, M. H. (2014). *Cognition* (4th ed.). Boston, MA: Pearson Education.

Rideout, V. J., Foehr, U. G., & Roberts, D. F. (2010). *Generation M2: Media in the lives of 8- to 18-year-olds*. Henry J. Kaiser Family Foundation. Retrieved from www.kff.org/other/event/generation-m2-media-in-the-lives-of

Schunk, D. H. (2012). Social cognitive theory. In K. R. Harris, S. Graham, & T. Urdan (Eds.), *APA educational psychology handbook. Vol. 1: Theories, constructs, and critical issues* (pp. 101–123). Washington, DC: American Psychological Association.

Weinstein, C. E., & Mayer, R. E. (1986). The teaching of learning strategies. In M. C. Wittrock (Ed.), *Handbook of research on teaching* (3rd ed., pp. 315–327). New York, NY: Palgrave Macmillan.

Weinstein, C. E., Palmer, D. R., & Schulte, A. C. (1987). *LASSI: Learning and study strategies inventory*. Clearwater, FL: H & H.

Zimmerman, B. J. (1998). Academic studying and the development of personal skill: A self-regulatory perspective. *Educational Psychologist, 33*, 73–86.

7.11 Problem solving

R. Taconis

Introduction

Problem solving is "any goal-directed sequence of cognitive operations" (Anderson, 1980, p. 257). Problems may vary in a multitude of dimensions such as familiarity, complexity, being open or closed, the amount of information available, and the type of cognitive activities required (or useful) to solve the problem (Jonassen, 2000; Taconis, Ferguson-Hessler, & Broekkamp, 2001). Problems may be ill-defined or well-defined. Ill-defined problems may consist of just a rough and incomplete description or may even require that the problem be extracted from a context by the problem solver.

It is important to note that the term *problem* in many cases is relative. A situation may be a problem to one person in the sense that it requires a goal-directed sequence of cognitive operations, but the solution may be immediately apparent to an expert. It strongly depends on the distance between the knowledge, skills, and metacognition required to solve the problem and the problem solver's resources. Moreover, different kinds of problems may require different mental resources (Jonassen, 2000). Solving a problem typically is a complex, demanding, and lengthy process (Sweller & van Merriënboer, 2005), and thus persistent effort may be needed to keep all necessary cognitive resources available and high levels of concentration and confidence. This is particularly so when faced with a large-scale, ill-defined, complex problem, without others providing much cognitive emotional support.

Research evidence

Teaching students adequate cognitive strategies and bringing them to use these in a systematic way in order to solve school problems turn out to be quite difficult. A large number of researchers who have focused on problem solving have a background in cognitive psychology. They usually focus on fundamental and general aspects of problem solving, often employing problems of a general nature. This has led to a range of general theoretical approaches such as the gestalt approach (Duncker), the behaviorist approach (Skinner), the cultural-historical approach (Vygotsky), and cognitive psychological approaches (Simon, Newell). Much attention has been paid to the process of problem solving, its (desired) sequencing, problem solving strategies, and heuristics for solving problems. Besides this, a large group of researchers have investigated problem solving from a domain-bound perspective. Often the way experts solve problems is investigated and compared to the approach taken by novices in order to find ways to facilitate or teach expert-like behavior (Chi, Glaser, & Farr, 1988).

More recently, cognitive research, brain research, artificial intelligence, and computer modeling have contributed insight into problem solving. The cognitive load approach employs aspects of information processing theory and emphasizes the inherent limitations of working memory. Individuals differ in cognitive processing capacity, and instructional designers may need to limit cognitive load as overload makes problems difficult to solve and ineffective for the acquisition of knowledge and understanding (Sweller, 1988).

Cognitive outline: skills base and knowledge base

Obviously, problem-solving activities need to be practiced before the student becomes fluent and makes few errors. Practice both strengthens the structure of the so-called skills base and leads to automation. However, school subjects such as physics, mathematics, and geography are semantically rich domains, meaning that the performance of cognitive strategies strongly depends on the domain knowledge and the understanding of these domains. Therefore, it seems just as necessary to work on the perfection of the knowledge and understanding of the domain as on the problem-solving skills.

Both skills and knowledge range from general to specific. Some may be general (such as reading skills or general knowledge of what determines valid arguments); others may be more generic (such as the need for proof in mathematics or knowledge of science words) or even specific to a small class of problems (such as skills in solving differential equations or knowledge of Einstein's general relativity). Successful problem solving in semantically rich domains requires both skills (the ability to perform) and an adequate knowledge base (knowing what, when, and how) (Taconis et al., 2001). For example, analyzing a problem (skill) can only be performed in a semantically rich domain when one has knowledge of what to look for and what information to discard. Since problem solving implies a complex and prolonged effort involving the coordinated use of a variety of cognitive activities, problem solving also requires strategic knowledge (knowledge of the approaches that could be fruitful in a particular situation), as well as metacognitive (regulative) abilities.

Analyzing the scarce evidence in a quantitative meta-study comparing the actual learning results on science (school) problem solving obtained in a range of empirical studies (1980–1996), Taconis et al. (2001, p. 43) asked the question "Which learning activities contribute to the learning of science problem solving?" They focused on three characteristics of the treatments: (a) the learning tasks and their relation to the task of problem solving (same, akin, different, only a specific part of the problem-solving process), (b) the type of knowledge focused on, and (c) the learning conditions. The problems involved in this study were of varying complexity, from various science domains, and required different types of cognitive activities.

Effects on cognitive factors

Treatments concentrating on problem-solving strategy without giving attention to the knowledge used in the solution tended to have little or no learning effect. When parallel attention was given to the quality of the knowledge base, however, the effect increased. Treatments focusing on the quality of the knowledge base of the subjects were the most effective. This conclusion appears to be valid for school problems of varying complexity, requiring either problem-solving skills or skills in formulation and testing of hypotheses (Taconis et al., 2001). Tasks that strengthen the knowledge base (e.g., help the construction of adequate schemata) contribute to the mastery of problem solving more effectively. Examples of such tasks include eliciting information, removing misconceptions, qualitative analysis, assessing possible solutions, categorizing problems, and concept mapping (Nesbit & Adesope, 2006). Particularly powerful is studying worked examples or explaining worked examples to other students (Sweller, 2006).

Learning conditions

Learning conditions include immediate feedback to the learners and external guidelines on *what to do* and explicit criteria for *what to reach*. Having students work in small groups does not improve problem-solving education unless the group work is combined with other measures that have been shown to be effective, such as attention to schema construction, external guidelines, and immediate feedback. Group work may even show a significantly negative effect, and it may be that collaborative learning is only beneficial for very complex tasks. Among the don'ts of problem-solving education are focusing too much on isolated aspects of problem solving or phases within the problem-solving process and denying guidance, criteria, or feedback to students, particularly in unstructured group work.

Metacognition, self-regulation, and epistemological beliefs

Both aspects of metacognition are clearly important in problem solving: that is, metacognitive knowledge and awareness (e.g., insight into the progress being made, a view of the difficulties ahead related to the resources available, and criteria for an adequate and complete solution) and metacognitive control (the ability to adapt plans if necessary) (Shin, Jonassen, & McGee, 2003). Lesh and Zawojewski (2007) conclude that the way metacognitive skills steer mathematical problem solving, for example, depends on the phase of the problem-solving process. Pajares (1996), however, finds that self-regulation has no direct effect on mathematical problem solving but has an indirect effect through self-efficacy only. Thus, it is important that students have opportunities to experience successes in solving problems, both to learn from and to build up a self-efficacy high enough to energetically and effectively encounter new challenges. In the background of self-regulation, epistemological beliefs are active. For example, inadequate personal beliefs, such as that problem-solving ability in science is a gift and cannot be learned, may hinder the acquisition of problem-solving achievement.

Motivational and emotional factors

Theories on problem solving have not always emphasized the role of motivation (Mayer, 1998 p. 56). Given that problem solving is often a long and demanding process, it may be that interest, motivation, and self-efficacy will be critically important when solving problems.

Task perception, task valuing, and interest

Students learn more meaningfully when they are interested. When they consider a problem as meaningful and worth solving, they will engage more completely/deeply in solving it and can mobilize their cognitive resources more effectively (Jonassen, 2000).

Cultural issues and beliefs

Processes like problem solving are interwoven with various aspects of cultures (Nisbett, Peng, Choi, & Norenzayan, 2001). One's cultural heritage may emphasize particular problem-solving approaches (Guss & Wiley, 2007) that may or may not line up with Western modern science. What if, for instance, the idea of individually isolating a problem in order to subsequently solve it analytically is alien to a student's (indigenous) cultural background? Cultural issues may hinder collaboration in teams or asking for help or may comprise (epistemological) beliefs contrasting with those enclosed in the school problems that are usually embedded in the culture of Western modern science.

Summary and recommendations

Optimizing students' achievement in problem solving should aim at a balanced mix of various factors (Jonassen, 2010). It can be fostered most effectively if the teacher:

- Ensures that there is enough understanding *before* demanding that students solve (difficult) problems, thus fostering self-efficacy and preventing cognitive overload.

- Programs exercises aimed at building an adequate knowledge base, such as concept mapping and studying worked examples.
- Uses problems that are interesting, worthwhile, and manageable in the eyes of the students and that match their individual cognitive resources. Since students differ in their cognitive capacities, styles, and preferences, this points in the direction of an adaptive, individual approach in which the problems are tuned to the actual competence of the students.
- Varies problems (their types and their presentation), which will probably help learning.
- Provides ample social and emotional support, adequate guidelines on what to do, and criteria for the result (what to aim for).
- Gives instructions (and feedback) that focus on knowledge and understanding as well as on the strategies, skills, and self-regulation necessary for problem solving.
- Has a keen eye for individual and cultural differences between students.

Adaptive computer training programs using problems perceived as relevant and manageable by the learner could be a practical approach. It could be the medium for delivering a variety of learning tasks, worked problems, and exercise problems that focus on strengthening the knowledge base and thinking skills. Guidelines and immediate feedback could be implemented to create an adequate learning environment for science problem solving.

References

Anderson, J. R. (1980). *Cognitive psychology and its implications*. New York, NY: Freeman.
Chi, M. T. H., Glaser, R., & Farr, M. J. (Eds.). (1988). *The nature of expertise*. Hillsdale, NJ: Erlbaum.
Guss, C. D., & Wiley, B. (2007). Meta cognition of problem solving strategies in Brazil, India, and the United States. *Journal of Cognition and Culture, 7*, 1–25.
Jonassen, D. H. (2000). Toward a design theory of problem solving. *Educational Technology Research and Development, 48*(4), 63–85.
Jonassen, D. H. (2010). *Learning to solve problems: A handbook for designing problem-solving learning environments*. New York: Routledge.
Lesh, R., & Zawojewski, J. (2007). Problem solving and modeling. In F. K. Lester (Ed.), *Second handbook of research on mathematics teaching and learning* (pp. 763–804). Reston, VA: National Council of Teachers of Mathematics.
Mayer, R. E. (1998). Cognitive, meta-cognitive, and motivational aspects of problem solving. *Instructional Science, 26*, 49–63.
Nesbit, J. C., & Adesope, O. O. (2006). Learning with concept and knowledge maps: A meta-analysis. *Review of Educational Research, 76*, 413–448.
Nisbett, R. E., Peng, K., Choi, I., & Norenzayan, A. (2001). Culture and systems of thought: Holistic versus analytic cognition. *Psychological Review, 108*(2), 291–310.
Pajares, F. (1996). Self-efficacy beliefs and mathematical problem-solving of gifted students. *Contemporary Educational Psychology, 21*, 325–344.

Shin, N., Jonassen, H. D., & McGee, S. (2003). Predictors of well-structured and ill-structured problem solving in an astronomy simulation. *Journal of Research in Science Teaching, 40*(1), 6–33.

Sweller, J. (1988). Cognitive load during problem solving: Effects on learning. *Cognitive Science, 12*, 257–285.

Sweller, J. (2006). The worked example effect and human cognition. *Learning and Instruction, 16*(2), 165–169.

Sweller, J., & van Merriënboer, J. J. G. (2005). Cognitive load theory and complex learning: Recent developments and future directions. *Educational Psychology Review, 17*(2), 147–177.

Taconis, R., Ferguson-Hessler, M. G. M., & Broekkamp, H. (2001). Teaching science problem solving: An overview of experimental work. *Journal of Research in Science Education, 38*, 442–468.

Summary table: influences from teaching strategies

Category	Variable	Considerations
Cognitive/ Motivational	**Metacognitive strategies** represent the skills that students need to be able to control what they do, and to think about their thinking. Metacognitive strategies support students' abilities to understand and control the types of specific strategies that they will use while engaged with various academic tasks.	*Metacognitive strategy usage is very clearly related to academic achievement. Examples of metacognitive strategies include monitoring, planning, self-questioning, and evaluating. Students can be taught metacognitive strategies – teachers should teach and model the strategies, gradually supporting the students' independent use of the strategies.*
	Goal orientations represent the reasons students do what they do in schools.	*Although there are several models of goal orientations, the most typical consists of two goals. There are two types of mastery goals: mastery approach (where the goal is to master a task) and mastery avoid (where the goal is to avoid misunderstanding). There also are two types of performance goals: performance approach (where the goal is to demonstrate one's ability) and performance avoid (where the goal is to avoid appearing less competent than others). Research on relations of both mastery and performance goals to achievement have produced mixed results, although research consistently indicates that performance avoid goals are related to lower achievement.*

(Continued)

Category	Variable	Considerations
	When students **set goals**, they achieve at higher levels.	There are many different kinds of goals that students can set. Goals are more strongly related to achievement when students feel self-efficacious (i.e., confident) about being able to successfully achieve the goal that has been set.
Instructional	**Direct instruction** is a model of teaching that includes a sequenced curriculum that allows for mastery of topics and feedback as students are learning; teachers provide clear, often scripted instruction, and students have opportunities to see worked examples and engage in deliberate practice.	Direct instruction yields achievement gains for both regular and special education students. Its effects may occur because the direct instruction by teachers may reduce the cognitive load that students must devote to tasks that involve more independent discovery- or problem-based learning.
	Reciprocal teaching is a technique that enhances reading comprehension. RT includes four strategies (summarizing, questioning, clarifying, and predicting).	RT is effective when teachers and students engage in dialogue throughout the process. Students take on greater responsibility for the dialogues over time.
	Cooperative learning (CL) is a strategy in which students work in small groups and share responsibility for group success.	There are several approaches to CL. (CL is not simply putting students into groups to work together). Competitive and individualistic lessons can be enjoyable, but CL consistently enhances achievement.
	Peer tutoring (PT) is a strategy in which peers assume the roles of tutor and tutee and use specific procedures to interact with each other.	PT leads to achievement gains, partially because students learn material at a deeper level when they are asked to actually teach the material to someone else (e.g., to a peer). When using PT, it is important to carefully consider students' roles, establish trust between partners, and align tutoring with curriculum.
	Students can be taught **problem-solving** strategies.	There are many different types of problems (e.g., ill defined vs. well defined). To facilitate students' abilities to solve problems, teachers should (a) ensure that students have adequate background knowledge and understanding before attempting problems, (b) use problems that are meaningful and interesting, (c) vary the types of problems that students solve, (d) provide support and instruction while students are solving problems, and (e) be aware of individual and cultural differences among students.

(Continued)

Category	Variable	Considerations
	Problem-based learning occurs when small groups of students, guided by a tutor, engage with authentic problems.	Research has been primarily in health-related fields. Research to date suggests that PBL may be effective for the learning of clinical skills, whereas more traditional techniques are more effective for learning basic science knowledge.
	Feedback reduces discrepancies between a student's current understanding/performance and the desired performance.	Not all types of feedback are effective. In order to positively affect achievement, feedback should be specific, should offer suggestions for improvement (e.g., other strategies that a student can use), and should support students' use of appropriate self-regulatory strategies. Feedback also must be carefully aligned with the students' goals and the goals for a particular lesson.
	Individualized instruction (II) occurs when instruction is personalized for each student.	To be effective, teachers need to be trained in providing II. Effects are small but positive. II may be particularly useful with culturally and linguistically diverse students. Educators are reluctant to utilize individualized instruction in an era of high-stakes testing.
	Worked examples (i.e., learning from examples) involve providing step-by-step instructions for the procedures needed to solve a problem or complete a task.	Worked examples are particularly effective during the early stages of learning new material. As students become more proficient, they can transition into more independent problem solving. Worked examples enhance achievement because they reduce the cognitive load (i.e., the amount of mental effort) required for the problem; thus, students can focus specifically on the actual problem.
	Students learn more effectively when they are given multiple opportunities to **practice** newly learned material over time.	Students should be given opportunities to practice and review content over time; presentation of material only once does not lead to effective learning. Students should be encouraged to reread materials from a textbook multiple times.
	Achievement is enhanced when teachers **ask questions** related to class content.	Deep questions (i.e., questions that encourage students to both recall and use information) are more effective than shallow questions (e.g., simple yes/no or basic recall questions).
	Teacher immediacy is an instructional style wherein the teacher focuses on effective nonverbal communication with students.	Examples of aspects of behaviors that can be changed to increase immediacy include (a) increased eye contact, (b) reducing physical distance, (c) smiling, (d) vocal variation, and (e) relaxed posture.

(Continued)

Category	Variable	Considerations
	Time on task refers to the amount of time that students spend engaged with an academic task.	*In general, when students are able to spend greater amounts of time on a task, learning is improved. However, teachers must consider how the time is spent (e.g., if the student is struggling with the task and does not receive support, learning will not occur) and the fact that the amount of time that a student needs with a particular task may vary dramatically across students.*
	Students achieve at higher levels when they utilize appropriate **study skills** (also known as **study strategies**).	*Students can be taught to use effective study skills. Skills/strategies that may be effective for learning facts and procedures might include rehearsal strategies and the use of mnemonics; skills for learning more complex skills might include summarizing and self-questioning. Study skills should ideally be taught as part of classroom content, rather than as a separate topic.*
	Matching instruction to a student's preferred **learning style does not improve achievement**.	*Despite its widespread appeal and popularity, there is virtually no empirical evidence supporting the idea of matching instructional techniques to students' preferred learning styles (e.g., auditory, visual, kinesthetic).*
	Home schooling occurs when students are taught at home, usually by a parent or guardian.	*On average, students who are home-schooled perform as well or better than students who attend traditional schools. This may be due to the fact that (a) they receive much individualized attention, (b) parents are more involved in all aspects of their children's education, and (c) parents who choose to home-school their children tend to be more educated than other parents.*
	Reading achievement can be improved for **students with learning disabilities** when **evidence-based programs** are used.	*Programs that include both strategy and direct instruction tend to improve reading comprehension; programs that use direct instruction tend to improve word recognition.*
Technological	**Simulations** are a form of computer-based instruction that provide virtual environments that allow for the application of knowledge in realistic conditions.	*Simulations have larger effects on achievement when teachers serve as facilitators (i.e., teachers don't simply allow students to work independently) and when teachers are confident in the use of the needed technology.*

(Continued)

Category	Variable	Considerations
	Multimedia learning involves learning with both words and pictures, often via computer technology.	Effective multimedia instructional materials (a) limit words and pictures to those that are the most essential, (b) provide cues indicating the essential content, (c) place corresponding words close to related graphics on the screen, (d) are presented in segments, and (e) are presented in a conversational style.
	Overall, the use of **technology** has a small but positive effect on achievement, but technology must be used in specific ways.	Technology is more effective when it is used to support, rather than to provide, instruction.

Note: This table summarizes information presented by authors who contributed chapters to section 8 of the first edition of The International Guide to Student Achievement, as well as to revised chapters included in the present chapter.

Additional references

Dent, A. L., & Koenka, A. C. (2016). The relation between self-regulated learning and academic achievement across childhood and adolescence: A meta-analysis. *Educational Psychology Review, 28*(3), 425–474. https://doi-org.proxy.lib.ohio-state.edu/10.1007/s10648-015-9320-8

Ergen, B., & Kanadli, S. (2017). The effect of self-regulated learning strategies on academic achievement: A meta-analysis study. *Eurasian Journal of Educational Research (EJER)*, (69), 55–74. https://doi.org/10.14689/ejer.2017.69.4

Pressley, M., & Harris, K. R. (2008). Cognitive strategies instruction: From basic research to classroom instruction. *Journal of Education, 189*(1–2), 77–94.

Richardson, M., Abraham, C., & Bond, R. (2012). Psychological correlates of university students' academic performance: A systematic review and meta-analysis. *Psychological Bulletin, 138*(2), 353–387.

Index

Note: **Boldface** page references indicate tables. *Italic* references indicate figures.

Abbott, R. D. 224
Abbott, S. P. 224
Abedi, J. 129
Aber, J. L. 69
ability beliefs 107
ability grouping 79–83, 120, **185**
academic achievement 2; *see also* achievement
academic motivation *see* motivation
academic self-concept 9–10, **46**
academic tasks and classroom context 118–119
achievement: attainment of knowledge and 3; defining 2–3; emotion in classroom and 145–148; ethnicity and 8; gap 27, 30–31n1, 93; home influences on 4, 51–52; improvement in knowledge and 3; influences on 3–4; measures of 3; overview 1–2, 4; pedagogical content knowledge and 141–142; prior 10, **47**; school transitions and 104–105; valuing 2; *see also specific influence*
Achilles, C.M. 88
active processing principle 293
Adams, G. 278
affective goals 2–3
Akerhielm, K. 87
Albanese, M. A. 270–271
Alexander, C. 99, 102
Alfieri, L. 280
Allan, A. 15
Allen, M. 265
Allen, R. 175
Allnutt, J. 175
alternate route (AR) teachers' field experiences 178
alternatively certified (AC)/licensure programs 120, 177, **186**

alternative teacher training 173–179
Alter, P. J. 21–22
Anderman, E.M. 9, 105, 241, 286
Anderson, J. F. 264
animation of pump workings 291, *292*
anxiety 145–146
Applebee, A. N. 233
Appleton, J. J. 219
Archer, K. 306
architectural design of schools 100–101
Arellano, B. 219
Asian students 122–123
attitudes: student 6, 9–10, **44–46**; teacher 116–117, **181**
authoritative style of parenting 53, 57, 68, **72**
autonomy, student 119, 168–169, **183**

Bagley, W. C. 160
Baker, K. 205
Ball, D. L. 141
Barrett, P. 100
Barrows, H. S. 270
Baumert, J. 142
Beaubien, J. M. 287
Bedouin schools 26
behavioral engagement 10, **45**
behavioral involvement 58
behaviors: parents' 53–54, 57–58, **72–73**; students' 160
behaviors; *see also* classrooms, management of
beliefs: ability 107; competence 53, 57, **72**; education 53, **72**; efficacy 117; epistemological 117, **181**, 317–318; expectancy 167–168;

Index

mind-set 42, 169–170; parents' 52–53, 56–57, **72**; problem solving and 318
Ben-Peretz, M. 163
Bereiter, C. 223
Berkson, L. 272
Berninger, V. W. 224
between-class ability grouping 78, 83, 106, **113**
Bidjerano, T. 35
Big-Fish-Little-Pond effect 11, **48**
Big Five theory of personality 33, 36
bilingual education programs 203–207
bilingual teachers 175
Binici, S. 233
Black, A. E. 168
Black, P. 128–129
Blackwell, L. S. 169–170
Blaga, M. 289
Blake, R. L. 271
Blatchford, P. 89
Bloom's taxonomy 260
Boer, H. D. 161
Borko, H. 140
Borman, G. D. 279
Bottoms, G. 178
Boyd, D. 177
Boyd-Zaharias, J. 88
Bradshaw, Catherine 75
Breed, F. 160
Brekelmans, M. 155
Brewer, D. 176
Brewer, D. J. 88
Brinkman, B. A. 174
Brookhart, S. M. 130
Brophy, J. 161, 287–288
Brown, A. 253, 297
Brown, J. L. 69
Brown, S. D. 41
Buijs, G. J. 240
Buisonje, C. D. 270–271
Burns, M. K. 219

Cahen, L. S. 88
calculators 193, **246**
career and technical education (CTE) 178
caregivers *see* parents
Carver-Thomas, D. 173
Casper, T. P. 233
causal mechanisms 82–83, 298–300
Chamorro-Premuzic, T. 34, 36
change, conceptual 10, **46**
Chapman, S. 259
charter schools 77, **110**
Charters, W. W. 127
Cheema, J. R. 196

Cheung, A. 205, 305–306
Chiari, G. 163
Chinese medical education 274
Chung, H. Q. 129
clarifying strategy 299
classic goal orientation 285
classroom-based intervention programs 256
classrooms: collaboration in 132–136, **185**; context of 117–120, **182–185**; cultural diversity in 155; emotion in 145–150; management of 22, 160–164; person-centered 161; questioning by teacher and 261–262; size of 86–89, **111**; social relationships in 118; teacher-centered 161; traditional 161; *see also* teacher/classroom influences
"closing the gaps" policy 27, 30–31n1
coaching **112**, 199
co-construction of knowledge 133
cognitive abilities 224, 316–317
cognitive capacity 42
cognitive development 10, 42, **47**, 105, 133
cognitive differences 61; *see also* learning difficulties
cognitive elaboration perspective 133
cognitive goals 2–3
cognitive influences 10, **46–47**
cognitive involvement 58
cognitively guided instruction (CGI) 198
cognitive/metacognitive skills 311
cognitive/motivational strategies 250–251, **320–321**
cognitive referents 42–43
cognitive theory of multimedia learning 292–293
Cohen, H. L. 67
coherence principle 293
Coleman Report 92–94
collaboration in classroom 132–136, **185**
Collier, V. 204
Colliver, J. A. 270–272
colored lights 102
Comenius, John Amos 291
Commeyras, M. 233
communication behaviors, teachers' 264–268
competence in writing 224
computer technology (CT) 303, **324**; *see also* technology-supported learning
conceptual change 10, **44**, 46
conflict 134–135
Connell, M. L. 162
conscientiousness 34–35
Consistency Management & Cooperative Discipline® (CMCD) 162–163

consulting **112**
content-based curricula 211
content knowledge 140
content knowledge for teaching mathematics (CKT-M) 141–142
context of classroom 117–120, **182–185**
contextual knowledge 140
contextual learning 197
Cook, A. 306
cooperative learning (CL) 133–134, 178, **321**
Cooper, H. 121–122
Corcoran, J. 240
Cornelius-White, J. 28, 161
Craig, S. D. 261
Crawford, L. 305
creativity 161, **182**, 192, **243**, 259, 306–307
Creemers, B. 163
Crow Island School 101
cueing principle 293
cultural factors and motivation 42
cultural issues and problems solving 318
curriculum influences: achievement and 4, 189, 191–192; bilingual education programs 203–207; content-based 211; discussion in reading comprehension 231–236, **245**; entries from previous edition 189–191; general/overarching 191–192, **243–247**; genre-based 212; handwriting 225; health education, adolescent 238–241, **246**; language 192–193, 210–214, **244–245**; mathematics 193–200, **246**; Multitiered Systems of Support 216–220, **244**; overview 189–194; response to intervention 216–220, **244**; science 193–194, **246**; spelling 225; summary table **243–246**; writing instruction 222–228, **245**

Dai, D. Y. 35
D'Angelo, J. H. 305
Darling-Hammond, L. 173, 176
Darling, N. 68
Davey, B. 261
Deci, E. L. 168
DeGroff, L. 233
de Jong, P. F. 225
de Kanter, A. A. 205
deliberate practice theory 141
demographics 8–9, **44**
Dempster, N. 28
den Brok, P. 155
DeNisi, A. 128
De Piccoli, N. 98
designing schools 98–102, **111**
Dewey, J. 197
Dexter, D. D. 218

dialogue 299–301
Ding, X. 274
direct instruction (DI) 277–282, **321**
Disabilities Education Improvement Act (IDEIA) 216–217
discipline 23, **47**, 160, 162–164; *see also* classrooms, management of
discrete emotions 146
discussion in reading comprehension 231–236, **245**
Dochy, F. 271–273
Dollinger, S. J. 36
Dolmans, H. J. M. 274
Donovan, J. J. 279
Doolard, S. 161
Dornbusch, S. M. 68
Driscoll, D. 261
dual channels principle 292–293
Duckworth, A. L. 36
Dutch Educational Priority Policy 163
Dweck, C. S. 169–170, 287
dynamic geometry software (DGS) 305
dynamics of teacher-child interactions 154–156
dynamic systems theory 155

Eccles, J. S. 167
ecological studies 161
educational outcomes 13, 16; *see also* achievement
Effective Teaching Profile (ETP) 29
efficacy 167–168
efficacy beliefs 117
efficacy of teachers **181**
Egelsto, P. 178
Eilam, B. 163
Elementary and Secondary Education Act (2015) 16
Elliot, A. 286
embodiment principle 294
emotion 145–150, 318
encoding 311
engagement of students 21–23, 28, **45**; *see also* discussion in reading comprehension
Engelmann, S. 278
England 163, 175
English/language arts (ELA) 177
English language learners (ELLs) 210–214, **245**
English as a second language (ESL) 210–214, 307, **308**
enthusiasm 117, **182**, **189**, 267
environmental/contextual skills 311
environment of home 55–59
epistemological beliefs 117, **181**, 317–318
Epstein, J. L. 67

Index

Equality of Educational Opportunity (Coleman Report) 92–94
essential processing 293
ethnicity 8–9, 26–30, 196
Evans, B. R. 178
Evans, P. 281
Eveleigh, E. 22
Every Student Succeeds Act (ESSA) (2015) 66, 216–218
expectancy beliefs 167–168
extraneous processing 293
extrinsic motivation 42
extrinsic rewards 94

faith-based schools 77, **110**
family structure **73**
Fan, H. 122–123
Fantuzzo, J. 67
Fan, W. 69
feedback: for students 41, **45–46**, 119, 126, 128–129, 168, 170, **185**, 226, **243–244**, 251, 256–257, 277–278, 282, 301, 313, 317, 319, **321–322**; for teachers 178, 240, 306
female academic success 15–17
female academic success, questions about 15–17
female underestimation 16–17
Fernandes, M. 128
Filby, N. N. 88
Fillespie, A. 225
financing schools 92–96, **111**
Finn, J. D. 88
Fiorell, L. 293–294
Firetto, C. M. 233
Fiske, E. B. 100
fixed mind-sets 42, 169
Flavell, John 253
Fontana, D. 128
formative assessment (FA): achievement and 126–130; description of 119; key elements of 127; overview 129–130; research evidence and 127–129; teacher/classroom influences and 126–130, **185**
Forness, S. R. 279
Foucault, M. 27
Fox-Turnbull, W. 129
Franklin, C. 240
Freeman, J. 23
Freiberg, H. J. 162, 164
French Ministry of Education 175
friendships, students' 11, **48**
Frymier, A. B. 265
Fuchs, D. 128
Fuchs, L. S. 128
Fuller, B. 87

Furnham, A. 34, 36
Furtak, E. M. 129

Gallup Organization 160
Galluzzo, G. 196
Galvao, T. F. 274
Gamoran, A. 233
Gavin, L. E. 239
gender: inequity in girls' schooling 13; influences/differences 12–18, **44**, 196; sex versus 12
gender gaps in student achievement 13
generative processing 293
genetic influences 56, **73**
genre-based language instruction 212
Gerber, S. B. 88
Gibb, S. J. 14
Gijbels, D. 271, 273
Gill, B. P. 88
Gilraine, M. 87
Ginns, P. 293–294
Glass, G. V. 86, 88
goal orientation 285–289, **320**
goals: cognitive 2–3; learning 2–3, 40; motivation and 41; psychomotor 2–3; setting 285, **321**; social 6, **48**
Goetz, T. 146
Goldberg, A. 306
Goldhaber, D. B. 176
Goldman, Z. W. 265–266
Gonzalez-DeHass, A. 66, 69
Goodboy, A. K. 265–266
Gottfried, A. E. 67
Gottfried, A. W. 67
GPA predictors 34–35
grade retention **113**
Graesser, A. C. 260
Graham, S. 224–225
Grant, H. 287
Greenberg, E. 176
Greene, J. P. 205
Grolnick, W. S. 66, 68, 168–169
Gröschner, A. 139
Grossman, P. 177
group functioning 133–134
growth mind-sets 42, 119–120, 169–170, **182–183**, 279
guided participation *see* scaffolding
guided practice 255, 277–278, 281, 300
Guilford, J. B. 233
Guskey, T. R. 2–3

Haas, M. 279
Haertel, G. D. 161
Hampton, V. 67

hands-on activities 191, **243**
handwriting 225
Harms, T. 161
Harris, K. R. 225, 313
Harwood, P. 16
Hashweh, M. Z. 140
Hattie, J. 28, 56, 277–278, 280, 311
health education, adolescent 238–241, **246**
Hembree, R. 146
Hennessey, M. N. 233
heterogeneous-ability grouping 78, 80–82, **113**
Higgins, K. 305
high-achieving mathematics programs 197–199
high-stakes accountability **185**
high-stakes assessment/testing 118–119, 181, **185**, 196
Hill, H. C. 141
Hill, N. E. 66–68
Hirn, R. G. 21–22
Hoglund, W. L. 69
Holbein, M. 66
home environment 55–59, **184**
home influences: achievement and 4, 51–52; entries from previous edition 52; environment of home 55–59; family structure **73**; genetics 56, **73**; maternal employment 54, **73**; overview 51–54; parent behaviors 53–54, 57–58, **72–73**; parent beliefs 52–53, 56–57, **72**; parent involvement 58, 66–70, **72**; parent social background 55–56; socioeconomic status 54, 61–63, **73**; structural 54, **73**; summary table **72–73**; television viewing 52, 54, **73**
home schooling 67, 69, **323**
home-school partnership model 67
homework assignments 119, 121–124
homogeneous-ability grouping 79–81, 83, **113**
Howe, James 231
Huang, B. 274
Huber, J. L. 36
Hughes, C. A. 218
Hulleman, C. S. 286–287
Hu, S. 67
Huzinec, C. 162
Hyde, J. S. 15

Iacono, W. G. 56
Ilies, R. 34
incentives, performance 94–95
inclusive education **111**
indigenous students 26–30, **44**
Individualized instruction (II) 83, 86, **322**
instructional context 83, **182**
instructional practices of teachers as influences 77–78, **112–113**, 136, **181–186**; *see also specific practice*

instructional strategies 251, **321–323**; *see also specific strategy*
interest and problem solving 318
interpersonal processes, debilitating 133–134
inter-thinking 235
intrinsic motivation 42
intrinsic rewards 94
I-R-E (initiates-responds-evaluates) pattern of classroom discourse 232–233
Ishikawa, S. 99, 102

Jacklin, C. N. 12
Jerusalem Schools Authority (Israel) 175
Jeynes, W. H. 58, 66–67
Johnson, W. 56
Jones, S. M. 69
Joseph, L. M. 22
Judge, T. A. 34
Jungert, T. 70
Junior Great Books discussion program 233

Kalyuga, S. 294
Kane, T. J. 177–178
Kappe, R. 36
Katz, Y. J. 163
Kim, J. H. 274
King, A. 261
Kiuhara, S. 225
Kluger, A. N. 128
knowledge: achievement and attainment of 3; acquisition of 98, 99; base 316–317; co-construction of 133; content 140; contextual 140; improvement in 3; pedagogical 140; pedagogical content 118, 139–143, **186**; telling 223
knowledge-transforming strategies 223
Kok, G. 240
Kong, L.-N. 274
Konrad, M. 22
Konstantopoulos, S. 87
Korpershoek, H. 161
Koster, M. 225
Krajcik, J. 140
Krenn, H. Y. 67
Krop, C. 88
Kuijk, M. v. 161
Kulkarni, A. 239

L2 students 210–214, 307, **308**
Lackney, J. A. 99
Lamborn, S. D. 68
Langer, J. A. 233
language: bilingual education programs 203–207; content-based instruction 211; curricula 192–193, 210–214, **244–245**;

329

genre-based curricular models and 212; second 210–214, 307, **308**; spoken at home 155; subject-matter instruction 211–212; technology-supported learning and 307, **308**
Lankford, H. 177
Lapointe, J. M. 164
Leahy, S. 129
learning: cognitive theories of 40; conditions 317; contextual 197; cooperative 133–134, 178, **321**; difficulties 20–24, **47**; goals 2–3, 40; mathematics 197; multimedia 291–295, **324**; outcomes 13; strategy 311; style 312, **323**; technology-supported 251–252, 303–308, **323–324**
Learning Policy Institute 179
Leary, H. 271, 273
Lee, H. 129
Lent, R. W. 41
Lesh, R. 317–318
Levy, J. 155
Lewis, R. 163
Li, D. 102
limited capacity principle 293
Li, Q. 304
literacy 224
load-reduction instruction (LRI) 281
local-area network (LAN), classroom-based 303
Loeb, S. 177
London Challenge schools 163
Longitudinal Study of Australian Children 51
Lorentz, J. 162
low academic success **47**

Macartney, H. 87
Maccoby, E. 12
MacSuga-Gage, A. S. 22
Madelaine, A. 280
Magnusson, S. 140
mainstreaming 21, **111**
male underachievement 14
Māori students 26, 28–29, 30–31n1
Marks, M. B. 313
Martin, A. J. 281
Martin, Andrew 52
Maslow, Abraham 40
mastery orientation 285–286
maternal employment 54, **73**
mathematics: achievement in 195–200, **246**, 304; cognitively guided instruction program and 198; content knowledge for teaching 141–142; curriculum influences 193–194, **246**; gender differences in 15, 196; high-achieving programs 197–199; learning 197; practice 198–199; predictors of achievement in 195–196; scores 174–175; technology-supported learning and 304–305, **308**
Matyja, A. M. 36
Ma, X. 67, 146, 304
Maxwell, L. E. 100
Mayer, R. E. 293–294, 311
McBride, S. 261
McCann, C. 36
McGrath, K. F. 154
McGue, M. 56
McIlveen, P. 37
McKeown, D. 225
McMaster University 270
McMillan, R. 87
McMullen, F. 280
McWayne, C. 67
mediating factors in emotion in classroom 147
medical education 271–274
Meek, A. 101
Mehrabian, Albert 264
Meister, C. 259, 298
Mellanby, A. R. 239
mental spatial rotation 13
mentoring 41, **112**, 177
Mercer, N. 235
metacognition 300, 317–318
metacognitive strategies 253–257, 300, **320**
middle school transitions 104–108, **111**, 184
Middleton, M. J. 156
Midgley, C. 156
mind-set beliefs, students' 42, 169–170
minoritized students 26–30, **44**
Mississippi Subject Area Test (MSAT) 174
Mitchell, S. 270–271
mixed-ability grouping 80
mixed-grade classrooms **110**
mnemonics 313
Mockler, N. 177
modality principle 294
moderators of emotion in classroom 147–148
Moore, E. E. 174
Morganfield, B. 155
motivation: classroom context and 119; cultural factors and 42; extrinsic 42; goals and 41; intervention for promoting 41–42; intrinsic 42; mind-set beliefs and 42; problem solving and 318; student 6, 40–43, **45**, 105, 117, 166–171, 312; teachers' 117, **181**
motivational/affective skills 311
Mueller, C. M. 175
Mueller, T. E. 239
multimedia learning 291–295, **324**

330

multimedia principle 291
Multitiered Systems of Support (MTSS) **112**, 192, 216–220, **244**
Multon, K. D. 41
Murayama, K. 286
Murphy, P. K. 233

National Assessment of Educational Progress (NAEP) 176
National Board of Medical Examiners (NBME) 272
National Center for Educational Evaluation and Regional Assistance 219
National Center for Educational Statistics 210
National Education Longitudinal Study (NELS) 87, 176
National Institute for Direct Instruction (NIFDI) 278
National Network of Partnership Schools (NNPS) 69
National Reading Panel 256
Nation, M. 239
Navajo reservation schools 26
Netherlands medical education 273
Newberry, M. 156–157
Newcombe, R. G. 239
New York City Teaching Fellows program 178
No Child Left Behind Act 216
Noftle, E. E. 34
Nokes-Malach, T. J. 279
nontraditional teacher preparation 173–179
nonverbal immediacy 266–268
nonverbal messages 266
normative goal orientation 285
North Carolina's state education policies 175
Nystrand, Martin 231, 233

Obama, Barack 216
O'Connor, M. C. 34
office discipline referrals (ODRs) 23
Oliver, M. E. 37
Opuni, K. A. 162
oral language abilities 224
Orbis Pictus 291–292
Organisation for Economic Co-operation and Development (OECD) studies/reports 16, 216
outdoor education 192, **243**

Pajares, F. 318
Palincsar, A. S. 297
parents: authoritative 53, 57, 68, **72**; behaviors 53–54, 57–58, **72–73**; beliefs 52–53, 56–57, **72**; competence beliefs 53, 57, **72**; education beliefs 53, **72**; involvement of 58, 66–70, **72**; maternal employment 54, **73**; social background 55–56; socioeconomic status of 54, 61–63; *see also* home influences
Park, D. 170
Paulussen, T. G. W. M. 240
Paunonen, S. V. 34
Payne, S. C. 287
pedagogical content knowledge (PCK) 118, 139–143, **186**
pedagogical knowledge 140
peer interactions 118, 132–133, **184**
peer tutoring (PT) **321**
Pekrun, R. 41, 147–148, 286
Pennings, H. J. M. 155
Perera, H. N. 37
performance incentives 94–95
performance orientation 287–288
Perin, D. 225
Perry, A. 160
personal involvement 58
personality 33–37, **44**
personalization principle 294
person-centered classroom management 161
Person, N. 260
Peters, L. W. H. 240
Phi Delta Kappan 160
phonics instruction 193, **244**
physical activity **48**
Piaget, J. 10, 133
Pilegard, C. 294
Pintrich, P. R. 35
planning process in designing schools 100
Pomerantz, S. 15–16
positive behavior supports and interventions (PBIS) 23–24
Postmes, T. 289
postsecondary education 3, **48**, 304
practice, student 20, **44**, 126, 128–129, 198–199, 224, **245–246**, 256, 277–279, 281–282, 300–301, 304, 316, **321–322**
predicting strategy 299
preschool experience **47**
Pressley, M. 313
preterm infants **44**
pretraining principle 294
prior achievement 10, **47**
problem-based learning (PBL) 270–275, **322**
problem solving 315–319, **321**
process approach to writing instruction 226–227
process-outcome (product) studies 161
Program for International Student Assessment (PISA) 14–15, 80, 254

Progress in International Reading Literacy
   Study (PIRLS) 80
progress, perceptions of 41
Prokosch, N. 162
prosocial programs 162
PsychINFO search 145
psychomotor goals 2–3
Purdue, N. 311

questioning strategy 259–262, 299
Qui, X. 163

Raby, R. 15–16
Radosevich, D. J. 279
Ramírez, D. J. 204
Rashedi, R. 129
reading achievement and technology-supported
   learning 305–306, **308**
reading comprehension 231–236, **245**
reciprocal teaching (RT) 297–301, **321**
redundancy principle 293
Rees, J. 239
reform, school 161–162
regrouping 80
Reichardt, R. 88
relationship development phases 156
relationship between student and teacher
   153–157, **183**
relevance of emotion in classroom 148
Renold, E. 15
repeated reading 193, **244**
response to intervention (RTI) **112**, 192,
   216–220, **244**
Rhodes, D. 176
Richey, J. E. 279
Roberts, R. D. 36
Robins, R. W. 34
Roderiguez, M. 155
Rogers, Carl 40
Rollero, C. 98
Rolstad, K. 205
Romi, S. 163
Ronevich, P. 279
Roorda, D. L. 154
Rosenshine, B. 259, 298
Rosen, Y. 307
Rossell, C. H. 205
Rowan, B. 141
Ruiz de Castilla, V. 175
Ruiz-Primo, M. A. 129
Russell, M. 306
Ryan, R. M. 168–169

Salomon, G. 307
Sanche, T. 219

Sandberg, Sheryl 17
Sanders, M. G. 69
Sass, H. 178
Sass, T. R. 177
scaffolding 126, 133, 225–226, 271,
   281, 300
Scardamalia, M. 223
Schabmann, A. 100
Schmidt, H. G. 273
Schoenfeld, A. 196
school-based mental health **111**
School Design and Planning Laboratory 98
school influences: ability grouping 79–83, 120,
   185; achievement and 4, 75; class size 86–89,
   111; entries from previous edition 75–76;
   financing schools 92–96, **111**; instructional
   practices of teachers 77–78, **112–113**; layout/
   design of schools 98–102, **111**; middle school
   transitions 104–108, **111**; organizational
   features of school 77, **110–111**; overview
   75–78; services provided by school 78,
   111–112; summary table **110–113**
schooling outcomes see achievement;
   educational outcomes
schools: architectural design of 100–101; charter
   77, **110**; class size in 86–89, **111**; daylight/
   views in 101; environments, best 105–106,
   162; faith-based 77, **110**; financing 92–96,
   111; hard-to-staff 173; instructional practices
   of 78, **112–113**; layout/design of 98–102, **111**;
   learning difficulties and 23–24; movement/
   circulation in 101; organizational features
   of 77, **110–111**; parental involvement and
   57–58; reform 161–162; services provided
   by 78, **111–112**; single-sex **110**; transitions to
   104–108, **184**
School-Wide Positive Behavior Interventions
   and Supports (SWPBIS) 23, **112**
Schunk, D. 128–129
science curriculum 193–194, **246**
Scott, T. M. 21–22
Scriven, M. 126–127
Segers, M. 271
segmenting principle 294
Seidel, T. 139
Sekino, Y. 67
self-concept, student's academic 9–10, **46**
self-determination theory 265
self-efficacy, student 9, 41, **46**, 119, 167–168, 312
self-evaluation 128
self-image, student 15–16
self-regulation 35, 311, 317–318
Senk, S. 197
serotonin 102
service learning **112**

setting practice 80–81
sex versus gender 12
Shavelson, R. J. 139
sheltered instruction observation protocol (SIOP) 211
Shen, J. 67
Shen, T. 87
Shepard, L. 196
Shin, I. S. 274
Shulman, L. S. 139–140
signaling principle 293
Silverstein, M. 99, 102
Simonsen, B. 22
single-sex schools **110**
Sirin, S. R. 55
skills base 316–317
Skinnerian research 161
Slavin, R. E. 81, 205, 305–306
Slowiaczek, M. L. 66, 68
Smith, M. L. 86, 88
Smits, P. B. A. 270–272
social goals 6, **48**
social influences 6, 11, **47–48**
social interactions, expert-led 300
social relationships and classroom context 118
social skills, teaching 133, 192, **243**, 280
socioeconomic background (SEB) 79–81
socioeconomic status (SES) 54, 61–63, **73**, 142, 312
socioemotional learning (SEL) 78, **113**, 164
Somers, C. L. 239
Sommer, R. 99
Soter, A. O. 233
spatial contiguity principle 293
Spearman, C. F. 178
special education **111–112**, 128, 173, 216, 218–219, 279–280, 297–298, **321**
spelling 225
SQ4R (survey-question-read-recite-record-review) 311
stage-environment fit problem 105
Stancavage, F. 176
Stehouwer, J. D. 219
Steinberg, L. 68
Stein, T. 162
STEM (science, technology, engineering, math) 14–15, 193; *see also* mathematics
Stipek, D. J. 196
strategy-focused approach to writing instruction 226–228
streaming 79–80
structural influences 54, **73**
student achievement *see* achievement
student-centered classroom management 163
student influences: academic self-concept 9–10, **46**; achievement and 4, 6; attitudes/dispositions 6, 9–10, **44–46**; cognitive 10, **46–47**; defining 6; demographics 8–9, **44**; entries from previous edition 7–8; ethnicity 26–30; gender 12–18, **44**; indigenous/minoritized students 26–30, **44**; learning difficulties 20–24, **47**; motivation 6, 40–43, **45**, 117, 166–171, 312; overview 6–11; personality 33–37, **44**; social 6, 11, **47–48**; summary table **44–48**
student outcomes 28; *see also* achievement
students: ability beliefs of 107; academic self-concept of 9–10, **46**; Asian 122–123; attitudes of 6, 9–10, **44–46**; autonomy of 119, 168–169, **183**; behavior of 160; engagement of 21–23, 28, **45**; expectancy beliefs of 167–168; feedback for 41, **45–46**, 119, 126, 128–129, 168, 170, **185**, 226, **243–244**, 251, 256–257, 277–278, 282, 301, 313, 317, 319, **321–322**; friendships of 11, **48**; indigenous 26–30, **44**; L2 210–214, 307, **308**; learning difficulties of 21; low academic success of **47**; mind-set beliefs of 42, 169–170; minoritized 26–30, **44**; motivation of 6, 40–43, **45**, 105, 117, 166–171; peer interactions and 118, 132–133, **184**; physical activity of **48**; practice for 20, **44**, 126, 128–129, 198–199, 224, **245–246**, 256, 277–279, 281–282, 300–301, 304, 316, **321–322**; preschool experience of **47**; progress and, perception of 41; relationships between teachers and 153–157, **183**; self-efficacy of 9, 41, **46**, 119, 167–168, 312; social goals of 6, **48**; teacher discourse with 136
Student-Teacher Achievement Ratios (STAR) study (Tennessee) 87, 93
study skills 310–313, **323**
subject-matter language instruction 211–212
Sugrue, B. 273
Sullivan, W. C. 102
summarizing strategy 299
summary tables: curriculum influences **243–246**; home influences **72–73**; school influences **110–113**; student influences **44–48**; teacher/classroom influences **181–186**; teaching strategy influences **320–324**
summative assessment (SA) 126
summer school **112**
Sun, K. L. 170
Surmann, A. T. 239
Sutcher, L. 173, 179
Swanson, H. L. 219, 279
Sy, S. R. 67

Taconis, R. 317
Tamim, R. M. 303–304

Index

Tanner, C. Kenneth 98–99
task perception and problem solving 318
task valuing and problem solving 318
Taylor, A. P. 100
Taylor, L. C. 66
Teach for America (TFA) 174–175
teacher-centered classroom management 161
teacher/classroom influences: ability grouping 120, **185**; achievement and 4, 114; attitudes/beliefs of teachers 116–117, **181**; collaboration in classrooms 132–136, **185**; context of classrooms 117–120, **182–185**; emotion in classrooms 145–150, **184**; entries from previous edition 114–116; formative assessment 126–130, **185**; homework 121–124; management of classrooms 160–164; nontraditional teacher preparation 173–179; overview 114–120; pedagogical content knowledge 118, 139–143, **186**; preparation/professional development of teachers 120, **186**; relationship between student and teacher 153–157, **183**; summary table **181–186**
teacher immediacy 264–268, **322**
teachers: alternatively certified 120, 177, **186**; attitudes/beliefs of 116–117, **181**; bilingual certification and 175; classrooms and questioning by 261–262; communication behaviors of 264–268; discourse with students 136; efficacy beliefs of 117; efficacy of **181**; epistemological beliefs of 117, **181**; feedback for 178, 240, 306; indigenous/minoritized students and 27; instructional practices of 77–78, 136; learning difficulties and 21–22; motivation 117, **181**; nontraditional preparation of 173–179; pedagogical content knowledge of 118; performance incentives for 94–95; preparation/professional development of 120, **186**; quality 94; relationship between students and 153–157, **183**; shortages in hard-to-staff schools 173; teaming practice and 106; traditionally certified 177
Teach First 175
teaching strategy influences: achievement and 4, 247; cognitive/motivational 250–251, **320–321**; direct instruction 277–282, **321**; entries from previous edition 247–249; goal orientation 285–289, **320**; instructional 251, **321–323**; metacognitive strategies 253–257, 300, **320**; multimedia learning 291–295, **324**; overview 247–252; problem-based learning 270–275, **322**; problem solving 315–319, **321**; questioning 259–262; reciprocal teaching 297–301, **321**; study skills 310–313, **323**; summary table **320–324**; teacher immediacy 264–268, **322**; technology-supported learning 251–252, 303–308, **308, 323–324**
teaming practice 106
technology 303, **324**; *see also* technology-supported learning
technology-supported learning 251–252, 303–308, **323–324**
Te Kotahitanga project 28
television viewing 52, 54, **73**
Templeton, S. M. 162
temporal contiguity principle 293
Ten Dam, G. T. M. 240
Tennessee Student-Teacher Achievement Ratios (STAR) study 87, 93
"territoriality of place" 101
test performance 106
Texas Education Assessment of Minimal Skills (TEAMS) 162
texts, discussion of 193, **244**
text structure approach to writing instruction 226
theory-based programs 240
Third International Mathematics and Science Study (TIMSS) 87
Thomas, M. A. M. 177
Thomas, W. P. 204
Thompson, D. 197
time on task **323**
tracking 79–80, 120, **185**
traditional classrooms 161
traditionally certified (TC) teachers 177
training in child development 11, **47**
Tran, L. 219
Treisister, E. S. 162
Tribushinina, E. 225
Tripp, J. H. 239
Troops for Teachers 174
Trzesniewski, K. H. 169–170
Turkish behavioral teaching programs 163
Turner, Julianne 114
Tyler, R. W. 127
Tyson, D. F. 67–68

Uhn, J. 178
underweight infants **44**
United Nations (UN) 216
United Nations Educational, Scientific and Cultural Organization (UNESCO) 216
University of Georgia 99, 101
University of Texas at Austin 143
UTeach program 143
utilization deficiency 312
Utman, C. H. 286–287

values 41
van Bergen, P. 154

van den Bergh, H. 225
van den Bossche, P. 271
van der Flier, H. 36
van Vliet, W. 101
van Yperen, N. W. 289
verbal messages 266
Verbeek, J. H. A. M. 270–271
Vernon, D. T. A. 271
"Victor" (Howe) 231–232
Virginia Standards of Learning (SOL) 174
Vlastos, G. 100
vocabulary 193, 211–213, 222, **245**
voice principle 294
von der Embse, N. 146
Vygotsky, L. S. 133

Walberg, H. J. 161
Walker, A. 271, 273
Wang, M. C. 161
Weber, K. 265–266
Weinstein, C. E. 311
West, M. R. 87
What Works Clearinghouse (WWC) 211
Wheeless, V. E. 265
Whitaker, D. 224
Widdowson, H. 213
Wigfield, A. 167
Wiliam, D. 128–129

Wilkinson, I. A. G. 233
Willems, P. 66
Williams, C. M. 69
Willig, A. C. 205
within-class ability grouping 78–79, 82–83, **113**
Witt, P. L. 265
Wößmann, L. 87
Woessmann, L. 95
Wohlwill, J. F. 101
worked examples 278, 280–282, 317, 319, **321–322**
working memory capacity 223
writing instruction 222–228, **245**
writing and technology-supported learning 306–307, **308**
Wubbels, T. 154–156
Wyckoff, J. 177

Yankelevitch, E. 163
Ye, X. 176
Youngcourt, S. S. 287
Yuan, J. 67

Zawojewski, J. 317–318
Zepeda, C. D. 279
Zhang, Y. 274
Zhao, Y. 307
Zimmerman, B. J. 311